Due Return Date Date	Due Return Date Date

CONTEXTS OF DRYDEN'S THOUGHT

CONTEXTS
OF DRYDEN'S THOUGHT

Phillip Harth

THE UNIVERSITY OF CHICAGO PRESS
CHICAGO AND LONDON

LIBRARY OF CONGRESS CATALOG CARD NUMBER: 67–30129

THE UNIVERSITY OF CHICAGO PRESS, CHICAGO & LONDON
THE UNIVERSITY OF TORONTO PRESS, TORONTO 5, CANADA
© 1968 BY THE UNIVERSITY OF CHICAGO
ALL RIGHTS RESERVED. PUBLISHED 1968
PRINTED IN THE UNITED STATES OF AMERICA

For Sydney

PREFACE

The primary concern of this study is with Dryden's religious thought. For Dryden, however, as for most of his contemporaries, religious questions are inevitably linked to the respective claims of reason and revelation. On this premise, the truth of revelation cannot be considered apart from the validity of reason, and the province of faith can only be surveyed in relation to the adjacent boundaries of knowledge, secular as well as religious. In chapter 1, therefore, I have had to explore the subject of Dryden's "scepticism" and of his attitude toward reason and its activities as a preliminary to any discussion of his religious thought in the following chapters.

Dryden introduces religious ideas into his writings frequently, but in three quite different ways which must be kept distinct. First of all, he makes dramatic use of religious ideas in several of his plays, particularly in *The Indian Emperor* and *Tyrannic Love*. Religious ideas of this kind are to be explained, not by reference to Dryden's own beliefs, but by an understanding of the part they play in revealing character or in supplying the motivation for dramatic action. They are therefore irrelevant to a study of Dryden's religious thought and I have deliberately avoided discussing them in this book. Secondly, Dryden expresses his own ideas on particular religious questions briefly in a number of his lives and prefaces. These notions, thrown off in the course of discussing other matters, are neither systematic nor inherently important, but they are sometimes revealing and can be used to throw additional light on certain areas of his more systematic thought. Finally, Dryden's religious thought is embodied in two of his longest and most important poems, *Religio Laici* and *The Hind and the Panther*. It is with the interpretation and elucidation of these two poems that I am principally concerned in this study. They are the primary contexts in which his religious thought is to be understood.

The essential preliminary to such a task, of course, is an understanding of these primary contexts themselves: the logical contexts in which his terms acquire whatever meaning they possess, and the artistic contexts, or particular poems, in which Dryden's religious ideas appear, not as discrete opinions possessing interest solely for the biographer, but as the material ingredients of carefully planned formal structures. It is a matter of crucial importance whether we approach *Religio Laici* and *The Hind and the Panther* as poetic versions respectively of the religious confession, the sceptical discourse, the theological treatise, or the polemical tract, for our interpretation of the ideas offered in these poems will vary accordingly. In chapter 2, therefore, I have discussed the purpose of these poems and the strategies appropriate to them.

In the remainder of the book I have analyzed Dryden's religious thought as it appears in these two poems. Chapters 3 to 6 consist of a detailed analysis of *Religio Laici* which attempts to clarify the issues, often elusive to the modern reader, that stand in the way of a proper understanding of one of Dryden's greatest poetic achievements. Chapters 7 and 8 contain a discussion of the religious issues in *The Hind and the Panther,* a much longer poem which, nevertheless, I have been able to treat more briefly, both because approximately half the poem is concerned with political matters outside the scope of this study and because the religious issues presented there will already be familiar to the reader from my fuller analysis of the earlier poem.

By examining Dryden's religious ideas as component parts of these two poems, I have tried to keep them in the setting of the primary contexts to which they belong. But I have been equally concerned in this study with restoring his religious ideas to their appropriate secondary contexts: the historical circumstances in which Dryden conceived and expressed them. This book is in no sense what a well-meaning but mistaken reviewer described an earlier study of mine as being: "a history-of-ideas exercise in the Basil Willey tradition." I have made no attempt to construct a single seventeenth-century background, or intellectual milieu, or world picture to explain the rich complex of Dryden's ideas on a wide variety of religious subjects. I could have done so only at the risk of blurring important distinctions and of discussing other people's answers to questions Dryden never raised. I have been content to recover the specific historical contexts in which Dryden considered certain clearly defined questions familiar to his contemporaries and offered answers with which they were also acquainted. To have approached the problem in the manner popularly associated with the "history of ideas," beginning with contemporary "climates of opinion" and attempting to show how these affected Dryden's thought, would have been to lose sight of the very particularity which makes his thought more interesting and more memorable than that of many of his contemporaries who shared the same ideas. Insead, my procedure has been to begin in every case with Dryden's own ideas as expressed in their particular literary contexts and then to search for individual historical movements of thought which can help to define his own thought more precisely and to identify its specific orientation. When looked at in this way, even a single poem such as *Religio Laici* reveals a multiplicity of historical contexts which may become indistinguishable if reduced to some convenient generalization about the poem's background, intellectual milieu, or "climate of opinion."

I wish to thank Northwestern University, which provided a summer grant at the beginning of my research for this study, and the John Simon Guggenheim Memorial Foundation, which awarded me a fellowship in order to complete it.

CONTENTS

I

THE SCEPTICAL CRITIC

Most discussions of Dryden's characteristic thought are governed by a set of assumptions about his scepticism and its relation to his other ideas which have been accepted, with very few exceptions, by most students of the poet for the past thirty years. This conception of Dryden is so familiar that it can be reviewed very briefly.

It begins with the hypothesis that Dryden was a Pyrrhonist, or antirationalist, and proceeds to use this hypothesis to explain his public behavior and poetic thought in a great many widely different areas. Dryden—so runs the explanation—was not so much unable to make up his mind as unwilling to do so. The most significant parallel to this attitude is to be found in the essays of Montaigne, and its intellectual antecedents are to be sought in the two-thousand-year-old tradition of philosophical scepticism. Since Dryden was convinced that reason and the senses are essentially unreliable, he concluded that knowledge is uncertain and speculation vain. Unwilling to commit himself on any questions to which more than one answer could be suggested, he had recourse to that perennial suspension of judgment which Montaigne recommends in his essays by precept and example.

Once we view Dryden in this light (it is suggested) much that was previously obscure in his writings or inexplicable in his behavior will become clear and consistent. Thus, his habit of juxtaposing positions which are contrary to each other, as in *An Essay of Dramatic Poesy* and *The Hind and the Panther,* will be seen to be the confirmed sceptic's penchant for balancing conflicting opinions. Again, Dryden's political conservatism can be explained as a fear of change and a distrust of novelty to which

1

he was predisposed by his philosophical scepticism. For it is a corollary of the distrust of human reason that the Pyrrhonist casts a sceptical eye upon Utopias, ideas of reform, and suggestions for human betterment. Such plans are, in his view, as chimerical as any other speculations, and not worth exchanging for the established system of government at the cost of upheavals and possibly even bloodshed. Thus we should expect the sceptic to be just such a supporter of stable forms of government as Dryden in fact is. Finally, Dryden's conversion to the Catholic faith will cease to draw accusations of inconsistency and time-serving once we perceive that this was merely the highly predictable outcome of a long search for infallible authority as a substitute for fallible reason in matters of religion.[1]

It has been some years since this interpretation was first offered, and its wide acceptance in recent years is undeniable. In biographies of Dryden, in editions of his poems, and in studies of his individual works, his Pyrrhonism has become one of those commonplaces, like the date of his birth or the shortcomings of his wife, to which reference can be made, but for which no further proof need be attempted.[2] We can easily guess at some, at least, of the reasons for the popularity of this hypothesis. It offers, as no other theory has been able to do, a single, relatively simple explanation for a highly complex series of thoughts and actions for which Dryden was responsible. It allows us to predict these in advance, as logical consequences of Dryden's antirationalism,

[1] The fullest argument for this view is presented by Louis I. Bredvold, *The Intellectual Milieu of John Dryden* (Ann Arbor: University of Michigan Press, 1934).

[2] See, for example, *The Best of Dryden,* ed. Louis I. Bredvold (New York: Thomas Nelson, 1933), pp. xxvi–xxxiv; Mildred E. Hartsock, "Dryden's Plays: A Study in Ideas," *Seventeenth Century Studies, Second Series,* ed. Robert Shafer (Princeton: Princeton University Press, 1937), pp. 71–176; James M. Osborn, *John Dryden: Some Biographical Facts and Problems* (New York: Columbia University Press, 1940), p. 106; *The Poetical Works of Dryden,* ed. George R. Noyes (2d ed.; Boston: Houghton Mifflin Co., 1950), pp. xlix–1; Bonamy Dobrée, *John Dryden* (London: Longmans, 1956), pp. 10–12; Charles E. Ward, *The Life of John Dryden* (Chapel Hill: University of North Carolina Press, 1961), p. 15; *Selected Poems of John Dryden,* ed. Roger Sharrock (London: William Heinemann, 1963), p. 6; Selma Assir Zebouni, *Dryden: A Study in Heroic Characterization* (Baton Rouge: Louisiana State University Press, 1965), pp. 43–45. Miss Hartsock's study is intended as an "extension" to Professor Bredvold's, and she devotes an entire chapter to Montaigne's influence on Dryden; yet she consistently identifies the latter's "Pyrrhonism" with religious scepticism, or agnosticism (see, for example, pp. 160 and 173–76). Her views are therefore much closer to those of Sir Walter Scott (see *The Works of John Dryden,* ed. Sir Walter Scott and George Saintsbury [Edinburgh: William Paterson, 1882–93], I, 263 [hereafter referred to as *Works*]).

much as we can produce corollaries from a given proposition. "It is obvious," we are told, "that the man who in that century found himself inclined to philosophical scepticism was likely to find his views to some extent determined thereby in such distantly related subjects as religion and politics."[3] Clearly, Dryden's Pyrrhonism is a premise which leads to many conclusions.

Sceptics—of a rather different kind—have nevertheless been heard to complain, from time to time, that some of these conclusions seem to be derived from altogether different premises. It has been some years since Hoyt Trowbridge argued that the theoretical foundations of Dryden's criticism suggested a mind which had been schooled not in philosophical scepticism but upon the logical treatises of Aristotle.[4] More recently, two critics, working independently, have both suggested that Dryden's views in *Religio Laici* owe nothing to the tradition of Christian scepticism.[5]

Doubts such as these concern the consistency between some of Dryden's articulated ideas and the antirationalism which is supposed to be responsible for them. Similar difficulties occur when we consider whether Dryden's public behavior is consistent with his supposed allegiance to Pyrrhonism. For one thing, the conservatism for which the sceptic is notorious in politics has its counterpart in religion. Montaigne, so often cited as a kind of paradigm of Christian scepticism, could boast that as a consequence of his Pyrrhonism he enjoyed "a certain steadfastness of opinion" and had "not much altered those that were original and native with me." This had produced the same tranquillity in religion as he pursued in politics. "In this way I have, by the grace of God, with no perturbation and disturbance of conscience, preserved my faith intact in the ancient beliefs of our religion, amid so many sects and divisions that our age has produced."[6] That faith was the Catholic one, since he lived in France. But who can doubt that if Montaigne had lived in England and belonged to the Established Church, the same attitude would have made him hold fast to the state religion of that country and reject

---

[3] Bredvold, *Intellectual Milieu*, p. 153.

[4] See his very perceptive study of "The Place of Rules in Dryden's Criticism," *Modern Philology*, 44 (1946): 84–96.

[5] See Elias J. Chiasson, "Dryden's Apparent Scepticism in *Religio Laici*," *Harvard Theological Review*, 54 (1961): 207–21, and Thomas H. Fujimura, "Dryden's *Religio Laici*: An Anglican Poem," *PMLA*, 76 (1961): 205–17.

[6] "Apology for Raimond Sebond," *The Essays of Michel de Montaigne*, trans. Jacob Zeitlin (New York: Alfred Knopf, 1935), II, 233.

all those sects, including the Catholic one, which threatened its tranquillity? Dryden's behavior, in leaving the Established Church to join and stubbornly adhere to a despised and persecuted minority, is so contrary to this as to be inexplicable if he was indeed of Montaigne's mind.

Or again, the hypothesis that Dryden was a Pyrrhonist does not accord at all well with the frequent and enthusiastic praise he offers the new science and the contempt he expresses for that of the ancients. Montaigne, confronted with the arguments between the Copernicans and the supporters of the Ptolemaic system, could only wonder: "What lesson does this have for us, except that it does not matter to us which of the two opinions is true? And who knows but that a third, a thousand years hence, will overthrow the two former?"[7] In contrast to such studied indifference, Dryden can only exclaim that freeborn reason, long enslaved by the ancients, has at last been set at liberty by the new philosophy to accomplish the hopeful predictions he makes for it.

These may not be decisive objections to the theory of Dryden's Pyrrhonism, although I suspect that any attempt to answer them effectively would require appeals to that very quality of inconsistency in Dryden's character which this theory was designed to disprove. What these objections do suggest, however, is that this hypothesis does not "solve the phenomena," as Dryden's contemporaries would have put it, nearly as well as it is reputed to do, and that it must have depended upon some confirmatory argument in order to win acceptance.

The nature of this argument is not hard to discover. On three widely separated occasions, Dryden drew attention to what he chose to refer to as his "scepticism." If he had not done so, it is hard to imagine that the hypothesis we are considering would ever have been offered. But "scepticism" is a highly ambiguous term which has more than one meaning in the seventeenth century, as anyone who cares to consult the *Oxford English Dictionary* can easily confirm. What the advocates of the theory that Dryden was a Pyrrhonist have done is to deny any ambiguity to the term by appealing not to the logical contexts in which Dryden uses the term, as we might expect them to do, but to his intellectual milieu. They have argued that philosophical scepticism, or Pyrrhonism, was a pervasive influence in the seventeenth century, that Dryden could scarcely have avoided coming in contact with

[7] *Ibid.*

4

it, and that his references to scepticism consequently can be taken only in this sense.

But to argue in this way is to proceed in the manner which R. S. Crane recently described when he referred to the method of those critics of Book IV of *Gulliver's Travels* who "suppose that there is a kind of probative force in [one] preferred formula for [a] period which can confer, a priori, if not a unique at least a privileged relevance on one particular hypothesis about a given work of that period."[8] To do so has meant, in this case, ignoring both the logical contexts of Dryden's remarks about his own scepticism and the possibility of there being other intellectual traditions in his own time which might better account for his use of this term.

To begin with Dryden's statements concerning his scepticism, there is a rather remarkable similarity about the contexts in which they appear. The first of these is a famous passage in his "Defence of *An Essay of Dramatic Poesy*" (1668), an answer to the charges which Dryden's brother-in-law, Sir Robert Howard, had leveled against the *Essay* in the preface to *The Duke of Lerma*. Among other things, Howard had accused him of setting himself up as a legislator for the drama and of enacting rules which all playwrights were expected to obey, so that the *Essay* is nothing less than an "attempt to infringe the Liberty of Opinion by Rules" and an arrogant assumption of the right to "dictate Lawes for *Dramatick Poesie*."[9] Dryden replies:

He is here pleased to charge me with being magisterial, as he has done in many other places of his preface. Therefore, in vindication of myself, I must crave leave to say that my whole discourse was sceptical, according to that way of reasoning which was used by Socrates, Plato, and all the Academics of old, which Tully and the best of the Ancients followed, and which is imitated by the modest inquisitions of the Royal Society. That it is so, not only the name will shew, which is *An Essay*, but the frame and composition of the work. You see it is a dialogue sustained by persons of several opinions, all of them left doubtful, to be determined by the readers in general.[10]

8 "The Houyhnhnms, the Yahoos, and the History of Ideas," *Reason and the Imagination: Studies in the History of Ideas 1600–1800,* ed. J. A. Mazzeo (New York: Columbia University Press, 1962), p. 240.

9 "To the Reader," *The Great Favourite, or, The Duke of Lerma* (London, 1668), sig. A4v.

10 *Of Dramatic Poesy and Other Critical Essays,* ed. George Watson (London: J. M. Dent and Sons, 1962), I, 123. (Hereafter referred to as *Essays.*)

The term "sceptical" here is being used to describe a "way of reasoning," or mode of inquiry, applicable to a wide variety of philosophers, not a theory of knowledge with which several of them would have had no wish to be associated. It is a method of "modest inquisition" which consists in investigating a question in an open and unbiased manner and in letting the reader make up his mind for himself.

The next time Dryden spoke of scepticism in connection with himself he was anticipating the same charge of being magisterial that Howard had leveled against him and answering it in advance. He begins the preface to *Religio Laici* (1682) by admitting that

a POEM with so bold a Title, and a Name prefix'd, from which the handling of so serious a Subject wou'd not be expected, may reasonably oblige the Author, to say somewhat in defence both of himself, and of his undertaking. In the first place, if it be objected to me that being a *Layman*, I ought not to have concern'd my self with Speculations, which belong to the Profession of *Divinity* . . . I pretend not to make my self a Judge of Faith, in others, but onely to make a Confession of my own; I lay no unhallow'd hand upon the Ark; but wait on it, with the Reverence that becomes me at a distance. . . . Being naturally inclin'd to Scepticism in Philosophy, I have no reason to impose my Opinions, in a Subject which is above it: But whatever they are, I submit them with all reverence to my Mother Church.[11]

Howard had called him a dictator of laws for dramatic poesy; here Dryden makes sure that no one shall call him a judge of faith. Again his defense is a rather exaggerated modesty, the diffidence of one who is content to make a confession of his own faith without presuming to meddle with that of the reader. The words "being naturally inclin'd to Scepticism in Philosophy" have often been quoted out of their context and, by an equation of "Scepticism in Philosophy" with "philosophical scepticism," have been treated as an admission on Dryden's part to Pyrrhonism. But to do this is to ignore the parallel elements in his sentence: "Scepticism" is contrasted with "to impose my Opinions," "Philosophy" with "a Subject which is above it," or theology. Dryden is simply offering the a fortiori argument that, as one who is instinctively diffident in matters inferior to faith, he is even less inclined to grow magisterial in a higher sphere and to become a judge of

[11] *The Poems of John Dryden,* ed. James Kinsley (Oxford: Clarendon Press, 1958), I, 302. (Hereafter referred to as *Poems.*)

faith, where he possesses no special competence. Once again he is drawing our attention to his way of reasoning, not to his theory of knowledge.

Dryden's final allusion to his sceptical temperament occurs three years later in the "Preface to *Sylvae*" (1685), where he is describing the "distinguishing Character" of Lucretius, whom he had translated. This character emerges as just such a magisterial one as he had previously denied to be his own. Lucretius, Dryden writes, is remarkable for

a certain kind of noble pride, and positive assertion of his Opinions. He is every where confident of his own reason, and assuming an absolute command not only over his vulgar Reader, but even his Patron *Memmius*. For he is always bidding him attend, as if he had the Rod over him; and using a Magisterial authority, while he instructs him. . . . he seems to disdain all manner of Replies, and is so confident of his cause, that he is before hand with his Antagonists; Urging for them, whatever he imagin'd they cou'd say, and leaving them as he supposes, without an objection for the future. All this too, with so much scorn and indignation, as if he were assur'd of the Triumph, before he enter'd into the Lists. . . . These are the considerations which I had of that Author, before I attempted to translate some parts of him. And accordingly I lay'd by my natural Diffidence and Scepticism for a while, to take up that Dogmatical way of his.[12]

The opposite of Dryden's own natural diffidence and scepticism, then, is a manner of inquiring into a subject, and a method of presenting one's conclusions, which he describes as positive assertion, magisterial authority, and a dogmatical way. It consists in a supreme confidence in one's own judgment, the putting forward of private opinions as indisputable truths, and an arrogant attempt to impose these views upon the reader. For such overconfidence, the only remedy is the modesty of the honest seeker after truth who welcomes discussion and stands ready to yield to better judgment, modifying his own conclusions accordingly.

I believe we must conclude that in none of these personal references to scepticism is Dryden alluding to a theory of knowledge. This is not to deny that Dryden knew the writings of Montaigne, admired him as an essayist, and could quote him on occasion—as has many another writer who did not share Montaigne's Pyrrhonism. Nor is it to deny that, having read widely among the

12 *Ibid.*, p. 395.

classical authors and made the acquaintance of Diogenes Laertius and of Thomas Stanley's *History of Philosophy*, Dryden was perfectly familiar with the teachings of ancient scepticism under both its forms.[13] This is readily apparent from his lives of Plutarch and Lucian, where, in several passages which are simply paraphrases of the more learned commentators upon whom he is drawing, he describes the beliefs of the Pyrrhonists and of the New Academy as the doctrines of two ancient sects which claimed the allegiance of Lucian and Plutarch respectively.[14] But because of the historical and biographical context in which they appear, Dryden can assume that the terms "Sceptic" and "sect of Sceptics" which he introduces into the "Lives" will be taken as referring to an ancient school of philosophy.[15] When, in an altogether different context, Dryden alludes to his own "natural Diffidence and Scepticism" or "sceptical way of reasoning," and contrasts this with a "Magisterial" or "Dogmatical" manner, he assumes the reader's familiarity with these terms in a quite separate sense. This latter conception of two modes of logical procedure, offered to the reader by means of two kinds of discourse, invites some sort of historical explanation, as does Dryden's assumption that the names of scepticism and dogmatism which he gives them will be readily understood.

I think we can see what such a historical explanation would require. It would have to find, not a tradition of attacking the reliability of reason and the senses, but a habit of presenting two opposite ways of reasoning, one of which is recommended, under

[13] " 'Tis true that Diogenes Laertius, and our learned countryman Mr. Stanley, have both written the lives of the philosophers; but we are more obliged to the various principles of their several sects than to any thing remarkable that they did for our entertainment" ("The Life of Lucian," *Essays*, II, 209–10).

[14] See *ibid.*, p. 210, and "The Life of Plutarch," *Works*, XVII, 31–32. The late E. N. Hooker assumed that in the latter passage Dryden undertook to describe a position which he shared with Plutarch. He therefore concluded that Dryden professed the modified scepticism of the New Academy (see "Dryden and the Atoms of Epicurus," *ELH*, 24 [1957]: 184). George Watson, however, has excluded the passage from his edition of Dryden's criticism on the grounds that it is simply a recasting of "material explicitly translated or adapted from continental treatises and commentaries" (*Essays*, I, xvii), and A. E. Wallace Maurer has shown that Dryden is indebted to Jean Ruault for the entire passage (see "Dryden and Pyrrhonism," *Notes and Queries*, 202 [1957]: 251–52).

[15] In both lives, Dryden reserves the term "Sceptic" for a member of the Pyrrhonist sect. His name for one who professes the scepticism of the New Academy is "an Academic, that is, half Platonist, half Sceptic" ("The Life of Plutarch," *Works*, XVII, 72). This obviously contradicts Hooker's thesis that Dryden's references to his own scepticism are intended as synonyms for Academic probabilism.

the name of scepticism, as a kind of modesty and diffidence, while the other is condemned, under some such name as dogmatism, as a kind of positiveness of opinion. And this historical explanation would have to show, not simply that this tradition was a pervasive influence in the seventeenth century, or part of the intellectual climate of that age which the English presumably shared with the French, but that it was a body of opinion with which Englishmen in the 1660's and 1670's were readily familiar and which Dryden could take for granted in his own rather casual references to scepticism in these years. It would require, in other words, a search, not for world pictures or intellectual milieus, but for particular contexts.

I should like to suggest that such a body of opinion can be discovered in some of those books which began to appear at about the time the Royal Society was founded and which sought to publicize the activities of that group or actually to put into effect some part of its program. One of the matters which receives special emphasis in these books is the method of reasoning which the members of the Royal Society use, and the manner in which they offer the results of this reasoning to others. Joseph Glanvill described their procedure in *Plus Ultra* as one which

renders them *wary* and *modest, diffident* of the *certainty* of their *Conceptions,* and averse to the *boldness* of *peremptory asserting.* So that the *Philosopher thinks much,* and *examines* many things, separates the *Certainties* from the *Plausibilities, that* which is *presumed* from *that* which is *prov'd,* the *Images* of *Sense, Phansie,* and *Education,* from the *Dictates* of *genuine* and *impartial Reason.* This he doth before he *Assents* or *Denies;* and *then* he takes with him also a Sense of his own *Fallibility* and *Defects,* and never concludes but upon resolution to alter his mind upon contrary evidence. Thus he conceives *warily,* and he speaks with as much *caution* and *reserve,* in the humble Forms of *So I think,* and *In my opinion,* and *Perhaps 'tis so*—with great [deference] to *opposite* Perswasion, candour to *dissenters,* and *calmness* in *contradictions,* with *readiness* and *desire* to *learn,* and great delight in the Discoveries of Truth, and Detections of his *own* Mistakes.[16]

This was published in 1668, the very year in which Dryden was describing his own way of reasoning in the *Essay* in closely similar terms, and likening it to "the modest inquisitions of the Royal Society." The opposite of such a way of reasoning, according to

[16] *Plus Ultra* (London, 1668), pp. 146–47.

the members of the Royal Society, was that of the ancients, especially Aristotle, which consisted in a haughty confidence in one's
own opinions and an arrogant attempt to impose them upon
others. The most common term for this was dogmatism, and
under this name it was frequently denounced by the advocates of
the new philosophy. They had several names for their own way
of reasoning, and one of these was scepticism.

A particularly striking parallel to Dryden's habit of contrasting
dogmatism and scepticism as two opposite ways of reasoning is
offered by Glanvill's earliest book. This popular work has as its
subject the two ways of reasoning and of offering opinions which
we are concerned with. It undertakes to condemn the ancient
practice of laying down the law of nature as a thing already understood and ratified, and to advocate in its place a more diffident
form of inquiry. When the book appeared the first time, in 1661,
Glanvill chose a title which would stress the method he condemned, and he called his discourse *The Vanity of Dogmatizing*.
But when he reissued the book in a new form in 1665, three years
before Dryden's "Defence of *An Essay of Dramatic Poesy*," he
decided to give a more positive emphasis to the title, and he
renamed it *Scepsis Scientifica*, in reference to the method espoused
in the book. It was dedicated this time to the Royal Society,
because, Glanvill wrote, "regarding Your *Society* as the strongest
Argument to perswade a *modest* and *reserved diffidence* in opinions, I took the boldness to borrow that deservedly celebrated
name, for an *evidence* to my Subject."[17] With this idea in mind,
Glanvill proceeded in his book to urge his readers to adopt "the
Scepticism which consists in *Freedome* of *inquiry*," and to assure
them that *"Scepticism*, that's the only way to *Science."*[18] Nevertheless, Glanvill was careful to point out that if he was sceptical, he
was no Pyrrhonist, and that in advocating modesty, diffidence, and
freedom of inquiry under the name of scepticism he was far
from "endeavouring to discourage *Philosophical* enquiries, by
introducing a *despair* of *Science"* in the manner of the ancient
Sceptics. He went on to declare firmly: "I desire it may be taken
notice of once for all then, that I have nought to do with that
shuffling Sect, that love to doubt eternally, and to question all
things. My profession is *freedom* of *enquiry*, and I own no more

[17] "To the Royal Society," *Scepsis Scientifica* (London, 1665), sig. A4.
[18] *Ibid.*, p. 56, and "Sciri tuum nihil est," *ibid.*, p. 12.

Scepticism then what is concluded in the *Motto* which the ROYAL SOCIETY have now adopted for theirs, NULLIUS IN VERBA [on the word of no one]."[19]

Robert Boyle, the most prominent member of the Royal Society during its early years, placed a similar stress upon modesty and diffidence and upon freedom of inquiry; he too sometimes described his method as "sceptical." In one of his earliest books, *Certain Physiological Essays* (1661), he considered it a matter for special remark "that in almost every one of the following essays I should speak so doubtingly, and use so often, *perhaps, it seems, it is not improbable,* and such other expressions, as argue a diffidence of the truth of the opinions I incline to, and that I should be so shy of laying down principles, and sometimes of so much as venturing at explications."[20] His emphasis here upon modesty of expression is complemented by the importance he gives to freedom of inquiry in another of his early books, also published in 1661. *The Sceptical Chymist, or, Chymico-Physical Doubts and Paradoxes* is, like Dryden's *Essay of Dramatic Poesy,* a "dialogue sustained by persons of several opinions," one of Boyle's favorite literary forms. In this dialogue, the sceptical chemist of the title, representing Boyle's own point of view, proposes doubts concerning the currently accepted alchemical theories. But like Glanvill, Boyle is careful to point out that it is possible to be sceptical without sharing the theory of knowledge of the ancient Sceptics.

For though sometimes I have had occasion to discourse like a Sceptick, yet I am far from being one of that sect; which I take to have been little less prejudicial to natural philosophy than to divinity itself. I do not with the true Scepticks propose doubts to persuade men, that all things are doubtful and will ever remain so (at least) to human understandings; but I propose doubts not only with design, but with hope, of being at length freed from them by the attainment of undoubted truth; which I seek, that I may find it; though if I miss of it in one opinion, I proceed to search after it in the opposite, or in any other where it seems more likely I should meet with it.[21]

It is this emphasis upon doubts (*scepses*) that led the members

[19] "Sciri tuum nihil est," *ibid.,* p. 3.
[20] *Certain Physiological Essays, The Works of the Hon. Robert Boyle,* ed. Thomas Birch (2d ed.; London, 1772), I, 307.
[21] Appendix to *The Sceptical Chymist, ibid.,* p. 591. This appendix was added to the second edition of 1679.

11

of the Royal Society to apply to their own procedure the terms "sceptical" and "scepticism" also adopted by the Pyrrhonists.[22] But as Boyle, Glanvill, and Thomas Sprat in his *History of the Royal Society* (1667) all make clear, there is an enormous difference between themselves and the Pyrrhonists in the use which they make of doubts.[23] The Pyrrhonists, because of their theory of knowledge, "love to doubt eternally," and "propose doubts to persuade men that all things are doubtful." The doubts proposed by the members of the Royal Society, on the other hand, are merely temporary, the initial ingredients of a method of procedure which will lead ultimately to "the attainment of undoubted truth."

This method of preliminary doubt was inherited from Bacon, as the members of the Royal Society frequently stressed.[24] It is a conception which Bacon expressed in an oft-quoted remark in *The Advancement of Learning:* "If a man will begin with certainties, he shall end in doubts; but if he will be content to begin with doubts, he shall end in certainties."[25] In urging this method of temporary doubt, and attacking those who "render sciences dogmatic and magisterial" in the manner of Aristotle, who "laid down the law on all points," Bacon is as careful as his successors later in the century to distinguish the doubts he recommends from those of the Pyrrhonists.[26] In one of many such passages which abound in his works, he writes:

It will also be thought that by forbidding men to pronounce and to set down principles as established until they have duly arrived through the intermediate steps at the highest generalities, I maintain a sort of suspension of the judgment, and bring it to what the Greeks call

[22] Like Dryden (see note 15 above), the other members of the Royal Society, when referring to the ancient sceptical sects, reserved the term "Sceptics" for the Pyrrhonists and designated the sceptics of the New Academy by the name of "Academics." See Henry Oldenburg's practice in the *Philosophical Transactions,* 7 (1672): 5081, and 11 (1676): 791. According to Richard H. Popkin, this was the common practice of most writers of the sixteenth and seventeenth centuries. See *The History of Scepticism from Erasmus to Descartes* (Assen, The Netherlands: Van Gorcum, 1960), pp. xii–xiii.

[23] For an extended discussion of this difference, see Thomas Sprat, *The History of the Royal Society* (London, 1667), pp. 101, 106–8.

[24] The Royal Society's debt to Bacon in this and other respects is thoroughly discussed by Richard Foster Jones in *Ancients and Moderns* (St. Louis: Washington University Press, 1936).

[25] *The Advancement of Learning,* in *The Works of Francis Bacon,* ed. J. Spedding, R. L. Ellis, and D. D. Heath (London: Longman and Co., 1857–74), III, 293.

[26] *Novum Organum,* in *ibid.,* IV, 69.

Acatalepsia,—a denial of the capacity of the mind to comprehend truth. But in reality that which I meditate and propound is not *Acatalepsia,* but *Eucatalepsia;* not denial of the capacity to understand, but provision for understanding truly; for I do not take away authority from the senses, but supply them with helps; I do not slight the understanding, but govern it.[27]

It is this conception of doubt as a temporary mental discipline, the preliminary stage in every inquiry which must ultimately lead to certitude, that distinguishes the new scientists from the Pyrrhonists. The scepticism of the Royal Society is an essential ingredient, not of a theory of knowledge, but of a scientific method; yet it is squarely based upon an optimistic epistemology which denies and contradicts the tenets of philosophical scepticism.[28]

In the passages I have quoted, Boyle and Glanvill describe the scepticism of the Royal Society sometimes as modesty and diffidence, sometimes as freedom of inquiry. Both characteristics are derived from the importance which they attach to doubt, and therefore both are properly described as "sceptical." Freedom of inquiry, which the members of the Royal Society had learned from Bacon to claim as their right, consisted in taking *Nullius in Verba* as their motto and questioning the opinions of the ancients. Their first doubts, then, concerned the scientific principles inherited from the past, and, as Sprat wrote, "out of a just disdain, that the *Antients* should still possess a Tyranny over our Judgements, [they] began first to put off the reverence that men had born to their memories."[29] But that which rendered these inherited principles dubious in their eyes was the fact that the ancients themselves had lacked a capacity for self-doubt. "The

[27] *Ibid.,* pp. 111–12. Other passages in the *Novum Organum* which stress the differences between the Baconian method of doubt and philosophical scepticism occur on pp. 39, 53, and 68–69. See also *The Advancement of Learning,* in *ibid.,* III, 293, and *Instauratio Magna, ibid.,* IV, 32.

[28] See the illuminating discussion by Sir Karl Popper of the contrast between the "optimistic epistemology" underlying the Baconian and Cartesian methods of doubt and the "pessimistic epistemology" of Montaigne and the other philosophical sceptics in *Conjectures and Refutations* (London: Routledge and Kegan Paul, 1963), pp. 3–30. For the survival of this optimistic epistemology among later seventeenth-century scientists before Newton, see Ralph M. Blake, "Natural Science in the Renaissance," *Theories of Scientific Method: The Renaissance through the Nineteenth Century,* ed. Edward H. Madden (Seattle: University of Washington Press, 1960), pp. 3–21; the same author's "Isaac Newton and the Hypothetico-Deductive Method," *ibid.,* pp. 119–43; and Edward Grant, "Hypotheses in Late Medieval and Early Modern Science," *Daedalus,* 91 (1962): 599–616.

[29] *History of the Royal Society,* p. 29.

greatest occasion of our dissenting from the *Greek Philosophers,* and especially from *Aristotle,*" according to Sprat, "was, that they made too much hast to seise on the prize, before they were at the end of the Race: that they fix'd, and determin'd their judgements, on general conclusions too soon, and so could not afterwards alter them, by any new appearances, which might represent themselves."[30] Their very dogmatism had made them immune to that self-criticism which is essential to every seeker after truth.

It was not enough, therefore, simply to doubt the teachings of the ancients. The members of the Royal Society must doubt their own conclusions and cultivate a diffidence of opinion, striving to overcome that "impatience of doubt, and haste to assertion without due and mature suspension of judgment" which Bacon had condemned, but to which all men unfortunately are subject.[31] "They love not a long and a tedious doubting," Sprat remarked, "though it brings them at last to a real certainty: but they choose rather to conclude presently, then to be long in suspence, though to better purpose."[32] Modesty and diffidence, as pursued by the members of the Royal Society, represent a deliberate attempt to overcome this natural tendency and to encourage the same scepticism toward their own efforts as they directed toward those of their predecessors. "Wherever [the reader] finds that I have ventur'd at any small Conjectures, at the causes of the things that I have observed," another prominent member of the Society warned in 1665, "I beseech him to look upon them only as *doubtful Problems,* and *uncertain ghesses,* and not as unquestionable Conclusions, or matters of unconfutable Science; I have produced nothing here, with intent to bind his understanding to an *implicit* consent."[33] If scepticism was an antidote for the dogmatism of the ancients, it was also a preservative against the same malady among the moderns.

These two characteristics, then, of freedom of inquiry and of modesty and diffidence were the essential ingredients of that method of investigation which was given the name of "scepticism" in the mid-seventeenth century. It was these same two characteristics which Glanvill, in his essay "Of Scepticism and Certainty"

[30] *Ibid.,* p. 30. For a similar complaint against the ancients' lack of diffidence, see Boyle, *Certain Physiological Essays, Works,* I, 302.

[31] *The Advancement of Learning,* in *Works of Francis Bacon,* III, 293.

[32] *History of the Royal Society,* p. 32.

[33] Robert Hooke, *Micrographia* (London, 1665), sig. b1.

14

(1676), selected as justifying the use of the term "scepticism" in connection with the Royal Society. The "modern free philosophers," he wrote, can be described as "sceptical" because (1) they "dare dissent from the *Aristotelian* Doctrines, and will not slavishly subscribe [to] all the Tenents of that *Dictator* in *Philosophy*"; and (2) they "proceed with wariness and circumspection without too much forwardness in establishing Maxims, and positive Doctrines."[34] If Dryden's "way of reasoning" in his *Essay of Dramatic Poesy* was in imitation of "the modest inquisitions of the Royal Society," his description of the *Essay* as a "sceptical discourse" was appropriate and accurate.

We could probably account for Dryden's knowledge of this conception of scepticism, and his sympathy for it, by pointing to his temporary membership in the Royal Society and to his friendship with some of its other members, such as Thomas Sprat and Walter Charleton.[35] This is the usual explanation for the interest in the new philosophy he expresses at about this time in "To my Honour'd Friend, Dr. Charleton," *Annus Mirabilis*, and *An Essay of Dramatic Poesy*. But I should like to suggest that Dryden's membership in the Royal Society was itself a result of his attitude toward the new science, rather than its cause. I believe it began much earlier, when he was a student at Trinity College, Cambridge, from 1650 to 1654.

Scant attention has been paid to Dryden's years at Cambridge, not only because we possess little positive information about his activities there, but also because the Cambridge influence has

---

[34] "Of Scepticism and Certainty," *Essays on Several Important Subjects in Philosophy and Religion* (London, 1676), pp. 43–45.

[35] This is the explanation suggested by Laura Johnson Wylie (*Studies in the Evolution of English Criticism* [Boston: Ginn and Co., 1894], pp. 36–41) and R. F. Jones ("Science and Criticism in the Neo-Classical Age of English Literature," *Journal of the History of Ideas*, 1 [1940]: 384), both of whom recognize the similarity between Dryden's notion of scepticism and that of the Royal Society. Earl Miner has recently challenged the view that Dryden was an admirer of this group, and has suggested that his allusion to "the modest inquisitions of the Royal Society" indicates disapprobation rather than sympathy. He writes: "Dryden can hardly be called a fervent supporter of the new science in the face of a declaration that its 'inquisitions' were so modest and imitative of five groups of Ancients. The really significant fact seems to be that in spite of his response to almost everything that moved him in his age, he wrote no Cowleyan ode on the Royal Society, as he surely would have, if he had placed his strongest hopes in the new science" ("Dryden and the Issue of Human Progress," *Philological Quarterly*, 40 [1961]: 121). If Dryden wrote no Cowleyan ode on the Royal Society, his praise of the new science in other works, discussed later in this chapter, would seem to be an adequate substitute.

15

been dismissed as having slight importance as far as his later attitude toward the new philosophy is concerned.[36] This is scarcely surprising. Until quite recently, both universities have been pictured as offering little encouragement, if not a positive hindrance, to the growth of the new science in the early seventeenth century.[37] By assuming that the actual course of studies at the two universities was limited to the Scholastic curriculum provided by the statutes, historians have presented Oxford and Cambridge as intellectual backwaters.[38] Several recent studies, however, have revised—and indeed reversed—this estimate of their importance. Mark H. Curtis, in particular, has shown that the curriculum provided by the Elizabethan statutes of 1570, for Cambridge, and by the Laudian Code of 1636, for Oxford, was considerably modified and modernized in actual practice, besides being supplemented by a significant number of extrastatutory studies.[39] His evidence is particularly important in regard to the new philosophy, for it supports and amplifies the testimony of Seth Ward, one of the earliest members of the Royal Society, who in 1654, on the basis of twelve years' experience at Cambridge and of half as many at Oxford, published a book testifying that the new science was in a flourishing condition at both universities.[40] Professor Curtis'

[36] Thus, Dryden's most recent biographer covers his career at Cambridge in three paragraphs, confines his discussion of the university's intellectual climate to the contributions of the Cambridge Platonists, and adds the curious suggestion that this group may have been responsible for Dryden's Pyrrhonism. See Ward, *Life of John Dryden,* pp. 14–16.

[37] For a typical statement of this position, see Godfrey Davies, *The Early Stuarts, 1603–1660* (2d ed.; Oxford: Clarendon Press, 1959), pp. 354–56.

[38] For the content of this statutory curriculum at Cambridge, see William T. Costello, S.J., *The Scholastic Curriculum at Early Seventeenth-Century Cambridge* (Cambridge, Mass.: Harvard University Press, 1958).

[39] See *Oxford and Cambridge in Transition, 1558–1642* (Oxford: Clarendon Press, 1959), pp. 115–25 (the modification of the statutory curriculum) and 126–48 (extrastatutory studies). In an appendix to his *Intellectual Origins of the English Revolution* ([Oxford: Clarendon Press, 1965], pp. 301–14), Christopher Hill has challenged many of Professor Curtis' views. Whatever the merits of his case, Mr. Hill does not deny the scientific atmosphere at Cambridge in the 1650's, but in fact confirms it. He writes: "It is true of the fifties that 'the universities, despite their statutes, were teaching the results of recent findings in mathematics and science.' But the statement is not true of the period before the end of the civil war, or at least its truth has not been demonstrated, and the mass of contemporary evidence seems to be against it" (p. 310).

[40] See *Vindiciae Academiarum* (London, 1654). The book was written in answer to the charges of John Webster and Thomas Hobbes that the universities were bound wholly to tradition and taught the Peripatetic philosophy exclusively. A preface to the book by John Wilkins, one of the founders of the Royal Society, confirms Ward's testimony.

own conclusion is that "just as the universities did more in disseminating new scientific discoveries and in training the experimental or new philosophers than has heretofore been realized, so they also contributed more to the assault on intellectual dogma and authority than has been credited to them."[41]

The chief reason for Professor Curtis' revision of previous estimates of the universities' importance is that he has assembled considerable evidence to show that the lectures and disputations in the public schools of the universities—the bulwark of the statutory curriculum—had fallen into desuetude by the beginning of the seventeenth century as the colleges assumed an increasingly greater share of the instruction.[42] The collegiate instruction offered to the students included not only the guidance of the tutors but also a complementary system of college lectureships duplicating as well as supplementing the subjects covered by the university professorships. By the middle of the seventeenth century, the colleges had replaced the public schools of the universities as the center of academic activity. Since the greatest part of the student's training took place within the walls of his own college, it is here, rather than in the university at large, that most of the formative influences to which he was subject are to be sought. In Dryden's case, the intellectual conditions of Trinity College, customarily ignored, are a far more important consideration than the possible influence of the Cambridge Platonists of Emmanuel College, on which his biographers have spent their speculations.

Trinity in the early 1650's, when Dryden was a student there, was the most important outpost of the new science at Cambridge. It is probably no exaggeration to say that its role at Cambridge was in many ways similar to that of Wadham College at Oxford, where, under the wardenship of John Wilkins, the Invisible College, out of which the Royal Society was to emerge, was holding its meetings during these very years. It was entirely appropriate, in fact, that Wilkins should have left Wadham to assume the mastership of Trinity, Cambridge, in 1659, and that the young Isaac Newton, coming up to Cambridge two years later, should have enrolled at Trinity as a student. For Trinity had been Fran-

[41] *Oxford and Cambridge in Transition*, p. 250. Professor Curtis' chapter on "The Universities and the Advancement of Learning" (*ibid.*, pp. 227-60) is a masterly account of the role of the universities in the growth of the new science. See also Phyllis Allen, "Scientific Studies in the English Universities of the Seventeenth Century," *Journal of the History of Ideas*, 10 (1949): 219-53.

[42] See *Oxford and Cambridge in Transition*, pp. 100-115.

cis Bacon's college, and his spirit persisted there. When Dryden came up to Trinity from Westminster School in 1650, he entered a college where Bacon's ideals were not only honored, but actually pursued by some of its fellows.[43] Here, in the chambers of one of its fellows, John Nidd, members of the college met to conduct discussions and carry out experiments similar to, though less famous than, those of the Invisible College in Wilkins' lodgings at Wadham.[44] The group included two fellows of the college who were later to rank among the most illustrious members of the Royal Society: Isaac Barrow, the mathematician, and John Ray, the botanist. Both men at this time were college lecturers in the subjects which Dryden, like all the students at Trinity, was required to follow.

From the teaching of such men as these we can reasonably expect the undergraduates to have acquired some idea of the new science. In fact, such evidence as survives indicates that the young men were buying and reading such books as Bacon's *Advancement of Learning* and Wilkins' *Mathematical Magic* along with the more traditional classics recommended by their tutors.[45] It is scarcely surprising, then, that Dryden's fellow students during his time at Trinity included a number of future scientists, such as the physicians John Mapletoft and Thomas Allen, the zoologist Francis Willughby, and the embryologist Walter Needham, all of whom were to become fellows of the Royal Society and take their place along side such older graduates of Trinity as the mathematician John Pell and the astronomer Walter Pope. Of these young men who shared the same environment with Dryden at Trinity in the early 1650's, Walter Needham is particularly significant. Needham and Dryden had been students together at Westminster School. Both were chosen for scholarships at Trinity in 1650, both studied under the same tutor, John Templer, during the next three and a half years, and both graduated together early in 1654. Subject to the same influences as Dryden during these years, Needham developed a lively interest in science and

[43] For a very illuminating account of the flourishing condition of the new science at Trinity during the early 1650's, see Charles E. Raven, *John Ray, Naturalist: His Life and Works* (2d ed.; Cambridge: At the University Press, 1950), pp. 43–71.

[44] For information on Nidd's circle and its activities, see *ibid.*, pp. 47–50. Nidd did not live to become a member of the Royal Society. He died in 1659.

[45] See "The Expense Book of James Master of Trinity College, Cambridge," *The Flemings in Oxford,* ed. John Richard Magrath (Oxford: Oxford Historical Society, 1904), I, 374–91. Master was an undergraduate at Trinity from 1646 to 1648.

began at Trinity, in the year of his graduation, the experiments which led to his contributions to embryology.[46] Another of Templer's students at this time, his namesake John Templer, was later to contribute papers to the *Philosophical Transactions*.

I am not suggesting, of course, that Dryden received a scientific training at Trinity. This was not the province of the arts course which undergraduates at both universities followed. What I do suggest is that the conversation about experiments and enthusiasm for the new science provided later by the meetings of the Royal Society, which have been credited with inspiring in Dryden an interest in the new philosophy, were already available to him in his own college a decade earlier. I have emphasized the large number of scientists and future scientists who were at Trinity during the time that Dryden was a student there. But Professor Curtis has pointed out that Oxford and Cambridge acted as nurseries of the new philosophy in the early seventeenth century, not only by training the new scientists themselves, but by "helping to create an intellectual class which could encourage and support the works of genius."[47] The fact that there was an unusual degree of interest in the new science at Trinity simply increases the probability that this college played no small part in the creation of such a class. Besides the scientists, there were others, like Sir Robert Paston and Dryden himself, who left Trinity with enough interest in the new philosophy to join the Royal Society later as spectators and supporters of experiments in which they took no active part themselves. It is probably no coincidence that the two poets who wrote verses eulogizing the Royal Society during its infancy, Dryden and Cowley, were both graduates of Trinity College, Cambridge.[48]

Our immediate concern, however, is not with Dryden's later enthusiasm for the Royal Society but with the possibility of his having become acquainted this early with the ideal of scepticism later associated with the Royal Society, consisting in freedom of

[46] We have Needham's own testimony for this. See his *Disquisitio Anatomica de Formato Foetu* (London, 1667), sig. A3, where he declares that the experiments reported in the book were to a great extent ("*magnam partem*") begun at Trinity in 1654 before he migrated to Queens' College to begin his medical studies.

[47] *Oxford and Cambridge in Transition*, p. 258.

[48] Cowley belonged to the "Philosophical Society," E. S. de Beer's term for the group that became the Royal Society in 1662, by which date Cowley was no longer a member. His ode "To the Royal Society" was written for Sprat's *History of the Royal Society* in 1667.

inquiry and in modesty and diffidence of opinion. I think we can answer without hesitation that he did. These two characteristics, although not yet commonly described as scepticism, are neverthe- less essential to the very conception of the new science, and a nec- essary part of Bacon's legacy. No student who was in any degree exposed to the new science could have been ignorant of those atti- tudes of dissent from the ancients and of caution in establishing new principles which lay behind the new philosophy. Fortunately, we need not leave the matter to speculation. One of Barrow's lec- tures at Trinity has survived, delivered in 1652 while Dryden was an undergraduate there. Whether or not Dryden heard this par- ticular lecture is unimportant. What is significant is that it reveals that both ingredients of what was later to be called scepticism were being presented to the members of the college as ideals which ought to be adopted. Freedom of inquiry, in Barrow's view, is an essential requirement for progress in the sciences. For many ages, he tells his audience, and almost until their own times, "the principles and dictates of Aristotle alone prevailed." But these have at last been rejected, and "the minds of men have awakened from a deep slumber or lethargy." As a result, natural philosophy has begun to revive, along with medicine, mathematics, and the other arts, which now occupy the attention of "many ingenious men."[49] But this is not all. Barrow also speaks of the importance of modesty and diffidence in all inquiries, and of the caution with which opinions ought to be offered. This, he reminds the men of Trinity, had been the counsel of "our own Bacon" (*Verulamius noster*). "For several times in his *Novum Organum* he prudently cautioned against all universal hypotheses" and warned his readers to avoid principles urged by violent argument and "born of the brain of individual men."[50] Thus the ideals of freedom of inquiry and of cautious diffidence bequeathed by Bacon were as much a part of the contribution Trinity College made to the new science as were the experiments conducted in the chambers of some of its members.

Dryden seems to have carried a belief in both these sceptical ideals with him when he left Cambridge, for they appear again and again in his writings of the 1660's and early 1670's. We

[49] "Cartesiana hypothesis de materia et motu haud satisfacit praecipuis naturae phaenomenis," *The Theological Works of Isaac Barrow,* ed. Alexander Napier (Cam- bridge: At the University Press, 1859), IX, 80. My translation.
[50] *Ibid.,* p. 86. I have translated freely from Barrow's Latin.

noticed earlier his allusions to modesty and diffidence—the capacity for self-doubt—in statements about his own scepticism. But freedom of inquiry—the privilege of doubting accepted theories propounded by others—plays an equally important part in his earlier writings. It appears as early as 1662, in "To my Honour'd Friend, Dr. Charleton."

This short poem, written a few months before Charleton proposed Dryden for membership in the Royal Society, is often cited as revealing Dryden's interest in, and sympathy for, the new science. Undoubtedly it affords evidence of these feelings and also of the fact, which I have been stressing, that these sentiments preceded and were responsible for, not a result of, his joining the Royal Society. But it has greater relevance to our subject than this.

In recent years it has been argued that this poem is concerned with two "themes," one scientific, the other political. According to this suggestion, the poem begins with a "survey of science from Aristotle to Charleton" and ends with a "panegyric on the King." Yet both themes—so runs the explanation—are present throughout the poem, their relative positions gradually shifting, until the political theme, which was at first submerged, ultimately becomes the more important. In this view, the first stanza introduces a "historical sketch of science," which, because it is expressed by means of political metaphors, must be intended to imply a parallel between Aristotle and Cromwell, Columbus and General Monck. In the second stanza the survey of science is continued, but science and the state now "become equivalent subjects." Finally, in the last stanza, the political theme becomes dominant, for "the ultimate objective of the epistle is to celebrate the Stuart reign in so far as it is confirmed by the providential correspondence of political developments and the progress of the new science. . . . Science, then, is not the central theme of the poem; it is only a function of the theme, and to detach it is to falsify the poem."[51]

One can readily agree that "science is not the central theme of the poem" without necessarily opting in favor of politics. For to be forced into choosing between a "commentary on the new science" and a poem written "to celebrate the Stuart reign" is to be made the victim of a false dichotomy. "To my Honour'd Friend,

[51] Earl R. Wasserman, "Dryden's Epistle to Charleton," *Journal of English and Germanic Philology,* 55 (1956): 201–12.

Dr. Charleton" is a commendatory verse epistle. Like Dryden's earlier ventures in this minor genre, "To his friend the Authour, on his divine Epigrams," written for John Hoddesdon's *Sion and Parnassus* (1650), and "To my Honored Friend, Sir Robert Howard, On his Excellent Poems," contributed to Howard's *Poems* (1660), these verses were meant to be prefixed to another author's book; and like these earlier poems, it is a panegyric, not of the new science or of Charles II, but of the author who requested the poem and especially of the book in which it was to appear. The book in this case was Walter Charleton's *Chorea Gigantum, or, The most Famous Antiquity of Great-Britain, Vulgarly called Stone-Heng, Standing on Salisbury Plain, Restored to the Danes* (1663). The full title of Dryden's poem makes its subject clear: "To my Honour'd Friend, Dr. Charleton, on his learned and useful Works; and more particularly this of STONE-HENG, by him Restored to the true Founders."

Dryden's problem was to find a way of complimenting Charleton on his book, and the method he chose was the common one of enhancing his subject by encomiastic analogy. For such a purpose, a "historical sketch of science" would have been entirely inappropriate. Charleton's book is not a scientific treatise in any sense recognized at that time. We might classify the subject as archaeological, and hence scientific, but this is to make use of the categories of a later age. In the seventeenth century science was natural philosophy, and no study of human monuments could qualify as scientific. The book for which Dryden wrote his poetic tribute was a historical, or antiquarian, study, and its subject, as such, had nothing in common with the empirical discoveries of Gilbert, Boyle, Harvey, and Ent. What it shared with the experiments of these men, and with the explorations of Columbus as well, was an attitude of mind and a method of inquiry. Charleton's book was an attack upon the accepted theory, propounded earlier by Inigo Jones, that Stonehenge had been built by the Romans as a temple. Charleton refused to accept this account, proposed doubts to weaken its authority, and introduced a new hypothesis that Stonehenge was built by the Danes as a coronation place. The basis on which Dryden could compare Charleton's antiquarian treatise to the more famous exploits of Columbus and the English scientists was the fact that all these discoveries had resulted from the use of scepticism, in the sense of freedom of inquiry; for like these other discoverers, Charleton had rejected the authority of Jones's account, had insisted upon investigating the matter for himself, and had been rewarded with the discovery that the monument had a quite different origin—something which might never have been known had he been content to accept the received opinion. Accordingly, Dryden begins his poem by speaking of an analogous situation in which an accepted theory was proved wrong by one who, like Charleton, was sceptical and insisted on finding out for himself:

> THE longest Tyranny that ever sway'd,
> Was that wherein our Ancestors betray'd
> Their free-born *Reason* to the *Stagirite,*
> And made his Torch their universal Light.
> So *Truth,* while onely one suppli'd the State,
> Grew scarce, and dear, and yet sophisticate,
> Until 'twas bought, like Emp'rique Wares, or Charms,
> Hard words seal'd up with *Aristotle*'s Armes.
> *Columbus* was the first that shook his Throne;
> And found a *Temp'rate* in a *Torrid* Zone:
>
> .   .   .   .
>
> Had we still paid that homage to a *Name,*
> Which onely *God* and *Nature* justly claim;
> The *Western* Seas had been our utmost bound,
> Where *Poets* still might dream the *Sun* was drown'd:
> And all the *Starrs,* that shine in *Southern* Skies,
> Had been admir'd by none but *Salvage* Eyes.
>
> [ll. 1–20]

Dryden employs political metaphors here, certainly, in portraying Aristotle as a tyrant and Columbus as a rebel, but this is the conventional way of describing the rejection of the authority of the ancients in philosophy. In the statements of Sprat, Glanvill, and Barrow which I have quoted, the same political metaphors appear, and Aristotle is referred to as a tyrant or dictator, his followers as slaves. The gullible respect paid to his teachings is analogous, in Dryden's poem, to the easy acceptance of Inigo Jones's theory about Stonehenge. Columbus, although no scientist, is nevertheless the prototype of those who, like Charleton later, depend for their knowledge "on the word of no one." Unwilling to pay "homage to a *Name,*" he was sceptical of the Aristotelian geography and, upon investigation, "found a *Temp'rate* in a *Torrid* Zone."

In the next stanza, Dryden turns to the use which the English have made of this same freedom of inquiry:

> Among th' *Assertors* of free Reason's claim,
> Th' *English* are not the least in Worth, or Fame.
> The World to *Bacon* does not onely owe
> Its *present* Knowledge, but its *future* too.
> *Gilbert* shall live, till *Load-stones* cease to draw,
> Or *British* Fleets the boundless Ocean awe.
> And noble *Boyle,* not less in *Nature* seen,
> Than his great *Brother* read in *States* and *Men.*
> The *Circling* streams, once thought but pools, of blood
> (Whether Life's fewel, or the Bodie's food)
> From dark Oblivion *Harvey*'s name shall save;
> While *Ent* keeps all the honour that he gave.
> Nor are *You,* Learned Friend, the least renown'd;
>
> [ll. 21–33]

Dryden continues, at some length, referring to the reasons for Charleton's renown: his "learned and useful Works," many of them scientific treatises like those of his contemporaries and predecessors whom Dryden has just mentioned; the cures he has wrought as a physician; and finally *Chorea Gigantum,* in which "STONE-HENG, once thought a *Temple,* You have found / A *Throne,* where Kings, our Earthly Gods, were Crown'd." What all of Charleton's disparate activities share in common is the same quality which justifies their comparison to the undertakings of other famous Englishmen: that initial scepticism of a received opinion which leads to a new discovery. Thus, the circling streams of blood "once thought but pools" which Harvey disclosed are paralleled with the coronation throne of Stonehenge "once thought a *Temple,*" which Charleton has revealed. All such knowledge discovered by the "*Assertors* of free Reason's claim," Dryden declares, the world owes to Bacon, since it was he who first proclaimed to Englishmen the ideal of freedom of inquiry.

In the final short stanza, Dryden employs a conceit which compliments both Charleton and the King. Stonehenge has been changed from a temple to a throne by a twofold restoration: that of Charleton himself, who has "Restored to the true Founders" this ancient monument, and that of the King as well. For Stonehenge, by sheltering Charles' "Sacred Head" when he rested there after the Battle of Worcester, was for a brief space a temple in fact as well as in theory. "But, *He* Restor'd, 'tis now become a

24

Throne," where "our *Soveraign* here above the rest might stand." Dryden has simply found the basis for a new similitude which in no way affects the unity of the poem. The subject remains throughout Charleton and his book, for which Dryden is free to find more than one means of praise.

"To my Honour'd Friend, Dr. Charleton," which cites some of the achievements of the new science among the important discoveries to which freedom of inquiry can lead, was published in *Chorea Gigantum* within a few weeks of Dryden's election to the Royal Society on November 19, 1662. His next writings to refer to these accomplishments, *Annus Mirabilis* (1667), with its *"Apostrophe to the Royal Society,"* and *An Essay of Dramatic Poesy* (1668), with its complimentary references to the new philosophy, were both published after Dryden's name had been dropped from the rolls of the Royal Society on October 29, 1666, for nonpayment of dues. As Louis I. Bredvold pointed out some years ago, the fact that *Annus Mirabilis* was written in the latter part of 1666, when Dryden was already in arrears, indicates that his leaving the Royal Society was not occasioned by any change of attitude toward the importance of its activities.[52] Dryden's interest in the "directing, judging, conjecturing, improving and discoursing upon experiments," described by Sprat as the chief business of its meetings, may very well have waned, but his belief in the significance of the discoveries to which such experiments would lead and in the value of the sceptical attitude which made them possible continued unabated, as his subsequent writings show.

In *Annus Mirabilis,* Dryden ignores the scepticism underlying the new philosophy and refers exclusively to scientific inquiries, in order to concentrate on the utilitarian outcome of such investigations as applied to shipping and navigation. This is perfectly appropriate, considering the context in which his remarks appear. They climax a *"Digression concerning Shipping and Navigation"* (stanzas 155 to 166) in which Dryden begins by tracing the history of shipping and navigation "from small beginnings" down to his own time, continues with hopeful predictions of the great progress in these matters which "shall in this Age to *Britain* first be shown," and ends with an *"Apostrophe to the Royal Society"*

[52] See "Dryden and Waller as Members of the Royal Society," *PMLA,* 46 (1931): 954–57 (an answer to Claude Lloyd, "John Dryden and the Royal Society," *ibid.,* 45 [1930]: 967–76).

in which he suggests that it is this Society which will be responsible for the accomplishment of his prophecy.

A well-known passage in *An Essay of Dramatic Poesy* has also been frequently cited as evidence for Dryden's continuing interest in the new science. Undoubtedly it does afford such information, but an exclusive attention to this incidental intelligence has obscured its real importance. It appears in the course of the first of the three debates recounted in the *Essay* and should be considered in the context of the argument in which it figures.

This debate is carried on between Crites, who considers the Ancients superior to the Moderns in every branch of poetry, and Eugenius, who judges that the Moderns "equal the Ancients in most kinds of poesy, and in some surpass them." Because the subject is too broad to debate profitably, the two speakers agree to "limit their dispute to dramatic poesy." But we ought to bear in mind that the positions of the two opponents on this particular subject originate in the general attitudes which each expresses at the beginning of the debate. According to Crites, the Ancients possess an authority and esteem in the realm of poetry which no succeeding generation can hope to challenge. In every kind of poetry the Ancients are "those whom it is our greatest praise to have imitated well," while in the more special field of dramatic poesy "all the rules by which we practise the drama at this day . . . were delivered to us from the observations which Aristotle made of those poets, which either lived before him, or were his contemporaries."[53] For Eugenius, on the other hand, the modern poets are capable of surpassing their predecessors by substituting industry and the observation of nature for an excessive reverence for antiquity. As for the Ancients, he declares,

we own all the helps we have from them, and want neither veneration nor gratitude while we acknowledge that to overcome them we must make use of the advantages we have received from them: but to these assistances we have joined our own industry; for (had we sat down with a dull imitation of them) we might then have lost somewhat of the old perfection, but never acquired any that was new. We draw not therefore after their lines, but those of nature; and having the life before us, besides the experience of all they knew, it is no wonder if we hit some airs and features which they have missed.[54]

[53] *Essays*, I, 27.
[54] *Ibid.*, p. 32.

The basic premises of the two antagonists on the question of the progress of poetry are clearly similar to those of the "dogmatists" and the "free philosophers," respectively, on the matter of the advancement of science. Like the scientific dogmatists, Crites emphasizes before everything else esteem for the Ancients and respect for the rules of dramatic poesy "which Aristotle made." Eugenius, in turn, is opposed, like the sceptical scientists, to an excessive reverence for antiquity which would substitute imitation for industry and the authority of the Ancients for nature herself. It is scarcely surprising, therefore, that both men make use of an argument from analogy with the sciences, although for different ends.

The very first argument which Crites offers on behalf of the ancient drama is based on the theory that each age has been characterized by a common aptitude for a single pursuit in which it has excelled all other periods. "It has been observed of arts and sciences," he declares, "that in one and the same century they have arrived to a great perfection; and no wonder, since every age has a kind of universal genius which inclines those that live in it to some particular studies: the work then being pushed on by many hands, must of necessity go forward," He then introduces the analogy which has so often been quoted apart from its context:

Is it not evident in these last hundred years (when the study of philosophy has been the business of all the virtuosi in Christendom), that almost a new nature has been revealed to us? that more errors of the school have been detected, more useful experiments in philosophy have been made, more noble secrets in optics, medicine, anatomy, astronomy discovered, than in all those credulous and doting ages from Aristotle to us? so true it is, that nothing spreads more fast than science, when rightly and generally cultivated.[55]

Greatly as Crites esteems the Ancients for their poetry, he is quite ready to admit that they have been excelled by the Moderns in natural philosophy. But he tries to use this concession to support his argument. The Moderns have made such great advances in science because this is where their common talent has lain "these last hundred years." The universal genius of the Ancients was for dramatic poesy, and they have surpassed all other ages in this art as completely as the modern era has triumphed in science.

In drawing his analogy between ancient drama and modern sci-

[55] *Ibid.*, p. 26.

ence, however, Crites has made a fatal admission which Eugenius is quick to turn to his own advantage. Although he attributes the scientific advances of the past century to the genius of the age, Crites describes them in terms which emphasize the importance of method. "Nothing," he admits, "spreads more fast than science, when rightly and generally cultivated." And this method, where the sciences are concerned, has consisted in detecting the errors of the school, investigating nature herself, and generally rejecting the authority of "all those credulous and doting ages from Aristotle to us." As Eugenius loses no time in pointing out, if such a method has succeeded so well for the sciences, why may it not lead to equally important results for the arts, and particularly for dramatic poesy? The analogy between the arts and the sciences is indeed a good one, but it favors the Moderns:

I deny not what you urge of arts and sciences, that they have flourished in some ages more than others; but your instance in philosophy makes for me: for if natural causes be more known now than in the time of Aristotle, because more studied, it follows that poesy and other arts may, with the same pains, arrive still nearer to perfection; and, that granted, it will rest for you to prove that they wrought more perfect images of human life than we; which, seeing in your discourse you have avoided to make good, it shall now be my task to show you some part of their defects, and some few excellencies of the Moderns.[56]

Progress in the arts and sciences is to be attributed not to the genius of any particular age but to a proper application of study and industry. Permitted the same freedom as the scientists, the modern poets will be at liberty to recognize the defects of ancient drama and to advance beyond the limits attained by their predecessors. Crites had argued that "to imitate the Ancients well, much labour and long study is required; which pains, I have already shown, our poets would want encouragement to take, if yet they had ability to go through with it."[57] Eugenius too stresses the necessity of painstaking labor and study, but not to imitate the Ancients; rather, to outdistance them and "arrive still nearer to perfection."

When, a few months later in his "Defence of *An Essay of Dramatic Poesy*," Dryden described the *Essay* as a sceptical discourse, he was referring specifically, as we have seen, to the "frame and

[56] *Ibid.*, p. 32.
[57] *Ibid.*, p. 27.

composition of the work," which set forth his opinions in a modest and diffident fashion. But the *Essay* is just as truly a sceptical discourse to the extent that Eugenius demands the same privilege of doubt and dissent that was taken for granted in the "modest inquisitions of the Royal Society." His role in the *Essay* is essentially the same as that of Boyle's interlocutor in *The Sceptical Chymist,* for both speakers challenge the authority of received opinions in the name of free inquiry.

Eugenius appears to have the better argument in this debate and almost certainly expresses Dryden's own views on the question. His analogy with the new science is an obvious one, for Crites' excessive deference to the Ancients offers the same check to advancement in "poesy and other arts" which Bacon had been concerned with opposing in the sciences. But as Dryden had suggested in "To my Honour'd Friend, Dr. Charleton," reverence for the Ancients is not the only form which authority can take. The theory of Inigo Jones on the origin of Stonehenge was a quite recent one, yet its ready acceptance had threatened to hinder further investigation quite as much as had the homage paid to Aristotle's name. On two occasions during the next few years, Dryden, speaking in his own voice, repeated Eugenius' analogy between dramatic poetry and the new philosophy to justify his plea for freedom. But on these occasions he dissented from a more recent authority than that of the Ancients.

The first such occasion occurs in the preface to *An Evening's Love* (1671), where Dryden finds fault with some of Ben Jonson's comedies. He deplores the tendency of some of his critics to demand absolute deference to the authority of Jonson in the drama and to permit no criticism of him to be offered.

I know I have been accused as an enemy of his writings; but without any other reason than that I do not admire him blindly, and without looking into his imperfections. For why should he only be exempted from those frailties from which Homer and Virgil are not free? Or why should there be any *ipse dixit* in our poetry, any more than there is in our philosophy?[58]

Dryden's analogy is a good one. To reverence Jonson as an authority in the drama whose theory and practice of comedy must be "admired blindly" is to pay "that homage to a *Name,* / Which onely *God* and *Nature* justly claim." *Nullius in Verba* is a motto

<hr>

[58] *Ibid.,* p. 148.

to which poets have as much right as the members of the Royal Society, for scepticism is not the exclusive prerogative of the scientists.

The following year, Dryden returned to his attack on the tyranny of authority and broadened the target to include not only Jonson but Shakespeare, Fletcher, and all the older dramatists. The occasion this time occurred in his "Defence of the Epilogue, or, An Essay on the Dramatic Poetry of the Last Age" (1672), where he once again claims for poetry the privilege, already enjoyed by the other arts and sciences, of rejecting the errors inherited from the past. He had been severe with the faults of the earlier dramatists in the "Epilogue to the Second Part of *Granada*," and here he defends his right to criticize them.

I would ascribe to dead authors their just praises in those things wherein they have excelled us; and in those wherein we contend with them for the preeminence, I would acknowledge our advantages to the age, and claim no victory from our wit. This being what I have proposed to myself, I hope I shall not be thought arrogant when I inquire into their errors. For we live in an age so sceptical, that as it determines little, so it takes nothing from antiquity on trust. And I profess to have no other ambition in this essay than that poetry may not go backward, when all other arts and sciences are advancing.[59]

Here at last, in applying the term "sceptical" to the age in which he lived and to his own efforts at the same time, Dryden gives us a complete and unambiguous definition of scepticism. It consists of the same two ingredients which Glanvill was to specify a few years later in describing the scepticism of the "modern free philosophers." On the one hand, it consists in the avoidance of dogmatizing, the modesty and diffidence of "determining little" to which Dryden alluded in his other references to his own scepticism. On the other hand, it involves that freedom of inquiry which "takes nothing from antiquity on trust" and which he was to emphasize in his investigations of dramatic poetry.

As these statements make clear, Dryden did not abandon the ideals of the Royal Society when he relinquished his membership in that organization. Rather, he carried these ideals with him into another sphere. He saw his own role in poetry and criticism as analogous to that of the "modern free philosophers" in science. Scepticism, in Dryden's view, is an attitude and a mode of inquiry

[59] *Ibid.*, p. 169.

which can prove fruitful in many areas besides those which were the proper business of the meetings at Gresham College. The advancement of learning which Bacon predicted from his method need not be confined to natural philosophy; it can be extended to all the arts and sciences, including poetry. In this vision of progress and achievement there is as great a need for a sceptical critic as for a sceptical chemist, for a Dryden as for a Boyle.

Unquestionably, scepticism is an important part of Dryden's characteristic thought. But it is a very different matter from the Pyrrhonism with which it has been so long identified. Indeed, it is in certain important respects the very opposite. Far from being a sign of Dryden's "antirationalism," his scepticism is a confident affirmation of the powers of human reason. When unexamined opinion is accepted as a substitute for honest investigation, Dryden believed, reason is betrayed and truth made captive. But when the pursuit of knowledge is "rightly and generally culti-vated," errors will be detected and truth prevail. In his repeated expression of this hopeful belief, Dryden is not the least among the "*Assertors* of free Reason's claim."

2

A KIND OF LAW-GIVER

Scepticism, as Dryden and the other members of the Royal Society used the term, plays an important part in his thought during the 1660's and 1670's, as we have seen. But it leads to no corollaries in his political or religious thought. Once we have abandoned the idea that "the deepest intellectual bond between Dryden and his age was the Pyrrhonism which he said he was naturally disposed to, and which served him so usefully in clarifying and justifying his opinions on politics and religion,"[1] it would be a serious mistake simply to substitute our new conception of scepticism for the old, while continuing to believe that this was somehow connected with Dryden's politics and religion.

Dryden's faith in freedom of inquiry served him well in criticism; he could appreciate the success to which it had led the members of the Royal Society in natural philosophy, and he believed that it could promote the advancement of all the arts and sciences. Beyond these boundaries, however, he never sought to extend it. Had he applied to the political and religious spheres this freedom of inquiry which "takes nothing from antiquity on trust," questioning accepted beliefs and traditions, he would presumably have been a Whig in politics, a freethinker in religion. But neither Dryden nor the other members of the Royal Society who espoused this ideal considered it universally applicable.

The other ingredient of their scepticism—the cautious attitude toward their own conclusions which leads them to express themselves with modesty and diffidence—is often taken to be Dryden's

[1] Louis I. Bredvold, ed., *The Best of Dryden* (New York: Thomas Nelson, 1933), p. xxxiv.

habit of mind even when he is not writing as a critic. No one, certainly, has questioned the force and thrust of his political poems, such as *Absalom and Achitophel* and *The Medal,* where he states his own position with conviction and gives no quarter to his opponents. But the "natural Diffidence" to which Dryden laid claim would clearly be out of place in satire, and his critics have therefore made an understandable exception in the case of these writings. His poems on religion, on the other hand, are frequently considered as modest expressions of private opinion not dissimilar to *An Essay of Dramatic Poesy. The Hind and the Panther* particularly, with its interchange of opposing views, is often regarded as a dialogue very close in technique to the *Essay,* which Dryden himself described as a sceptical discourse.[2]

It is easy to exaggerate Dryden's modesty and diffidence in *An Essay of Dramatic Poesy.* He calls it a dialogue; we can more accurately describe it as a debate, or rather a series of three debates. In the case of each of the three, the question or "dispute" is announced at the outset: whether ancient or modern drama is superior, whether French or English drama is better, and whether rhyme is or is not proper for the stage. On each question, only two of the four speakers are heard, each of the two delivering a set speech on behalf of one side of the dispute. No interruptions are allowed, no rebuttal permitted, no decision rendered. But the fact that no prizes are awarded does not mean that there are no victors. We know Dryden's own position on these questions from his other critical writings and particularly from the "Defence of *An Essay of Dramatic Poesy,*" where he enlarges upon these matters in his own person. He clearly considered modern drama superior to the ancient, English drama better than the French, and rhyme appropriate to the stage. In each of the three debates, the defender of the position Dryden privately opposes speaks first. He is answered by a spokesman for Dryden's views who has all the advantages. As the second speaker in a debate without rebuttals, he is able to answer his opponent's arguments in detail without having to extend him a similar privilege. He has the last word in the argument and he speaks at far greater length than his opponent. The speeches of Eugenius and Neander which con-

---

[2] See Louis I. Bredvold, *The Intellectual Milieu of John Dryden* (Ann Arbor: University of Michigan Press, 1934), pp. 13–14; Earl Miner, "The Significance of Plot in *The Hind and the Panther,*" *Bulletin of the New York Public Library,* 69 (1965): 454.

clude the first two debates are in fact twice the length of their antagonists', while Neander's speech on behalf of rhyme is some four times as long as the one he answers. It would be a dull reader who could not decide which speaker had the advantage of such arguments.

If Dryden's diffidence is minimal it is nevertheless sufficient to justify his comparing the *Essay* to "the modest inquisitions of the Royal Society." He has preserved the character of a modest inquirer by putting his views into the mouths of other speakers, by presenting them as opinions rather than as rules, and by studiously avoiding any appearance of partiality in rendering a decision between uneven combatants: "they differed in their opinions, as 'tis probable they would; neither do I take upon me to reconcile, but to relate them . . . without passion or interest; leaving your Lordship to decide it in favour of which part you shall judge most reasonable."[3]

Such detachment is appropriate and even desirable on questions such as these, which are the proper subject of free inquiry. It has no place, however, in the discussion of topics to which this freedom does not apply. The justification for sceptical modesty and diffidence is that it accompanies the expression of provisional opinions in an open investigation where dogmatizing would hamper freedom and terminate inquiry. In religion, however, to Dryden and his contemporaries, dogmas are appropriate, traditional beliefs should be accepted, and a doubting attitude ought to be discouraged. Firm conviction, not timorous caution, was called for in matters of religion which were not the discoveries of an individual nor the opinions of a scattered few.

This difference is noticeable in those dialogues by members of the Royal Society which are concerned with religious questions. Walter Charleton's *The Immortality of the Human Soul* (1657), Henry More's *Divine Dialogues* (1668), and Robert Boyle's *A Discourse of Things above Reason* (1681) all make use of the dialogue form.[4] But although these dialogues are, like Dryden's *Essay,* "sustained by persons of several opinions," the views expressed are not, as in the *Essay,* "all of them left doubtful, to

---

[3] *Of Dramatic Poesy and Other Critical Essays,* ed. George Watson (London: J. M. Dent and Sons, 1962), I, 16. (Hereafter referred to as *Essays.*)

[4] Boyle's authorship of *A Discourse of Things above Reason* has been questioned by C. C. J. Webb in "Some Bodleian Memories," *Bodleian Library Record,* 4 (1953): 277–79. The solution to the problem does not, in any case, affect my discussion of the pamphlet.

be determined by the readers in general."[5] In each of these dialogues there is one speaker who reflects the position, not simply of the author, but of his church: Athanasius in Charleton's book, Philotheus in More's dialogues, and Sophronius in Boyle's discourse. Each is engaged in a Socratic dialogue rather than a formal debate with one or more antagonists who hold views antithetical to the Christian religion. The author's spokesman is not only given the longest speeches and the best arguments but is awarded the decision as well; for he succeeds in converting or effectually silencing his opponents and in winning the applause of the neutral bystanders. Clearly the popularity of the dialogue form among members of the Royal Society when engaged in religious controversy points to other advantages than those of modesty and diffidence.

These advantages are mentioned in the "Advertisement to the Reader" prefixed to *The Immortality of the Human Soul* of Dryden's friend Charleton. James M. Osborn has argued, very persuasively I believe, that it was Dryden who wrote this advertisement, while he was employed by Henry Herringman, the printer of the book.[6] Whether it is by Dryden or by Herringman himself, who signed it, the advertisement considers the reasons that induced the ancient philosophers "to deliver their opinions and documents, as wel Physical as Moral, in the plain and familiar way of *Dialogue*." The principal reason was that

they thereby gave themselves the advantage of freely alleaging the various and different Conceptions and Perswasions of Men, concerning the subject, which they had designed to discuss: Which in the stricter method of Positive and Apodictical Teaching, they could not with equal conveniency do; And how much better we may judge of the truth of any Theorem, when we have heard as wel the principal Reasons that impugne, as those that assert it, is obvious to common observation.[7]

The dialogue, then, is an excellent form in which to present not only an inquiry but an argument as well, for in the latter case it permits the author to air the possible objections to his proposition and to answer them fully. In religious controversy it was a particularly useful form in which to present the false positions which the author wished to assail.

[5] *Essays*, I, 123.
[6] See *John Dryden: Some Biographical Facts and Problems* (New York: Columbia University Press, 1940), pp. 174–75.
[7] *The Immortality of the Human Soul* (London, 1657), sig. b4.

In Parts II and III of *The Hind and the Panther,* Dryden presents two separate dialogues between the Hind, signifying the Catholic church, and the Panther, symbolizing the Church of England. If we carefully examine one of these dialogues—that offered in Part II—we shall see that it is very far from being a "balancing of conflicting ideas." This is not a formal debate, as in *An Essay of Dramatic Poesy.* It is a dramatic series of alternate speeches put forward by the two participants. But as in the *Essay,* all the advantages are given to one side—in this case, that of the Hind—and the contest on this occasion is more uneven than it was in the *Essay.* The Panther, as the aggressor, speaks first, so that the Hind is always in the position of answering her antagonist and is favored with the last word. Of the 648 lines given to the speeches of the two animals in Part II, the Hind is allotted 575 lines, the Panther only 73.

Departing from his practice in the *Essay,* Dryden makes no pretense of impartiality. As in the prose dialogues on religion by members of the Royal Society, the decision is clearly awarded to the side the author favors. Otherwise, however, there is little similarity between the urbane discussion among friends offered in these genuine dialogues and the heated exchanges between the antagonists in *The Hind and the Panther* which Dryden describes as "sharp debates." There are ten of these exchanges in Part II, and a glance at the number of lines given to the antagonists in each of them will reveal the way in which Dryden prepares a crushing defeat for the Panther.

	Panther	Hind
1	17	20
2	6	16
3	10	67
4	8	23
5	4	4
6	5	31
7	4	6
8	6	69
9	8	84
10	5	255

It is noticeable that while most of the Hind's replies are considerably longer than the Panther's speeches the difference increases as the debate proceeds, so that in the last three exchanges the Panther is overwhelmed by her opponent. At the end of the first of these particularly uneven exchanges—the eighth, in which the Hind has delivered a reply of 69 lines—the Panther is practically reduced to helplessness: "nor cou'd the *Panther* well enlarge/ With weak defence against so strong a charge" (II, 297–98). She resorts instead to a brief objection which initiates the ninth exchange, in which she is rewarded with an even longer reply, at the end of which the Panther can only manage a question which is prefaced by a concession to her opponent. The stage is set for the Hind's triumph: "The Dame, who saw her fainting foe retir'd,/With force renew'd, to victory aspir'd" (II, 394–95). The Hind's great speech of 255 lines follows, at the end of which a remarkable phenomenon takes place:

> Thus, while with heav'nly charity she spoke,
> A streaming blaze the silent shadows broke:
> Shot from the skyes a chearfull azure light;
> The birds obscene to forests wing'd their flight,
> And gaping graves receiv'd the wandring guilty spright.
>
> [II, 649–53]

No earthly judge, but Heaven itself, has proclaimed the Hind's victory, and the Panther, stupefied by this sign of divine partiality, preserves a sullen silence.

The pattern of the dialogue in Part III is similar. Another series of exchanges displays the same disparity in length between the speeches of the Hind, who is given a total of over 800 lines, and those of the Panther, who is allowed little more than 300, most of them spent in relating the parable of the swallows. Again the Hind manages to silence her opponent who, unable to make further answer, is yet unwilling to concede defeat, "But, with affected Yawnings at the close,/Seem'd to require her natural repose" (III, 1291–92).

Dryden's choice of the dialogue form in *The Hind and the Panther* is clearly dictated neither by generosity to the other side nor by a desire to state both positions as fairly as possible, but by a time-honored rhetorical consideration. It is to the advantage of the side he is defending to forestall possible objections and replies by bringing them forward at once, presenting them as unfounded accusations or honest misunderstandings, and offering a full and decisive answer. In this way the reader is supposed to be better able to perceive the impregnability of the Hind's position, having "heard as wel the principal Reasons that impugne, as those that assert it."

Religio Laici, Dryden's other poem on religion, is susceptible to the same kind of misunderstanding as *The Hind and the Panther.* Although it is not written in dialogue form, this poem too has been compared to *An Essay of Dramatic Poesy* on the grounds that in these two widely separated works Dryden reveals a similar degree of caution. The poem is taken to be the expression of his private opinions on the subject of religion—a kind of religious confession or apologia. So one critic sees *Religio Laici* as a product of "self-questioning," in which Dryden was "to repeat exactly the method that he had followed" in the *Essay.* "As in the case of the drama, he now attempted to think the matter [of religion] out and make clear in his own mind what was the best course for him to follow. *Religio Laici* was thus his 'Essay of what I can believe'."[8] Another critic of the poem, who also feels that the "other work to which it has most resemblance in method and spirit is the *Dramatick Poesie,*" agrees with the view that it is an expression of Dryden's personal opinions: "He now writes the *Religio Laici* to make sure as well as he can where he stands as a churchman. The poem was wholly spontaneous. He assumes 'an honest layman's liberty' and argues out his problems for the peace of his own mind."[9]

It must be said at once that Dryden himself has been in part responsible for this view of his poem. The self-effacement of his title, *Religio Laici, or, A Laymans Faith,* has tended to support this interpretation, suggesting as it does the kind of private essay on religion represented by Sir Thomas Browne's *Religio Medici.* Even more important is the diffidence he assumes in that passage from the preface to the poem which we noticed in the last chapter, where he denies any intention "to impose my Opinions." But this phrase is not an accurate description of the contents of the poem, nor was it intended as such.

In offering the public a poem on religion, Dryden was confronted with a problem which he could not afford to ignore. He was a layman writing on a subject which was the special province of divines. This in itself was no insuperable difficulty. Other

---

[8] Osborn, *John Dryden,* p. 106.

[9] David Nichol Smith, *John Dryden* (Cambridge: At the University Press, 1950), pp. 60–61. For another expression of the same view, see Roger Sharrock, ed., *Selected Poems of John Dryden* (London: William Heinemann, 1963), p. 136.

laymen, some of them his own friends and acquaintances, were in the habit of writing on religious subjects. Walter Charleton had dealt with such topics in *The Darkness of Atheism* and *The Immortality of the Human Soul,* and Robert Boyle had done so in numerous treatises. But these were learned men who were accustomed to addressing the public on any number of serious subjects, among which religion found a fitting place. This was hardly Dryden's case, whose previous role as the author of satires and plays, including some rather dubious comedies, in no way entitled him to put himself forward as a religious controversialist.

Dryden overcame this obstacle at the very outset by devoting the first part of his preface to what Aristotle calls a "remedial introduction"—one which is concerned with the author himself and directed to removing prejudice—in this case, against a poem on religion whose title page announced that it was "Written by Mr. Dryden." "A Preface," he remarked in a similar forward to *The Hind and the Panther,* "is but a bespeaking of Favour." That is his purpose here. He begins at once by stating the objection which he must answer: "A POEM with so bold a Title, and a Name prefix'd, from which the handling of so serious a Subject wou'd not be expected, may reasonably oblige the Author, to say somewhat in defence both of himself, and of his undertaking."

Dryden begins with a defense of himself, and of the modest role which he professes to have assumed:

In the first place, if it be objected to me that being a *Layman,* I ought not to have concern'd my self with Speculations, which belong to the Profession of *Divinity;* I cou'd Answer, that perhaps, Laymen, with equal advantages of Parts and Knowledge, are not the most incompetent Judges of Sacred things; But in the due sense of my own weakness and want of Learning, I plead not this: I pretend not to make my self a Judge of Faith, in others, but onely to make a Confession of my own; I lay no unhallow'd hand upon the Ark; but wait on it, with the Reverence that becomes me at a distance.

His attitude could hardly be more disarming. He disclaims all title to the public authority of those whose profession is divinity, and even declines the sanction accorded to such laymen as Charleton and Boyle, "with equal advantages of Parts and Knowledge," who can compete with churchmen on the same terms. Instead, he solicits as a favor the respectful hearing he cannot demand as a right.

Having justified himself, Dryden takes up the defense of his undertaking:

In the next place I will ingenuously confess, that the helps I have us'd in this small Treatise, were many of them taken from the Works of our own Reverend Divines of the Church of *England*; so that the Weapons with which I Combat Irreligion, are already Consecrated; though I suppose they may be taken down as lawfully as the Sword of *Goliah* was by *David*, when they are to be employed for the common Cause, against the Enemies of Piety.

Dryden insures a favorable reception for the religious ideas in his poem by suggesting that they are the offspring of better minds, toward which he stands in the relation of a foster parent. If the arguments in the poem were fashioned into verse by a weak and unlearned layman, they are nevertheless for the most part not of his devising. They are borrowed helps, "many of them taken from the Works of our own Reverend Divines of the Church of *England*," and as such they are "already Consecrated" and deserving of the sanction and authority accorded to their authors. The sources to which Dryden refers are clearly not devotional works nor even theological treatises. They are the controversial writings of religious apologists which have provided him with "the Weapons with which I Combat Irreligion" in a polemical poem directed "against the Enemies of Piety."

Dryden adds to this defense some remarks which have contributed to the common misunderstanding about the nature of his poem. Having made certain Anglican divines responsible for many of the arguments in his poem, he continues:

I intend not by this to intitle them to any of my errours; which, yet, I hope are only those of Charity to Mankind; and such as my *own* Charity has caus'd me to commit, that of *others* may more easily excuse. Being naturally inclin'd to Scepticism in Philosophy, I have no reason to impose my Opinions, in a Subject which is above it: But whatever they are, I submit them with all reverence to my Mother Church, accounting them no further mine, than as they are Authoriz'd, or at least, uncondemn'd by her.

This is the kind of disclaimer which is common to many prefaces. In acknowledging his indebtedness to others for help, the author proceeds to lay exclusive claim to any errors the work may contain. Dryden adds as well the safeguard from formal heresy, common also in religious writings of the period, which refers all disputed opinions to the final decision of the author's "Mother Church." Those who have read *Religio Laici* as a "spontaneous" poem, the expression of the poet's private views on religion, apparently believe it consists entirely of these opinions which he quite properly declines to impose on the reader. But Dryden clearly indicates that these opinions are only a few notions of his own which he has occasionally introduced in the course of amplifying his arguments, and which may possibly be erroneous. He refers to only one of them, occasioned by his "Charity to Mankind." This is his suggestion in the poem that St. Athanasius grew "too eager in dispute" with the Arians, "flew high; and as his *Christian* Fury rose / Damn'd all for *Hereticks* who durst *oppose*."

Dryden reinforces the distinction he makes between the greater part of his arguments, which are assuredly true in view of their origin, and the occasional opinions of his own, which are liable to error:

And, indeed, to secure my self on this side, I have us'd the necessary Precaution, of showing this Paper before it was Publish'd to a judicious and learned Friend, a Man indefatigably zealous in the service of the Church and State: and whose Writings, have highly deserv'd of both. He was pleas'd to approve the body of the Discourse, and I hope he is more my Friend, than to do it out of Complaisance: 'Tis true he had too good a tast to like it all; and amongst some other faults recommended to my second view, what I have written, perhaps too boldly on St. *Athanasius*: which he advised me wholy to omit.

It has been suggested that this "judicious and learned Friend" was John Tillotson, at that time Dean of St. Paul's.[10] Whoever he was, he apparently occupied a position of some eminence, and by his sanction was able to confer upon the "body of the Discourse" a vicarious authority which Dryden himself was unable to bestow. By carefully excepting his own opinions, such as that on St. Athanasius, from this sanction, Dryden once again exhibits a proper diffidence toward his private views, while emphasizing that most of his arguments are not matters of opinion but the standard weapons of Anglican controversialists, consecrated by long use and requiring no apology.

In *Religio Laici*, then, as in *The Hind and the Panther*, Dryden

---

[10] See Nichol Smith, *John Dryden*, pp. 88–89. Nichol Smith states categorically that the friend was Tillotson, but offers no evidence. The suggestion has been amplified by David Brown, "Dryden's 'Religio Laici' and the 'Judicious and Learned Friend'," *Modern Language Review*, 56 (1961): 66–69.

is mostly engaged in defending what he considers to be certain and indubitable truths, and only occasionally concerned in proffering tentative suggestions. His role in such an enterprise is very different from that of the sceptical critic who, in the essays, exhibits the wary caution of an independent inquirer. The role that he takes in his polemical poems on religion is best described in his own words at the end of the preface to *Religio Laici*, where he is justifying the style of his poem, which is that of Horace's *Epistles* rather than of heroic poetry:

The Expressions of a Poem, design'd purely for Instruction, ought to be Plain and Natural, and yet Majestick: for here the Poet is presum'd to be a kind of Law-giver, and those three qualities which I have nam'd are proper to the Legislative style. The Florid, Elevated and Figurative way is for the Passions; for Love and Hatred, Fear and Anger, are begotten in the Soul by shewing their Objects out of their true proportion; either greater than the Life, or less; but Instruction is to be given by shewing them what they naturally are. A Man is to be cheated into Passion, but to be reason'd into Truth.

Dryden's conception of the poet as "a kind of Law-giver" is very far from the modern notion of his function, but it is nevertheless a common one in the seventeenth century.[11] It is a conception of the poet as a rhetorician. In a poem such as *Religio Laici* or *The Hind and the Panther*, "design'd purely for Instruction," the poet's business is not to usurp the function of the philosopher or theologian and to engage in new speculations. His task is to borrow his arguments from elsewhere, to enhance them with the power of poetic expression, and to fashion them into a poetic discourse whereby men may be "reason'd into Truth." If the "Legislative style" of such an enterprise reminds us of the "Magisterial authority" which Dryden condemned in Lucretius, there is this important difference: Lucretius' fault was a "positive assertion of his Opinions"; Dryden's purpose is the enforcement of "*Sacred Truth.*"

His description of the rhetorical end of these poems as one of reasoning men into truth points to his choice of logical argument

---

[11] For an excellent study of this conception of the poet, with particular attention to Dryden, see K. G. Hamilton, *The Two Harmonies: Poetry and Prose in the Seventeenth Century* (Oxford: Clarendon Press, 1963). The only previous study of Dryden's place in the rhetorical tradition is that of Lillian Feder, "John Dryden's Use of Classical Rhetoric," *PMLA*, 69 (1954): 1258–78, which is mostly concerned with his prose.

as the principal means of persuasion. But it does not exclude the other available means at his disposal. Having been schooled in the rhetorical tradition, he was certainly aware that, as Aristotle points out, the rhetorician "must not only try to make the argument of his speech demonstrative and worthy of belief; he must also make his own character look right and put his hearers, who are to decide, into the right frame of mind."[12] In other words, the speaker or writer who hopes to convince his audience must pay attention to all the available means of persuasion: not only to *logos*, or argument ("the Weapons with which I Combat Irreligion"), but also to *ethos*, or the impression his character makes on his listeners, and to *pathos*, or the feelings of his audience. To concentrate exclusively on compelling arguments while ignoring the audience's frame of mind and its assessment of the speaker is to risk winning a battle and losing a war.

A proper consideration of *ethos* requires that the rhetorician win the trust and confidence of his audience. If he is making a speech or writing a tract or poem in which he offers his arguments in his own voice, he must solicit these feelings for himself by attention to subjective *ethos*. In the case of a tract or poem, however, some imaginary speaker may be employed to present his arguments instead, and in this case the rhetorician must win the respect of the audience for this fictitious person by concentrating on objective *ethos*. In either case, the qualities of character which the speaker must reveal in order to inspire the listener's trust and confidence will depend on the nature of his appeal. The qualities expected of a person engaged in logical argument are those of moderation, reasonableness, and modesty. Dryden takes special pains to create an *ethos* out of these very ingredients in his two poems on religion.

In *The Hind and the Panther*, Parts II and III, the arguments are carried on between the Hind and the Panther themselves, and here Dryden's problem is one of creating an objective *ethos* for each speaker which is appropriate to his purpose of making the Hind's arguments credible to the audience, and those of the Panther unconvincing. The character and motivation of these two combatants are as opposite as the positions they adopt in their dispute.

[12] *Rhetoric*, in *The Basic Works of Aristotle*, ed. Richard McKeon (New York: Random House, 1941), p. 1379.

43

The qualities of character which the Panther reveals are those, not of moderation, reasonableness, and modesty, but of passion and prejudice. Throughout the course of the debates, "the *Panther* full of inward discontent" betrays violent emotions whenever she speaks, "her glowing eye-balls glitt'ring in the dark." The position she adopts in her controversy with the Hind stems not from reasonable conviction but from a whole complex of ill-natured passions:

> Disdain, with gnawing envy, fell despight,
> And canker'd malice stood in open sight.
> Ambition, int'rest, pride without controul,
> And jealousie, the jaundice of the soul;
> Revenge, the bloudy minister of ill,
> With all the lean tormenters of the will.
>
> [III, 70–75]

Dryden's ascription of such an *ethos* to the Panther is clearly calculated to alienate the readers' sympathies so that they will discount her arguments.

In deliberate contrast to the malice, passion, and violence of the Panther, the qualities of character exhibited by the Hind are those of courtesy, reasonableness, and restraint. More interested in correcting her opponent than in triumphing over her, she speaks in moderate accents. Confronted with her furious antagonist, Dryden writes, the Hind could not be goaded into an angry retort, "But strove with Anodynes t'asswage the smart, / And mildly thus her med'cine did impart" (III, 82–83). We have noticed that the Hind is granted signs of divine favor in the course of her debate with the Panther; yet the modesty of her behavior receives special emphasis. Even her great speech at the close of Part II, in which she puts forward her claims to be considered the true church, is prefaced by the line: "Then thus the matron modestly renew'd." In this guise of a mild and reasonable appellant, the Hind evinces a character designed to insure the readers' sympathy, and a respectful hearing for her arguments.

In *Religio Laici* Dryden must create a similar *ethos* in order to promote the acceptance of his arguments, but here his problem is compounded by two considerations. In the first place, since the arguments in this poem are offered in his own voice, he must establish subjective *ethos*, a subtler and more difficult task than that of creating objective *ethos*. In such a case, he can seldom rely on explicit self-description; more often he must reveal his character implicitly through his tone and manner. Secondly, he possesses none of the inherent advantages, and consequent authority, of the Hind, who is not simply an advocate for her church, but that church itself. To the extent that Dryden is only a voluntary spokesman for his church in *Religio Laici*, and a layman as well, a greater degree of modesty is expected of such a speaker, who must present his arguments with considerable diffidence.

Dryden's solution is to capitalize on his inferiority as a layman and even to emphasize it in the course of creating a sympathetic *ethos*. If he cannot seriously pose as an authority on the matters under discussion, it is better to understate his competence and to appear in the role of an arbitrator, advancing his arguments under the guise of happy solutions to the honest difficulties of his opponents. So, having anticipated and attempted to answer an objection to his position, he comments: "Thus far my Charity this path has try'd; / (A much unskilfull, but well meaning guide:)" (ll. 224–25) and he goes on to refer to the notions he has just presented as "these crude thoughts." His answer to another anticipated objection begins with this modest demur:

> Shall I speak plain, and in a Nation free
> Assume an honest *Layman's Liberty?*
> I think (according to my little Skill,
> To my own Mother-Church submitting still:)
> [ll. 316–19]

In such lines, kept to a judicious minimum in the poem, Dryden resorts to explicit self-description: he is "an honest *Layman*," "a much unskilfull, but well meaning guide"; usually his ethical appeals are less patent, a matter of implicit tone rather than of explicit statement. In either case, Dryden tries to create the impression that he is a person of good will whose very status as a layman guarantees his disinterestedness, since he has none of the professional obligations of a clergyman to defend his church's position.

The poem closes with a particularly explicit ethical appeal:

> Thus have I made my own Opinions clear:
> Yet neither Praise expect, nor Censure fear:
> And this unpolish'd, rugged Verse, I chose;
> As fittest for Discourse, and nearest Prose:

For, while from *Sacred Truth* I do not swerve,
Tom Sternhold's, or *Tom Shadwell*'s *Rhimes* will serve.

[ll. 451–56]

He leaves the reader with a final reminder that he is disinterested: he will "neither Praise expect, nor Censure fear." There is no hint here that the arguments he has presented in the poem "were many of them taken from the Works of our own Reverend Divines of the Church of *England*," as he frankly admits in the preface. For what they are worth, they are simply "my own Opinions," set in "unpolish'd, rugged Verse" by an honest layman. Such modesty is similar to the Hind's, although more prominent, in keeping with his role as a layman. The attitude of both stems not from self-doubt or a fear of correction but from a confidence in never swerving from "*Sacred Truth*" which permits them to rely on courteous efforts at persuasion. In both cases, this is not the effect of Dryden's "natural Diffidence" but a rhetorical posture assumed for the occasion.

Any good rhetorician, of course, must have his audience constantly in mind; the modes of persuasion he adopts and the form in which he presents them must be appropriate to the particular group for whom they are intended and to his specific purpose in addressing them. Dryden gives careful consideration to his audience in all of his rhetorical poetry. In each of his two poems on religion, the poetic form he adopts is admirably suited to his prospective audience, to his own relationship with these readers, and to the persuasive purpose for which the poem is designed.

In *Religio Laici* Dryden's audience is not the enemies of piety whom he is attacking, but a very different group. It consists, as the preface makes clear, of his fellow Anglicans. The fact that he is exclusively addressing himself to the members of his own church emerges first of all from the nature of his appeals. Only an Anglican reader would be impressed by the information that the poet had borrowed much of his material from "the Works of our own Reverend Divines of the Church of *England*," or be reassured as to the poem's orthodoxy by being told that it had met with the approval of "a Man indefatigably zealous in the service of the Church and State." Even more significant is Dryden's invariable practice throughout the preface of using the first person plural to refer to the Church of England, the third person plural to refer to the enemies of piety whom he mentions. The Church of England is consistently referred to as "our Church" or "our Religion," while that of some of his adversaries is "their Church" or "that Religion." Similarly, the Anglican clergy appear as "our own Reverend Divines," "our venerable *Hooker*," or "a Reverend Prelate of our Church," in contrast to those of other churches who are described as "their Clergy," "their Champion *Bellarmine*," "their Father *Cres*," or "an Adversary to our Religion." The effect of Dryden's language is to suggest a close bond between him and his readers which consists in their sharing a common religion as well as a mutual contempt for the enemies of piety.

In his choice of audience, Dryden does not differ from numerous Anglican apologists who wrote in prose. Not only books and pamphlets, but countless sermons by Restoration divines were expended in denouncing atheism, Catholicism, and Dissent. To profess amusement at such efforts on the score that atheists, Catholics, and Dissenters were absent from the congregations which listened to these sermons is to miss the point. Their purpose was not to reach and convert the atheists in their coffee houses or the Dissenters and Catholics in their conventicles and private places of worship. These sermons were deliberately addressed to the Anglican faithful in the hope of preventing further defections; the elaborate arguments of which they consist were intended to impress the wavering and the doubtful, not those who had already lapsed.

The same purpose informs the many books and pamphlets which appeared as confutations of Hobbes's *Leviathan* or of various books by prominent Dissenters or Catholic apologists, although their approach is different. Instead of addressing the Anglican laity directly, they may take the form of a dialogue involving imaginary speakers, or of a "letter to a friend" who is experiencing difficulty in defending his beliefs. Quite often they are offered as a "reply" or "answer" which pretends to engage directly with some adversary. But these are merely exhibition matches for the edification of the faithful, who were accustomed to being addressed directly on the same subject from the pulpit. Few Anglican apologists could have been so sanguine as to expect a recantation from their opponent. Their hopes were more modest: to confirm their coreligionists in the beliefs they already held and to provide them with a reasonable basis for their religion.

Similarly, Dryden cannot seriously have expected *Religio Laici* to win proselytes among the "Enemies of Piety" he engages in the poem. The efforts of his deliberative rhetoric were expended, not on conversion, but on a less ambitious goal. As a "well meaning guide," he would offer his fellow laymen a "preservative" or "antidote," in the language of so many religious pamphlets of the time, against the doubts and difficulties encouraged by the enemies of piety. But his approach must be suitable to his own abilities and profession. A sermon in verse, addressed directly to the members of his own church, would be a presumptuous undertaking, as well as an artistic failure. A direct assault upon his more learned adversaries would be a task beyond his powers. As a poet, his recourse was not to imitate the method of those prose works which provided him with his arguments, but to adopt some poetic model appropriate to his purpose. In his preface, Dryden declares:

> It remains that I acquaint the Reader, that the Verses were written for an ingenious young Gentleman my Friend; upon his Translation of *The Critical History of the Old Testament,* compos'd by the learned Father *Simon:* The Verses therefore are address'd to the Translatour of that Work, and the style of them is, what it ought to be, Epistolary.
>
> If any one be so lamentable a Critique as to require the Smoothness, the Numbers and the Turn of Heroick Poetry in this Poem; I must tell him, that if he has not read *Horace,* I have studied him, and hope the style of his Epistles is not ill imitated here.

Whether or not Dryden was on terms of close acquaintance with the "ingenious young Gentleman" whose name was Henry Dickinson need not concern us at this time. It is enough that Dryden presents him in the role of the "Friend" to whom Horatian epistles are conventionally addressed, and that this friend shared Dryden's own status as a layman of the Church of England. As such, he can serve as an excellent surrogate for Dryden's more numerous audience, consisting of Anglican laymen as well, who can identify themselves with Dickinson and experience with him the persuasive force of the poet's arguments. In the role of one who is addressing a coreligionist in the easy accents of a Horatian epistle, Dryden can express these arguments in the guise of spontaneous opinions, the effect of a sturdy common sense which refuses to be dismayed by the assaults of the enemies of piety on the poet's "Mother-Church."

In *The Hind and the Panther,* Dryden's audience has not changed, but his own relationship to that audience has altered radically. His prospective readers still consist, by and large, of

Anglicans, who made up the greatest share of the reading public; but he now addresses them, not as a fellow Anglican, but as the member of a despised and persecuted minority. The comparatively brief preface which he wrote for this poem suggests the intended audience and something of the strained relationship he feels toward them. In *Religio Laici* he faced nothing more serious than the mild objection "that being a *Layman,* I ought not to have concern'd my self with Speculations, which belong to the Profession of *Divinity.*" Such criticisms were easily met by a friendly preface. But in his new situation Dryden can expect nothing less than active hostility, and he abandons at the outset any hope of dispelling these feelings by the kind of "remedial introduction" he had provided for his earlier poem. He begins:

The Nation is in too high a Ferment, for me to expect either fair War, or even so much as fair Quarter from a Reader of the opposite Party. All Men are engag'd either on this side or that: and tho' Conscience is the common *Word,* which is given by both, yet if a Writer fall among Enemies, and cannot give the Marks of *Their* Conscience, he is knock'd down before the Reasons of his own are heard. A *Preface,* therefore, which is but a bespeaking of Favour, is altogether useless. What I desire the *Reader* should know concerning me, he will find in the Body of the Poem; if he have but the patience to peruse it.

Although his poem is intended for the members of the Panther's church, Dryden could have hoped to win few proselytes among them. A kind of grudging silence was the best the Hind could win from the Panther herself, after all; but this was no small concession from so dangerous a beast. It was enough that she

> civily drew in her sharpn'd paws,
> Not violating hospitable laws,
> And pacify'd her tail, and lick'd her frothy jaws.
> [II, 718–20]

Similarly, Dryden was attempting to persuade his Anglican readers to grant religious tolerance as well as political toleration to the members of his new church.

To achieve this purpose he depends on two principal methods in this long "Poem, in Three Parts." The first is what he himself describes in the preface as satire, employed through the beast characters in Part I and the two "Episodes, or Fables" in Part III, and directed against the Dissenters in general and the more extreme factions among both Anglicans and Catholics in the hope

49

of appealing to the more moderate Anglicans. The effect is to isolate the Dissenters, renounce the actions of the more extreme Catholics, and question the motives of the more intransigent Anglicans in the expectation of arriving at some kind of accommodation between men of good will in the Anglican and Catholic camps.[13] Dryden's second method is the dialogue between the Hind and the Panther in Parts II and III. The dialogue in Part III on the subject of political toleration is presented, as Dryden remarks in the preface, in the "hope, that the Church of *England* might have been perswaded to have taken off the *Penal Lawes* and the *Test,* which was one Design of the Poem when I propos'd to my self the writing of it." The dialogue in Part II, on the other hand, is, as he points out, "chiefly concerning Church Authority," and here his purpose is to persuade Anglican readers, if not to adopt the Catholic view of this question, at least to accord some measure of religious tolerance to those who accept a position which has been shown to be not unreasonable.

Dryden's chances of succeeding in these designs were severely hampered, however, by the fact that he could expect more than the ordinary hostility felt by Anglicans for Catholics at a time when the nation was in ferment and moving inexorably toward revolution. The author of *The Hind and the Panther,* whose identity was an open secret, was not only a Catholic, but a recent convert from the Church of England. In the eyes of Anglicans he was a renegade and apostate who had even less right to expect a fair hearing than most members of his newly adopted church. Any poetic form such as that of a Horatian epistle which focuses attention on the poet's own personality, invites trust, and sugggests a sharing of common interests was therefore out of the question. Instead, Dryden distracts attention from himself throughout most of *The Hind and the Panther.* His role as narrator allows him to remain discreetly in the background at most times. The beast

[13] In the preface to the poem, Dryden declares that his satire is not "any way intended" for "many of our Sects, and more indeed then I could reasonably have hop'd, who have withdrawn themselves from the Communion of the *Panther;* and embrac'd this Gracious Indulgence of His Majesty in point of Toleration." The Declaration of Indulgence to which he refers had caught him by surprise, however, as he admits later in the preface, "about a Fortnight before I had finish'd" the poem. This event, as is well known, had rendered much of Dryden's strategy in the poem obsolete. His course there had been to isolate the Dissenters without exception and to appeal to the Anglicans to form an alliance with the Catholics. The King's new policy, to which Dryden tries to fit his poem in the preface, was to abandon the Anglicans and effect an alliance with the Dissenters.

characters in Part I are, of course, offered in his own voice, but these, quite as much as the "two Episodes, or Fables" in Part III to which he alludes in the preface, are "Common Places of *Satyr*, whether true or false, which are urg'd by the Members of the one Church against the other," and as such "are not of my Invention." The "matters of dispute" handled in Parts II and III, however, are something else again. Here he avoids the spectacle of a recent convert presuming to speak authoritatively on behalf of his new church while proceeding to attack his former "Mother-Church." Instead, he puts the dialogue into the mouths of invented characters, creating for each an appropriate objective *ethos*, as we have seen.

Nevertheless, the reader cannot be expected to ignore the identity of the poetic narrator entirely, and some effort must be made to alleviate the prejudice he bears him. In declining to defend himself by means of a remedial introduction in the preface, Dryden declared that "what I desire the *Reader* should know concerning me, he will find in the Body of the Poem." He is referring, not to information about himself, in the usual sense, but to two passages in the poem which draw attention to himself in order to establish subjective *ethos*. They are dictated in this case, not simply by the normal demands of ethical appeal, as in the corresponding passages of *Religio Laici* we noticed earlier, but by the special needs created by his relationship to his audience. He could expect two principal accusations to be made against him by Anglican readers, and the attacks which followed the appearance of *The Hind and the Panther* only confirmed the accuracy of his prediction. The first was that of being a turncoat whose morals were of no advantage to any church, but who had chosen to abandon his coreligionists at a time when the accession of a Catholic king had exposed them to unusual peril. The second was that of having joined the new king's church out of hopes of personal profit. Each of the two ethical appeals Dryden introduces into the "Body of the Poem" is devoted to answering one of these charges.

Early in Part I, where he has been presenting satirical beast characters of the Independents, Quakers, atheists, and Baptists, which Anglicans could relish quite as well as Catholics, Dryden turns to the Socinians and raises for the first time an issue which the majority of his readers would find offensive. He makes the introduction of the Socinians an excuse for a defense of the

51

Catholic doctrine of Transubstantiation which suggests that Protestants, including the Anglicans, adopt toward this doctrine the point of view of the Socinians whom they despised. But before launching this discussion, he comes forward and offers a prayer of petition asking for the gift of faith and of an unswerving loyalty to his new church.[14] The prayer includes the following lines:

> My thoughtless youth was wing'd with vain desires,
> My manhood, long misled by wandring fires,
> Follow'd false lights; and when their glimps was gone,
> My pride struck out new sparkles of her own.
> Such was I, such by nature still I am,
> Be thine the glory, and be mine the shame.
>
> [I, 72–77]

Since the time of Scott, these lines have been considered fair game by Dryden's biographers, who have seen in them an account of the successive stages of his religious conviction, although they have quarreled over the details. Yet the purpose of this passage is not autobiographical, but rhetorical. The virtue of such a passage is that it forcefully conveys the impression that Dryden's recent conversion was final and represents a turning of his back on his own past. It anticipates, and answers beforehand, those very charges of insincerity and reminders that he was the author of *The Spanish Friar* as well as of *Religio Laici* which were to be leveled against him for the rest of his life. By phrasing his defense as a prayer rather than a protestation, Dryden enhances the impression of sincerity and humility; by proceeding in the following line to declare "Good life be now my task: my doubts are done," he suggests that he has undergone a conversion of morals as well as of faith. Paul is no longer Saul.

In Part III occurs another passage which, although it is spoken by the Hind, is a second ethical appeal on behalf of Dryden himself, as he explains in the preface. He writes: " 'Tis evident that some part of [the poem] was only occasional, and not first intended. I mean that defence of my self, to which every honest man is bound, when he is injuriously attacqu'd in Print," and he

---

[14] There are two other passages in the poem where Dryden comes forward in his own person, but neither of these involves an ethical appeal. The first (II, 658–62), labeled *"Poeta loquitur"* in the margin, is a personal testimony to having seen "the pleasing triumphs of the sky / For *James* his late nocturnal victory" at the Battle of Sedgemoor. The second (III, 1–25) is a defence of his choice of the beast fable.

goes on to refer to Stillingfleet's recent attack on him in *A Vindication of the Answer to Some Late Papers*. The passage (III, 221–305) is a long one, in which, after alluding to the controversy between the two men, the Hind proceeds to defend Dryden against the charges brought against him by Stillingfleet, before going on to attack the latter in another lengthy passage (III, 306–40). The accusation against Dryden which she refutes is the common one that he had joined the new king's church from motives of profit. Including him at first with her other recent accessions, she declares:

> Now for my converts, who you say unfed
> Have follow'd me for miracles of bread,
> Judge not by hear-say, but observe at least,
> If since their change, their loaves have been increast.
> The *Lyon* [James] buyes no Converts, if he did,
> Beasts wou'd be sold as fast as he cou'd bid.
> Tax those of int'rest who conform for gain,
> Or stay the market of another reign.
>
> [III, 221–28]

Later, however, she singles Dryden out among "my sons accus'd," and explains how "I discipline a son / Whose uncheck'd fury to revenge wou'd run" against the unjust charges of Stillingfleet. The counsel she offers him is a remarkable example of ethical appeal which successfully avoids the danger always present in subjective *ethos* that self-praise will alienate the reader. Dryden's self-defense is not only spoken by someone other than himself but conveys the impression of humility by being expressed as counsel unwillingly received by one who "champs the bit, impatient of his loss, / And starts a-side, and flounders at the cross." Yet Dryden obviously accepts her advice, and the Hind's words of counsel redound to his credit:

> If joyes hereafter must be purchas'd here
> With loss of all that mortals hold so dear,
> Then welcome infamy and publick shame,
> And, last, a long farewell to worldly fame.
> 'Tis said with ease, but oh, how hardly try'd
> By haughty souls to humane honour ty'd!
> O sharp convulsive pangs of agonizing pride!
> Down then thou rebell, never more to rise,
> And what thou didst, and do'st so dearly prize,
> That fame, that darling fame, make that thy sacrifice.
> 'Tis nothing thou hast giv'n, then add thy tears

For a long race of unrepenting years:
'Tis nothing yet; yet all thou hast to give,
Then add those *may-be* years thou hast to live.
Yet nothing still: then poor, and naked come,
Thy father will receive his unthrift home,
And thy blest Saviour's bloud discharge the mighty sum.

[III, 281–97]

The allusion, once more, to the sin of pride to which he had confessed in the prayer in Part I, "such was I, such by nature still I am," serves to remind the reader of the struggles that accompanied his change of heart, the sacrifices this entailed, and the disinterested spiritual motives which led to his conversion. To point out the rhetorical effectiveness in the poem of such reminders is not to question the sincerity of Dryden's declaration or the genuineness of his feelings. It is simply to recognize that these passages serve a deliberate rhetorical function as a mode of persuasion carefully subordinated to Dryden's general purpose in the poem and to his awareness of his audience. No one who recalls the eleventh and twelfth chapters of the Second Epistle to the Corinthians needs to be told that subjective *ethos* is no less sincere for being deliberate, and that no appeal is the worse for being offered with consummate skill.

If the question is asked, then, whether it is possible to make any reliable inferences about Dryden's thought from two such polemical poems as I have tried to show *Religio Laici* and *The Hind and the Panther* to be, the answer must surely be a qualified affirmative. We can infer a great deal about his religious ideas from these poems, but we must be constantly alert to rhetorical strategy and recognize that the demands of a work of religious apologetics, whether in poetry or prose, are very different from those of a carefully weighed exposition of personal belief. The forceful arguments of a debate are not to be equated with the judicious statements of a dispassionate discourse. In both these poems Dryden is engaged in particular religious disputes where, as the representative of one party to the controversy, he is committed to the defeat of the opposite side; his arguments, therefore, are polemically oriented, the "Weapons," he calls them, "with which I Combat Irreligion." Arguments of this kind characteristically offer an exaggerated counterpoise to the opponent's position in order to redress the balance of opinion. An explanation of this procedure is offered by the most prominent Anglican lay apologist of Dryden's time. In *The Excellency of Theology* Robert Boyle attempted to combat the tendency of some of his fellow scientists to slight theology in their pursuit of natural philosophy. As a result, the leading member of the Royal Society appears in this book to be disparaging scientific investigation in comparison to the study of Scripture. He explains this paradox in the preface to his book, beginning with a piece of advice which readers of Dryden's poems on religion would do well to remember:

In such kind of discourses, as the ensuing, it may justly be hoped, that equitable readers will consider, not only what is said, but on what occasion, and with what design it is delivered. Now it is plain by the series of the following discourse, that the physeophilus, whom it most relates to, was by me looked upon as a person, both very partial to the study of nature, and somewhat prejudiced against that of the scripture; so that I was not always to treat with him, as with an indifferent man, but according to the advice given in such cases by the wise, I was (to use *Aristotle*'s expression) to bend the crooked stick the contrary way, in order to the bringing it to be strait, and to depreciate the study of nature somewhat beneath its true value, to reduce a great over-valuer, to a just estimate of it.[15]

This procedure of "bending the crooked stick" is used by Dryden just as often as it is by Boyle and their contemporaries when they are engaged in debate. To understand his poems on religion properly, therefore, we must heed Boyle's advice and "consider, not only what is said, but on what occasion, and with what design it is delivered." In other words, we must interpret Dryden's arguments in the context of the poem in which they appear and see the poem itself in the context of the religious controversy to which it belongs.

In the following chapters I shall consider Dryden's religious thought in all these contexts, logical, artistic, and historical, and explain "on what occasion, and with what design it is delivered" in *Religio Laici* and, more briefly, in *The Hind and the Panther*.

[15] *The Works of the Hon. Robert Boyle*, ed. Thomas Birch (2d ed.; London, 1772), IV, 3.

3

THE CHRISTIAN APOLOGIST: CHALLENGE

In the preface to *Religio Laici,* Dryden expresses his resolve to combat "Irreligion" in the poem and pictures himself as engaged in "the common Cause against the Enemies of Piety." He neglects to provide a catalogue of these enemies of piety in the preface, however, and there has been considerable disagreement over their number and identity. One critic declares that there are four of these enemies in the poem and identifies them as Epicurean atomism, deism, Catholicism, and Puritanism.[1] Another eliminates the first and declares that there are only three.[2] An imposing list of people who might be described as "Enemies of Piety" could be drawn up from stray allusions in the poem, but there is no reason to suppose that all of them are the targets of Dryden's arguments. Epicurean atomism, for example, is only briefly mentioned in two lines (18–19) of a stanza in which Dryden is developing an argument against an altogether different opponent and citing various examples, including this one, in support of his thesis. A much clearer idea of Dryden's targets in *Religio Laici* can be gained by considering its form and structure as a Horatian epistle.

I pointed out in the last chapter that the form of the Horatian epistle was admirably suited to Dryden's ethical argument. Without some adaptation, however, it was less appropriate to his logical arguments. The *Epistles* of Horace are loosely organized, informal poetic discourses scarcely suited to the development of closely reasoned logical proofs. Furthermore, like all epistles and other

---

[1] See E. N. Hooker, "Dryden and the Atoms of Epicurus," *ELH,* 24 (1957): 177–90.
[2] See Donald R. Benson, "Theology and Politics in Dryden's Conversion," *Studies in English Literature,* 4 (1964): 395.

forms of monologue, they do not permit the presence of a participating adversary to offer the "principal Reasons that impugne" the author's own position, which we noticed as one of the advantages of the dialogue. To circumvent these disadvantages, Dryden adapted and modified the Horatian epistle to serve his argumentative purpose.

In the first place, while Dryden is careful to preserve what he considers to be the style of Horace's *Epistles*—"Plain and Natural, and yet Majestick"—he has not hesitated to modify the structure of his own epistle significantly, producing a coherent, carefully organized sequence of ideas which has no counterpart in his original. Secondly, he has taken a recurrent feature of Horace's *Epistles* and greatly magnified its importance. In the absence of any participating adversary in his *Epistles,* Horace sometimes introduces a rhetorical interlocutor to pose a question or offer an objection. He imagines some brief comment which might be interposed by a fancied individual and immediately adds his own rejoinder. These interjected remarks often consist of no more than one or two sentences, but they are introduced in the form of direct discourse.[3] In *Religio Laici* Dryden adopts and considerably expands these rhetorical interjections, turning them into short speeches of his imagined adversary which summarize the position he is attacking, or raise, and permit him to forestall, the most considerable objection to his own argument. The identity of these rhetorical adversaries reveals the specific "Enemies of Piety" against whom the poem is directed.

Religio Laici is divided into two halves of almost exactly the same length, in each of which Dryden is engaged in attacking a different position. The earlier half, consisting of the first 223 lines of the poem, contains no direct address to Dickinson or mention of the book he had translated. The second half, consisting of 227 lines, begins with a stanza which the marginal rubric identifies as a *"Digression to the Translatour of Father Simon's Critical History of the Old Testament."* Here Dryden breaks off his discourse to speak directly to his supposed correspondent for the first time in the poem and to mention the book which has been respon-

---

[3] The use of these rhetorical interlocutors, or "nonce adversaries," by Horace and Pope is briefly discussed by John M. Aden, "Pope and the Satiric Adversary," *Studies in English Literature,* 2 (1962): 276. Aden's examples from Horace are all taken from the monologues in the first book of the *Satires.* Equally good examples can be found, however, in *Epistles* i. 16 and i. 19.

sible for the reflections he has just finished making. When he resumes his discourse after this digression he proceeds to discuss some of the arguments in Father Simon's book. The poem concludes with a brief stanza of six lines referring to both halves of *Religio Laici.*

In each half of the poem, Dryden follows exactly the same pattern in his use of rhetorical interlocutors. He imagines in each case two speeches which his fancied adversary might be expected to make. The first such speech in each half of the poem expresses at the very outset the position which Dryden proceeds to attack; the second, introduced later on, raises the most considerable objection to Dryden's arguments, which he then goes on to answer. These imagined speeches are in the form of direct discourse which, in the absence of inverted commas, is indicated by marginal rubrics. As a consequence of this method of interpolating imaginary speeches into an epistle to a friend, Dryden alternates between addressing Dickinson directly ("'Tis true, my Friend") and apostrophizing his rhetorical adversary ("Dar'st thou, poor Worm"), in a manner familiar to readers of Pope's *Essay on Man.*

In the second half of *Religio Laici,* Dryden's fancied opponent is, as we might expect, Father Simon, expressing the arguments offered specifically in his own book and more generally in works of Catholic apologetics. His first speech (lines 276–81) is introduced with the words, "Oh but says one," and presents Simon's (and the Catholic church's) over-all view *"Of the Infallibility of Tradition, in General"* in the words of the marginal rubric. His second, and longer, speech (lines 305–15) presents an imagined rejoinder on his part, labeled in the margin as *"Objection in behalf of Tradition; urg'd by Father* Simon." There is, indeed, a *"Second Objection"* later (lines 356–57), but this is referred to by Dryden in his own words, not given to Father Simon as a speech.

In the first half of his poem, however, Dryden is concerned with attacking an altogether different position from that of Father Simon and the Catholic church, as the identity of his rhetorical interlocutor makes clear. Here Dryden is attacking deism, and the fancied adversary is a spokesman for this position, not otherwise identified than as "the Deist." His first speech, introduced with the words, "The *Deist* thinks he stands on firmer ground," is a long stanza of direct discourse (lines 42–61), setting forth, as the rubric explains, the *"Systeme of Deisme."* His second speech (lines 168–83), beginning with the words "But stay: the *Deist* here will urge anew," presents his imagined rejoinder to Dryden, identified in the margin as the *"Objection of the Deist."*

The failure to understand Dryden's choice of this adversary in the first half of his poem, or to recognize the implications of this choice in the arguments he uses there, has been responsible for most of the confusion about the meaning of *Religio Laici*. There are several reasons for this. In the first place, the logical unity of a poem which attacks both deism and Catholicism is not immediately clear; I shall discuss this question in a later chapter. Even more obscure to readers of the poem has been the historical occasion for Dryden's attack on deism. Whereas the allusion to Dickinson's translation of Father Simon's *Critical History* as well as the long-standing controversy between Anglicans and Catholics makes perfectly clear Dryden's choice of antagonist in the second half of his poem, no historical occasion has been identified which would explain his decision to attack the deists at this time and in the same poem.

In order to understand the specific position which Dryden is attacking in the first half of his poem, we can begin with the Deist's opening speech in which he sets forth the *"Systeme of Deisme."* In the first forty-one lines of the poem, Dryden has discussed some of the difficulties and conflicting answers which have resulted from attempts to solve religious questions by reason alone, without recourse to revelation. At this point, he imagines an interruption:

> The *Deist* thinks he stands on firmer ground;
> Cries ἐυρεκα: the mighty Secret's found:
> *God* is that *Spring* of *Good; Supreme,* and *Best;*
> *We,* made to *serve,* and in that Service *blest;*
> If so, some *Rules* of Worship must be given,
> Distributed alike to all by Heaven:
> Else *God* were *partial,* and to *some* deny'd
> The Means his Justice shou'd for *all* provide.
> This *general Worship* is to PRAISE, and PRAY:
> One part to *borrow* Blessings, one to *pay:*
> And when frail Nature slides into *Offence,*
> The *Sacrifice* for *Crimes* is *Penitence.*
> Yet, since th' Effects of Providence, we find
> Are variously dispens'd to Humane kind;
> That *Vice Triumphs,* and *Vertue suffers* here,
> (A Brand that Sovereign Justice cannot bear;)
> Our Reason prompts us to a *future* State:

The *last Appeal* from *Fortune,* and from *Fate*:
Where God's all-righteous ways will be declar'd;
The *Bad* meet *Punishment,* the *Good, Reward.*

[ll. 42–61]

With remarkable economy of language Dryden has managed to distill in this speech of only nineteen lines the essential features of deism. The basis of the Deist's speech is his proclamation, with dogmatic confidence, of the Five Catholic Articles which were the pentalogue of that religion which all men supposedly professed. These five articles, as they are expressed in this speech, are as follows: (1) there is a God, the *"Spring* of *Good, Supreme* and *Best";* (2) we have been "made to *serve"* God, and are "in that Service *blest"* when we worship Him; (3) "this *general Worship* is to PRAISE [God] and PRAY" to Him; (4) "when frail [human] Nature slides into *Offence"* against God, "the *Sacrifice* for *Crimes* is *Penitence"* for our sins; (5) "Our Reason prompts us to a *future* State . . . where God's all-righteous ways will be declar'd; / The *Bad* meet *Punishment,* the *Good Reward."*

The other essential ingredients of deism are stated or implied in the logical links among the five articles in the Deist's speech. Three of these ingredients are particularly important. First of all, "Our Reason prompts us" to discover these five articles of religion, without benefit of revelation. Consequently, these five articles are catholic, or universal, for they are available to all mankind, who have but to consult their own faculties in order to perceive them. Second, the *"Rules* of Worship" must be "Distributed alike to all by Heaven: / Else *God* were *partial,* and to *some* deny'd / The Means his Justice shou'd for *all* provide." Therefore, these five articles which all men can discover for themselves comprehend all necessary religion and are sufficient for salvation. Finally, it follows that a particular historical revelation, making known to only a part of mankind further religious duties necessary for salvation, would have been neither necessary nor just. Christianity, therefore, is essentially a restatement of the Five Catholic Articles, along with various corruptions and additions introduced through superstition and priestcraft. This final notion, which rejects Christianity as unnecessary and unjust, does not appear in the Deist's first speech, but is the basis of the objection which he raises to the Christian Scriptures later on:

But stay: the *Deist* here will urge anew,
No *Supernatural Worship* can be *True*:
Because a *general Law* is that alone
Which must to *all*, and every *where* be known:
A Style so large as not *this* Book can claim
Nor ought that bears *reveal'd* Religions *Name*.
'Tis said the sound of a *Messiah's Birth*
Is gone through all the habitable Earth:
But still that Text must be confin'd alone
To what was *Then* inhabited, and known:
And what Provision cou'd from *thence* accrue
To *Indian* Souls, and Worlds discover'd *New*?
In other parts it helps, that Ages past,
The Scriptures there were *known*, and were *imbrac'd*,
Till Sin spread once again the Shades of Night:
What's that to these who never *saw* the Light?

[ll. 168–83]

As a brief, cogent, yet reasonably complete account of the deist religion, these two speeches, taken together, could scarcely be bettered. Here, as so often in his controversial writings, Dryden displays a gift for distinguishing the essential from the merely adventitious in his opponent's position. So clear a perception of the deist system could hardly have depended on rumor and report; it indicates a first hand acquaintance on Dryden's part with some of the deist writings. This seems an obvious conclusion, at least until we begin to inquire what deist books were available in 1682.

The enormous volume of books for and against deism which marked the longest and most heated religious controversy of the eighteenth century began to appear in the 1690's, about a decade after the publication of *Religio Laici*. The most striking feature of Dryden's attack on deism is the date of its appearance: 1682. Had it been written fifteen years later, toward the close of his life, it would still have been an early contribution to the controversy, but not apparently unique. As it is, Dryden's decision to attack the deists when there does not appear to have been any occasion for such a polemic seems at first glance a remarkable example of historical foresight.

If the battle of the books between the deists and their opponents did not begin until the closing decade of the seventeenth century, the basic ingredients of the deist position had nevertheless already

61

found their way into print during the second quarter of that century in a series of books by Lord Herbert of Cherbury which commenced with the publication of his *De Veritate* in Paris in 1624. All histories of deism beginning with John Leland's *View of the Principal Deistical Writers* (1754) have considered Herbert the "father of English deism," whose intellectual offspring were posthumous by many years.[4] For by general consent, the second English deist is considered to be Charles Blount, whose *Oracles of Reason* (1693) is credited with starting the deist controversy. Since *Religio Laici* appeared during the interval of more than half a century that separates the father of English deism from his earliest acknowledged disciple, it is a critical commonplace to assume that "the Deist" whom Dryden is answering in the first half of his poem is Lord Herbert.

There are several features of Dryden's poem which seem at first sight to suggest that he had Herbert in mind. First of all, there is the title of the poem itself. One of Herbert's later works in which he developed the deist principles of his *De Veritate* is entitled *Religio Laici* (1645).[5] It has been suggested therefore that Dryden deliberately adopted for the title of his answer to Herbert the name of one of his books to which he objected.[6] Even if Dryden was aware of this book and knew its contents, however, the wisdom of giving his poem the same title appears questionable. He had long been the victim of ugly rumors that he was not a Christian. As early as 1670 he had complained that "I am charged by some ignorant or malicious persons with no less crimes than profaneness and irreligion."[7] A few years later he expostulated against the unsavory reputation which he and his friends

[4] The fullest account of English deism is still that of Sir Leslie Stephen in his *History of English Thought in the Eighteenth Century* (London: Smith, Elder and Co., 1876).

[5] This work is often referred to as *De Religione Laici*. This is the title given the book by its editor and translator, Harold R. Hutcheson (*Lord Herbert of Cherbury's "De Religione Laici"* [New Haven: Yale University Press, 1944]). The work was first published along with Lord Herbert's *De Causis Errorum* in 1645, and Hutcheson and others have taken the name of the former from the joint title page, which reads *De Causis Errorum: Una Cum tractatu de Religione Laici*. The Latin syntax obviously requires the form "*de Religione Laici*" here, since it modifies the noun "*tractatus.*" However, the running title "*De Causis Errorum*" in the first half of the volume is replaced by "*Religio Laici*" on p. 127, where the second treatise begins, and this continues as the running title for the remainder of the book.

[6] See James Kinsley, ed., *The Poems of John Dryden* (Oxford: Clarendon Press, 1958), IV, 1933, for this suggestion. (Hereafter referred to as *Poems.*) Like Hutcheson, he calls Lord Herbert's book, *De Religione Laici*.

[7] "Preface to *Tyrannic Love*," in *Of Dramatic Poesy and Other Critical Essays,* ed. George Watson (London: J. M. Dent and Sons, 1962), I, 139.

had incurred from "those wretches [who] paint lewdness, atheism, folly, ill-reasoning, and all manner of extravagances amongst us."[8] The rumors that he had begun his career as "a declard patron of Atheism" nevertheless persisted.[9] Indeed, Narcissus Luttrell, who bought a copy of *Religio Laici* on November 28, 1682, inscribed "Atheisticall" on the title page above the words "Written by Mr. Dryden."[10] It seems unlikely that Dryden would consciously have adopted the title of a deistic book and risked giving the impression of having imitated, rather than answered, Lord Herbert's book to those, like Luttrell, who were willing to judge the poem from its title page alone. A more plausible explanation for his choice of title would seem to be the fact that there was a well-established tradition of giving informal works on religion similar titles indicative of the author's status or position: witness Sir Thomas Browne's *Religio Medici* (1642), Sir George Mackenzie's *Religio Stoici* (1665), and the anonymous *Religio Clerici* (1681).[11] Dryden's decision to emphasize and even capitalize on his position as a layman, which we have already noticed, would surely have suggested the choice of this particular title within the general tradition.

Whether Dryden knew of Lord Herbert's deistic books or had read any of them is a matter of which we have no certain knowledge. The only one of Herbert's books with which we can be sure that Dryden was acquainted is *The Life and Reign of King Henry the Eighth*, to which he refers in the preface to his own *Religio Laici* in support of his assertion that Tindale's translation of the Bible had been the occasion of numerous heresies. Harold R. Hutcheson has pointed out that the gist of Herbert's *Religio Laici* appears in a passage of this book which is purported to be a speech delivered in the House of Commons in 1529.[12] Yet the fact that it has remained for a modern commentator to make this discovery casts doubt on the likelihood that Dryden's notice was attracted by the same passage or that he reached the same conclusion about its implications. Hutcheson has also made the

8 "Dedication to *The Assignation*," ibid., I, 186. This was addressed to Dryden's friend Sir Charles Sedley and appeared in 1673.

9 From the letter of a Mr. Fowke quoted by Charles E. Ward in his *Life of John Dryden* (Chapel Hill: University of North Carolina Press, 1961), p. 233.

10 See Hugh Macdonald, *John Dryden: A Bibliography of Early Editions and of Drydeniana* (Oxford: Clarendon Press, 1939), p. 33, n. 2.

11 *Religio Stoici* was proposed as a possible model by David Nichol Smith in *John Dryden* (Cambridge: At the University Press, 1950), p. 62. *Religio Clerici* was suggested by E. N. Hooker in "Dryden and the Atoms of Epicurus," p. 182.

12 See Hutcheson, *Lord Herbert of Cherbury's "De Religione Laici,"* pp. 53–54.

63

interesting suggestion that the opening words of Dryden's Deist, "ἔυρεκα: the mighty Secret's found," possibly echo a passage in another of Herbert's deistic books, *De Religione Gentilium*, where the author boasts that "I found those five [Catholic] Articles I have so often mention'd, and thought my self far more happy than *Archimedes*."[13] This certainly suggests the possibility that Dryden was acquainted with some of Herbert's deistic writings, nor is it unreasonable to suppose that this may have been the case. But the possibility that he was aware of the fact that Herbert was a deist in no way establishes that the first half of Dryden's *Religio Laici* is an answer to this individual, as the second half of the poem is a reply to Father Simon, or that "the Deist" who speaks on two occasions is supposed to represent Herbert.

Unquestionably, the principal basis for this common assumption is the fact that Lord Herbert not only expressed the general position which the Deist expounds in Dryden's *Religio Laici* but formulated the Five Catholic Articles which we have noticed as the basis of the first speech in the poem. Herbert could honestly claim that "I found those five Articles I have so often mention'd," for although he believed that they had been implicit in the minds of all men in all ages, he was certainly the first to dispose them into a systematic formula. He first proclaimed the Five Catholic Articles rather briefly in an appendix to *De Veritate* (1624) where, as an outgrowth of his discussion of the celebrated "Common Notions" in the body of his book, he proceeds to enumerate the five common notions concerning religion which the human mind "has been able in every age and place to apprehend." At the same time, he set forth the essential ingredients of deism which I have enumerated and which appear in the two speeches of the Deist in Dryden's *Religio Laici*. For by virtue of the fact that these Five Catholic Articles are common notions, which have been "clearly accepted at all times by every normal person," they are the product, not of revelation, but of human reason alone. They are, furthermore, entirely sufficient, for "if we set aside superstitions and legends, the mind takes its stand on my five articles, and upon nothing else." Indeed, "the only Catholic and uniform Church is the doctrine of Common Notions which comprehends all places and all men. . . . and it is only through this Church that salvation is possible." It follows, therefore, that

---

[13] See *ibid.*, pp. 49 and 57.

no historical revelation, limited to certain ages and particular peoples as in the case of Christianity, can be true, except insofar as it contains, like all religions, these common notions. "The true Catholic Church is not supported on the inextricable confusion of oral and written tradition to which men have given their allegiance. Still less is it that which fights beneath any one particular standard, or is comprised in one organization so as to embrace only a restricted portion of the earth, or a single period of history."[14]

Had Lord Herbert written nothing else after *De Veritate*, the exposition of religious principles to be found there would have justified his title as "the father of English deism." But he was not content to have expounded his religious notions in what was, after all, only an afterthought to a treatise on epistemology. Some twenty years later, therefore, in 1645, he published two books together, in the first of which, *De Causis Errorum*, he expanded the epistemology which was the proper subject of *De Veritate*, while in the second treatise, *Religio Laici*, he developed the religious notions contained in the appendix to his earlier book. Here Herbert repeated his Five Catholic Articles and explained them more fully in the course of setting forth the principles of deism. After Herbert's death appeared his *De Religione Gentilium* (1663), where the Five Catholic Articles were once more repeated and explained. Indeed, he seems to have been obsessed with the Five Catholic Articles, for he discussed them at some length in two other works which were not published in the seventeenth century. One of these is his *Dialogue between a Tutor and His Pupil*, first published in 1768. The other work, also called *Religio Laici*, has only come to light in recent years and is apparently an earlier, abandoned version of the treatise which he published under the same name in 1645.[15] Since Herbert alone, apparently, was responsible for formulating and constantly reiterating the Five Catholic Articles during the half century before Dryden's *Religio Laici* appeared, the conclusion has seemed inescapable that, as one commentator has remarked, "it is impossible to assign any major source but Herbert's five articles to the pas-

---

[14] See the translation by Meyrick H. Carré, *De Veritate by Edward, Lord Herbert of Cherbury* (Bristol: J. W. Arrowsmith, 1937), pp. 289–307.

[15] This work was discovered in manuscript and published by Herbert G. Wright in "An Unpublished Manuscript by Lord Herbert of Cherbury Entitled 'Religio Laici'," *Modern Language Review*, 28 (1933): 295–307. The title "Religio Laici" on the manuscript, in Lord Herbert's own hand, adds considerable probability to the conjecture that this, rather than "De Religione Laici," was the title he gave to his later work.

sage" in the poem where the Deist presents his position.[16]

The hypothesis that Dryden is answering Lord Herbert in the first half of *Religio Laici* appears persuasive until we begin to consider the difficulties which it raises. In the first place, it is very hard to explain Dryden's reticence about naming Herbert if he is the target against whom the poet is directing his arguments. Dryden is not usually shy about naming his adversaries. His target in the second half of the poem is not "the Catholic," but "Father Simon." If he felt no qualms about naming a living adversary, why should be have hesitated to name a man who had been dead for more than thirty years? Furthermore, "the Deist" seems an appropriate name for Herbert only to modern readers, approaching the poem with the advantage of historical hindsight; there is little reason to suppose that Dryden or his contemporaries enjoyed any such advantage. The habit of considering Herbert "the father of English deism" began much later. It commenced with John Leland's *View of the Principal Deistical Writers*, published in 1754, at a time when the deist movement had been in existence long enough for its history to be written and its origins traced back to a writer of the Jacobean and Caroline period. I know of no single piece of evidence that Herbert was referred to as a deist before 1682 or considered the founder of the deist movement. Dryden's use of the term "the Deist" is reminiscent of the character writing of his time and suggests that, as in the case of the popular prose characters, the author is describing, not an individual, but a type.

A more formidable objection to Lord Herbert as "the Deist" arises when we stop to consider whether his *De Veritate*, or any of his other deist books, could conceivably have been the historical occasion, in any meaningful sense of that term, for Dryden's attacking deism in 1682. *De Veritate*, first published in Paris in 1624, seems to have enjoyed a mild popularity during the next three decades, for it went through three subsequent editions during that time, being republished in London in 1633, 1645, and 1656. It was not published again in the seventeenth century, so that more than a quarter of a century elapsed between the last edition of *De Veritate* and the first edition of Dryden's *Religio Laici*. Herbert's other deist books reveal a similar history. His

[16] Hutcheson, *Lord Herbert of Cherbury's "De Religione Laici,"* p. 57. See also *Poems*, IV, 1933, for the same conclusion.

66

Religio Laici, published with *De Causis Errorum* in London in 1645, enjoyed three editions that year, but was republished only once in the seventeenth century, in 1656, the same year as the last edition of *De Veritate*. His *De Religione Gentilium* was not published in England at all in the seventeenth century. It was first published in Amsterdam in 1663, and the only subsequent edition appeared in the same city two years later. Herbert's other deist books remained unpublished until long after Dryden's death. All the available evidence indicates that if Herbert's deist books were not being published during the quarter of a century preceding Dryden's *Religio Laici*, they were also not being read. He seems to have received more attention on the Continent, where several of his books had been first published, than in England. The only answer to Herbert published in England before 1682 was made by Richard Baxter, the Presbyterian divine, in his *More Reasons for the Christian Religion* which appeared in 1672 (and which nowhere refers to him as a deist).

To conclude that Dryden interrupted his activities in 1682 to launch an attack on the little noticed and long forgotten writings of a Caroline philosopher who had died while the poet was still at school is to make an unwarranted assumption about his habits as a writer for which there is no parallel in his entire career. In all of his poems which deal with issues of public interest, Dryden habitually writes as an "occasional" poet in the best sense of that term. He seizes upon some occasion which has aroused excitement or controversy and makes it the subject of a poem which he publishes before the public's interest has subsided. In his early period, he writes a poem to elegize the Lord Protector who has recently died ("Heroique Stanzas"), or to celebrate within a few weeks of the event the restoration of the monarch (*Astraea Redux*) or his coronation (*To His Sacred Majesty*). His idea of "an historical poem" (*Annus Mirabilis*) is one which recounts the events of the preceding year. When he returned to writing poems of this kind in the enormously productive period of 1681–82, Dryden resumed the habit of his earlier years. *Absalom and Achitophel* appeared within a few months of the dissolution of the Oxford Parliament, and *The Medal* was published within an even shorter interval following Shaftesbury's acquittal. *Religio Laici*, written and published the very year in which the translation of Father Simon's *Critical History* appeared, conforms to the same pattern of immediacy in its answer to the French Oratorian. It is highly probable, therefore, that Dryden's arguments in the first half of the poem were also occasioned by some recent controversy of general interest, rather than by some unexplained antiquarian interest on Dryden's part.

We must also remember that all of Lord Herbert's books dealing with religion which appeared during the seventeenth century were written and published in Latin, and that no English translation of any of these works came out until after Dryden's death.[17] Herbert's choice of Latin for these works is due in part to the fact that several of them were first published abroad and were addressed to an international audience. But his choice also reflects the fact that his religious and philosophical works were not written for popular consumption but were intended for a comparatively small number of learned readers. The only one of his works which enjoyed real popularity in Dryden's time was, in fact, his sole book in English to be published in the seventeenth century, the *Life and Reign of King Henry the Eighth* (1649), which was frequently republished, two editions appearing in 1682.[18] The matter is not without significance. The fact that Herbert's works on religion were in Latin would have been no handicap to Dryden, but it would have been such to the popular audience to which his *Religio Laici* was addressed. There is no single instance in the Restoration period of a book, written in Latin and not translated into English, arousing public controversy, except in connection with other works in English by the same author. It was Hobbes's *Leviathan,* written and published in English, which excited the greatest controversy of the century, not his Latin works, except as these provided his enemies with further ammunition. This is perfectly understandable when we recall that the many books of religious apologetics which appeared in the seventeenth century were not academic disputations but popular works written to quiet the apprehensions of the public and to safeguard

[17] The first English translation of *De Religione Gentilium,* entitled *The Antient Religion of the Gentiles,* was published in London in 1705. *De Veritate* and *Religio Laici* were first translated into English in 1937 and 1944 respectively. Two of Lord Herbert's works on religion were in English, but of these, the *Dialogue between a Tutor and His Pupil* was not published until 1768, and the earlier version of *Religio Laici* did not appear in print until 1933.

[18] Three editions had been published in 1672 and two more were to follow in 1683. Lord Herbert's *Autobiography* was not published until 1764. *The Expedition to the Isle of Rhe,* originally written in English, was known only in a Latin translation until 1860.

the convictions of the Anglican faithful at large. Such a purpose was best served, not by resurrecting forgotten attacks upon Christianity or by drawing attention to Latin books of whose dangers the public was mercifully ignorant, but by assailing and answering those English books which had excited some interest and had become matters for public concern. It was not, after all, Father Simon's *Histoire critique du Vieux Testament* which Dryden thought it necessary to answer, but Dickinson's translation of this book from French into English.

There is a final objection to the hypothesis that Dryden is answering Lord Herbert which has passed unnoticed until now, but which is particularly formidable. It is, in fact, a false assumption that Dryden has put into the Deist's opening speech the same Five Catholic Articles as Herbert had formulated. The original version of the Five Catholic Articles which Herbert laid down in the first edition of *De Veritate* is as follows:

1. There is some Supreme Authority (*Esse Supremum Aliquod Numen*).
2. This Supreme Authority ought to be worshipped (*Supremum Istud Numen Debere Coli*).
3. A due conformity of the faculties has always, by universal consent, been considered the principal part of divine worship (*Probam Facultatum Conformationem Ex Consensu Universali, Praecipuam Partem Cultus Divini Semper Habitam Fuisse*).
4. Vices and crimes of whatever kind ought to be expiated by repentance (*Vitia et Scelera Quaecunque Expiari Debere ex Poenitentia*).
5. There is a reward or punishment after this life (*Esse Praemium, vel Poenam Post Hanc Vitam*).[19]

If we compare these Five Catholic Articles with those which the Deist proclaims in Dryden's *Religio Laici,* we can see at once that, allowing for differences in wording, the first, second, fourth, and fifth articles are the same in both versions, but that the third is radically different in each case. These two versions present, indeed, two quite different articles.

Lord Herbert altered the wording of the Five Catholic Articles in each of his many repetitions of them. It is important, therefore, that we trace his several versions of the third article. In the third edition of *De Veritate,* which he revised extensively, Herbert expanded his third and fourth articles, the former now appearing as

[19] The Latin version is taken from *De Veritate* (Paris, 1624), pp. 198–206. The English version is my own.

3. Virtue joined with piety (which is described under the due conformity of the faculties in this work) is, and always has been, considered the principal part of divine worship (*Virtutem cum pietate conjunctam [quae sub proba Facultatum conformatione hoc in Opere describitur] praecipuam partem Cultus Divini habitam esse & semper fuisse*).[20]

The article in this version remains essentially the same, but for the Scholastic phrase "due conformity of the faculties [with their proper objects]" he has substituted the more explicit phrase, "virtue joined with piety." It is in this more specific version that Lord Herbert expresses his third article in his other Latin works, eliminating the earlier terminology completely. Thus, in the *Religio Laici* which he published the same year as the third edition of *De Veritate,* it appears as: "Virtue joined with piety is the best mode of divine worship (*Virtutem cum pietate conjunctam optimam esse rationem Cultus Divini*)."[21] Again, in his *De Religione Gentilium* the third article appears as "Virtue and piety are the principal parts of divine worship (*Virtutem, Pietatemque esse praecipuas partes Cultus divini*)."[22]

In his English versions of the Five Catholic Articles, Lord Herbert varies the form of the third article without in any way changing its nature. He simply adds several other internal dispositions to virtue and piety, all of which are to be found in his original discussion of this article in *De Veritate.* Thus, in *A Dialogue between a Tutor and His Pupil,* not published until 1768, the third article takes this form: "That the best worship of him [God] consists in virtue, piety, and charity conjoined with faith in, and love of God."[23] Another form of this version appears in the speech which Herbert attributes to a member of the Parliament of 1529 in his *Life and Reign of King Henry the Eighth.* The third of the five "Catholick or Universal Notions" which the seeker after pure religion will find is this:

Among many Rites, Ceremonies, and Volumes, &c. deliver'd us as Instruments or parts of His Worship [in any particular religion], He shall find Vertue so eminent, as it alone concludes and sums up the rest. Insomuch as there is no Sacrament which is not finally resolv'd

[20] *De Veritate* (3d ed.; London, 1645), p. 215. My translation.
[21] *De Causis Errorum: Una Cum tractatu de Religione Laici* (London, 1645), p. 152. My translation.
[22] *De Religione Gentilium* (Amsterdam, 1663), p. 2. My translation. The Five Catholic Articles are repeated, with only slight variations in wording, on pp. 186 and 210.
[23] *A Dialogue between a Tutor and His Pupil* (London, 1768), p. 7.

into it; Good life, Charity, Faith in, and Love of God, being such necessary and essential parts of Religion, that all the rest are finally clos'd, and determin'd in them.[24]

In both of these versions, virtue and piety ("Good life") have been joined by charity, faith in God, and love of God. Our final version, that of the earlier, unpublished *Religio Laici* by Herbert, is the fullest of them all and adds the virtue of hope to the other five:

That though diuers Rytes Misteryes and Sacra (as the Romans Call them) were introduced to ye worship of the Supreme God yet that there is noe vniuersall Consent or Agreement concerning them, But that a Pure and vntaynted minde as being Conscious in it selfe of noe vnworthynesse, a Vertuous and a pious life testifyed by the Expressions of Goodnes and Charity to all and accompanied with love Faith and hope in God were vndoubted wayes of serving him.[25]

Finally, the version of Herbert's Five Catholic Articles which Baxter quoted in his answer to him, the only other printed form in which they appeared before 1682, is a fairly literal translation of these articles as they appear in the first edition of *De Veritate*.[26]

Turning now to Dryden, let us consider his third article which the Deist expresses as: "This *general Worship* is to PRAISE, and PRAY: / One part to *borrow* Blessings, one to *pay*." We ought to consider first of all whether his very different version is simply a matter of poetic license. The question is easily settled, for in the preface to *Religio Laici* he has repeated the first and third articles, in the course of denouncing deism. His prose version of the third article is exactly the same: "that Praise and Prayer are his [God's] due Worship."

The third articles of both the Deist and Herbert set forth the proper form of that worship which the second article declares all men owe to God. For Herbert it consists in virtue and piety; that is to say, God is best worshiped when men lead righteous lives. In fact, what Herbert calls "worship" is really no more than obedience to the laws which God has written on men's minds. Without entering into all the details of Herbert's system, it should suffice to say that virtue and piety are the product of conscience, which distinguishes between good and evil and dictates the choice

---

[24] Reproduced in Hutcheson, *Lord Herbert of Cherbury's "De Religione Laici,"* p. 181.

[25] Wright, "An Unpublished Manuscript by Lord Herbert of Cherbury," p. 302.

[26] See Richard Baxter, *More Reasons for the Christian Religion* (London, 1672), p. 118.

of the former. When a person follows his conscience and practices virtue combined with piety, other internal dispositions are produced, including charity, faith, and love of God, which are a sufficient satisfaction to God to merit salvation.[27] For the Deist of Dryden's poem, on the other hand, the proper form of worship, which all men know instinctively that they ought to perform, consists in their communicating with God through prayer. This includes both prayers of petition ("one part to *borrow* Blessings") and prayers of praise and thanksgiving ("one to *pay*"); in either case it involves the offering of deliberate acts of tribute to God, not simply of implicit respect through obedience to His commands. This notion of active and explicit worship through prayer, which does not appear in Herbert's many versions of the third article or in his discussions of it, is important to Dryden's whole presentation of deism. The words "praise" and "pray" are given particular emphasis in the poem by being printed in capitals, and indeed it is this version of the third article which provides the grounds for part of Dryden's answer to deism, as we shall see in the next chapter.

Two conclusions seem obvious. One is that, in view of the fact that the Deist follows Herbert in four of his five articles both as to substance and order, Herbert's Five Catholic Articles are the ultimate source of the Deist's opening speech. The other is that, in view of the important discrepancy between the two versions of the third article, Dryden owes the Deist's speech to some quite different immediate source, although he may have had independent knowledge of Herbert's articles. The only alternative possibility, that Dryden is himself responsible for a major theological development in the deist creed, is not borne out by the facts which I am about to relate.

If we summarize the various objections to Lord Herbert as the Deist of Dryden's poem, we find that they all point in the same direction. They indicate the existence of more than one deist before 1682, perhaps even of a group of deists sufficiently numerous to justify Dryden's use of the term "Deist" to stand for a general type, as in the prose characters of the time. They suggest as well that the writings of these deists were in English and were the subject of current comment and discussion in 1682. They indicate finally that while these deist writings were ultimately derived

[27] See Carré's translation of *De Veritate*, pp. 183–87 and 296–97 especially.

from one or more books by Lord Herbert, they were not simply translations of the Caroline philosopher, but consisted of restatements, modifications, and new developments of his thought.

Our quest for these Restoration deists ought to begin with the man who is usually considered the "second English deist," Charles Blount. Although his last book, *The Oracles of Reason* (1693), was responsible for his greatest notoriety and is credited with providing the spark that ignited the deist controversy, he had, in fact, written and published several books before 1682 which are commonly described as "deist." Although they contain no mention of the Five Catholic Articles, they are sufficiently close in time to Dryden's *Religio Laici* to suggest that they could have been, in part at least, the occasion for the poem, if they can justify their reputation as deist books. The works in question are Blount's *Anima Mundi* (1679) and his *Great Is Diana of the Ephesians* (1680), to which we should add his translation of *The Two First Books of Philostratus* (1680), which includes notes by the translator.

Both the manner in which these books were published and their reception indicate that they were intended, and rightly considered, to undermine the established religion. *Anima Mundi* was first published in Amsterdam, according to the title page, and shortly afterwards republished in London in two editions. All three editions may, indeed, have been printed surreptitiously in London, for the date on the title page of the first edition, "Anno Mundi 00000," hardly establishes confidence in the imprint. The absence of the printer's name from the title pages of all three editions indicates that both author and publisher expected opposition from the authorities; and events proved them right. The Bishop of London, Henry Compton, wished to suppress the book, and it was, in fact, burnt during his absence from the capital.[28] A similar unfriendly reception seems to have greeted Blount's second book on religion, his *Great Is Diana of the Ephesians*, which was printed surreptitiously the following year without a printer's name or date, and bearing the fictitious place name of "Cosmopoli." Like its predecessor, it was reprinted the same year with the imprint "London, 1680," but without the name of the printer. Shortly afterwards, Blount published his translation of *The Two First Books of Philostratus*, also bearing the imprint

[28] See John Campbell's life of Blount in the *Biographia Britannica*.

73

"London, 1680," but suppressing the name of the printer.

It is easy to understand how these books, printed surreptitiously, received with hostility, and written by the man who was later responsible for *The Oracles of Reason,* have come to be regarded as deist books. In reality, however, they are not deist at all. The only word that accurately describes Blount at every stage of his career is "freethinker," that useful term which served Anglican apologists in denouncing any kind of anti-Christian writer from deists to outright atheists. A freethinker Blount certainly was throughout all of his adult life, but the form which his freethinking took varied in the course of his tempestuous career. However he may have ended his career, he began it as a follower of Hobbes, who was certainly not a deist. All three of Blount's books published before 1682 are Hobbesian rather than deist, and indeed their author was at this time a professed disciple of the detested philosopher who was frequently denounced from the pulpit and in print as an atheist. In 1678, the year before *Anima Mundi* was published, Blount sent the book in manuscript to Hobbes, accompanied by a letter in which he extolled him as "the great Instructor of the most sensible Part of Mankind in the noble Science of Philosophy."[29] The next year Hobbes died, and within a few months his young disciple had memorialized his master by publishing a broadside made up of extracts from the *Leviathan* and entitled *The Last Sayings, or Dying Legacy, of Mr. T. Hobbs of Malmesbury.*[30] It was during this period of his greatest enthusiasm for Hobbes that Blount wrote and published the three books we are considering, which easily explains their unfriendly reception.

Blount's manner of commemorating Hobbes, by reprinting extracts from his master's own writings, epitomizes his method as a writer. He was in no sense of the word an original thinker, nor even an original writer. In all of his books he is content to paraphrase or even to quote verbatim from the subject of his current enthusiasm. As a result, he has acquired the reputation of being a plagiarist. Yet it is doubtful whether he considered himself in this light. It is true that he does not identify the source of his individual quotations nor even mark them as such. But he is usually quite frank in acknowledging his general indebtedness to the

[29] The letter is printed in *The Oracles of Reason* (London, 1693), pp. 97–105.
[30] Printed in London, 1680.

writer whose words he is borrowing, and he seems to have considered himself the publicist, rather than the plagiarist, of other men's books. In this manner, he draws heavily upon Hobbes in his first three books on religion.

There is another source which plays almost as important a part as the works of Hobbes in these early books. The essays of Montaigne, particularly the *Apology for Raimond Sebond,* are responsible for many of the examples in Blount's *Anima Mundi,* a book written to show that there had never been any agreement on the question of whether the soul is immortal. The combination of Hobbes and Montaigne may appear eccentric, but in fact it is not. The general drift of Blount's early books is agnostic, following Hobbes's theme that religions are human institutions designed for politic ends. With such a subject, it is no difficult task for Blount to merge Hobbes's "agnosticism of unbelief" with Montaigne's "agnosticism of belief," eliminating the latter's fideist conclusion that since reason is powerless to discover anything relating to religion, we must rely instead upon divine revelation. Indeed, if Hobbes was Blount's religious master at this time, Montaigne was his philosophical mentor. He was so powerfully influenced by reading the *Apology for Raimond Sebond* that he professed at the beginning of his career a Pyrrhonist theory of knowledge. In a letter to John Wilmot, Earl of Rochester, written on February 8, 1680, Blount declares in the manner of Montaigne, "These, my Lord, are only such twilight Conjectures as our human Reason (whereof we yet so vainly boast) can furnish us with. . . . so that (indeed) all Philosophy, excepting Sceptism [*sic*], is little more than Dotage."[31]

It should be obvious that such sentiments as these are not only foreign to Lord Herbert's thought but actually contradict it. Deism is, by its very nature, a rationalist system which depends for its existence on an acknowledgment of the certitude and self-sufficiency of human reason in the form of common notions held by universal consent. Indeed, Herbert begins his *De Veritate* with an undisguised attack on Pyrrhonism, which "says that truth lies hidden in a well, that we know one thing only, namely that we know nothing," and on the fideism which Montaigne developed from this theory of knowledge: "a strange and unprecedented philosophy appeared in succeeding ages, which superseded reason

---

[31] The letter, addressed to "Strephon," is printed in *The Oracles of Reason,* p. 155.

altogether and sought to establish its doctrines upon the basis of an implicit faith; inclining, indeed, thereby to that school which taught that it was impossible to know anything. But such a doctrine is unacceptable to our reason, and severs our mental powers in two."[32] As long as he continued to write under the influence of Montaigne, and as a disciple of Hobbes, Blount was in no position to serve, even unwittingly, the cause of deism. The subject of *Great Is Diana of the Ephesians,* an attack on "priestcraft," was a favorite of both Hobbesians and deists. But the thesis of *Anima Mundi,* that there has never been any general agreement that the soul is immortal, undercuts Herbert's fifth article.

In the earliest of the answers to Blount's *Oracles of Reason, A Conference with a Theist* (1696), William Nicholls declared: "Now the Objections [to Christianity] which are urged in this Dialogue, are part of them taken from the Discourse of some Theistical [Deistical] men I have casually conversed with; but are mostly taken out of a Book lately published, called *Oracles of Reason,* the first Book I ever saw which did openly avow Infidelity."[33] Nicholls is using the term "Infidelity," in contrast with "atheism," as a synonym for deism. When he says that Blount's last book was the first he had ever seen that openly professed deism, he describes a situation which is very close to the truth. He is clearly unaware of Lord Herbert's Latin works published many years before, and he is ignorant of at least one book published after Dryden's *Religio Laici* and before *The Oracles of Reason.* But these omissions simply confirm our conclusion that Herbert's works no longer attracted notice during the Restoration period, and that *The Oracles of Reason* was the first printed work to receive general attention. Nicholls' remark, however, contains a further piece of information of the greatest importance. It reveals that if no deist books were being published during most of the Restoration period, there were nevertheless "some Theistical men" who did not hesitate to promote their ideas at least by way of conversation. We ought to investigate this group of freethinkers whose existence we have already suspected from Dryden's reference to a general type which he calls "the Deist." We can best learn of their existence through allusions to them by unfriendly antagonists, as in the case of Nicholls' statement.

[32] *De Veritate,* trans. Carré, p. 76.
[33] *A Conference with a Theist* (London, 1696), sig. A5v.

The terms which Nicholls uses for deists ("Theistical men") and for deism ("Infidelity") should offer us some caution at the outset of our search. The principal reason why the existence of any deists between Lord Herbert and Charles Blount has been ignored is the confusion of terminology for such people in the seventeenth century.[34] In the first place, the term "deist" itself was used very loosely at the time, and could be employed in two quite different senses. It could indeed mean one who subscribed to the position on religion expressed by Lord Herbert and by Dryden's Deist, but it was just as often used as a general term of abuse for freethinkers or, more specifically, for some particular group of freethinkers different from those whom we now call deists. The two uses of the word "deist" in England before 1682 recorded in the *Oxford English Dictionary*, for example, are so vague as to be meaningless. Both Robert Burton's statement of 1621 that "cosen-germans to these men [atheists] are many of our great Philosophers and Deists" and Robert Trail's remark in 1670 that "we have a generation among us . . . called Deists, which is nothing else but a new court word for Atheist" simply indicate that the authors refused to recognize any real distinction between deists and atheists. In his unpublished commonplace book, now in the British Museum, Ralph Cudworth, the Cambridge Platonist, includes an entry on deism; but the doctrine he describes there, "that we are generally inclined to religion by the prejudices of education," is Hobbesian rather than deist in the sense we are seeking.[35] The word "deist" continued to be used in this sense even after the publication of Dryden's *Religio Laici*. One of the earliest answers to deism, William Assheton's *Admonition to a Deist* (1685), is addressed to one who, while acknowledging that there is a God, denied the eternity of hell's torments and asserted that perhaps there is no afterlife or any account to be given in another world. This man, who denies Lord Herbert's fifth article, is obviously not a deist in our meaning of the word.

Just as the word "deist" does not always describe the followers of Lord Herbert in the seventeenth century, so other terms

[34] Hutcheson (*Lord Herbert of Cherbury's "De Religione Laici,"* pp. 56–57) argues that "Dryden's discussion of deism both in the preface and in the poem is too detailed to allow us to believe that, among laymen, Dryden had only Herbert and Blount in view." He uncovered no evidence, however, to support his suggestion that there were other deists between Herbert and Blount.

[35] BM Add MSS 4984.

besides "deist" were applied to this specific group. The two other words most commonly used were "antiscripturist" and "theist," the term we have noticed William Nicholls using. This latter word was, in fact, used just as frequently as "deist" until at least the end of the century. Keeping this varied terminology in mind, we can now proceed to look for explicit allusions to the men we are seeking.

The earliest reference I have been able to discover occurs in the Commonwealth period, within a few years of Lord Herbert's death, and implies the existence of a recognized group. Nathanael Culverwel, in his *Discourse of the Light of Nature* (1652), complains of "those lumps and dunghills of all Sects, I mean that young and upstart generation of gross Anti-Scripturists, that have a Powder-plot against the Gospel, that would very compendiously behead all Christian Religion at one blow, a device which old and ordinary Hereticks were never acquainted withall."[36] His description of this group as heretics, rather than atheists, who refuse to accept the Scriptures is, as far as it goes, an accurate description of Dryden's Deist; the further reference to the group as a "young and upstart generation" with whose beliefs "old and ordinary Hereticks were never acquainted" seems to indicate that it originated during Lord Herbert's lifetime.

Our next allusion belongs to the early years of the Restoration period. In 1665 John Sergeant, the Catholic apologist, offers an imaginary dialogue between a Protestant and a "Deist" who asks the Protestant "how you are certain that Book [the Bible] is God's word?"[37] It is clear that this individual believes in God but denies that a particular revelation is to be found in the Christian Scriptures. Another ten years elapses before the next allusion I have found. Other references may, and probably do, exist during this period, but they are certainly few and point to the conclusion that throughout the third quarter of the seventeenth century there existed a small number of Lord Herbert's followers who attracted only occasional notice. During the 1670's, however, they probably began to increase in number, and they certainly became more vociferous, for the allusions to them are much more frequent during the years immediately preceding the appearance of *Religio Laici*. By 1677 they had grown sufficiently important for Edward

[36] *An Elegant and Learned Discourse of the Light of Nature* (London, 1652), p. 172.
[37] *Sure Footing* (London, 1665), pp. 28–33.

Stillingfleet, the popular Anglican preacher, to publish *A Letter to a Deist,* written, in fact, two years earlier, for it is dated June 11, 1675. It is clear that Stillingfleet's Deist belongs to the same family as Dryden's, although the clergyman's answer is so different from the poet's that it is most unlikely that this was one of "the Works of our own Reverend Divines of the Church of *England*" from which Dryden borrowed his arguments. Stillingfleet writes: "This following Discourse was Written for the satisfaction of a particular Person, who owned the *Being* and *Providence* of *God,* but expressed a mean Esteem of the *Scriptures,* and the *Christian Religion.* Which is become so common a *Theme* among the *Scepticks* of this *Age.*"[38] Obviously we are dealing here with another "antiscripturist" like those described by Culverwel and Sergeant, but their objections have grown so frequent that they are a "common theme" of the age.

What is particularly significant about Stillingfleet's Deist and the others of his kind who are mentioned with increasing frequency during the five years preceding Dryden's *Religio Laici* is the fact that, in addition to the negative aspect of their opposition to the Scriptures, certain positive aspects of their beliefs begin to appear. We can postpone a consideration of these positive aspects as they apply to Stillingfleet's Deist for the moment, and turn to some of the other allusions. In 1679 William Outram asked in a sermon, "What theist was ever known to live according to the principles of natural religion?"[39] Here we have what is probably a direct allusion to some form of the Five Catholic Articles. The same year, the author of *The Spirit of Prophecy* presents a somewhat clearer picture of the deists:

What though the mystery of Godliness be (as without controversie it is) very great, yet the *Theists* of our Age have no reason on that account to disbelieve it: for though, perhaps, it is reasonable to expect that our Religion should befriend our Reason, yet not so far as to make it the Rule and measure of Divine Revelation.[40]

The sufficiency of reason in matters of religion and the rejection of any revelation which goes beyond the limits of reason emerge at this point as marks of "the *Theists* of our Age."

[38] *A Letter to a Deist* (London, 1677), sig. A3.

[39] The citation appears under "Theist" in the *Oxford English Dictionary* and is the only use of the terms "deist" or "theist" before 1682 quoted there which is relevant to our inquiry.

[40] W. H., *The Spirit of Prophecy* (London, 1679), p. 224.

In 1681, the year before Dryden wrote and published *Religio Laici,* the author of *Religio Clerici* was complaining that "this *Town* and *Kingdome* is infested with such swarms of *Deists, Socinians, Atheists,* and others, that not only violate the undoubted *Regalia,* but with treasonable Blasphemy dispute the Divine *Sovereignty* of *Jesus.*"[41] These deists, now grown so numerous, were apparently proclaiming some form of the Five Catholic Articles as being the whole of necessary religion, for the author describes them as "some licentious persons now a daies, willing to suspect that all Religion is but the general *Laws of Nature,* and (at the best) they reduce Christianity it self to the first stage from whence it long ago set out, *viz. Common Morality.*"[42]

Within a few short years deism had become a matter of some concern to Anglican apologists and was beginning to share attention with those perennial targets of the polemicists, atheism, Catholicism, and Dissent. Answers to the deists were slow to appear, however, and Stillingfleet's pamphlet is a rare exception. For a while, Anglican writers were content to denounce the deists in passing, as in the allusions I have quoted, or to make old arguments appear in new dress. Some time before his death in 1670, George Rust, the Cambridge Platonist, had written a *Discourse of the Use of Reason in Matters of Religion,* which was an attack on the more enthusiastic sects among the Dissenters, at that time the only important group who misunderstood, by denying, the use of reason in religious matters. When his friend Henry Hallywell edited and translated the manuscript a few months after Dryden's *Religio Laici* appeared, he saw fit to add the subtitle, "Shewing, That Christianity Contains Nothing Repugnant to Right Reason; against Enthusiasts and Deists." For in the interval, a second group had become prominent whose misuse of reason in religion was one of excess rather than defect. These deists, Hallywell explained in his preface to the book, were persons "pleading only for a Natural Religion in opposition to any Particular Mode or Way of Divine Revelation; And hence though they profess to acknowledge a God and Providence, yet have withal a mean and low esteem of the Scriptures and Christianity."[43] The description might have been drawn from the speeches

---

[41] *Religio Clerici* (London, 1681), p. 113.

[42] *Ibid.,* sigs. A4v–A5.

[43] "Preface to the Reader," *A Discourse of the Use of Reason in Matters of Religion* (London, 1683), sig. a1.

of Dryden's Deist, so closely do the two agree in their picture of this new and serious threat to Christianity.

The evidence is clear that an articulate group sharing the sentiments of Dryden's Deist was already in existence in 1682 and that these deists had achieved sufficient prominence during the years immediately preceding the appearance of *Religio Laici* to call for some kind of answer. We have confirmed our suspicion of their existence, but we have yet to consider the evidence in support of the further suggestion raised by Dryden's poem: that one or more English works by these deists, restating and modifying the notions of Lord Herbert, were circulating at this time and were available to Dryden. For it is unreasonable to suppose that so much concern could be elicited by conversation alone, or that these men should have made such unpopular, and indeed dangerous, opinions the burden of their private discourse with the Anglican clergy, who nevertheless became acquainted with these ideas.

I have called these opinions dangerous, and indeed they were, if only because of the opposition of those who exercised authority. As long as the various licensing acts continued in force, no book expressing deist or any other form of anti-Christian views could be lawfully published in England or imported from abroad, since all books were supposed to be passed for publication by the proper licensing authority, and no book could be licensed "wherein any doctrine or opinion shall be asserted or maintained which is contrary to the Christian faith or the doctrine or discipline of the Church of England."[44] It is no coincidence that the flood of deist books toward the close of the seventeenth century began shortly after the expiration of the last Licensing Act in 1695. Yet as the history of Charles Blount's early books makes clear, there were ways of evading the law. Not a few writers ignored the Licensing Act, and if a book was sufficiently dangerous it could be surreptitiously printed with a false imprint or the omission of the printer's name, in further violation of the law. The printing of books abroad for distribution in England, a method particularly favored by English Catholics, was another

[44] Licensing Act of 1662. See *English Historical Documents, 1660–1714,* ed. Andrew Browning (London: Eyre and Spottiswoode, 1953), pp. 67–69. This act was renewed biennially until 1679, when its place was taken by a royal proclamation enforcing similar provisions which continued in force until 1685, at which time the Licensing Act was again renewed.

evasion to which Lord Herbert, and perhaps Blount, resorted. The "Amsterdam" edition of Blount's *Anima Mundi* includes a preface from "The Printer to the Reader" which declares:

> The Free Use of the Press hath in these parts of Christendom, to the great advantage of Knowledge, been allow'd, till now of late it appears in some places so clogg'd with un-ingenious Restraints, as Necessitates those who would communicate Fancies not vulgar, either to bury them as an untimely Birth, or else to use them as men do pure Gold, mingling it with base Metal to make it the better endure Minting. But we of the *Low-Countries* [are more liberal]. . . . Therefore at this time, by reason of these present Commotions, very many of the *English* Nation being here amongst us, it was my fortune to meet with one of them, who lent me a Manuscript of this Treatise *de Anima Mundi,* lately written by an *English* Gentleman, one Mr. *Charles Blount.*[45]

Our Amsterdam printer may be Blount himself, but the state of affairs he describes is perfectly accurate. At no time in English history was the control of the press more rigorously enforced than during the quarter of a century following the passing of the Licensing Act of 1662. In his double role as licenser and surveyor of the press, the indefatigable Roger L'Estrange maintained a rigid censorship over those manuscripts submitted for his approval, at the same time seeking out and prosecuting those printers and booksellers who tried to escape his vigilance, or that of his informers. Surreptitious printing and the selling of unlicensed books from abroad were hazardous pursuits, only to be undertaken by those willing to risk arrest, imprisonment, and the pillory.[46]

The Licensing Act, however, applied only to the production and sale of *printed* books. It did not prohibit the circulation of manuscripts. A safer, if more tedious, method of publishing proscribed opinions was therefore available to those who would take the trouble to hand or send their works about in manuscript. Copies could soon multiply as friends and other interested readers transcribed the manuscript, or hired a scribe to do so, before passing it on to others. A chapter in the history of Restoration literature remains to be written on this second, largely ignored, method of "publication." The best-known example of such clandestine

---

[45] *Anima Mundi* (Amsterdam, 1679), sigs. A3–A3v.

[46] For an account of the severity with which the licensing acts were enforced during this period, see David Ogg, *England in the Reign of Charles II* (2d ed.; Oxford: Clarendon Press, 1956), II, 514–16.

publication is that of the several thousand verse satires against the government which circulated freely in manuscript throughout the Restoration period but only began to be printed, in the various collections known as *Poems on Affairs of State,* in 1689 following the Revolution.[47] The authors and propagators of such manuscripts, if safe from the Licensing Act, were nevertheless liable under the Treason Act if their writings were particularly objectionable, and Algernon Sidney was executed in 1683 for possessing a manuscript of his still unpublished *Discourses concerning Government.*[48] But such dangers accompanied the circulation of political "libels" to a greater degree than that of unorthodox religious opinions.[49]

Many of the writings on religion which could not obtain a license were circulated in the same manner as the political satires, although they were fewer in number. The manuscripts on religion which Lord Herbert left unpublished at his death were probably circulated among his friends. Hobbes's *Historical Narration concerning Heresy* was passing about in manuscript at least two years before it was published in 1680, for Blount read it in 1678, and his own *Anima Mundi,* which he sent to Hobbes in manuscript the same year, enjoyed widespread publication in this form before it was finally printed in 1679.[50] Such works were too lengthy to invite transcription, and after passing the holograph about among his friends for awhile, the author's only recourse was to incur the risks of unlicensed printing. Short prose tracts, however, could be multiplied as easily as were the verse satires on public figures, and in the form of numerous transcripts they could circulate among an ever growing audience for many years without employing the services of any printer. It was in this manner, I suggest, that the deists propagated their opinions and

[47] As Peter Laslett has brilliantly demonstrated, Locke's *Two Treatises of Government* was also being surreptitiously circulated in manuscript at this time, nearly a decade before it appeared in print. See "The English Revolution and Locke's 'Two Treatises of Government'," *Cambridge Historical Journal,* 12 (1956): 40–55.

[48] See Ogg, *England in the Reign of Charles II,* II, 649–50.

[49] For an interesting account of the circulation of the political poems in manuscript, and of the hazards involved, see George deForest Lord's introduction to his edition of *Poems on Affairs of State, Vol. I: 1660–1678* (New Haven: Yale University Press, 1963), pp. xxxii–xlii.

[50] For evidence that Blount had seen Hobbes's manuscript, see his letter to Hobbes referred to in n. 29 above. The information that *Anima Mundi* "had been long before handed about in manuscript by the acquaintance of its author" came from Blount's family and is recorded in Campbell's life.

attracted attention during the years immediately preceding the appearance of Dryden's *Religio Laici.*

If we turn back to Stillingfleet's answer to the deists, written seven years before Dryden's but not published until 1677, we shall find that at least one such deist tract was circulating in manuscript as early as 1675. For at the beginning of *A Letter to a Deist* Stillingfleet explains that he is answering some unpublished "papers" which a deist had the temerity to send him for perusal.[51] A good part of our knowledge of the very existence of such tracts must depend upon contemporary allusions of this kind, for many of them have undoubtedly disappeared. The great quantities of *Poems on Affairs of State* which are still extant in manuscript form owe their survival to the fact that after 1688 such criticisms of the former regime became treasured testimonials to Whig orthodoxy. No such radical change in the climate of religious opinion favored the deist tracts. Yet not all of these manuscripts have vanished.

In the British Museum are four manuscript tracts on religion, obviously the work of "freethinkers," which are now bound with several printed books in a single duodecimo volume.[52] Their appearance is interesting, for they reveal the care with which such manuscripts were transcribed for clandestine "publication." All four manuscripts are in the same hand, but each is a separate duodecimo pamphlet, without blots or corrections, carefully copied out with running titles and catchwords so as to resemble as closely as possible a small printed tract. Two of these pamphlets are Hobbesian; two are deist; all four are anonymous. The two Hobbesian tracts are entitled "Concerning the Arrians, Trinitarians and Councils" and "Of the Subversion of Judaism." The other two tracts carry the titles "A Summary Account of the Deists Religion" and "Of Natural Religion, as opposed to Divine Revelation." These last two pamphlets are brief, forcefully stated arguments on behalf of deism to which Lord Herbert could have subscribed without demur. But they are not by Herbert, nor are they simply paraphrases of his own treatises on religion. They are independent statements of the deist position by authors who had obviously read some of Herbert's writings, but had gone on to restate, and in one case even to modify and develop, his thought.

[51] See *A Letter to a Deist,* pp. 1–2.

[52] The volume, described on the spine as "Tracts on Religion," is in the Department of Printed Books and carries the press mark, 873 b 3.

"A Summary Account of the Deists Religion" is the less interesting of the two tracts for our purpose. The author obviously accepts the Five Catholic Articles, but he does not list them or offer any notions with which we are not already familiar in Lord Herbert. "Of Natural Religion," on the other hand, offers a decided breakthrough in the deist position. The author begins by listing the Catholic Articles, but instead of giving the customary five, he presents seven articles, not only adding to the original list but substantially altering it. He begins:

Natural Religion is the Belief we have of an eternal intellectual Being, & of the Duty which we owe to him, manifested to us by our Reason, without Revilation or possitive Law: The chief Heads whereof seem contained in these few particulars.
1. That there is one infinite eternal God, Creator of all Things.
2. That he governs yᵉ World by Providence.
3. That 'tis our Duty to worship & obey him as our Creator and Governour.
4. That our Worship consists in Prayer to him, & Praise of him.
5. That our Obedience consists in yᵉ Rules of Right Reason, the Practice whereof is Moral Vertue.
6. That we are to expect Rewards and Punishments hereafter, according to our Actions in this Life; which includes the Soul's Immortality, & is proved by our admitting Providence.
Seventhly, That when we err from yᵉ Rules of our Duty, we ought to Repent & trust in God's mercy for Pardon.[53]

The most remarkable feature of this new version of the Catholic Articles is the fourth, which offers the article concerning worship in the elusive form used by Dryden's Deist and in almost the very words which Dryden uses in the preface to *Religio Laici* when he says "that Praise and Prayer are his due Worship." This new version is obviously an expansion of Lord Herbert's, both fuller and clearer than the original.

The sixth and seventh articles of this author are Herbert's fourth and fifth, simply transposed. The first article in both versions is the same, except that our author has added certain divine attributes which Herbert reserves for his discussion of this article. The second article is a new and important addition to the list. It makes an explicit article of the belief in divine providence which was already implied, as the author suggests, in the expectation of

---

[53] Pp. [1–3]. The seven articles are underlined throughout.

rewards and punishments for our actions in this life. Finally, and most important, the author has noticed the discrepancy which I have already pointed out between Herbert's second article, which speaks of *worship,* and his third article, which defines this worship in terms which apply more properly to *obedience.* He has remedied this failure by expanding Herbert's second article to include obedience as well as worship among our duties to God. He has kept Herbert's third article concerning the practice of moral virtue, but has made it the expression not of our worship but of our obedience. Last of all, he has added a new article which makes praise and prayer the proper expression of the worship we owe to God, as moral virtue is of our obedience.

Either Dryden or some intermediary source has combined the two versions of the Catholic Articles to produce the *"Systeme of Deisme"* offered at the beginning of *Religio Laici.* An acquaintance with Lord Herbert's version is suggested by the fact that the seven articles have again been reduced to five, and that the sixth and seventh articles of the present version have been again transposed to the order in which Herbert offers them. But an acquaintance with the present version was clearly essential, for the new list of five articles is achieved by eliminating not only the new article concerning divine providence but also Herbert's third article, substituting for this the new article of the present version, concerning praise and prayer. Similarly, the twofold obligation of obedience and worship in this new version of Herbert's second article is comprehended under Dryden's single word "Service." As a result of these changes, Herbert's emphasis on a kind of natural law has been replaced in Dryden's version by a different stress, which places weight on deism as a system of worship. This change in emphasis, so important for the purpose of Dryden's own arguments, can be traced to the second version of the Catholic Articles.

It is impossible to say whether Dryden introduced these modifications himself on the basis of these two versions alone, or found them already made in some other deist pamphlet now lost. What is important is the fact that these two versions alone provide the necessary conditions for the Deist's opening speech, as well as for the objection which he raises later on in the poem. This objection against a particular revelation, and specifically against Christianity, is offered by Herbert in several passages of his works, but interspersed among various other matters with which Dryden's

Deist is not concerned.[54] In the pamphlet "Of Natural Religion," it is interesting to note, the substance of the Deist's second and concluding speech in *Religio Laici* follows without interruption the substance of his first speech. As soon as the author of this pamphlet has concluded his list of the seven articles, he immediately proceeds with an objection to the Christian revelation:

That Rule wch is necessary to our true Happiness, ought to be generally made known to all men.
But no Rule of Revealed Religion was, or ever could be made known to all men.
Therefore no Revealed Religion is necessary to future Happiness.
The Major is thus proved.
Our futur Happiness depends upon our Obeying, or endeavouring to fulfill ye known will of God.
But that Rule which is not Generally known, cannot be generally obey'd.
Therefore that Rule which is not generally known, cannot be ye Rule of our Happiness.
Now the Minor of the first Syllogism is matter of Fact, and uncontrovertible, that no Religion supernatural has been conveyed to all the World; Witness the large Continent of *America,* not discover'd till within this two hundred years; where if there were any Revealed Religion, at least it was not y^e *Christian.*[55]

This certainly contains the gist of the *"Objection of the Deist"* who argues in *Religio Laici* that "No *Supernatural Worship* can be *True:* / Because a *general Law* is that alone / Which must to *all,* and every *where* be known." Indeed, it offers the same example in support of this argument which the Deist uses when he asks, "And what Provision cou'd from *thence* accrue / To *Indian* Souls, and Worlds discover'd *New?*" While there is no reason to suppose that this pamphlet was the only deist tract that Dryden might have seen, the similarities in this case are so close that we are tempted to ask whether some form of the manuscript would have been available to Dryden before the middle of 1682.

This particular transcript, written in a late seventeenth-century hand, cannot be dated precisely and in any event it is probably only one of several which were made of the same manuscript. What is more important is the fact that new and expanded versions of Lord Herbert's Catholic Articles similar to this one were

[54] See, for example, *De Veritate,* trans. Carré, pp. 299–300 and 303; *Religio Laici,* trans. Hutcheson, p. 119.
[55] Pp. [4–6].

definitely being circulated in the 1670's. A careful examination of Stillingfleet's *Letter to a Deist* reveals that the "papers" sent him by a deist in 1675 contained yet another version of the Catholic Articles, of which again there are seven. This was apparently an altogether different pamphlet from the one we are considering, for the seven articles are not in every respect the same in the two versions. That which came to Stillingfleet's attention omits one of the articles in "Of Natural Religion," substituting another in its place, and presents the last two articles in the order in which Lord Herbert gives them. Nevertheless, we find here the article on divine providence, the separation of our duties of obedience and worship into two articles, and a similar version of the latter which states "That this God is to receive from us all Worship proper to Him, of Prayers, Praises, etc."[56] It is worth noting that Dryden could not have learned of the Catholic Articles from Stillingfleet's book any more than he could have taken his own answers from that source. Stillingfleet does not present these articles as the beliefs of his Deist, nor even make clear that they were expressed in the papers he was answering. He presents them as "things agreed upon between us," adding an eighth point of agreement for the sake of his argument, to the effect that the New Testament contains many excellent precepts. No one who did not have independent knowledge of the Catholic Articles would have any way of knowing that these were not points proposed by Stillingfleet himself to which the Deist had agreed as a common ground on which their dispute could proceed. For Stillingfleet does not challenge these articles, as we shall see Dryden doing, but accepts them and proceeds with his task of proving that the matters of fact reported in the New Testament are true, and that these in turn prove the divine origin of the doctrines which accompany them.

Without attempting to identify the specific deist tract, or tracts, which came to Dryden's attention, it is reasonable to conclude that brief pamphlets of this kind, expanding Lord Herbert's articles and presenting deism as a rational system of worship in rivalry with Christianity, were responsible for the growing disquiet in Anglican circles which led to Dryden's attack on the "Enemies of Piety." The later history of the four manuscript tracts now in the British Museum throws some light on the manner in which such works were circulated, and suggests a possible way in which some

[56] *A Letter to a Deist,* pp. 10–11.

of them may have come to Dryden's attention, for all four pamphlets were eventually printed in 1693 in *The Oracles of Reason,* and reprinted two years later in Blount's *Miscellaneous Works,* which included *The Oracles of Reason.*[57]

Blount's *Oracles of Reason* is a collection of miscellaneous tracts and letters concerning religion. All of its contents are frequently attributed to Blount, in spite of the fact that the title page clearly states that the pieces are by "Charles Blount, Esq., Mr. Gildon, and Others." The eighteen pieces in this collection comprise two distinct groups. One group of nine pieces consists of recent letters and essays by Blount and his young friend Charles Gildon written within a year or two of publication, the most notable being Blount's translation of several chapters of Thomas Burnet's *Archaeologiae Philosophicae* in an attempt to cast doubt on the biblical account of the creation. The other group of nine pieces consists of various essays and letters by Blount and other "freethinkers" written many years earlier, most of which had been in Blount's possession for at least fifteen years, and which he had been circulating clandestinely in manuscript long before he contributed them to the joint enterprise he undertook with Gildon in 1693. Blount's decision to publish these pieces at that late date was part of his successful effort to abolish censorship in England. In 1693 the Licensing Act came up for biennial renewal. Blount assumed an active role in opposing the bill and published two pamphlets, consisting for the most part of passages freely borrowed from Milton's *Areopagitica,* in which he pleaded for unlicensed printing.[58] At the same time he published another book, a carefully laid trap for the licenser of the press, Edmund Bohun, which was so successful that the unfortunate official was dismissed and imprisoned.[59] Largely as a result of his efforts, the Licensing Act,

[57] The two deist pamphlets, along with some other material from *The Oracles of Reason,* were reprinted in 1745 as *A Summary Account of the Deist's Religion* by an anonymous editor who declared that "Of Natural Religion," "I am *credibly* informed by a Gentleman of great Learning and Integrity, was penn'd by that *Eminent* Poet John Dryden, Esq." (sig. A3). It would be interesting to know the source of this curious attribution. In modern times, "Of Natural Religion" has usually been attributed to Blount because of its inclusion in *The Oracles of Reason.* But see Eugene R. Purpus, "Some Notes on a Deistical Essay Attributed to Dryden," *Philological Quarterly,* 29 (1950): 347–49.

[58] The two pamphlets were *A Just Vindication of Learning and of the Liberties of the Press* and *Reasons Humbly Offered for the Liberty of Unlicensed Printing.*

[59] The pamphlet was *King William and Queen Mary Conquerors.* For an account of this maneuver, see Leslie Stephen's life of Blount in the *Dictionary of National Biography.*

although renewed for a final two-year period, was no longer actively enforced, and Blount proceeded at last to defy the law with impunity by publishing the religious tracts which he had been circulating surreptitiously for many years, along with some of his more recent efforts.

The four manuscript pamphlets in the British Museum all belong to this former group of tracts which Blount had been sending about in the late 1670's and early 1680's. The letters from Blount which accompanied the lending of these manuscripts, the originals of which are now lost, are fortunately printed in many cases in *The Oracles of Reason*. They throw some light on the date and authorship of the tracts and reveal that the two Hobbesian tracts to which I have referred are by Blount himself, but that the two deist tracts are not. They also reveal Blount's part in their circulation.

"Concerning the Arrians, Trinitarians and Councils" was originally part of a long letter which Blount wrote to Hobbes in 1678 and which accompanied his loan of the manuscript of *Anima Mundi*. The references to Hobbes were later removed when it was transcribed as a tract for general circulation in manuscript. In December of the same year we find Blount sending the holograph of his own tract, "Of the Subversion of Judaism," to Lord Rochester, like Hobbes a notorious freethinker. On February 7, 1680, he sends Rochester the manuscript of another of his own tracts, "Concerning the Immortality of the Soul." At the same time, however, Blount was busily engaged in circulating manuscripts by other writers among his acquaintances. Thus, on February 8, 1680, we find Blount sending a transcript he had made of his father's unpublished "De Anima" to Lord Rochester, and on May 14, 1686, he sends a transcript of "A Summary Account of the Deists Religion," the work of an unknown author, to Thomas Sydenham, the noted physician. The letter which accompanied this manuscript illuminates Blount's activities as a clandestine "publisher" of religious tracts:

The last time I had the happiness of your Company, it was your Request that I would help you to a sight of the Deists Arguments, which I told you, I had sometimes by me, but then had lent them out; they are now return'd me again, and according to my promise I have herewith sent them to you.[60]

---

[60] *Oracles of Reason,* p. 87.

An impression begins to emerge that Blount was far more than simply the author of various pamphlets on religious subjects culled from the writings of other men. He was also a middleman for other freethinkers, the recognized means of transmission for their manuscripts. Presumably he performed a similar function in the case of the tract, "Of Natural Religion," sent to him by its author, whose initials were A. W., but about whom nothing else is known. Probably Blount shared this manuscript with his friends, and perhaps transcribed it, together with three brief papers by various authors expounding Epicureanism which are printed in *The Oracles of Reason.*

Blount's present-day reputation as a deist writer who indulged in plagiarism, therefore, is a distortion of the actual facts. In reality he was a publicist for, and propagator of, freethinking of any kind, whose activities took two different but simultaneous forms. On the one hand he was a popularizer of other men's works who freely adapted their writings to present needs. On the other hand he served as a promoter and lending librarian for unorthodox manuscript tracts on religion, much as the notorious Robert Julian was doing at the same time for the manuscript poems on affairs of state.[61] If these transcripts of other men's manuscripts, or even the digests of other men's books which Blount published under his own name, did not express a consistent point of view, this was no matter as long as they shared the common tactic of questioning accepted religious beliefs. The opinions of Pyrrhonists, Hobbesians, Epicureans, and deists, as well as the more sober investigations of Thomas Burnet into sacred history, were all equally welcome to Blount's enterprise.

One of the manuscripts containing unorthodox religious opinions which Blount managed to obtain was Lord Herbert's still unpublished *Dialogue between a Tutor and His Pupil.* The manuscript, which may have been circulating for some time, seems to have come into Blount's hands about 1680. He made use of it in writing his notes to *The Two First Books of Philostratus* in that year, favoring in particular those passages in which Herbert attacks "priestcraft," a subject dear to Hobbesians and deists alike.[62] Three years later he decided to popularize Herbert's reli-

[61] For a discussion of the role which men like Julian played as "clearing houses" for the political manuscripts, see Lord, *Poems on Affairs of State, Vol I: 1660–1678,* p. xxxviii.

[62] For a detailed discussion of Blount's use of Herbert's manuscript in writing these notes, see Hutcheson, *Lord Herbert of Cherbury's "De Religione Laici,"* pp. 72–74.

gious opinions in his usual manner; he published a book, under the title of *Religio Laici,* which is little more than a paraphrase of Herbert's exposition of deism. As usual, Blount made no mystery of the source from which he had borrowed his opinions and even purloined his title, modestly referring to his book as "this small *Piece,* which I Entitle by the Name of *Religio Laici,* from a Treatise of the *Lord Herbert* of *Cherburie*'s so called; whose *Notions* I have often made use of, and grounded the Chief of my Discourse upon his *Five Catholick* or *Universal Principles.*"[63] It is usually assumed that Herbert's *Religio Laici* is Blount's only source for this book, but in fact he was still using the unpublished manuscript he had obtained a few years earlier, for the "Five Catholick or Universal Articles of Religion" in Blount's book are copied directly, with slight changes in wording, from the list in *A Dialogue between a Tutor and His Pupil,* the only one of Herbert's many versions of these articles which agrees exactly with Blount's.[64] It is Blount's authorship of this book, plus the mistaken attribution to him of the deist tracts printed in *The Oracles of Reason,* which has been responsible for his reputation as a deist. But to think of Blount as having undergone a conversion to deism as a result of his becoming acquainted with Herbert's opinions is to misunderstand the man. Herbert was simply a temporary enthusiasm of Blount's, as Montaigne and Hobbes had been a little earlier, and as Thomas Burnet and the much despised Milton were to become a few years later. Blount "the second English deist" is an invention of the historians; Blount the principal organ for the dissemination of freethought, including deism, in the Restoration period is a figure of some importance.

Blount's *Religio Laici,* which followed Dryden's poem of that name by only a few months, is dedicated to the poet. The two men were certainly acquainted, and Blount professed himself Dryden's admirer and friend. It is doubtful, however, that Dryden reciprocated these feelings, or that they were as genuine on Blount's part as he pretended. Blount's first book, written when he was only seventeen, had been a defense of the poet entitled *Mr. Dreyden Vindicated* (1673). This juvenile effort coming from one who had yet to achieve notoriety may not have been unwelcome. But this was only the beginning of a succession of public compliments, expressed in his most offensive books, which

---

[63] Blount's *Religio Laici* (London, 1683), sig. A8v.
[64] See *ibid.,* pp. 49–50.

Blount continued to bestow on Dryden over the years. In *Anima Mundi* he illustrates a point by quoting a passage from *Tyrannic Love,* by "a modern most ingenious Poet."[65] In his notes to *The Two First Books of Philostratus* he turns to Dryden for illustration on two separate occasions.[66] To Dryden, already worried by accusations of impiety and even atheism, it can only have been an embarrassment to be quoted in such contexts and to be made a partner with Hobbes in these unsolicited testimonials of Blount's admiration. Neither was he likely to be so gullible as to assume that these discomfitures were offered without some tincture of malice. Certainly Dryden's only allusion to Blount, made after the younger man's death, is coldly ambiguous. In his "Life of Lucian" (1696) Dryden says of Blount, who had taken a hand in the translations to which the life was prefixed, "The wit of Mr. Blount, and his other performances, need no recommendation from me; they have made too much noise in the world to need a herald."[67]

Blount's dedication of his *Religio Laici* to Dryden in an "Epistle Dedicatory" swollen with fulsome praise was sufficiently embarrassing. What was worse, Blount pretended that this rehash of Lord Herbert's deist opinions was an appropriate sequel to Dryden's own *Religio Laici.* "I have endeavoured," he assured the poet, "that my Discourse should be onely a Continuance of yours; and that, as you taught Men how to *Believe,* so I might instruct them how to *Live.*" A little later he repeats the suggestion that his own efforts on behalf of deism had been inspired by Dryden's apparently similar enterprise in his poem: "Wherefore, I designed this Treatise of mine to be onely an *Addition,* or rather the *Consequence* of yours; encouraging Men to Live up to the *Vertue* of that *Doctrine* you teach."[68] Unless we are willing to suppose that Blount was obtuse in addition to his other failings, we cannot assume that his motives were innocent. Whatever he lacked in originality he made up for in a certain native shrewdness which is quite incompatible with his reading Dryden's poem as anything but a severe attack on the very principles Blount was now recommending. In reality, Blount's book is an answer to Dryden's

[65] *Anima Mundi* (London, 1679), p. 86.
[66] *The Two First Books of Philostratus* (London, 1680), pp. 80–81, 83.
[67] *The Works of John Dryden,* ed. Sir Walter Scott and George Saintsbury (Edinburgh: William Paterson, 1882–93), XVIII, 79.
[68] Blount's *Religio Laici,* sigs. All–Allv.

poem, disguised as a sequel. His maneuver was no more original than his title. He had learned it from one of his favorite books, Montaigne's *Apology for Raimond Sebond,* an onslaught against Sebond's treatise under the guise of a defense.

It is quite possible, though by no means certain, that Blount was responsible for supplying Dryden with the tract "Of Natural Religion" or similar deist pamphlets, that the poet proceeded to answer these arguments in *Religio Laici* as Stillingfleet had done on a similar occasion a few years before, and that Blount decided to serve his "friend" the same turn by his devious rejoinder. Whether or not he was the intermediary in this case, Blount's career reveals the existence of a religious underworld in Restoration London to complement the underworld of politics which is far better known. Dryden's acquaintance with this shadow world of political conspiracy and pamphleteering is obvious to every reader of his political poems. *Religio Laici* displays his familiarity with that other world where the "Enemies of Piety" exchanged their manuscripts in the shadow of the pillory.

4

THE CHRISTIAN APOLOGIST:
RESPONSE

By the beginning of 1682, the year in which Dryden wrote *Religio Laici*, the conditions which warranted his answers to both deism and Catholicism in that poem already existed. The long-standing controversy between Protestants and Catholics in England had increased and sharpened during the years following the Restoration, reaching an unprecedented intensity during the crisis over the Exclusion Bill beginning in 1679. To this well-entrenched topic for the polemicists had been added, more recently, the challenge of deism, swelling gradually until it had become "so common a *Theme* among the *Scepticks* of this *Age*" that it too required the attention of Anglican apologists.

Hardly any such apologists had yet appeared in the field against the deists, however, as we noticed in the last chapter. Stillingfleet's *Letter to a Deist,* almost the only effort of this kind, could offer Dryden little help.[1] Stillingfleet's procedure in his book had been to engage in a minute examination of details in order to answer his opponent's objections to the Scriptures. The Anglican churchman's concern with specific passages of the Bible is excusable in a treatise; it would be insufferable in a poem. Dryden's arguments

[1] Since this chapter was written, an article has appeared which suggests that Stillingfleet's *Letter to a Deist* was the source of Dryden's arguments in the first half of *Religio Laici*. The analogues cited occupy only a small portion of Stillingfleet's book and are of a kind which, as I show in this chapter, are common to Christian apologetics of the period. In the appendix to this book I have discussed seven works of Christian apologetics available to Dryden, any one of which contains more of his arguments than does *A Letter to a Deist*. This tradition is apparently unknown to the author of the article, who therefore concludes that there is a unique relationship between Stillingfleet's arguments and Dryden's. See Donald R. Benson, "Who 'Bred' *Religio Laici?,*" *Journal of English and Germanic Philology*, 65 (1966): 238–51.

are of a more general order, and more commonplace.

For convenience sake, I shall outline Dryden's arguments in the first half of *Religio Laici,* up to the point where the *"Digression to the Translatour"* signals the beginning of the second half:

I. Necessity of Revelation (ll. 1–125)
   A. Inadequacy of natural religion (ll. 1–92)
   B. Our dependence on revelation for the means of atonement (ll. 93–125)
II. Proofs That This Revelation Is Contained in the Bible (ll. 126–67)
   A. Superiority of its teachings to those of other religions in answering the ends of human life (ll. 126–33)
   B. Antiquity of its laws (ll. 134–37)
   C. Character and circumstances of its authors (ll. 138–45)
   D. Confirmation of its doctrines by miracles (ll. 146–51)
   E. Its remarkable reception in spite of so many hindrances, internal and external (ll. 152–67)
III. Answer to the Objection of the Deist (ll. 168–223)

No one has previously taken the trouble, I believe, to outline Dryden's arguments, and it is sometimes assumed that he has arranged them in a haphazard fashion which defies the common requirements of logical structure.[2] This outline, therefore, is worth some attention, for it reveals that Dryden's arguments form a coherent sequence of ideas in which each principal stage of the discourse depends on the one which immediately precedes it. Thus, his demonstration of the necessity of revelation leads to the question of where this revelation is to be found, and his affirmation that it is contained in the Bible leads to a consideration of the objection to this theory.

I have called these arguments commonplace, an assertion that I intend to prove to the reader's satisfaction in the course of this chapter. It is true that answers specifically addressed to the deists were still a rarity in 1682. But this offered no particular problem to anyone who chose to challenge their position, for as I have suggested, it was an easy matter to make old arguments appear in a new dress. They were already available as part of a common fund of religious apologetics which had long been popular in the Restoration period.

It is small wonder that this in some ways obvious source for Dryden's arguments should have been overlooked by previous

[2] See Donald J. Greene, " 'Logical Structure' in Eighteenth-Century Poetry," *Philological Quarterly,* 31 (1952): 315–36.

commentators on the poem. For as I indicated in chapter 2, some critics have assumed that *Religio Laici* is a poetic essay in which Dryden expresses his private opinions, and for these no other source need be sought than the poet's fertile imagination. On the other hand, the most popular interpretation of the poem, which seeks to relate it to some previous tradition, has directed attention away from the current of apologetics popular among English Protestants of the time. On the assumption that Dryden's poem expounds fideism, or the theory that reason is useless in religious matters (a notion relatively uncommon among members of the Church of England), the exponents of this interpretation have argued that *"Religio Laici* belongs historically rather to Roman Catholic than to Anglican apologetics."[3]

Undoubtedly, it is Dryden's discussion of the inadequacy of natural religion in the first ninety-two lines of his poem that has misled so many readers, offering, as it seems to do, concrete evidence for his fideism. A fideist is usually defined as one who denies that there is any such thing as natural religion, insisting that all matters pertaining to religion, even the existence of God, are unknowable by natural means and must be believed by faith alone. Now if Dryden was a fideist we should expect him to make just such an attack on the Five Catholic Articles—a form of natural religion—as we find him doing in the early stanzas of *Religio Laici.* On the basis of the many historical accounts of Renaissance and seventeenth-century fideism, it is a fairly easy matter to construct a hypothetical "model" of a fideist and to predict the responses such a model might be expected to make to a tract like "Of Natural Religion." The apparent identity between Dryden's

[3] Louis I. Bredvold, *The Intellectual Milieu of John Dryden* (Ann Arbor: University of Michigan Press, 1934), p. 47. See also pp. 73–129 for the first, and fullest, exposition of this popular theory. (For an example of its continued popularity, see the discussion of *Religio Laici* by Charles E. Ward in *The Life of John Dryden* [Chapel Hill: University of North Carolina Press, 1961], pp. 189–92.) For Bredvold, Dryden's fideism was a corollary of his Pyrrhonism. Nevertheless, the two positions are not inseparable, and Bredvold concedes that the fideist tradition, while congenial to Dryden because of his Pyrrhonism, was not itself Pyrrhonist. Although, in chapter 1 I have denied the antecedent proposition, that Dryden was a Pyrrhonist, this does not logically disprove the consequent that he was a fideist. Many Christian Pyrrhonists, such as Montaigne, were also fideists, but not all fideists have been Pyrrhonists. For recent studies that clarify the distinction between fideism and Pyrrhonism and show that the two positions can be independent of each other, see Paul H. Kocher, *Science and Religion in Elizabethan England* (San Marino, Calif.: Huntington Library, 1953), pp. 45–62, and Robert Hoopes, *Right Reason in the English Renaissance* (Cambridge, Mass.: Harvard University Press, 1962), pp. 96–122.

reactions at the beginning of *Religio Laici* and those we have predicted for our model could then be taken as a guarantee of the poet's fideism. Thus, we could predict that a fideist would disparage the power of reason in religious affairs, and then point to the oft-quoted lines with which *Religio Laici* opens: "DIM, as the borrow'd beams of Moon and Stars / To *lonely, weary, wandring* Travellers, / Is *Reason* to the *Soul*." We should expect to find a fideist stressing the divergent and even contradictory answers which philosophers have given to the questions of the existence of God or of the immortality of the soul, as Montaigne does in his *Apology for Raimond Sebond* and Blount in his *Anima Mundi* based on Montaigne's essay. Again we should find the first forty-one lines of *Religio Laici* repeating just such a pattern. Finally, we might hope that the outcome of these efforts would be the assertion that all such questions belong to the province of faith; and we could notice with some satisfaction that Dryden tells the Deist: "'Tis *Revelation* what thou thinkst *Discourse*."

I have made the strongest case I know how for Dryden's apparent fideism because it would be disingenuous to minimize the attraction of such a theory or the plausible evidence which has been derived from *Religio Laici* in its support. A case of this kind, based on similarity, acquires additional force by way of contrast. Fideism, a negative and minority view at best, has usually been set off in historical accounts against the majority view which, in the tradition of St. Thomas Aquinas and Richard Hooker, has always prevailed in the Catholic and Anglican churches. This position of what may be called "Christian rationalism" has always accepted a form of natural religion, discoverable by unaided human reason, but has denied its sufficiency, insisting on the necessity of revealed religion as well.[4] Adopting another hypothetical model, we might expect someone who subscribed to this latter position to go along with the Deist's version of natural religion, merely insisting on the addition of revelation. Dryden's failure to accept the Five Catholic Articles could then be taken as a sign that his own view of the matter was in marked contrast to this position.

All such arguments that Dryden is making a typical fideist response to the Deist, however, break off at the point where he

---

[4] I have discussed this position in some detail in *Swift and Anglican Rationalism* (Chicago: University of Chicago Press, 1961), pp. 21–36. However, the reader should be prepared to discount occasional allusions to Dryden as a fideist.

concludes his objections to the Five Catholic Articles. They fail to mention that he immediately proceeds to prove the necessity for revelation and to offer rational arguments for the divine authority of the Scriptures. Yet his arguments on behalf of revelation are an integral part of his answer to the Deist, and it is necessary to consider whether such arguments are consistent with the hypothesis that he was a fideist.[5]

To begin, we must discover why fideism has so often been condemned, officially and unofficially, by spokesmen for the Catholic and Anglican churches. Why should it matter to a Christian whether or not there is such a thing as natural religion, since all of its ingredients are repeated in the Scriptures? The importance of natural religion stems, not from any new beliefs which it can add to revelation, but from the logical grounds it provides for an acceptance of supernatural religion. It has been the traditional position of most Anglican and Catholic churchmen that there is a reasonable basis for Christian faith, and that these rational grounds for accepting the Christian revelation, or "preambles to faith," consist in our independent assurance that there is a God, that what He says is true, and that He has made a historical revelation which is to be found in the Bible. If a circular argument is to be avoided, these motives for belief must be sought outside the Scriptures themselves and ought to be a matter of rational conviction rather than of religious faith. As Hooker assured the Puritans, "Scripture teacheth us that saving truth which God hath discovered unto the world by revelation, and it presumeth us taught otherwise that itself is divine and sacred."[6] These inducements to assent to divine revelation depend in part on some of the ingredients of natural religion (the existence of God and the divine attributes of omniscience and veracity), but in part also on those rational proofs for the divine authority of the Scriptures which Dryden offers at some length in *Religio Laici*.

Now the essential feature of fideism is not simply the rejection of natural religion but the explicit denial that there are any

[5] Several recent articles have expressed doubts, on various grounds, concerning Dryden's fideism in *Religio Laici*. See Thomas H. Fujimura, "Dryden's *Religio Laici*: An Anglican Poem," *PMLA*, 76 (1961): 205–17, and, particularly, Elias J. Chiasson, "Dryden's Apparent Scepticism in *Religio Laici*," *Harvard Theological Review*, 54 (1961): 207–21.

[6] *Of the Laws of Ecclesiastical Polity* (London: J. M. Dent and Sons, 1954), I, 320 [III, viii, 13]. (All subsequent references to the *Laws* will be to book, chapter, and section, as in the reference here in brackets.)

rational motives for assenting to divine revelation. To assert that religious conviction must depend on a simple act of faith (*fides*) is to deny that there is any reasonable basis for religion and to substitute some nonrational motive for belief. This motive may be one of custom, based on a simple acceptance of the authority and teachings of the national church, as Montaigne recommends. The truly wise man, he writes, will avoid seeking reasons for his religion, instead "acknowledging his natural weakness, fit to receive from on high some strength not his own, unprovided with human knowledge and therefore more apt to admit divine knowledge, annihilating his judgment to make more room for faith, neither disbelieving, nor maintaining any dogma contrary to the common observances."[7] On the other hand, the fideist may maintain, in the manner of those Puritans whom Hooker opposed, that Scripture sufficiently provides its own supernatural inducement to assent in the "testimony of the Spirit" which is evident on every page. So, as an English Puritan wrote on the eve of the Restoration,

> How know we that the *Scripture* is the Word of God; how may others come to be *assured* thereof? The Scripture, say we, beares *Testimony* to it's selfe, that it is the Word of God; that Testimony is the witnesse of God himselfe, which who so doth not accept and believe, he doth what in him lyes to make God a lyar. . . . This *Truth* and consequently this *Authority,* is evidenced and made known to us, by the publick Testimony which is given unto it by the Holy Ghost speaking in it, with *divine Light* and Power, to the minds, soules, and consciences of men.[8]

Thus, rational proofs for the authority of the Scriptures such as Dryden offers in *Religio Laici* were worthless to the fideist, who discounted the efficacy of all considerations of this kind as a basis for belief. Efforts to prove the Bible to be the word of God met with the same objection as attempts to prove the existence of God or any of the other ingredients of natural religion: nature must not be expected to perform the work of grace. To all such arguments as Dryden's the Protestant fideist was wont to reply, as Hooker complained, that "if I believe the Gospel, there needeth no reasoning about it to persuade me; if I do not believe, it must

[7] "Apology for Raimond Sebond," *The Essays of Michel de Montaigne,* trans. Jacob Zeitlin (New York: Alfred Knopf, 1935), II, 166.

[8] John Owen, *Of the Divine Originall, Authority, Self- Evidencing Light, and Power of the Scriptures* (Oxford, 1659), pp. 87 and 99.

be the Spirit of God and not the reason of man that shall convert my heart unto him."[9]

Once we perceive that the essential feature of fideism is a denial of rational inducements for accepting the Christian religion, we are in a position to see that the entire course of Dryden's argument in the first half of *Religio Laici* is in direct contradiction to that view. Any attempt such as Dryden's to offer some part of the rational grounds for Christianity must presuppose an acceptance of the remaining parts. It is fruitless to argue, as Dryden does, that there are compelling reasons for believing that the Bible is the word of God unless one can assume a rational conviction that God exists and that what He says is true. In other words, an acceptance of natural religion is the essential basis of Dryden's logical scheme. Not custom, not the testimony of the Spirit, but reason alone provides the motives for belief in Dryden's view. "Let us be content at last, to know God, by his own Methods," he writes in the preface to *Religio Laici,* "at least so much of him, as he is pleas'd to reveal to us, in the sacred Scriptures; to apprehend them to be the word of God, is all our Reason has to do; for all beyond it is the work of Faith, which is the Seal of Heaven impress'd upon our humane understanding." Religion for Dryden is not initiated by an act of faith, as it is for the fideist; it is a system of worship which begins with reason and is ultimately crowned with faith. Thus grace does not destroy nature, but perfects it. It is true that "to apprehend [the sacred Scriptures] to be the word of God is all our Reason has to do," but this service, modest though it may be, is an essential undertaking which no substitute can perform.

The hypothesis that Dryden was a fideist breaks down, then, once we begin to consider the over-all structure of his arguments against the deists instead of concentrating exclusively on a single part. In order to understand why he appears to disparage natural religion in the course of offering rational arguments for Christianity, we must turn now to the tradition of popular apologetics for the Christian religion and to the role which natural religion played in that tradition.

Anyone who has read at all widely in the religious apologetics of Restoration England notices that this enormous industry takes two independent forms, both of which are often engaged in by the

[9] *Laws,* III, viii, 4.

same individuals, but on separate occasions. In the first place, there is a considerable body of what can be described as "confessional apologetics": defenses of the individual churches written by adherents of these communions for the benefit of their own laity. Here the subject of dispute turns on one or the other doctrinal differences among the various Christian churches, and the target of these polemics is some other Christian communion. So Anglican writers defend particular doctrines of the Church of England by assailing some Christian opponent who denies this belief. An espousal of the institution of the episcopacy, which the Catholics also accepted, will take the form of a polemical tract against the Dissenters, who rejected it; whereas an argument that the Bible alone is the "rule of faith," a doctrine shared by the Dissenters, will be directed against the Catholics, who denied it. Similarly, polemical tracts by dissenting ministers are often written separately against the Established Church or the Catholic church, and deal with very different subjects of dispute. Catholic writers, on the other hand, are ordinarily concerned with subjects wherein they differ from all Protestants, and often are not interested in distinguishing between Anglicans and Dissenters. The second half of *Religio Laici,* in which Dryden attacks the Catholics, necessarily draws upon such confessional apologetics, and when he writes in the preface that "the helps I have us'd in this small Treatise, were many of them taken from the Works of our own Reverend Divines of the Church of *England,*" he is referring particularly to the aid he required in the latter part of the poem for his assault on another Christian church.

There was another form of religious apologetics in Restoration England, however, which received just as much attention as this confessional literature and was often the work of the same authors. This can best be described as "Christian apologetics," for it consists of defenses of the Christian religion rather than of any particular church. Here the purpose is to show the faithful that there are reasonable grounds for accepting Christianity, by addressing a series of arguments to some supposed non-believer. Toward the end of the seventeenth century and for many years thereafter this antagonist was frequently a deist. During the period we are considering, however—the third quarter of the seventeenth century, when deism was only beginning to emerge—the target of these polemics was commonly an atheist. He was imagined as a well-meaning, reasonable person devoid of any religion, who had never heard, or at least had never seriously considered, the reasons which could be urged for the Christian religion. The treatises addressed to this individual were consequently closely argued courses of instruction in the only grounds of assent acceptable to one who was without religious faith: natural arguments amenable to human reason.

Now it should be obvious that these arguments on behalf of Christianity were not subject to confessional differences, being shared by all Christians, whether Anglican, Catholic, or nonconformist, who admitted that there are rational grounds for religion. On the other hand, a fideist, whatever his particular persuasion, would abjure any attempts to offer human arguments for divine matters. Dryden's friend Walter Charleton explained the distinction between these two points of view in one of his own contributions to Christian apologetics, written shortly before the Restoration:

Among Us, who are so happy, as to be Sacramentally engaged to fight under the Standard of the Crucified God, I observe, in the generall, two different perswasions concerning the nature of Faith. . . . The *First,* wholly refuse the assistance of their Reason, even where it offers it self and the subject is capable of illustration by the discourses it might raise thereupon; as judging any Fundamental of Religion much debased, and in a manner prophaned, if once it be brought to the Test of the Light of Nature, though meerly for Confirmation and more familiar admittance. The *Others,* humbly resign up their Assent to all Positions contained in Sacred Writ; and yet are glad, when they can bring up the Forces of their Reason to assist them in the conquest of their fleshly oppositions: And conceive they then make the best use of the talent of their Understanding, when they imploy it toward the ratification of Divine Traditions.[10]

As Charleton recognizes, neither of these two persuasions is the peculiar property of any one Christian communion. In a passage I have omitted above, he illustrates the first, or fideist, position by referring to those who "are ready to complain that they want Difficulties enough to exercise the strength of their Belief." This obvious allusion to Sir Thomas Browne's *Religio Medici* should

[10] *The Immortality of the Human Soul, Demonstrated by the Light of Nature* (London, 1657), pp. 56–57. The speaker in this dialogue is "Athanasius," the spokesman for Charleton's own ideas. This is the book for which James M. Osborn has suggested that Dryden wrote the "Advertisement to the Reader"; see *John Dryden: Some Biographical Facts and Problems* (New York: Columbia University Press, 1940), pp. 174–75.

serve to remind us that the exponents of this minority position included not only certain Puritans and several French Catholics but an occasional Anglican as well. On the other hand, when Charleton declares his own preference for the second, or traditional, view that reason is an important ally of faith, he does not hesitate to draw support from an official Catholic source:

> However, if you require farther justification of me; I refer you to the undeniable Authority of the *Lateran Council,* held under Pope *Leo* the tenth. Which having decreed the Anathematization of all Atheists, who durst question *the Being of God,* or *the Immortality of the Human Soul;* in the close of the Canon not only exhorteth, but expressly commandeth all Christian Philosophers to endeavour the demonstration of those sacred Truths, by solid and Physical Arguments. And, certainly, so pious and prudent an Assembly would never have prescribed that task, in case they had not conceived it both commendable and possible to be effected.[11]

Our exclusive attention to English Protestant writers should not blind us to the fact that many Catholics, especially on the Continent, also engaged in Christian apologetics. However, such works might give offense to English Protestants by alluding to more particular beliefs, and Catholic works on the subject were not numerous or popular in Restoration England.

On the other hand, the cause of Christian apologetics was served equally well among English Protestants by Dissenters as well as by Anglicans. We must not conclude from the position of some of the sects that all, or even most, Dissenters were fideists, any more than we should assume that Browne and Montaigne spoke for the Anglican and Catholic churches respectively. In 1676, fifteen nonconformist ministers published a pamphlet in which they stoutly denied that there was any difference of opinion between their own communions and the Church of England on the importance of reason in supplying the preambles to faith for a Christian.

> But the sense of the Question is, Whether it be a distance between Conformists and Non-conformists, Lutherans and Calvinists, or any otherly-named Parties of Protestants; whether, and how farr we must

---

[11] *The Immortality of the Human Soul,* p. 60. Athanasius is again the speaker. Charleton, one of the most prominent English Cartesians, is here almost certainly paraphrasing a passage in the dedication to the *Meditationes de Prima Philosophia* (1641) in which Descartes cites the same authority for maintaining that these questions can be demonstrated by rational arguments.

have, or give Reason for all our Religion, or Exercise Reason in discerning it; and in propagating, and defending it by Proof.
And we shall prove the Negative, 1. By those *Confessions* of the several Churches, and Parties, which notifie their Judgements. In all the *Corpus Confessionum* there is no Article on this Subject which is not commonly consented to by the rest of the Protestant Churches.[12]

When these Presbyterian and Independent ministers speak of the "Protestant Churches," however, they purposely exclude many of the sects. They are quite ready to admit that these latter groups do not believe it possible to "give Reason" for religious belief or to defend it by proof. "We deny not," they write, "that *Protestants* herein differ from *Enthusiasts,* or true Fanaticks."[13] The year before, Robert Ferguson, an Independent minister, had offered a similar defense of the nonconformists in *The Interest of Reason in Religion,* stressing the importance they attached to rational inducements to assent and pointing out "that the whole Party ought not to be Traduced, because of the Extravagancies of a few."[14] The state of affairs these ministers describe in the 1670's is an accurate one. The antirational bias of the Puritans in Hooker's day, which was an important phenomenon for several generations afterwards and has been the basis for all historical accounts of English fideism, dwindled after the Restoration to the point where it could be considered, even by many Dissenters, as the view of a lunatic fringe among English Protestants, the *"Enthusiasts,* or true Fanaticks"* who were the object of much scorn. On the other hand, Hooker's own position that the Christian religion is based on rational grounds had become by Dryden's day a view shared by the great majority of educated Protestants, whether Anglicans or Dissenters. The many works of Christian apologetics popular in Restoration England included, therefore, not only treatises from the pens of Anglican divines (and of laymen such as Charleton), but also translations of books by Continental Protestants and discourses by Presbyterian or Independent ministers such as Richard Baxter and William Bates, two of the subscribers to the statement quoted above.
It is in this body of Christian apologetics written by Protestants of every persuasion that we are likely to find the arguments Dry-

---

[12] *The Judgment of Non-conformists, of the Interest of Reason in Matters of Religion* (London, 1676), pp. 5–6. The question is printed in italics.
[13] *Ibid.,* p. 2.
[14] *The Interest of Reason in Religion* (London, 1675), p. 9.

den employs in the first half of *Religio Laici,* where he is attempting to answer one who does not believe in Christianity, just as his arguments against another Christian church in the second half of the poem are probably derived from the confessional apologetics of his own church. But these popular defenses of Christianity display a much wider scope of argument than Dryden found necessary, since they are addressed, not to a deist, but to an atheist.

I have pointed out that there are two separate questions involved in the preambles to faith for a Christian, each of which must be proved by distinct arguments. There is the question of the existence and veracity of God, a commonly accepted ingredient of natural religion; that is to say, it is a matter which could conceivably be discovered by someone who had never heard of Christianity. Secondly, there is the question of the divine authority of the Scriptures, Dryden's particular subject. This is not a matter of natural religion, since it could not even be posed by one who had never heard of the Bible. Nevertheless, it depends on natural religion, since one must be convinced that God exists before he can ask whether this Supreme Being has made a historical revelation which is to be found in the Scriptures. As Robert Ferguson pointed out, "our Belief of the Scripture supposeth the Existence of God, and therefore our knowledge of his Being must precede our Faith of the Divine Authority of the Bible."[15] Consequently, the Christian apologists of the Restoration period might deal with both these questions in their treatises or, if their design was less ambitious, with the first question only. But since these authors were supposedly addressing an atheist they could not simply ignore the first question and begin with the second.

There were many substantial treatises written during the second half of the seventeenth century which were confined to the first question alone. These were works on natural religion ostensibly addressed to an atheist but in reality designed to show the faithful that religion as such is a reasonable matter capable of demonstrative proof. Their subject is indicated by their titles, such as, *Of the Principles and Duties of Natural Religion* (1675), by John Wilkins, Bishop of Chester, and *Natural Theology, or the Knowledge of God from the Works of the Creation* (1674), by Matthew Barker, a nonconformist minister. Natural religion,

---

[15] *Ibid.,* p. 39.

as presented in these treatises, is by no means as extensive as it appears in the deist tract, "Of Natural Religion," or in the works of Lord Herbert of Cherbury. In the writings of most Restoration apologists, it consists of two ingredients only: the existence of God (including often His various attributes, such as veracity) and the immortality of the human soul. Sometimes these two ingredients are the subject of separate treatises. So Walter Charleton proved the existence of God at considerable length in *The Darkness of Atheism Dispelled by the Light of Nature* (1652) and then completed his task five years later with *The Immortality of the Human Soul Demonstrated by the Light of Nature*. Similarly, Henry More offered his arguments for the existence of God the same year as Charleton in *An Antidote against Atheism,* and followed it up with *The Immortality of the Soul* in 1659. More often, however, both matters were treated between the covers of a single book.

By the time he came to the end of one of these books, the Christian apologist would have brought his docile atheist to the point where he accepted natural religion but was still a long way from Christianity. The position of this imaginary convert would approximate that of the deist, although he would by no means believe as much as was contained in the Five Catholic Articles. Nevertheless, like a deist, he would now believe in a God who had given him an immortal soul, and he would be in a position to listen to arguments designed to show that this God has revealed His divine plan for mankind in the Bible. Sometimes the apologist would include a chapter briefly summarizing these arguments for the divine authority of the Bible, as Wilkins and Barker did in the books I have mentioned. But some, such as Charleton, were willing to leave this task to other hands, having accomplished their own design of demonstrating the foundations of Christianity.

Other apologists for Christianity, however, were more ambitious. They wrote treatises designed to lead some imaginary antagonist by a series of logical steps from the "darkness of atheism" to the supernatural light of Christianity. Such books usually consisted of two distinct parts. The first part was a discourse on natural religion exactly like those we have been considering. The particular choice of arguments in these discourses, as in the books devoted solely to natural religion, would vary according to the philosophical bent of the author. But all shared the common ingredient of attempting to prove the existence of God and the immortality of the soul by reason alone. The second part was a discourse on supernatural religion designed to prove the necessity of revelation and to offer convincing arguments that this revelation is to be found in the Scriptures. A typical arrangement of such books is indicated by Richard Baxter's *The Reasons of the Christian Religion* (1667). The first part is entitled "Of Natural Religion or Godliness," the second "Of Christianity and Supernatural Revelation." The lengths to which these treatises could run was often formidable. Sometimes the author chose to issue each of the two parts as separate books. So William Bates, the Presbyterian minister, published his *Considerations of the Existence of God, and of the Immortality of the Soul* in 1676, and the following year issued a sequel entitled *The Divinity of the Christian Religion Proved by the Evidence of Reason and Divine Revelation*. Similarly Sir Charles Wolseley's *The Unreasonableness of Atheism Made Manifest* appeared in 1669, to be followed three years later by his book on *The Reasonableness of Scripture-Belief*.

It should be obvious that anyone setting out to answer a deist rather than an atheist could find the arguments he needed in the second part of these treatises of Christian apologetics. The first part he would naturally ignore, since the deist already accepted the ingredients of natural religion set forth there—the existence of God and the immortality of the soul—as part of the Five Catholic Articles. But in the second part, on supernatural religion, the apologist could find an abundance of rational arguments to show that natural religion is not enough, that some supernatural revelation was necessary, and that this revelation is to be found in Holy Scripture—the very thesis, in fact, that Dryden attempts to prove in the first half of *Religio Laici*. The only part of Dryden's thesis which we should not expect to find in these answers to an atheist would, of course, be his reply to the objection of the Deist.

In 167 lines, naturally, Dryden could not hope to include all of the rational arguments for Christianity which were available to him, nor would there be any necessity to do so. So great is the variety of "reasons of the Christian religion" offered in these treatises, that some books adopt an approach which is entirely different from Dryden's. Nevertheless, one or more of his arguments, interspersed among others which he did not see fit to use, can be found in a respectable number of these treatises, and every one of them is contained somewhere in the Christian apologetics of the period. Needless to say, no two apologists introduce their arguments in exactly the same order. If Dryden had had the time and inclination, he obviously could have read a great many of these treatises, picking and choosing arguments as he saw fit, and arranging his selection according to a logical scheme of his own devising. However, his time was severely limited by his wish to publish his verses "address'd to the Translatour" of Father Simon's *Critical History* while the occasion was still fresh and within some months of the appearance of that book. Furthermore, the works in question were only part of the reading he had to do, since they only relate to the first half of his poem. Lastly, the many literary activities on which Dryden was engaged in 1682, one of his busiest years, left only a portion of his time free for work on *Religio Laici*. In such a predicament, his easiest recourse would have been to choose a single work of Christian apologetics, select what appeared to be some of its most telling arguments, and set these down in much the same order in which he found them, omitting some of the intervening arguments which he might decide to ignore.

My own reading of the works of Christian apologetics published in the Restoration period has convinced me that Dryden adopted this latter course. Some of his arguments appear in many of these works but, with a single exception, none of these books contains more than about half the proofs he offers, or presents them in exactly the order he adopts. The single exception is Sir Charles Wolseley's *The Reasonableness of Scripture-Belief: A Discourse Giving Some Account of Those Rational Grounds upon which the Bible is Received as the Word of God* (1672), the separately published second part of his complete system of Christian apologetics. This book has the novel distinction of containing every one of Dryden's arguments and of presenting them in precisely the same order. The similarity between Wolseley and Dryden is so striking that it is impossible to dismiss it as a fortuitous coincidence, particularly in view of the wide variation in the number and order of these arguments as they are found in the other works of Christian apologetics. In an appendix, I have presented the considerable evidence linking *Religio Laici* with *The Reasonableness of Scripture-Belief* and setting them apart from the works of other apologists. This similarity of logical proofs, reinforced by some remarkable verbal parallels, strongly suggests that Dryden used Wolseley's book extensively, not only as the source of his arguments, but as the basis for the thought pattern in which he presents them. This is not to say, of course, that Dryden was ignorant of the contents of some of the other works of Christian apologetics, or that he may not have used them occasionally in the composition of his poem. But his principal source, which provided him with the outline of his arguments, was unquestionably Wolseley's book.

Who was this man whose book played so important a part in the composition of *Religio Laici*? Sir Charles Wolseley was the same age as Dryden, but he achieved fame before the poet came to public notice and suffered an eclipse of fortune just at the time that Dryden was beginning to attract some attention. In 1653, while Dryden was still at the university, Wolseley was chosen a member of Cromwell's Little Parliament, although he was only twenty-two years old at the time. For the next seven years his success was phenomenal. He became the friend and counselor of Cromwell and, after the Protector's death, of Cromwell's son Richard. The Restoration, however, brought a sudden close to his promising career. He was pardoned by the King but received no further employment and retired to his country estate where, for more than half a century, he quietly occupied himself in various pursuits, among them the writing of books on religion. It is possible, though by no means certain, that, like Dryden and so many others, he conformed to the Established Church after the Restoration, although his warm support of the policy of toleration later pursued by James II shows that he remained at least sympathetic to the interests of the Dissenters.[16] At any rate he lived at peace with the authorities and became a close friend of the Archbishop of Canterbury, John Tillotson.[17]

Wolseley was also a friend of Dryden's. How early they became acquainted is unknown, but they were almost certainly introduced by Dryden's brother-in-law, Sir Robert Howard, or by some other member of his wife's family. Wolseley had long been a good friend of the Howard family, and at the Restoration it was Sir Robert Howard who intervened with the King to obtain a pardon for him. In the summer of 1680, Dryden went to stay with Wolseley

[16] Wolseley's *Liberty of Conscience* (1668) also indicates that the author, whether or not he had himself conformed, was an eloquent advocate of the nonconformists' right to worship as they pleased.
[17] In a holograph letter dated November 29, 1694, now in the British Museum, Wolseley gives the details of Tillotson's death and calls him "the *Archbishop* my old intimate friend" (BM MSS Stowe 747, f. 40).

110

at the latter's estate in Staffordshire.[18] This certainly suggests that the two men were on intimate terms. It is understandable, therefore, that Dryden should have been familiar with his friend's book and have turned to this defense of Christianity by a fellow layman when he required some "helps" in the first half of his poem.

Wolseley's two-part contribution to Christian apologetics in *The Unreasonableness of Atheism* and *The Reasonableness of Scripture-Belief* is one of the fullest, best-organized, and most lucid undertakings of this kind to appear in the Restoration period. It was, as we might expect, well received.[19] Matthew Barker did Wolseley the honor of modeling his own *Natural Theology* after the discussion of natural religion in *The Unreasonableness of Atheism,* and he warmly praised *The Reasonableness of Scripture-Belief* as the best book that had been written on that subject, "there having been so many Learned Pens already engaged herein, especially that *Honoured Knight,* whose worthy Book concerning the *Reasonableness* of receiving the Scriptures for the Word of God, doth justly add new Honour to Himself, and a great Confirmation to the Truth."[20]

In spite of the fact that it uses many of the same arguments as other works of Christian apologetics, the second part of Wolseley's defense of the Christian religion differs from these other books in one very important respect. We have noticed that these two-part treatises were addressed to an atheist and professed to lead this individual from a state of unbelief to the point at which he would accept Christianity. Even when the author issued the two parts separately under different titles, as William Bates did, the apologist normally resumed his argument with the same antago-

---

[18] This information, which was discovered by E. S. de Beer and reported by James M. Osborn in *John Dryden: Some Biographical Facts and Problems,* pp. 200–201, comes from a letter of Jacob Tonson to Narcissus Luttrell dated August 31, 1680, now in the library of All Souls College, Oxford (MS 181, No. 63).

[19] In *The Later Stuarts,* (2d ed.; Oxford: Clarendon Press, 1955), p. 31, Sir George Clark declares that Wolseley's *Reasonableness of Scripture-Belief* "alarmed his orthodox friends." This statement is completely false and apparently due to a hasty reading of Sir Charles Firth's life of Wolseley in the *Dictionary of National Biography* which mentions that a single friend, the Earl of Anglesey, criticized *Justification Evangelical,* an entirely different work of Wolseley's, in a letter to a friend. A reading of the letter, now bound in the Bodleian copy of this book (press mark 8° C345 Linc.), shows that Anglesey was merely expressing a personal opinion about a book which had been licensed by the Bishop of London, as were both *The Unreasonableness of Atheism* and *The Reasonableness of Scripture-Belief.*

[20] *Natural Theology, or the Knowledge of God from the Works of the Creation* (London, 1674), pp. 69–70.

111

nist in the second part. Wolseley, as usual, addressed *The Unreasonableness of Atheism* to such an individual. But when he wrote *The Reasonableness of Scripture-Belief* three years later, he chose a new antagonist. "There are but three sorts of men," he wrote at the beginning of his book, "by whom the Scriptures can, at any time, be generally Attact, and from whose principles their sacred Authority can receive an Universal Invasion. First, Such who wholly deny the being of God . . . such who wallow in the mire of an Atheistical profession." These "Monsters of Mankind" he dismisses at once, pointing out that "I have already contested with such, and dispatcht all my concernes with them" in *The Unreasonableness of Atheism.* "Secondly," he continues, "Such who admit the Being of God, and a supreme and first cause, but deny his providence, and believe he is no way concern'd about the World, nor troubles himself to exercise any Rule or Dominion at all over it."[21] He is referring, of course, to the Epicureans, who were normally answered in treatises against atheism, but whom Wolseley dispatches in 60 pages of this book of some 450 pages. He then turns to his proper antagonist: "Such who (in the third place) admit the being of *God,* of *Providence,* and *Religion,* but reject the *Christian-religion* and consequently the *Bible,* as not true, and close with some other in opposition to it, against those the whole of this discourse will chiefly tend."[22] This description might fit the members of any non-Christian religion, but we must remember that Wolseley was answering an English antagonist for the benefit of an English audience. The term which he regularly gives to this adversary throughout the rest of his book is "antiscripturist," one of the names used at this time for a deist, as we noticed in the last chapter.[23] It is, in fact, the deists whom Wolseley is answering in this book, but, in keeping with the practice which we noticed was the case until the late 1670's, he concentrates exclusively on their negative aspect as enemies of the Bible. He has nothing whatever to say of the positive system of religion which they offered as a substitute for Christianity, and nowhere does he mention the Five Catholic Articles. Nevertheless, setting aside the passing allusions to "antiscripturists" and "theists"

[21] *The Reasonableness of Scripture-Belief. A Discourse Giving Some Account of Those Rational Grounds upon which the Bible is Received as the Word of God* (London, 1672), pp. 6–7.
[22] *Ibid.,* pp. 68–69.
[23] See, for example, *ibid.,* pp. 82 and 195. Variations used by Wolseley are "Antiscriptural men" (p. 69) and "Antiscriptural opposition" (pp. 79 and 163).

which I described in the last chapter, Wolseley's *Reasonableness of Scripture-Belief,* published five years before *A Letter to a Deist,* is, so far as I can discover, the first English book written against deism.

The earliest deist pamphlet I have been able to find, apart from the works of Lord Herbert of Cherbury, is, the reader will recall, the manuscript tract, "Of Natural Religion," which I have suggested that Dryden may very well have been answering in *Religio Laici.* Now "Of Natural Religion" is itself an answer to Wolseley's *Reasonableness of Scripture-Belief,* the only attack on deism which the anonymous author mentions. It was probably written, therefore, within a few years of that book's appearance, since *The Reasonableness of Scripture-Belief* was never reprinted, and the anonymous author assumes the reader's familiarity with Wolseley's book. Brief as the pamphlet is, the author takes up and answers several of Wolseley's arguments in detail. But his principal answer to the entire book is that very *"Objection of the Deist"* which immediately follows his listing of the Catholic Articles and which Dryden refutes at considerable length in *Religio Laici.* I think it not unlikely that Dryden may be offering a rejoinder to this attack on his friend's book from which he was drawing his other arguments in the first half of his poem.

For Dryden, then, pressed for time and new to the occupation of a religious apologist, the choice of this book as a convenient aid to composition would have been practically inevitable. His friendship with Wolseley would have insured his knowledge of the book's existence and subject. His need for a series of arguments against the deists could not have been met so readily by any other book then in existence, for we have seen that Stillingfleet's approach in *A Letter to a Deist* was quite beside Dryden's purpose. The books against atheism, while they certainly contained the arguments he needed, would not have occurred as readily to a poet who, in his first approach to apologetics, was seeking an answer to deism. Wolseley, on the other hand, who had already shown his skill as a polemicist against atheism, could readily adapt these commonplace arguments of other apologists for use against a new antagonist, and it was through the intermediary of his book that many of the popular materials of Christian apologetics reached Dryden.

Wolseley is careful to limit his discourse to the rational grounds for accepting the divine authority of the Bible since, as he ex-

113

plains at some length, the kind of adversary he is answering will, like the atheist, only listen to natural arguments.[24] His thesis, therefore, is that a belief in the Scriptures is so reasonable a course that the antiscripturist is obliged, by his own terms, to accept it.

As the whole of Religion is declared to be a reasonable Service, and can be no other, so all the Principles of it in order to its being, must upon rational grounds necessarily be establish'd; what ever Belief is built upon the credit of any Revelation, ought to be ultimately resolved into a rational proof of that Revelation as such, and what ever appears to us upon those terms so to be, whatever can be sufficiently proved to be revealed to us from God, from the Soveraign Power of its Author, puts in but a reasonable claim to our assent, though the matter of it in some things exceed the bounds of a humane capacity.[25]

Two basic arguments, Wolseley explains, must be put forward in order to establish this reasonable claim to our assent, and these are the subject of his discourse:

First I will indeavour to render it a thing reasonable to be believed that there *should be some supernatural Law* revealed from God and given to mankind (in order to their present and future happiness) as the great *Guide* and *Rule* of all their actions towards God and towards each other. And that 'tis not a reasonable supposal that the world, in the posture we find it, should be left singly to the conduct of *Nature*. Secondly, That 'tis most rationally credible, upon all such grounds by which a judgment in this case ought to be established, That *this Book* we call the *Bible* is *this Revealed Law* superadded to our natural Light, and contains in it self that *compleat Systeme of Divine Truth* by which God will *Informe, Rule* and *Judge* the World.[26]

Lastly, he raises various objections to the Bible and proceeds to answer them.

A glance at the outline of Dryden's arguments earlier in this chapter will show why I have suggested that Dryden adopted Wolseley's logical scheme. The two basic arguments advanced by Wolseley and Dryden are identical, as is their common procedure of going on to raise and answer an objection to their thesis. The objections are not, of course, the same. The "doubts, queries, and difficulties" which Wolseley attempts to answer are the kind

---

[24] See *ibid.,* pp. 69–85. For a specific attack on the fideist method of rejecting rational arguments and appealing to the testimony of the Spirit, see pp. 79–82.
[25] *Ibid.,* sigs. A5–A5v.
[26] *Ibid.,* pp. 85–86.

THE CHRISTIAN APOLOGIST: RESPONSE

of cavils against the Bible with which Stillingfleet was concerned in *A Letter to a Deist*. The objection with which Dryden deals, on the other hand, had been raised after *The Reasonableness of Scripture-Belief* was published and in answer to that very book in the tract "Of Natural Religion."

With the famous opening lines of his poem, Dryden launches immediately into his first argument, the necessity of revelation:

> DIM, as the borrow'd beams of Moon and Stars
> To *lonely, weary, wandring* Travellers,
> Is *Reason* to the *Soul*: And as on high,
> Those rowling Fires *discover* but the Sky
> Not light us *here*; So *Reason's* glimmering Ray
> Was lent, not to *assure* our *doubtfull* way,
> But *guide* us upward to a *better Day.*
> And as those nightly Tapers disappear
> When Day's bright Lord ascends our Hemisphere;
> So pale grows *Reason* at *Religions* sight;
> So *dyes,* and so *dissolves* in *Supernatural Light.*
>
> [ll. 1–11]

These lines have often been interpreted as a disparagement of the power of human reason. It is important to notice, however, that Dryden is speaking only of reason's activity in one particular sphere. It is the light afforded by *"Reason* to the *Soul"* in its quest for salvation that is described as dim. Furthermore, it is dim only in comparative terms, when viewed in relation to supernatural light.

The metaphoric language of this passage, so often commented on, is actually a commonplace. Derived from the conventional description of reason as the "light of nature" and from the frequent scriptural metaphor of light for Christ or his Gospel, it is used repeatedly by religious writers of the seventeenth century, not to disparage human reason, but to offer a necessary caution in the course of emphasizing the importance of reason in religion.[27] Those who are fond of reminding us of the "increased" emphasis which the Cambridge Platonists and some of their contemporaries placed on the role of reason in religion, exalting it as "the candle of the Lord," sometimes forget that this metaphor is

---

[27] Archbishop Tillotson cites many instances of this metaphor in Scripture and explains its application to Christ or his Gospel in his sermon on "The Excellency and Universality of the Christian Revelation," *The Works of Dr. John Tillotson* (London: J. F. Dove, 1820), IX, 569–72.

intended to convey the relative insignificance of reason in relation to supernatural light. "A Lamp," Nathanael Culverwel observes, "is no such dazling object. A Candle has no such goodly light, as that it should pride and glory in it. 'Tis but a brief and compendious flame, shut up, and imprison'd in a narrow compasse. How farre distant is it from the beauty of a Starre? How farre from the brightnesse of a Sun?"[28] This caution appears in that classic of Christian rationalism, Culverwel's *Discourse of the Light of Nature,* but in a chapter significantly entitled "The Light of Reason is a Diminutive Light." Similarly, Matthew Barker, whose *Natural Theology* celebrates "that knowledge of God, and our duty to Him, which the Light of Nature may lead Man up to," is careful to include a chapter on "The Deficiency of Natural Theology Compared with the Scriptures" in which he speaks of "the *absurdity* of casting off Scripture-Light, and betaking our selves to the Light of Nature. Is not the Light of the Sun above that of the Moon? the one Ruleth the Day, and the other the Night. Those that have no Scripture-Light, live under the Dominion of Nature's *Moon-light,* and are but in the Night, feeling after God, as Men in the dark. It is Scripture-Light, through the Spirit, that makes the Day."[29] The metaphors of the moon for reason and of the sun for revelation are similar to Dryden's, but not identical.

The major difference between these conventional uses of light metaphors to express the comparative importance of reason and revelation in any era and the opening lines of *Religio Laici* is that Dryden is describing, in metaphorical terms, two distinct epochs of salvation history. In the first era, before the birth of Christ, mankind was in the condition of travelers in the night. With only "*Reason*'s glimmering Ray" to guide them, they lacked sufficient light to assure their halting progress toward salvation. All that the light of nature could do was to draw men's gaze upward in search of a better guide so that when, in the fulness of time, Christ appeared ("when Day's bright Lord ascends our Hemisphere"), they were prepared to accept him. The sun itself is a metaphor for Christ, who has provided a supernatural light, through revelation, which makes the Christian era a day, in con-

---

[28] *An Elegant and Learned Discourse of the Light of Nature* (London, 1652), p. 122.

[29] *Natural Theology,* p. 126. For another use of this metaphor, see J. M., *The Atheist Silenced* (London, 1672), p. 82. A similar, though earlier, usage by Donne is quoted in *The Poems of John Dryden,* ed. James Kinsley (Oxford: Clarendon Press, 1958), IV, 1936. (Hereafter referred to as *Poems.*)

trast to the night of the preceding epoch. In this bright daylight, the light of nature, although it continues to shine, is engulfed in the dazzling splendor of supernatural light.

Wolseley too, in the course of comparing the two epochs of salvation history, uses several of these metaphors. Speaking of the condition of mankind before the birth of Christ, he declares: "If we . . . take a view of what the *Wisest* and *Best* thought, what a poor product were all their *Notions,* compared with the *Bible!* What a *Midnight* were men in, in respect of *Religion,* in that clear *Sunshine* of *Humane Knowledge!*"[30] This may have suggested to Dryden the use of figurative language here, but it lacks most of the details of what becomes, in *Religio Laici,* a miniature parable of salvation history. As it happens, the exact parable is used by another Anglican layman, Richard Burthogge, in his *Causa Dei* (1675), where a lucid explanation is provided as well:

All the *Light* before Christ, whether that among the Jews, or that among the Gentiles, was but *Moon,* or *Star-light,* designed only for the *night* preceding; but it is the *Sun* must Rule by *Day.* Now the Gospel *dispensation* is the *Day,* and *Christ* the Sun that makes it; by whose Alone Light we must walk. For as in Nature, the *Light* afforded by the Moon and Stars, which is of great Advantage, and very much administers to our Direction, and Comfort in a Journey by night, yet in the day is *none;* The Moon and Stars that shine by night, and then make other things Visible, they are Invisible themselves, and Dark by day; So in the *Moral* world, not only the *Law* of *Moses* to the Jews, but that *Philosophy* and Wisdom among the Gentiles, that before the coming of the Lord Christ, while it was yet extream Dark, was of extraordinary Use and Benefit; *It* is no longer *now* of any to them, nor to be insisted on, since He is come. For now 'tis *broad Day.* One would be glad of Moon-light, or Star-light, that is to travel by night; but he delires, and is out of his Wits, that would preferr it before the Sun by Day.[31]

The identity of details between this passage and the opening lines of *Religio Laici* is remarkable. There is reason to believe, as we shall see, that Dryden had occasion to consult *Causa Dei* in seeking an answer to the objection of the Deist which Wolseley does not consider. I think it very likely that he marked this passage at the time and later decided to use its striking imagery for the beginning of his poem. It finds a fitting place in the argument

[30] *Reasonableness of Scripture-Belief,* p. 101.
[31] *Causa Dei* (London, 1675), pp. 195–96.

supplied by Wolseley; indeed, it simply elaborates Wolseley's own metaphor at the same stage of his discourse.

Having laid down the proposition that mankind before the coming of Christ was unable to arrive at any assurance about the means of salvation, Dryden proceeds to illustrate his thesis with examples. He begins by mentioning two matters of disagreement among ancient philosophers: first of all in their notions of a deity, and secondly in their attempts to account for the origin of the world:

> Some few, whose Lamp shone brighter, have been led
> From Cause to Cause, to *Natures* secret head;
> And found that *one first principle* must be:
> But *what,* or *who,* that UNIVERSAL HE;
> Whether some *Soul* incompassing this Ball
> *Unmade, unmov'd*; yet *making, moving All*;
> Or various *Atoms* interfering Dance
> Leapt into *Form,* (the Noble work of *Chance*;)
> Or this great *All* was from *Eternity*;
> Not ev'n the *Stagirite* himself could see;
> And *Epicurus Guess'd* as well as He.
>
> [ll. 12–22]

These three conflicting cosmologies are of course the Platonic conception of the World Soul, the Epicurean atomic theory, and the Aristotelian hypothesis of the eternity of the world respectively. Dryden refers in passing to several other souces of disagreement among the ancient philosophers ("As *blindly grop'd* they for a *future State*; / As *rashly Judg'd* of *Providence* and *Fate*") before going on thirdly to give examples of their contradictory notions of morality, or as the marginal rubric expresses it, the *"Opinions of the several Sects of Philosophers concerning the* Summum Bonum."

> But least of all could their Endeavours find
> What most concern'd the good of Humane kind:
> For *Happiness* was never to be found;
> But vanish'd from 'em, like Enchanted ground.
> One thought *Content* the Good to be enjoy'd:
> This, every little *Accident* destroy'd:
> The *wiser Madmen* did for *Vertue* toyl:
> A Thorny, or at best a barren Soil:
> In *Pleasure* some their glutton Souls would steep;

118

But found their Line too short, the Well too deep;
And leaky Vessels which no *Bliss* cou'd keep.

[ll. 25–35]

The three ethical systems are obviously those of the Stoics, Aristotle, and Epicurus respectively. Dryden concludes:

Thus, *anxious Thoughts* in *endless Circles* roul,
Without a *Centre* where to fix the *Soul*:
In this wilde Maze their vain Endeavours end.
How can the *less* the *Greater* comprehend?[32]
Or *finite Reason* reach *Infinity*?
For what cou'd *Fathom GOD* were *more* than *He*.

[ll. 36–41]

The plight of the pagan philosophers, then, was not an accidental misfortune, but the inevitable condition of humanity before the coming of Christ.

Dryden is following Wolseley fairly closely here, both in the nature and in the order of his argument. Wolseley spends some forty pages giving examples of the same three disagreements among the ancient philosophers. "When we view over the utmost products of all humane abilities," he writes, "and the greatest discoveries at any time made by natural light, we shall find the world without Revelation to have been greatly defective in these three things. First, in their *Divinity*, in their conceptions of the *Deity*, and their *Worship* of him. Secondly, In the account they gave to themselves of the worlds first *Production* and of the *Origine* of things. Thirdly, In their *Morality*, and in their *Ethical Institutes* of humane life, and the converse of mankind together."[33] He then proceeds to illustrate his thesis copiously, particularly drawing his examples, as Dryden does, from the Greek philosophers.

Montaigne's similar procedure for very different ends in his *Apology for Raimond Sebond* has obscured for many people the fact that this ancient and perfectly orthodox argument antedates the French Pyrrhonist by at least a thousand years, extending back to the patristic writers. Known as the argument *per errores philosophorum*, it has been used as a standard proof of the necessity of revelation by countless apologists who have appealed to the

[32] Cf. Wolseley: "The more Refined part lost themselves in a Wilderness of Abstracted Speculations about what they could never distinctly comprehend" (*Reasonableness of Scripture-Belief*, p. 113).
[33] *Ibid.*, pp. 87–88.

119

disagreements among the pagan philosophers as historical evidence that even the wisest of mankind were involved in fruitless speculations while deprived of the benefit of revelation. In Dryden's time, the argument was so well known that most apologists were content to allude to it, without treating it in detail as Wolseley did. So Matthew Barker, referring to the *Summum Bonum,* remarks: "There was nothing did more exercise the Minds of the wiser Heathens than this; to find out and enjoy this Good; and nothing were they more divided in their Judgments about. . . . But here the Scriptures again supply the defect of Nature's Light."[34] Likewise, Stillingfleet reminds his readers: "The World was almost lost in *Disputes* concerning the *nature, condition,* and *immortality* of the soul before *divine revelation* was made known to mankind by the Gospel of *Christ.*"[35]

This constant scanting of the natural religion of the heathens, not only by Dryden, but just as frequently by the other Christian apologists of the period, requires some explanation. At first sight it seems incompatible with the emphasis they place on natural religion elsewhere in their writings. When we recall that each of these apologists had devoted a sizable book, or portion of a book, to extolling the claims of natural religion, the fact that they begrudge such knowledge to the ancients appears perverse. But we must remember that there was an enormous difference between natural religion as taught to an atheist by Christian apologists seventeen centuries after the birth of Christ and natural religion as discovered for themselves by pagan philosophers five centuries before Christ. The advantages were all on the side of the modern atheist.

In the first place, the mind of a modern atheist, born and bred in a Christian land, was a kind of *tabula rasa* fit to be taught the rudiments of natural religion. His mind was unencumbered with all the rubbish of superstition which stifled the intelligence of the pagan philosopher, the product of a polytheistic culture. As Dryden explained in the preface to *Religio Laici,* mankind had at first been monotheistic, thanks to the original revelation made

---

[34] *Natural Theology,* p. 119. See pp. 119–26 for this argument.
[35] *Origines Sacrae, or A Rational Account of the Grounds of Christian Faith* (3d ed.; London, 1666), p. 608. For similar allusions, see Robert Boyle, *The Excellency of Theology, The Works of the Hon. Robert Boyle,* ed. Thomas Birch (2d ed.; London, 1772), IV, 6–16; John Tillotson, "The Excellency and Universality of the Christian Revelation," *Works,* IX, 596.

by God to Adam. This primitive revelation had survived for awhile, being transmitted from one generation to the next; but in course of time it had been corrupted, except among the people of Israel. He writes:

Truly I am apt to think, that the revealed Religion which was taught by *Noah* to all his Sons, might continue for some Ages in the whole Posterity. That afterwards it was included wholly in the Family of *Sem* is manifest: but when the Progenies of *Cham* and *Japhet* swarm'd into Colonies, and those Colonies were subdivided into many others; in process of time their Descendants lost by little and little the Primitive and Purer Rites of Divine Worship, retaining onely the notion of one Deity; to which succeeding Generations added others: (for Men took their Degrees in those Ages from Conquerours to Gods.)

This notion that polytheism was a corruption of the primitive revelation was a common one. Wolseley attributes "all that Rubbish of *Pagan Theology*" to "a corrupt Tradition of the Worlds first *original*, and the History of the *Creation*, and the *Flood*, and many passages both before and after the Flood, which *Noah* and his family first conveyed down to the world in its Repeopling, and the *Jews* from *Moses* afterward inform'd them of."[36] Burthogge writes in a similar vein:

In this Instance we have a lively *Pourtraict* of the *False Religion* of the Gentiles, and the plain *Reason* why it seemeth in so many things an Apish *Imitation* of the *True;* why it is so *diversified* in it self, and yet withall *Retaineth* such Resemblance and Conformity with Ours. It is because *that* all men came from one, and *that* not only *Adam,* but *Noah* did instruct his children in the Mysteries of the True Religion, and in the Rites of it, and these again *Reported* to theirs, and so onward. But we may easily believe it to have hapned in this Tradition, *as* it doth in all others, that there was almost in every *New* delivery and Transmission, (for the mentioned causes) some *departure* and Recess from the *Former.*[37]

Because of this corruption of the true religion, the pagan philosopher labored under a tremendous handicap. Like all men he was endowed with a natural capacity for rational knowledge of the existence of God and of the immortality of the soul; but in the midst of idolatry and superstition the chances of his attaining such knowledge were slight.

[36] *Reasonableness of Scripture-Belief*, p. 114.
[37] *Causa Dei*, p. 339.

The modern atheist also enjoyed a second advantage over the ancient philosopher where natural religion was concerned. He was not, after all, expected to discover for himself the existence of God and the immortality of the soul, for if this were the case, there would be no atheists and Christian apologetics would be needless. Natural religion was, on the contrary, a body of truths amenable to reason which was offered to him by one who was already a Christian. As taught by the apologists, it was simply the demonstration of the rational grounds of Christianity which might prove acceptable to an atheist and would certainly provide one who was already a Christian with the reasons for his religion. With the advantages of historical hindsight provided by the Christian revelation, the apologist could offer a much more extensive demonstration of the existence and attributes of God, of the immortality of the soul, and of similar matters than would otherwise have been possible. "I am apt to believe," Wolseley remarked, "that a *Supernatural* knowledg does much instruct us in the true extent of what is meerly Natural, and does much inkindle our natural Light, and we see many things *now* to be attainable by Nature, which the world (so farr as I can discerne) never found out without Revelation."[38] In the absence of such advantages, it was scarcely surprising that the natural religion which the pagan philosopher was able to discover by his own resources was a very small affair: hardly enough to fill a single chapter in the enormous tomes on natural religion which poured from the presses in seventeenth-century England.

When Dryden has concluded his account of the uncertain gropings of the heathen philosophers after natural religion, he turns in apparent contrast to the self-assured statements about religion which the modern deist makes and attributes to his own discovery. With the words "The *Deist* thinks he stands on firmer ground," he introduces the Deist's speech setting forth the Five Catholic Articles which I discussed in the last chapter. At the conclusion of this speech, Dryden offers his own comment:

> Thus Man by his own strength to Heaven wou'd soar:
> And wou'd not be Oblig'd to God for more.
> Vain, wretched Creature, how art thou misled
> To think thy Wit these God-like Notions bred!
> These Truths are not the product of thy Mind,

[38] *Reasonableness of Scripture-Belief*, p. 113.

But dropt from Heaven, and of a Nobler kind.
Reveal'd Religion first inform'd thy Sight,
And *Reason* saw not, till *Faith* sprung the Light.
Hence all thy *Natural Worship* takes the *Source*:
'Tis *Revelation* what thou thinkst *Discourse*.

[ll. 62–71]

Dryden is suggesting, of course, that the modern deist shares the same advantages we have just been noticing that the Christian apologist enjoys in discoursing on natural religion. The Deist, product of a Christian culture, benefits from the same supernatural knowledge as does the Christian. He too can "see many things *now* to be attainable by Nature, which the world never found out without Revelation," but in his pride he attributes all to his own reason.

Dryden proves this assertion by referring once again to the heathen philosophers:

Else, how com'st *Thou* to see these truths so clear,
Which so obscure to *Heathens* did appear?
Not *Plato* these, nor *Aristotle* found:
Nor He whose Wisedom *Oracles* renown'd.
Hast thou a Wit so deep, or so sublime,
Or canst thou lower dive, or higher climb?
Canst *Thou*, by *Reason*, more of *God-head* know
Than *Plutarch, Seneca*, or *Cicero*?
Those Gyant Wits, in happyer Ages born,
(When *Arms*, and *Arts* did *Greece* and *Rome* adorn)
Knew no such *Systeme*: no such Piles cou'd raise
Of *Natural Worship*, built on *Pray'r* and *Praise*,
To One sole GOD.

[ll. 72–84]

Here Dryden introduces an a fortiori argument: if, as he has already shown, these religious notions were but obscurely known to Plato, Aristotle, Socrates, and the other ancient philosophers, "those Gyant Wits, in happyer Ages born," it is even less likely that they should have owed their discovery to the Deist, that "vain, wretched Creature," as Dryden calls him. The supposed ingredients of natural religion put forward by the deist pamphleteers must therefore have a supernatural origin.

Of course the deists did not claim to have discovered the Five Catholic Articles. They insisted that they were simply formulating principles which were truly catholic because they had been

123

known in every age and country and by every class and condition of men. But this does not affect Dryden's argument that the Five Catholic Articles had a supernatural origin. If they were indeed held by men before the Christian revelation was proclaimed, then they must have been derived from the primitive revelation. In the preface to his poem he suggests that whatever true ideas of God may have been known to the ancients, including the philosophers, were simply the survival of some scattered remains of the primitive revelation in the midst of its more degenerate forms. Having explained how "succeeding Generations" gradually corrupted the original truth into polytheism, as we have seen, he continues:

If my supposition be true, then the consequence which I have assum'd in my Poem may be also true; namely, that Deism, or the Principles of Natural Worship, are onely the faint remnants or dying flames of reveal'd Religion in the Posterity of *Noah:* And that our Modern Philosophers, nay and some of our Philosophising Divines have too much exalted the faculties of our Souls, when they have maintain'd that by their force, mankind has been able to find out that there is one Supream Agent or Intellectual Being which we call God: that Praise and Prayer are his due Worship; and the rest of those deducements, which I am confident are the remote effects of Revelation, and unatainable by our Discourse, I mean as simply considerd, and without the benefit of Divine Illumination. So that we have not lifted up our selves to God, by the weak Pinions of our Reason, but he has been pleasd to descend to us: and what *Socrates* said of him, what *Plato* writ, and the rest of the Heathen Philosophers of several Nations, is all no more than the Twilight of Revelation, after the Sun of it was set in the Race of *Noah.*

Dryden's assumption is a reasonable one if, as he says, his previous supposition be admitted, according to which the primitive revelation was passed down from one generation to another. If the popular religion of the heathens was to be explained as a corruption of this revelation, the more exalted ideas of their contemporaries might reasonably be supposed to be a purer survival of the same tradition. Wolseley falls back on the same assumption to explain "the Judgment of some particular persons amongst them, who have uttered here and there some fragments of *Truth,* and have sometimes spoken in justification of these *Main Points.*"

So *Plato* and others have spoken somewhat of *One God* (Though it ought to be noted that the Being of *One God* was never generally and distinctly acknowledged in any *Heathen Country,* nor was there ever a *Law* made in any *Heathen State* to establish the Being and Worship of *one God.* Nay, some have supposed that no particular *Person* did ever purely by *Natural Light,* determine that there was *but one God:* But that such who have spoken of it had it from a *Tradition* originated in *Revelation*).[39]

He goes on to speak of such refined notions as "sparks of Divine Truth" which, "though under much Rubbish, have been there secretly kept alive," just as Dryden calls them "faint remnants or dying flames" of the primitive revelation.

It is not enough, however, for Dryden simply to suggest that there is another explanation for these religious ideas beside that proposed by the Deist, and that a primitive revelation may just as easily account for them as human reason. That would not be to disprove the Deist's theory but merely to show that it is not a necessary explanation. Dryden goes on to argue that the assumed cause (human reason) is insufficient to produce the observed effects (the Five Catholic Articles). He sets out to show that these notions must be "the remote effects of Revelation" because they are "unatainable by our Discourse," and these two alternatives exhaust the possible causes which can be suggested. It lay beyond the limits of human understanding itself for mankind to have "been able to find out that there is one Supream Agent or Intellectual Being which we call God," that is to say, a personal, intelligent being corresponding to the Christian notion of God, and thus to offer *"Pray'r* and *Praise, / To One sole* GOD."

Repeatedly, both in the poem and in the preface, Dryden affirms the limited character of man's knowledge of God as provided by unaided human reason. In the poem, speaking of the heathen philosophers, he declares that some few "found that *one first principle* must be," but not *"what,* or *who,* that UNIVERSAL HE." Later he asks: "How can the *less* the *Greater* comprehend? / Or *finite Reason* reach *Infinity?"* To this he adds the remark that "what cou'd *Fathom* GOD were *more* than *He."* In the preface, he expands on these notions:

That there is some thing above us, some Principle of *motion,* our Reason can apprehend, though it cannot discover what it is, by its own Vertue. And indeed 'tis very improbable, that we, who by the strength of our faculties cannot enter into the knowledg of any *Bee-*

[39] *Ibid.,* pp. 109–10.

ing, not so much as of our *own,* should be able to find out by them, that Supream Nature, which we cannot otherwise define, than by saying it is Infinite; as if Infinite were definable, or Infinity a Subject for our narrow understanding.

These statements can be reduced to the following propositions: man's reason, being finite, cannot comprehend an infinite being such as God; it can only apprehend God as a first principle; it can perceive that God exists, but not who or what He is.

These restrictions on reason are severe, but they will appear excessive only to those who exaggerate the role that reason is assigned in the tradition of Christian rationalism. There is not a single one of these propositions which is not asserted, for example, by Thomas Aquinas in the course of explaining and qualifying his well-known thesis that the existence of God can be demonstrated by reason.[40] In Dryden's own day these qualifications were regularly mentioned by apologists who expounded the importance of natural religion. So Wolseley declares: "That God is, and that he is to be *Served,* my *Reason* will tell me; But *What* he is! and after what *Manner* he Exists . . . I must be taught from *above.*"[41] Robert Boyle points out: "We may indeed know by the consideration of his works, and particularly those parts of them that we ourselves are, both that he is, and in a great measure what he is not; but to understand thoroughly what he is, is a task too great for any but his own infinite intellect."[42] This particular distinction, which Dryden employs in lines 14–15 of his poem, is a commonplace which would have been recognized by every reader.[43]

These limitations, which are due to the disparity between a finite intelligence and an infinite being, apply equally to the modern deist and to the ancient philosopher; indeed, they extend to all mankind. It is, therefore, an easy matter for Dryden to use

[40] For the proposition that a finite intelligence cannot comprehend an infinite being, see the *Summa contra Gentiles,* III, 55, and the *Summa Theologiae,* I, 12, 7; for the statements that God can be known only as a first principle and that our reason can discover only whether He exists, not who or what He is, see *Summa Theologiae,* I, 12, 12; for the errors and limited notions of the ancient philosophers concerning God, see *Summa Theologiae,* I, 1, 1; II IIae, 1, 8 ad 1; II IIae, 2, 4.

[41] *Reasonableness of Scripture-Belief,* pp. 128–29.

[42] *A Discourse of Things above Reason, The Works of the Hon. Robert Boyle,* IV, 408. Concerning the disputed authorship of this tract, see chapter 2, note 4 above.

[43] For other uses of this distinction by Archbishop Laud and Bishop Lucy, see *A Relation of the Conference betweene William Lawd and Mr. Fisher the Jesuite* (London, 1639), pp. 111–12, and William Lucy, *Observations, Censures and Confutations of Notorious Errors in Mr. Hobbes His Leviathan* (London, 1663), pp. 240–41.

Wolseley's commonplaces to discount the Five Catholic Articles which Wolseley never mentions. He stresses another limitation on men's natural knowledge of God, however, for which he is not indebted to Wolseley and which was particularly useful against the deist theory.

Lord Herbert had presented the Five Catholic Articles as examples of common notions. Now common notions, according to Herbert, do not depend for their discovery on sense experience or logical enquiry. They are the product of natural instinct. Consequently, these religious common notions, like all others, are innate ideas recognized by psychological intuition and universally agreed upon by all men possessing normal, healthy minds.

Dryden, on the other hand, insists, both in *Religio Laici* and in his preface to the poem, that man's natural knowledge of God is confined to demonstration. At no point does he concede that mankind possesses an innate or instinctive idea of God. Instead, he mentions two ways by which some men have been able to arrive at a knowledge of God's existence. Both are modes of inductive argument from sense experience to some first principle. In the poem itself he declares that "Some few, whose Lamp shone brighter, have been led / From Cause to Cause, to *Natures* secret head; / And found that *one first principle* must be." In the preface he remarks: "That there is some thing above us, some Principle of *motion,* our Reason can apprehend." In the first case, he refers to the argument from efficient causation; in the second, to the argument from motion. These are the first two of the famous five inductive proofs for the existence of God of Thomas Aquinas; their popularity among Christian apologists in Dryden's time was considerable, particularly the fifth proof, the argument from design, which became a kind of trademark of the physico-theologians.[44] By insisting that the existence of God can only be known by demonstration, Dryden not only implicitly denies that this idea is innate in the human mind, he also disqualifies it as a Catholic Article, for demonstrations of this kind are beyond the capacity of most men.

This will become clearer if we examine Richard Baxter's use of the same tactic against Lord Herbert. Replying to Herbert's

[44] See *Summa Theologiae*, I, 2, 3. The two arguments Dryden mentions, if not quite as prominent as the argument from design, were nevertheless perfectly common in his time. They are, for example, the first two arguments introduced by Wolseley in *The Unreasonableness of Atheism*.

assertion that the Five Catholic Articles are sufficient in themselves as a basis for religion, Baxter declares that revelation was
necessary for the following reasons:

First, Most men are naturally dull. Secondly, Few have leisure by
Learning to improve their intellects. Thirdly, And fewer have leisure
& disposition to exercise them by long searches & argumentation upon
every thing that they should know. Fourthly, And therefore where
Revelation was not, few were wise or virtuous; And the Philosophers
themselves were all to pieces among themselves, and their disagreements and doubtfulness tended to the gulfe of utter Scepticisme. . . .
Now if all the Poor unlearned Men and Women in the World must
have known all these things only by *natural discourse,* how little
Religion would have been in the World, when the Philosophers knew
so little themselves. And though your learning and understanding
made the immortality of the Soul so clear to you and the rewards and
punishments of another life, as that you number it with the *common
notices;* yet were not the old Philosophers themselves, so commonly
agreed on it as they should have been; much less all the common
People. And if you say that now almost all the world believeth it, I
answer it is Gods great mercy that it is so. But consider whether it
be not more by the way of believing, than of naturall instinct or
knowledge.[45]

Baxter's method of procedure here, while more elaborate than
Dryden's, is essentially the same. He refuses to admit that these
ideas are common notices, as Herbert contends, and insists that
without revelation mankind "must have known all these things
only by *natural discourse.*" Every one of the particular reasons he
offers on behalf of revelation is based on this assumption that the
natural knowledge of God's existence can only be attained by
laborious demonstrations ("argumentation") of which relatively
few men are capable. These reasons are copied directly, although
without acknowledgment, from Thomas Aquinas, who argued in a
similar context that without revelation the existence of God could
only have been known by long and wearisome demonstrations
beyond the ability or inclination of most men.[46] Like Dryden,
Baxter concludes that in the absence of these pretended common
notices, mankind in general must have received their religious
ideas, not by "naturall instinct or knowledge," but "by the way

[45] *More Reasons for the Christian Religion* (London, 1672), pp. 144–45.
[46] Baxter's source is either *Summa contra Gentiles,* I, 4, or *Summa Theologiae,* II
IIae, 2, 4.

of believing" in revealed truths.[47]

Dryden confronts the Deist's argument, then, not by denying natural religion, but by insisting on its essentially a posteriori and inductive character which, by limiting its availability to a restricted few, would make it an unacceptable substitute for revelation even if it were capable of disclosing more than the sparse number of rudimentary truths it actually comprises. His position is part of a long tradition which extends from Thomas Aquinas, through Hooker, to the physico-theologians of Dryden's own day. This tradition is shared by all those who, from the basis of an empirical theory of knowledge, conceive of natural religion not as the instinctive recognition of those truths with which all men are born but as the careful construction of inductive proofs for the existence of God from sense experience. In Dryden's time there were many apologists, often scientists as well and members of the Royal Society, who felt that one of the benefits of their natural studies was the additional evidence these could provide for natural religion. They strongly believed that, as Boyle declared, "we may indeed know [God] by the consideration of his works," but by no other method, short of revelation. Whether or not Dryden was acquainted with Baxter's answer to Herbert, his convictions on this matter could only have been confirmed, not suggested, by his reading of that author. His training at Cambridge, his membership in the Royal Society, and the whole course of his early interest in experimental science which we noticed in the first chapter had assured his familiarity and sympathy with this religious by-product of the study of nature.[48]

There was another Christian position on natural religion popular in Dryden's day, however, which was also part of a long tradition that extended from John Damascene and Anselm, through Descartes, to many apologists of the Restoration period.[49] Accord-

[47] Burthogge too denies that the "Points of Religion, wherein all men all the World over commonly agree" are *"Innate Idea's,* or Notions ingrafted and imprinted on the Minds of Men by Nature, but (as I have evinced them) *main and substantial Points of the first Tradition" (Causa Dei,* pp. 340–41).

[48] Richard Westfall has discussed the popularity of this tradition during the Restoration period in *Science and Religion in Seventeenth-Century England* (New Haven: Yale University Press, 1958).

[49] I have discussed the differences between these two traditions in this respect, as found in Dryden's time, in *Swift and Anglican Rationalism,* pp. 144–53. For the earlier history of this second tradition, see Etienne Gilson, *Etudes sur le rôle de la pensée médiévale dans la formation du système cartésien* (Paris: J. Vrin, 1951), pp. 9–50.

ing to this belief, the existence of God is a common notion, or innate idea, in the human mind. As Henry More declared, "there is in man an *Idea* of a *Being absolutely and fully perfect*. . . . And this notion is naturall and essentiall to the soul of man, & cannot be washt out . . . so long as the mind of man is not craz'd, but hath the ordinary use of her own faculties."[50] Consequently, the existence of God, at least, is a Catholic Article of belief held by all men at all times. Ralph Cudworth, for example, wrote "that the *Generality* of Mankind in all Ages, have had a *Prolepsis* or *Anticipation* in their Minds, concerning the *Real* and *Actual Existence* of such a Being [as God]."[51] I have quoted several Cambridge Platonists, and this group as a whole taught such a doctrine; but the notion was not restricted to this particular group. There were many other Protestants, such as Charleton and Stillingfleet, who employed the Cartesian arguments from the idea of God in the human mind and helped popularize the theory that the existence of God was a matter of general consensus among mankind.[52]

It is churchmen such as these whom Dryden criticizes in the preface to *Religio Laici*, referring to them as "some of our Philosophising Divines" who, in company with "our Modern Philosophers" (Descartes and the other rationalist philosophers), "have too much exalted the faculties of our Souls, when they have maintain'd that by their force, mankind has been able to find out" that there is one God to whom praise and prayer are due. Dryden does not make the mistake of confusing these churchmen with the deists, of course. He was well aware that they were perfectly orthodox divines who insisted on the necessity of revelation to supplement natural religion. But he suggests with some justice that

---

[50] *An Antidote against Atheism* (2d ed.; London, 1655), p. 10.

[51] *The True Intellectual System of the Universe* (London, 1678), p. 634.

[52] John W. Yolton produces considerable evidence for his thesis that this idea enjoyed wide popularity among many Restoration divines besides the Cambridge Platonists in *John Locke and the Way of Ideas* (London: Oxford University Press, 1956), pp. 26–48. Wolseley, too, shows the Cartesian influence on much of English apologetics of the period. In *The Unreasonableness of Atheism* (2d ed.; London, 1669), p. 168, he writes of "some *innate Idea* we have in our souls, of [God]. And this we are as sure of, as that *we think;* which is the thing, in the world, we can be most sure of." While Dryden is indebted to Wolseley for his presentation of traditional Christian arguments, his poetic version of these arguments is remarkably free of the Cartesian language and presuppositions in which his friend had expressed them, and reflects, I believe, his lack of sympathy for the epistemology of the Cartesians and Cambridge Platonists.

by their constant emphasis on the religious common notices shared by all mankind these men were lending unintentional support to the deist theory of Catholic Articles. His suggestion is not as gratuitous as it might appear to be. One of the Cambridge Platonists, for example, actually appeals to Lord Herbert for support. In his *Discourse of the Use of Reason in Matters of Religion,* George Rust introduces Herbert's theory of natural instinct and its product, common notions, in order to buttress his own thesis about the manner in which reason serves as a source of religious knowledge.[53] This little book appeared a few months after *Religio Laici* was published, but it simply makes explicit an affinity with some of Herbert's philosophical views which had been apparent for some time in certain Anglican divines.

It is not, then, because these churchmen supported natural religion, as is sometimes suggested, that Dryden criticizes them, but because of the basis they offered for its support.[54] The misunderstanding of Dryden's rebuke here comes from reading this passage as if it were a confrontation between fideism and "Latitudinarianism" instead of recognizing it for what it actually is: the criticism of one tradition of Christian rationalism from the standpoint of another. From the time that Thomas Aquinas rejected the doctrine of innate notices of God taught by Damascene, there had always been members of this tradition who were severely critical of the other.[55] In Dryden's day, several churchmen such as Nathanael Culverwel and Samuel Parker included in their own discourses on natural religion a strongly worded attack on the

[53] See *A Discourse of the Use of Reason in Matters of Religion* (London, 1683), pp. 31–32.

[54] Kinsley, for example, identifies the "Philosophising Divines" with the Cambridge Platonists, but on the grounds that their "defence of reason laid them open to uninformed criticism" (*Poems,* IV, 1933–34). Along with most commentators, Kinsley identifies "our Modern Philosophers" with the deists. I think this most unlikely. Herbert was a philosopher, but the deist pamphleteers most certainly were not, and Dryden would hardly have dignified them with the title. The term "Modern Philosophers" here embraces not only Herbert but Descartes, Cudworth, and all such seventeenth-century philosophers (like Dryden's friend Charleton) who taught an epistemology which "too much exalted the faculties of our Souls."

[55] See *Summa contra Gentiles,* I, 10–11, and *Summa Theologiae,* I, 2, 1. The criticism was not often reciprocated in Dryden's day. Many of those who popularized this notion of religious common notices were themselves members of the Royal Society and admired and used the inductive proofs for the existence of God. They insisted, however, that the best evidence for this truth was to be found in the idea of God in the human mind.

131

theory of innate religious notices taught by some of their fellow divines.[56]

Dryden criticizes the "Philosophising Divines" on another score as well in the preface to *Religio Laici*. Still speaking of the same churchmen, he goes on to write:

They who wou'd prove Religion by Reason, do but weaken the cause which they endeavour to support: 'tis to take away the Pillars from our Faith, and to prop it onely with a twig: 'tis to design a Tower like that of *Babel,* which if it were possible (as it is not) to reach Heaven, would come to nothing by the confusion of the Workmen. For every man is Building a several way; impotently conceipted of his own Model, and his own Materials: Reason is always striving, and always at a loss, and of necessity it must so come to pass, while 'tis exercis'd about that which is not its proper object. Let us be content at last, to know God, by his own Methods; at least so much of him, as he is pleas'd to reveal to us, in the sacred Scriptures; to apprehend them to be the word of God, is all our Reason has to do; for all beyond it is the work of Faith, which is the Seal of Heaven impress'd upon our humane understanding.

In order to understand Dryden's criticism of those "who wou'd prove Religion by Reason," we must notice the careful distinction he makes throughout this passage between reason and faith. It is the province of reason to convince us that the Scriptures are the word of God. To this extent it is possible to "prove Religion by Reason," as Dryden himself is engaged in doing in the first half of *Religio Laici*. But "all beyond it is the work of Faith"; that is to say, the truths contained in Scripture are those which God "is pleas'd to reveal to us" and which reason itself could never have discovered. Here it is useless for reason to be "exercis'd about that which is not its proper object." The prov-

---

[56] See Samuel Parker, *A Demonstration of the Divine Authority of the Law of Nature and of the Christian Religion* (London, 1681), pp. 5–7; Richard Burthogge, *Organum Vetus & Novum* (London, 1678), pp. 54–60; Nathanael Culverwel, *Discourse of the Light of Nature,* pp. 92–96. Culverwel, often erroneously described as a Cambridge Platonist himself, was particularly severe on the "Platonists" of his day for holding that all men share a "connate species" of God, and he insisted that He must be discovered inductively. He, too, couples their teaching with that of Lord Herbert, but he is more harsh to the Platonists than to Herbert, concluding that the latter's theory of common notions is less absurd philosophically than the crude notions of some of the churchmen, and even a preferable alternative for those for whom the "discursive [inductive] way will not suffice." He is not, of course, concerned here with the religious implications of Herbert's teachings.

ince of faith includes all those revealed truths which are believed, not because they are self-evident or can be demonstrated, but solely on the authority of the divine proponent, Who cannot deceive. In Hooker's words, "We all know that many things are believed, although they be intricate, obscure, and dark, although they exceed the reach and capacity of our wits, yea although in this world they be no way possible to be understood. . . . whoso assenteth to the words of eternal life, doth it in regard of his *authority* whose words they are."[57] This is Dryden's meaning when he urges us to "be content at last, to know God, by his own Methods." His whole conception of the two distinct orders of reason and faith stems from the tradition of Thomas Aquinas, Hooker, and many of his contemporaries.

If we turn to the group whom Dryden is criticizing, however, we find a very different conception. Here there is a tendency to confuse these two orders, to consider faith a rational act, and to attempt to demonstrate matters of belief.[58] Following in the footsteps of Anselm, the "Philosophising Divines" of Dryden's day went to great lengths to "prove Religion by Reason." They admitted, of course, that reason was incapable of discovering the Christian mysteries, but they argued that once they had been revealed by God these truths were amenable to rational proof. Ralph Cudworth's *True Intellectual System of the Universe* (1678) offers many instances of such efforts which were by no means unusual.[59] In rebuking the divines for attempts which "do but weaken the cause which they endeavour to support," Dryden again reflects a long-standing criticism of one tradition of Christian rationalism by the other. Culverwel, for example, declares:

I know there are some Authors of great worth and learning, that endeavour to maintain this Opinion, that revealed truths, though they could not be found by reason, yet when they are once revealed, that Reason can then evince them and demonstrate them: But I much rather encline to the determinations of *Aquinas,* and multitudes of others that are of the same judgement, that humane Reason when it has stretcht it self to the uttermost, is not at all proportion'd to them,

---

[57] *Laws,* V, xxii, 8. See also V, xxii, 5, and V, lxiii, 1.

[58] I have discussed the difference between these two traditions in this respect in *Swift and Anglican Rationalism,* pp. 41–51.

[59] A more convenient sampling of such efforts can be found in Rust's *Discourse of the Use of Reason,* pp. 42–46.

but at the best can give only some faint illustrations, some weak adumbrations of them.[60]

This is not to decry reason, but in the same author's words, "to give unto *Reason* the things that are *Reasons,* and unto *Faith* the things that are *Faiths*; to give *Faith* her full scope and latitude, and to give *Reason* also her just bounds and limits."[61] As a description of Dryden's treatment of reason in *Religio Laici,* these words could scarcely be bettered.

At the same time we must remember the polemical orientation of Dryden's statements concerning natural religion in *Religio Laici.* In the face of an adversary who advocates natural religion exclusively, Dryden responds by "bending the crooked stick," stressing the importance of revelation while conceding no more than the minimum to reason. Nevertheless, there is a minimum, which he scrupulously concedes. Confronted with a different opponent, an atheist who denied natural religion, Dryden would necessarily have found himself in the position of urging the maximum case for natural religion. But again we can assume that there would be a limit to this maximum beyond which he would be unwilling to go. For anyone who argues on other than purely pragmatic grounds, there is a certain latitude between the permissible bounds of his own convictions. Within this latitude he can move freely, emphasizing now one side, now the other, as the occasion of his argument requires. But beyond these borders he will not go. In Dryden's case, the permissible bounds of his religious convictions are clear. Beyond them, on the one side, lies the position of the Christian fideists, willing to deny natural religion and to eschew all appeals to reason and every use of argument in matters of religion. On the other side lies the position of the "Philosophising Divines," eager to make natural religion a matter of common notions easily available to all mankind. For neither of these extremes does Dryden ever evince the least sympathy.

As it happens, it is possible to map the boundaries of Dryden's convictions on natural religion very accurately. We have been

[60] *Discourse of the Light of Nature,* p. 175. For the same criticism of some of their contemporaries, see Robert Ferguson, *Interest of Reason in Religion,* p. 35, and Meric Casaubon, *Of Credulity and Incredulity, in Things Divine and Spiritual* (London, 1670), pp. 16–17. Casaubon gives a close paraphrase of the classical statement of his and Dryden's position by Thomas Aquinas in *Summa Theologiae,* I, 32, 1.

[61] *Discourse of the Light of Nature,* p. 1.

exploring the minimal side as it appears in *Religio Laici* and its preface, where Dryden concedes that "some few" have been able to reason their way inductively to some first principle but not "to find out that there is one Supream Agent or Intellectual Being which we call God," a notion "unatainable by our Discourse." A few months later he wrote his "Life of Plutarch" (1683). Here again we find him engaged in argument at one point. But this time he is opposing the notion that Plutarch was a polytheist; he is drawn, therefore, to make the strongest case he can in support of his thesis that this ancient moralist was a monotheist. He writes:

I have ever thought, that the wise men in all ages have not much differed in their opinions of religion; I mean, as it is grounded on human reason: for reason, as far as it is right, must be the same in all men; and truth being but one, they must consequently think in the same train. Thus it is not to be doubted but the religion of Socrates, Plato, and Plutarch was not different in the main; who doubtless believed the identity of one Supreme Intellectual Being, which we call GOD.[62]

This is not so much a contradiction as it is a shift in emphasis, occasioned by different argumentative needs. The question of whether God's unity could be discovered by natural means was a debatable one, as Wolseley indicated when he wrote that "some have supposed that no particular *Person* did ever purely by *Natural Light,* determine that there was *but one God.*" When he is opposing the deists, Dryden sides with this minimal view; when he is urging the case for Plutarch's monotheism, he does not. But even here he is unwilling to concede that all "mankind has been able to find out" by reason that there is one God, as the "Philosophising Divines" maintained. It is "the wise men in all ages"— philosophers such as Socrates, Plato, and Plutarch—who have made this discovery. A little later he writes that Plutarch "believed no more than what he could deduce from the principles of nature." It was by this means—demonstrative reasoning beyond the capacity of the majority of mankind—that Plutarch and the other wise

[62] *The Works of John Dryden,* ed. Sir Walter Scott and George Saintsbury (Edinburgh: William Paterson, 1882–93), XVII, 33. Watson omits this section of the "Life" from his edition of the *Essays* on the grounds that it consists for the most part of "material explicitly translated or adapted from continental treatises and commentaries" (*Of Dramatic Poesy and Other Critical Essays,* ed. George Watson [London: J. M. Dent and Sons, 1962], I, xvii). This particular passage, however, is quite clearly the expression of Dryden's own views.

men discovered the existence of the one God, not by means of any common notices of God found in the human mind. Dryden still insists that natural religion is a matter of demonstration, as he does several years later in the "Preface to *Sylvae*" (1685), where he refers to the other branch of natural religion, the immortality of the human soul. Here he is arguing against Lucretius' "Opinions concerning the mortality of the Soul," which "are so absurd, that I cannot if I wou'd believe them." On this occasion he confronts one who "was so much an Atheist, that he forgot sometimes to be a Poet." He emphasizes natural religion, therefore, as much as he had minimized it in opposing the Deist. He writes: "I think a future state demonstrable even by natural Arguments," and he proceeds to offer one of the common arguments on its behalf.[63] But again, he insists that this is a matter of demonstration, not of intuitive recognition available to all mankind. Between the opposite shoals of fideism and the excessive rationalism of the "Philosophising Divines," Dryden steers a course which keeps to the midstream of his own firmly held convictions.

Up to this point, Dryden has been speaking exclusively of natural religion. He now turns to another matter as he introduces his second argument for the necessity of revelation. This argument, like his first, is framed as an attack on the Deist's Catholic Articles.

Not all of the Five Catholic Articles pertain to natural religion as this was usually understood, in spite of the claim implicit in the title of such a deist pamphlet as "Of Natural Religion." As used by Christians, the term "natural religion" or "natural theology" refers exclusively to certain religious truths, the knowledge of which can be attained by natural means alone. But "by matters of Religion," as Robert Ferguson explained, "we mean in general as well the *Agenda* as the *Credenda* of it; What we are to perform as well as what we are to believe."[64] Now the Five Catholic Articles comprehend both of these matters. Such articles of belief as the existence of God and the immortality of the soul, the subject of the first and fifth articles, are *credenda* which find a fitting place in anyone's conception of natural religion. But the *"Rules of Worship"* laid down in the third article and the means of reconciliation with God described in the fourth pertain not simply to knowledge but to action. They are the *agenda* of a religious

---

[63] *Poems*, I, 395–96. The entire passage is in italics.
[64] *Interest of Reason in Religion*, p. 29.

system which includes rites and observances as well as matters of belief. It is not true that "to Dryden," as one critic has written, "deism meant natural religion."[65] His quarrel with deism is not only that it grossly exaggerates the extent and importance of genuine natural religion, but that it professes to discover the terms of service and adoration which only God can reveal and no natural religion can pretend to. He never uses the phrase "natural religion" in connection with deism. Instead, he speaks in the preface of "Deism, or the Principles of Natural Worship," and in the poem itself he regularly uses *"Natural Worship"* as a synonym for deism. As the phrase implies, the *"Systeme of Deisme"* which he opposes is a rival to Christianity which pretends to tell us "what we are to perform as well as what we are to believe."

Just as he concentrates attention on the Deist's first article, the existence of God, in order to deny that this system can adequately provide us with what we must believe, so in rejecting the claim that deism can tell us what we must perform he chooses the Deist's fourth article, "the *Sacrifice* for *Crimes* is *Penitence*." In a remarkably smooth transition Dryden turns from the inability of the ancients to reach any clear notion of the "Godhead" to pursue his a fortiori argument against deism in another direction. "Those Gyant Wits," he had remarked, "knew no such *Systeme*: no such Piles cou'd raise / Of *Natural Worship*, built on *Pray'r* and *Praise*, / *To One sole* GOD." He continues:

> Nor did Remorse, to Expiate Sin, prescribe:
> But slew their fellow Creatures for a Bribe:
> The guiltless *Victim* groan'd for their Offence;
> And *Cruelty*, and *Blood* was *Penitence*.
> If *Sheep* and *Oxen* cou'd Attone for Men
> Ah! at how cheap a rate the *Rich* might Sin!
> And great Oppressours might Heavens Wrath beguile
> By offering his own Creatures for a Spoil!
> [ll. 85–92]

If we compare these last four lines with Dryden's source, we can see how closely he sometimes follows Wolseley. In the course of developing the same argument, Wolseley had written: "What a

[65] Harold R. Hutcheson, *Lord Herbert of Cherbury's "De Religione Laici"* (New Haven: Yale University Press, 1944), p. 57. Like Kinsley, Hutcheson assumes that the phrase "our Modern Philosophers" refers to the deists and that the reference to "some of our Philosophising Divines" is "clear proof that, in Dryden's mind, deism had already infected the Church itself."

trifle is the *Blood* of a *Sheep* or an *Oxe* to satisfie for an Offence against an Infinite Justice! At how *easie* and *cheap* a rate might men *Sin,* and God be *satisfied!*"[66] These two sentences reappear almost intact in two lines of the poem. And yet, Dryden is never content simply to paraphrase, even when he is following his source most closely. By altering "men" to "the *Rich,*" and developing this new idea in two additional lines, Dryden amplifies Wolseley's argument that such repentance would be too easy by adding the further objection that it would be unjust, since the poor would be at a decided disadvantage in making atonement for their sins.

Leaving the ineffectual efforts of the ancients to make atonement, Dryden returns to the Deist and argues that no means of reparation devised by man's own wit can ever be adequate:

> Dar'st thou, poor Worm, offend *Infinity?*
> And must the Terms of Peace be given by *Thee?*
> Then *Thou* art *Justice* in the *last Appeal:*
> *Thy easie God* instructs Thee to *rebell:*
> And, like a King remote, and weak, must take
> What Satisfaction *Thou* art pleas'd to make.
>
> [ll. 93–98]

Wolseley had developed at some length this notion that the terms of reconciliation must be offered by the one against whom the offense was committed, not by the offender. "No man," he writes, "(should he study over all the Volumes of Nature) unless it be told him from *Heaven,* can certainly know upon what *terms* God will proceed in *pardoning* and *punishing* the sins of the World! . . . If we should ransack all the particulars that Humane invention can reach in this kind, we could never be fully assured, that the *Expiation* of mens *Sin* lay in *any,* or in *all* of them."[67]

A revelation of the terms of peace between God and man would be necessary, therefore, in any case. But a simple revelation, as by a voice from Heaven, would not be enough. For the magnitude of an offense is determined by the importance of the person to whom it is offered, not by that of the person who commits it. A sin committed against an infinite being is by its very nature an infinite offense, requiring an infinite atonement greater than man can make.

---

[66] *Reasonableness of Scripture-Belief,* p. 162.
[67] *Ibid.,* pp. 157–58.

> But if there be a *Pow'r* too *Just*, and *strong*
> To wink at *Crimes*, and bear unpunish'd *Wrong*;
> Look humbly upward, see his Will disclose:
> The *Forfeit* first, and then the *Fine* impose:
> A *Mulct thy* Poverty cou'd never pay
> Had not *Eternal Wisedom* found the way:
> And with Coelestial Wealth supply'd thy Store:
> *His Justice* makes the *Fine, his Mercy* quits the *Score*.
> [ll. 99–106]

At this point, Dryden begins to narrow his argument from the necessity for *some* revelation to the necessity for the particular revelation recorded in the New Testament, and for the circumstances from which it arose.

Since an infinite atonement was necessary for man's sin, only God was capable of offering it. Hence the necessity of the Incarnation on which the imputed righteousness proclaimed by the Gospel depends.

> See God descending in thy Humane Frame;
> Th' *offended,* suff'ring in th' *Offenders* Name:
> All thy Misdeeds to him imputed see,
> And all his Righteousness devolv'd on thee.
>   For granting we have Sin'd, and that th' offence
> Of *Man,* is made against *Omnipotence,*
> Some Price, that bears *proportion,* must be paid;
> And *Infinite* with *Infinite* be weigh'd.
> See then the *Deist lost*: *Remorse* for *Vice,*
> *Not* paid, or *paid, inadequate* in price:
> What farther means can *Reason* now direct,
> Or what Relief from *humane Wit* expect?
> *That* shews us *sick*; and sadly are we sure
> *Still* to be *Sick,* till *Heav'n* reveal the *Cure*:[68]
> [ll. 107–20]

Wolseley, too, had dwelt on the need for an infinite atonement which would satisfy God's justice as well as His mercy:

What will *procure Mercy,* or what will *satisfie Justice,* or how they will be made to *meet* in *one Divine Act,* when both *perfect,* and nothing of either can be *abated*; because not consistent with their perfection! are things utterly impossible to be known without *Revelation*. If God for-

---

[68] Cf. Wolseley: "The *Philosophers* abounded with *remedies* for this *Epidemical Disease*. . . . But alas, The right way of doing it has lain hid from *Ages* and *Generations* till God himself made it known, and revealed it from Heaven" (*ibid.,* p. 162).

give *absolutely* without any *satisfaction*; what becomes of his *Justice,* which should secure and vindicate the Honour of his Laws? And should he only forgive men when they themselves make a *Plenary satisfaction* to Justice, where were his *Mercy*? And how could such a plenary satisfaction to infinite Justice for mens disobedience be ever *found out?* . . . The truth is, the evil of the world being in its Nature an offence against God, and the guilt arising from it relating to his Tribunal, where no Sentence can pass but what is the result of infinite and perfect Attributes, the terms of our pardon must come from God.[69]

Once this has been established, all that remains is to turn to the source which reveals the terms of our pardon and to consider its claim to be the word of God. Dryden concludes with these lines:

> If then *Heaven's Will* must needs be understood,
> (Which must, if we want *Cure,* and *Heaven,* be *Good*)[70]
> Let all Records of *Will reveal'd* be shown;
> With *Scripture,* all in equal ballance thrown,
> And *our one Sacred Book* will be *That one.*[71]
>
> [ll. 121–25]

Up to this point, in attempting to prove the necessity of revelation Dryden has proceeded by way of demonstration. When he turns to the task of establishing the fact that this revelation is to be found in the Christian Scriptures, he must vary the form of his arguments. Demonstration is out of the question; indeed, this section of his poem opens with the words: *"Proof* needs not here." It was generally accepted in Dryden's time that the truth of the Christian religion could not be demonstrated like the existence of God or the immortality of the soul. Since the genuineness of the Christian revelation pertained to a matter of fact long past, its proof must depend upon historical evidence which falls short of demonstration. The best that could be offered was a series of moral arguments sufficient to convince a reasonable man that there

[69] *Ibid.,* pp. 159–60. For the same argument, see Barker, *Natural Theology,* pp. 111–18; Ferguson, *Interest of Reason in Religion,* pp. 64–65.

[70] Cf. Wolseley: "If there be such a thing as a *Revelation* made to the World (as that which the goodness of God, and the *wants* of men seem necessarily to call for) If God have given to Mankind a Law supernatural, *Where* is this Divine Law to be found? 'Tis but reasonable to suppose it *somewhere* or other upon Record" (*Reasonableness of Scripture-Belief,* pp. 163–64).

[71] Cf. Wolseley: "If it be acknowledged there is any where extant a *Revelation* from God to the *World,* let it be *produced.* Let the best *rival* to the *Bible* upon that account, or all its *Competitors* together be brought forth. . . . and the *Bible* must needs be *Predominant,* and prevail against all *Competition*" (*ibid.,* p. 178).

is the greatest probability that the Christian religion is true. In establishing the authority of Scripture, as Bishop Ward pointed out, "we are not here to expect the necessity of demonstrations, but must content our selves with such arguments as the nature of our subject will admit."[72] William Bates explained the nature of such arguments when he wrote: "The proofs of the truth of Christian Religion are of a moral nature; and though not of equal clearness with the testimonies of Sense, or a Mathematical Demonstration, yet are so pregnant and convincing, that the considering dispassionate spirit fully acquiesces in them."[73]

Dryden offers five moral arguments for the authority of the Scriptures in *Religio Laici,* all of them culled from Wolseley. But whereas Wolseley had presented these arguments (along with many others) in a carefully arranged scheme, Dryden deliberately offers them as a haphazard collection of spontaneous arguments. He makes a virtue of the fact that proof, in the sense of demonstration, is impossible and states at the outset that it is unnecessary. By a series of clauses beginning "whether," he gives the impression that he is choosing at random from among dozens of moral arguments, any one of which should be sufficient to convince a "considering dispassionate spirit" of the divine authority of the Bible. He begins:

> *Proof* needs not here, for whether we compare
> That Impious, Idle, Superstitious Ware
> Of *Rites, Lustrations, Offerings,* (which before,
> In various Ages, various Countries bore)
> With *Christian Faith* and *Vertues,* we shall find
> None answ'ring the great ends of humane kind
> But *This one Rule of Life: That* shews us best
> How *God* may be *appeas'd,* and *Mortals blest.*
>
> [ll. 126–33]

Dryden's reason for placing this argument first is clear enough. It follows directly from his proposal in the preceding stanza that "all Records of *Will reveal'd* be shown; / With *Scripture,* all in

[72] Seth Ward, *A Philosophicall Essay towards an Eviction of the Being and Attributes of God* (5th ed.; Oxford, 1677), p. 87.

[73] *The Divinity of the Christian Religion Proved by the Evidence of Reason and Divine Revelation* (London, 1677), p. 41. For Wolseley's expression of the same position, see *Unreasonableness of Atheism,* pp. 24–26, and *Reasonableness of Scripture-Belief,* pp. 84–85. For the same view from a Continental Protestant, see Hugo Grotius, *The Truth of Christian Religion,* trans. Simon Patrick (London, 1680), p. 94.

equal ballance thrown." When this is done, he now declares, the comparison bears out his prediction that the Bible best answers "the great *Ends* of *Mankind*," in Wolseley's phrase, "relating to *this life* and a *future*." That is to say, the Christian Scriptures, in Wolseley's words, "furnish mankind with all those necessary Requisites to their own present and future happiness" which Dryden (and Wolseley) have previously shown that nature alone is unable to supply.[74]

Dryden continues:

> Whether from length of *Time* its worth we draw,
> The *World* is scarce more *Ancient* than the *Law*:
> Heav'ns early Care prescrib'd for every Age;
> First, in the *Soul*, and after, in the *Page*.
>
> [ll. 134–37]

"If we consider the Revelation Historically contained in this Book," Wolseley writes, "'tis what was from the *beginning*, and of the same *Date* with the *World* it self." For it is but reasonable to suppose, he points out, "that Gods Revelations were as early as mans *necessities*, That there was no time wherein man stood in need of Supernatural Instruction and help, but that God affords it to him." This revelation was not at first written down, he explains, since Moses "was the first introducer of *Letters* as well as the first Writer of *Books*," who set down these laws in the Pentateuch, "God pleasing so to order it, that although the Revelations he made to the World were not *written* from the beginning, yet they were written long before any *other Writings* were extant."[75]

With the words "Or, whether more abstractedly we look, / Or on the *Writers*, or the *written Book*," Dryden turns to what Wolseley calls the "*way* and *manner*" of the Bible's "conveyance to us," which he too had divided into "the *Instruments* God imploied in the writing of it" and the book itself. Beginning with the writers, Dryden asks:

[74] See *Reasonableness of Scripture-Belief*, pp. 181–84. Cf. John Wilkins, *Of the Principles and Duties of Natural Religion* (London, 1675), pp. 403–7; Bates, *Divinity of the Christian Religion*, pp. 10–33; Ferguson, *Interest of Reason in Religion*, pp. 76–86; Grotius, *Truth of Christian Religion*, pp. 62–80.

[75] *Reasonableness of Scripture-Belief*, pp. 200–227. Cf. Wilkins, *Principles and Duties*, pp. 399–400; Ferguson, *Interest of Reason in Religion*, pp. 88–91.

Whence, but from *Heav'n*, cou'd men unskill'd in Arts,
In several Ages born, in several parts,
Weave such *agreeing Truths?* or *how*, or *why*
Shou'd *all* conspire to cheat us with a *Lye?*
Unask'd their *Pains, ungratefull* their *Advice,*
Starving their *Gain*, and *Martyrdom* their *Price.*

[ll. 140–45]

In these six lines he skillfully combines three separate considerations about these writers, each of which Wolseley discusses in detail. "Many of the *Prophets*," he writes, "and most of the *Apostles* were men Illiterate, and of Parts and Education so *mean*, that they seem no way *capable* to write so profoundly, to lay so *deep* a Contrivement of mischief, or by the single strength of their own abilities to bid so fair to delude the World." Furthermore, "the world affords not an instance, that ever so many *Men* that lived in so many several and *distinct Ages,* so exactly agreed about *any one thing,* much less to *cheat* and *abuse* the *World.*" Finally, it was not in the interest of these writers to have attempted such a deception, since "the most of those that God imploied in that work actually exposed themselves by the doing of it to all the *Persecutions, Hazards* and *Contempts* imaginable; And some of them . . . with the loss of their own *Lives* published their Doctrine."[76]
Taking up the product of these men's efforts, Dryden writes:

If on the Book it self we cast our view,
Concurrent Heathens prove the Story *True*:
The *Doctrine, Miracles*; which must convince,
For *Heav'n* in *Them* appeals to *humane Sense*:
And though they *prove* not, they *Confirm* the Cause,
When what is *Taught* agrees with *Natures Laws.*

[ll. 146–51]

Here Dryden briefly refers to Wolseley's argument elsewhere, that the events related in the Bible are confirmed by pagan historians, and then proceeds to discuss in some detail his friend's argument that the Bible's doctrine has been shown to be true by the miracles which accompanied its proclamation. In regard to the latter, he

[76] *Reasonableness of Scripture-Belief*, pp. 228–40. Cf. Wilkins, *Principles and Duties,* p. 400; Parker, *Demonstration of the Divine Authority,* pp. 184–99; Ferguson, *Interest of Reasons in Religion,* pp. 101–18; Grotius, *Truth of Christian Religion,* pp. 55–59, 116–18; Bates, *Divinity of the Christian Religion,* pp. 108–15.

goes on to declare the conditions necessary for a miracle to confirm a cause. Wolseley had considered at some length the question "Whether *miracles* simply in themselves are always an unquestionable proof of that Doctrine they are brought to Confirme." Like Dryden, he answers that if the doctrine is not "opposite to that Natural Duty we owe [God], They *are*. But if otherwise, if they come in direct Competition with the Law of Nature, They are *not*."[77]

Dryden next produces his final argument:

> Then for the *Style*; *Majestick* and *Divine*,
> It speaks no less than God in every Line:
> *Commanding words*; whose *Force* is still the same
> As the first *Fiat* that produc'd our Frame.
> All Faiths *beside*, or did by *Arms* ascend;
> Or *Sense* indulg'd has made *Mankind* their *Friend*:
> This *onely* Doctrine does our *Lusts* oppose:
> Unfed by Natures Soil, in which it grows;
> Cross to our *Interests*, curbing Sense, and Sin;
> Oppress'd without, and undermin'd within,
> It thrives through pain; its own *Tormentours* tires;
> And with a stubborn patience still aspires.[78]
>
> [ll. 152–63]

He has saved for last, and expounded at greatest length, what had been traditionally considered the most forceful argument on behalf of the Christian religion.[79] Dryden's allusion to the Bible's style at the beginning of the stanza may obscure the nature of his argument here. The majestic style of the Scriptures, which "speaks no less than God in every Line," is the basis of a separate argument which Wolseley expounds elsewhere.[80] But he repeats

[77] *Reasonableness of Scripture-Belief*, pp. 240–63. Cf. Wilkins, *Principles and Duties*, p. 402; Parker, *Demonstration of the Divine Authority*, pp. 266–83; Ferguson, *Interest of Reason in Religion*, pp. 101–18; Grotius, *Truth of Christian Religion*, pp. 50–54; Bates, *Divinity of the Christian Religion*, pp. 85–115.

[78] Cf. Wolseley: "The *Christians* at that time Tired out the Inventions of their Enemies in finding out ways to torment them, and by their constant and patient suffering the utmost of humane misery even wearied out their Executioners" (*Reasonableness of Scripture-Belief*, p. 269).

[79] See *ibid.*, p. 295: "Had I no other consideration to induce me to believe the *Bible* but what ariseth from hence, this one seems singly sufficient to me to justifie its Divinity, against all reasonable suspition of Imposture, and for ever to silence all the doubts that can be at any time made about it." In expounding this argument in the thirteenth century, Thomas Aquinas had also declared it the most potent evidence on behalf of Christianity. See *Summa contra Gentiles*, I, 6.

[80] See *Reasonableness of Scripture-Belief*, pp. 179–81.

it more briefly later in his book, in the course of developing the argument Dryden offers at this point, which concerns the remarkable reception of the Christian revelation in spite of numerous internal and external hindrances. In the absence of any external helps to spread the Christian religion, Wolseley notes, this doctrine could depend on "no other Cause, but its own Innate worth, and the Divine evidence from Heaven attending it."

This Book and the Religion it contains, as it avows it self to be solely from God, and comes to us with a commanding voice from Heaven, speaks to us in God's own Name, and upon that single account requires our obedience; And those that wrote it, neither had nor pretended to have any other Authority but what was Divine and from Above; So it has introduced it self by Means suitable thereunto. Never was there at first any Force used to compel men, nor any Arts practised to deceive men about this matter. No man can prove out of any Story that ever the Apostles or the Primitive Professors of this Religion raised Arms to introduce or promote it.

Not only was this religion unaccompanied by any helps, he explains, but it was faced with formidable hindrances, both internal and external. Internally, it had little to recommend it, being "a Religion directly opposite to the whole corrupt interest of humane Nature, and calling men to the highest Mortification and Self-denial, upon the account of an Invisible World to come." Externally, "all the force of the *Roman Empire* was every where violently at work for its total Suppression and Extirpation." Never, he declares, "was any Religion so begun and propagated by such indefatigable sufferings." Indeed, "it swims down to these latter Ages in whole streams of Blood that ran from its Primitive Martyrs."[81]

Arguments such as the five he has presented, Dryden concludes, must induce the assent of all reasonable men to the divine authority of the Scriptures:

> To what can *Reason* such Effects assign
> Transcending *Nature*, but to *Laws Divine?*
> Which in that Sacred Volume are contain'd;
> Sufficient, clear, and for that use ordain'd.
>
> [ll. 164–67]

[81] See *ibid.,* pp. 289–97. Cf. Wilkins, *Principles and Duties,* p. 403; Parker, *Demonstration of the Divine Authority,* pp. 239–66; Grotius, *Truth of Christian Religion,* pp. 86–93; Bates, *Divinity of the Christian Religion,* pp. 145–52.

Having shown that there must be some revelation and that this revelation is to be found in the Bible, Dryden has completed his immediate task.

He has not finished with the Deist, however, for the latter has an objection in reserve, as we noticed in the last chapter, which must be answered before the case against deism is complete. At this point Dryden parts company with Wolseley, who had dealt with other objections, to exploit a different tradition which I shall discuss in the next chapter.

5

DEFENDER OF THE FAITH:
LATITUDINARIAN vs. CALVINIST

I pointed out in the last chapter that two different traditions lie behind the two halves of *Religio Laici*: in the first half, where Dryden is answering a non-Christian opponent, he draws upon a broad tradition of Christian apologetics common to most Anglicans, Dissenters, and Catholics; while in the second half of the poem, where he is opposing another Christian communion, Dryden must turn to the confessional apologetics of his own church. We might expect him to continue to use the common fund of Christian apologetics when, after offering his arguments for the reasonableness of Christianity, he anticipates and answers the objection of the Deist before turning his attention to Father Simon. This is not, however, the case. In replying to the objection of the Deist, Dryden begins to deal with matters which divided the Christians of his time, and this continues to be his procedure throughout the remainder of the poem. The failure to realize this early change of tactics has been responsible for the common misunderstanding of Dryden's answer to the Deist.

With the words "But stay: the *Deist* here will urge anew," he introduces the Deist's second speech, discussed in chapter 3, which offers the objection that "No *Supernatural Worship* can be *True:* / Because a *general Law* is that alone / Which must to *all*, and every *where* be known." On the assumption that Christians are committed to the belief that none can be saved to whom the Gospel has not been preached, the Deist asks "what Provision cou'd from *thence* accrue / To *Indian* Souls, and Worlds discover'd *New*?" By the logic of their own position, he argues, Christians are committed to impugning divine justice, by making God responsible for condemning a large part of mankind for the accidents of their time or place of birth. Dryden refuses to accept the terms of the Deist's argument, however, which would force him into the uncomfortable position of defending an economy of salvation manifestly unjust. Instead, he argues that the Christian dispensation is perfectly compatible with divine justice because those who have never heard the Gospel preached are nevertheless offered the possibility of salvation.

The position Dryden takes in answering the Deist has been repeatedly condemned in recent years on both logical and theological grounds. On the one hand he has been charged with inconsistency and with contradicting his own position on the necessity of revelation earlier in the poem. So one recent critic complains that "he not only contradicts some of the implications he was at pains to suggest in the first section but also, at times, exceeds even orthodox claims for reason."[1] On the other hand he is accused of misrepresenting the Christian position and of defending it with heterodox arguments. It is charged that in his anxiety to meet the Deist on his own grounds, Dryden has ended by accepting the deist position himself. So another critic declares that "Dryden not only dismisses revelation in summary fashion, but he asserts the adequacy of natural reason for salvation." It is small wonder that he suggests such tendencies might logically have led "in the direction of Toland's *Christianity not Mysterious*."[2]

It is not only critics of *Religio Laici* who feel that the position Dryden adopts in answering the Deist's objection is seriously "unorthodox." The most famous expression in English literature of the position Dryden takes here is to be found in *Joseph Andrews*. In the course of a heated conversation with another clergyman, Parson Adams attacks the doctrine of the atonement taught by George Whitefield, leader of the Calvinist Methodists, and opposes to this "my own Opinion, which hath always been, that a virtuous and good Turk, or Heathen, are more acceptable in the sight of their Creator than a vicious and wicked Christian,

[1] Donald R. Benson, "Theology and Politics in Dryden's Conversion," *Studies in English Literature*, 4 (1964): 400.

[2] Thomas H. Fujimura, "Dryden's *Religio Laici:* An Anglican Poem," *PMLA*, 76 (1961): 208–9, 216–17. Even as discerning a historian of Anglicanism as the late Norman Sykes discusses Dryden's answer to the objection of the Deist, along with Pope's *Essay on Man*, as examples of the vogue of deism among the poets of the time; see *From Sheldon to Secker: Aspects of English Church History, 1660–1768* (Cambridge: At the University Press, 1959), pp. 158–61.

though his Faith was as perfectly Orthodox as St. Paul himself."[3] For this expression of charity toward the heathen, Adams has been posthumously tried, found guilty of Pelagianism, and condemned as a heretic in a recent study of Fielding's novel.[4] There seems to be a fairly widespread belief among literary historians that any disposition among Anglicans of the seventeenth and eighteenth centuries to include the heathen within the terms of salvation is a certain sign of deism, Pelagianism, or Arminianism (described as a popular "heresy" of the time).[5]

The facts, however, are quite otherwise, and it is curious that such a misconception should be current at the present day. The question of the salvation of the heathen is as old as Christianity itself. In every period of the Christian Era theologians have debated whether the atonement extends to the pagans of antiquity and to those more recent pagans to whom the Gospel has never been preached. The complex history of this question has been traced before, but it is apparently unknown to students of seventeenth- and eighteenth-century English literature.[6] Otherwise it would have been impossible for them to assume that there was a single "orthodox" position on this question among Christians of that time, and that this position consisted in a cheerful acquiescence in the damnation of the heathen.

At the time of the Reformation—to begin no earlier—the Protestant and Catholic churches met the question of the salvation of the heathen with completely opposite answers. In each case the answer was a corollary of the respective positions of the two churches on one of the major issues of the Reformation: the problem of justification. The Protestant doctrine of justification by faith alone offered no comfort to the infidel who was denied this faith by the circumstances of his time or place of birth. Except for Zwingli, the Protestant reformers of the sixteenth century

---

[3] *Joseph Andrews*, Book I, chap. xvii. Fielding puts identical sentiments into the mouth of Heartfree in *Jonathan Wild* (Book IV, chap. i).

[4] See Martin Battestin, *The Moral Basis of Fielding's Art: A Study of Joseph Andrews* (Middletown, Conn.: Wesleyan University Press, 1959), pp. 95–97. See also p. 21, where Battestin declares that "this Pelagian doctrine corresponded to the deism, for example, of Lord Herbert of Cherbury, who had refused to believe that a benevolent God would condemn those ignorant of scriptural revelation."

[5] For descriptions of Arminianism as "heresy," see the works by Fujimura and Battestin cited above in notes 2 and 4 respectively.

[6] See Louis Capéran, *Le Problème du salut des infidèles: essai historique* (2d ed.; Toulouse: Grand Séminaire, 1934). The history was originally published in 1912.

taught in common that, in the absence of an explicit faith in Christ, the works of the pagans were without any merit and their condemnation certain. To Calvin, for whom the atonement was limited to the elect, the fact that the heathen had been denied the light of the Gospel was itself a sign of their reprobation. Throughout the sixteenth century and well into the seventeenth, this continued to be the common doctrine of English Protestants as well, whether Puritans or members of the episcopal party.

An excellent summary of this position by an enlightened member of the Church of England writing shortly before the Restoration can be found in Nathanael Culverwel's *Discourse of the Light of Nature* (1652). A Calvinist, as were most members of the Church of England before the Restoration, Culverwel will concede no saving merit to the pagans of antiquity. Admittedly, some pagans were better than others, "nor is there any doubt but that some of the Heathen pleased God better then others. Surely *Socrates* was more lovely in his eyes then *Aristophanes, Augustus* pleased him better then *Tiberius, Cicero* was more acceptable to him then *Catiline*." Such pagans had their reward: in this life they received temporal blessings denied to the vicious; in the next, they "shall have more mitigations of punishment then the other."

Socrates shall taste a milder cup of wrath, when as *Aristophanes* shall drink up the dregs of fury; if divine justice whip *Cicero* with rods, 'twill whip *Catiline* with Scorpions. An easier and more gentle worm shall feed upon *Augustus,* a more fierce and cruel one shall prey upon *Tiberius.*[7]

Such doubtful consolations are the best Culverwel can offer those to whom God chose to deny that faith which alone can justify men, render their actions meritorious, and win salvation.

This is not to say that God may not have chosen a few of His elect from among the pagan nations; but if He did so it was by revealing Christ to them in an extraordinary manner and as a result, not of any meritorious actions on their part, but of His own free election. Culverwel writes of these favored individuals:

You must be sure not to entertain such a thought as this, that the excellency of their intellectuals and morals did move and prevail with the goodnesse of God to save them more then others of the Heathen ... whereas you must resolve it only into the free grace of God, that did thus distinguish them here in time, and might more distinguish

[7] *An Elegant and Learned Discourse of the Light of Nature* (London, 1652), p. 204.

them eternally, if it pleased him to bestow a Saviour upon them. Which grace of God is so free, as that it might save the worst of the Heathens, and let go the rest; it might save an *Aristophanes* as well as a *Socrates,* nay before a *Socrates.* . . . Yet I am farre from the minde of those Patrons of Universal Grace, that make all men in an equal propinquity to salvation, whether Jewes, or Pagans, or Christians. . . . 'Tis an evident signe that God intends more salvation there, where he affords more means of salvation; if then God do choose and call an Heathen, 'tis not by universal, but by distinguishing grace.[8]

If a less rigorous view of the question was taken by Catholic theologians, this was made possible by their doctrine of justification by faith and good works together. Good works, while not alone sufficient to merit salvation, are viewed as preparing men for the reception of faith. Furthermore, the atonement was universal; since God willed the salvation of all men, He did not intend to exclude from His mercy those who, from invincible ignorance, have had no opportunity to embrace the Christian religion. According to a popular Scholastic maxim, "God does not refuse grace to one who does what he can" *(Facienti quod in se est, Deus non denegat gratiam).* If the ancient or modern heathen do not have the Gospel, they nevertheless have the law of nature. By observing this law diligently, they will find favor with God and receive the gift of His grace with sufficient faith to merit salvation.

A good account of the common Catholic position on the salvation of the heathen can be found in Dryden's own words. It occurs in a passage of his translation of *The Life of St. Francis Xavier* by Dominique Bouhours (1688), made after his conversion to the Catholic faith. Speaking of the period of Xavier's missionary activities, when he had made many converts among the Japanese, Bouhours refers to "the sorrow of the Japonians for having been bereft for so many ages of Christian knowledge," and to their fears for the salvation of their ancestors. He declares that we have the saint's own account of how "he had the good fortune to give them comfort, and put them in a way of more reasonable thoughts";

for he shewed them in general, that the most ancient of all laws is the law of God, not that which is published by the sound of words, but that which is written in hearts by the hand of nature; so that every one who comes into the world, brings along with him certain precepts, which his own instinct and reason teach him. . . . "Suppose an infant bred up in forests among the beasts, far from the society

[8] *Ibid.,* pp. 209–10.

of mankind, and remote from the civilized inhabitants of towns, yet he is not without an inward knowledge of the rules of civil life; for ask him, whether it be not an evil action to murder a man, to despoil him of his goods, to violate his bed, to surprise him by force, or circumvent him by treachery, he will answer without question, 'That nothing of this is to be done.' Now if this be manifest in a savage, without the benefit of education, how much more may it be concluded of men well educated, and living in mutual conversation? Then," added the holy man, "it follows, that God has not left so many ages destitute of knowledge, as your Bonzas have pretended." By this he gave them to understand, that the law of nature was a step which led them insensibly to the Christian law; and that a man who lived morally well, should never fail of arriving to the knowledge of the faith, by ways best known to Almighty God; that is to say, before his death, God would either send some preacher to him, or illuminate his mind by some immediate revelation.[9]

In spite of the fact that both Culverwel and Xavier refer to the possibility of a special revelation, the two positions have nothing in common. For Culverwel this revelation would simply be an exception to the general rule that the heathen are condemned to reprobation; such an action on God's part would be purely arbitrary, without regard to the heathen's behavior. For Xavier, on the other hand, this revelation, or some such means of salvation, will be offered to every virtuous heathen who observes the law of nature, in order that the benefits of the atonement may be extended to all mankind.

In the course of the seventeenth century, the simple division of opinion between Protestants and Catholics on the question of the salvation of the heathen became confused. Within each of the two churches a minority opinion appeared which favored the views on this question traditionally associated with the opposite communion. In the Catholic church in France from 1640 onwards, the

---

[9] *The Works of John Dryden,* ed. Sir Walter Scott and George Saintsbury (Edinburgh: William Paterson, 1882–93), XVI, 339–40. The saint (or his biographer) is closely following a *locus classicus* of the Catholic view of the question, the famous passage in which Thomas Aquinas writes that although an explicit faith is necessary for salvation, this does not work to the detriment of anyone, even one "bred up in forests or among the beasts; for it is the care of divine providence to furnish everyone with whatever is necessary for salvation, as long as it is not prevented by the individual himself. So if someone brought up in this manner followed the guidance of natural reason in seeking good and avoiding evil, it most certainly must be held that God would either by internal inspiration reveal to him what had to be believed, or would send him some preacher of the faith as He sent Peter to Cornelius" (*Quaestiones Disputatae: De Veritate,* XIV, 11). My translation.

followers of Jansenius adopted a position on limited atonement and on the sinfulness of good works unaccompanied by faith which was practically indistinguishable from that of the Calvinists. With perfect consistency, they accepted the traditional Protestant view that the heathen are excluded from any participation in grace and are consequently predestined to reprobation. Although it was repeatedly condemned as heretical by the Catholic church, Jansenism continued to find favor with an important minority of French Catholics for many years. On the other hand in the Dutch Reformed church shortly after the beginning of the century, Arminius and his followers developed a position on the universality of the atonement and on the efficacy of good works as a preparation for faith which was very close to that of the Catholics. Indeed, they were accused of propagating the teachings of Cardinal Bellarmine among the Dutch. In any case, they logically shared the Catholic view on the salvation of virtuous infidels which followed from their position on the atonement. Rejected as a heresy by the Synod of Dort in 1619, Arminianism nevertheless continued to exercise considerable influence on the Continent.

The Church of England was not exempt from this realignment of minorities within the several churches during the seventeenth century. Like the Dutch Reformed church, it had its share of members who began to challenge the Calvinist doctrine of the atonement traditionally held by their church and to express sympathy for the more liberal doctrine which had previously been the almost exclusive preserve of their Catholic opponents. It is customary to refer to this liberal minority within the Church of England as "Arminians," and it must be said that there is considerable warrant for this practice in the writings of their contemporaries. If the term is intended as nothing more than a metaphor, it will serve quite well, for there is a decided similarity between the views of these Anglicans and those expressed by the followers of Arminius in the Netherlands. Yet if the emergence of anti-Calvinism within the Church of England had its counterpart in Dutch Protestantism, it was nevertheless of independent growth. Clarendon showed more perception than many of his contemporaries when he described the religious differences which divided the national church on the eve of the civil wars:

Some doctrinal points in controversy had been in the late years agitated in the pulpits with more warmth and reflections than had used

153

to be; and thence the heat and animosity increased in books *pro* and *con* upon the same arguments: most of the popular preachers, who had not looked into the ancient learning, took Calvin's word for it, and did all they could to propagate his opinions in those points: they who had studied more, and were better versed in the antiquities of the Church, the Fathers, the Councils and the ecclesiastical histories, with the same heat and passion in preaching and writing, defended the contrary. But because, in the late dispute in the Dutch churches, those opinions were supported by Jacobus Arminius, the divinity professor in the university of Leyden in Holland, the latter men we mentioned were called Arminians, though many of them had never read [a] word written by Arminius. . . . The archbishop [Laud] had all his life eminently opposed Calvin's doctrine in those controversies, before the name of Arminius was taken notice of or his opinions heard of; and thereupon, for want of another name, they had called him a Papist.[10]

The growth of "Arminianism" in the Church of England, then, is simply part of a general movement during the seventeenth century in which a minority within each of the Protestant churches attempted to soften the rigors of Calvinism by assimilating some of the notions on justification which the early reformers had condemned as Catholic errors.[11]

If this movement assumes greater importance in the Church of England than in some of the other Protestant churches of the seventeenth century, this is because the efforts of its Anglican adherents were crowned with early and lasting success. By the end of the century, the minority had become a majority which eventually embraced nearly the entire church membership until, in the early eighteenth century, "Arminianism" was accepted as a matter of course by most of the bishops, clergy, and laity of the national church.[12] The crucial period of transition was the Restoration era, during which Calvinism gradually but steadily waned

[10] *History of the Rebellion and Civil Wars in England,* ed. W. Dunn Macray (Oxford: Clarendon Press, 1888), I, 123–24.

[11] Among the French Calvinists, an important, but less far-reaching, modification of this kind was known as Amyraldism, after Moise Amyraut. Among the English Presbyterians of the Restoration period a similar movement was called Baxterianism, after Richard Baxter, who was often described as an Amyraldist on no better grounds than those on which Laud was called an Arminian.

[12] For two recent accounts of this change, see G. R. Cragg, *From Puritanism to the Age of Reason: A Study of Changes in Religious Thought within the Church of England, 1660 to 1700* (Cambridge: At the University Press, 1950), pp. 13–36, and Roland N. Stromberg, *Religious Liberalism in Eighteenth-Century England* (London: Oxford University Press, 1954), pp. 110–22.

while "Arminianism" slowly increased in importance. Unquestionably, the most vocal element responsible for this change was the Latitudinarians.

Such Latitudinarian characteristics as their interest in the new science, their emphasis upon the importance of reason in religion, and their efforts at securing comprehension for the Dissenters have received well-deserved attention in recent years, but they should not be allowed to obscure the important role which the Latitudinarians played in opposing Calvinism. To their contemporaries they were perhaps chiefly known for their unremitting opposition to the Calvinist doctrines on justification, reprobation, and the atonement; and much of their early unpopularity probably stemmed from members of their own church who held tenaciously to these doctrines. The earliest defense of the Latitudinarians, published in 1662, is careful to point out that there is not "any Article of Doctrine held forth by the Church, which they can justly be accused to depart from, unlesse absolute reprobation be one, which they do not think themselves bound to believe." It is principally due to "the new sect of Latitude-Men," the writer continues, that

the freedom of our wills, the universal intent of Christ's death, and sufficiency of Gods Grace, the conditions of justification, and many other points of the like nature, which have been almost exploded in these latter degenerate ages of the world, do again begin to obtain, though with different persons upon different accounts; some embrace them for their evidence in Scripture, others for the concurrent testimony of the primitive Church for above four hundred years; others for the reasonableness of the things themselves, and their agreement both with the Divine Attributes and the easy suggestions of their own minds.[13]

Joseph Glanvill, describing the Latitudinarians a few years later (1676), also stressed their settled opposition to the severe exclusiveness of the Calvinist doctrine of the atonement:

They took notice, what *unworthy* and *dishonourable Opinions* were publish'd abroad concerning *God,* to the disparagement of all his Attributes, and discouragement of vertuous Endeavours, and great trouble and dejection of many pious Minds; and therefore here they appear'd also to *assert* and *vindicate* the *Divine Goodness* and *love of Men* in its *freedom* and *extent,* against those Doctrines, that made

[13] S. P. of Cambridge, *A Brief Account of the New Sect of Latitude-Men* (London, 1662), pp. 9–10.

his *Love, Fondness;* and his *Justice, Cruelty;* and represented God, as the Eternal Hater of the far greatest part of his reasonable Creatures, and the designer of their Ruine, for the exaltation of *meer Power,* and *arbitrary Will:* Against these sowr and dismal Opinions They stood up stoutly, in a time when the Assertors of the Divine Purity and Goodness, were persecuted bitterly with nicknames of Reproach, and popular Hatred. . . . By *such* Principles as *These,* which are wonderfully fertile, and big of many great Truths, they undermined, and from the bottom overthrew the fierce and churlish *Reprobatarian* Doctrines.[14]

The bitter "persecution" of the Latitudinarians which Glanvill describes took place during the years immediately preceding the Restoration. If this persecution did not cease entirely, following that event, it nevertheless declined considerably after 1662, when the Presbyterians and Independents were excluded from the Church of England by the Act of Uniformity. Not all Calvinists joined in this exodus from the established church, of course, but they lost many of their supporters to Dissent, and Calvinist influence was certainly diminished greatly by this schism. One reason why Glanvill and the other Latitudinarians were able to persuade an ever increasing number of Anglicans to adopt their opinions was because they succeeded in identifying the Calvinist views on reprobation with the Puritans of the civil war period and with the Dissenters of their own day.

At the time Dryden wrote *Religio Laici* a very real division of opinion existed within the Church of England on the question of the salvation of the heathen, which reflected the divided Anglican views on the larger question of justification and reprobation. There were certainly rigid conformists who adhered to the traditional views increasingly associated with the Dissenters and who condemned the heathen to reprobation.[15] But as a Dissenter who

[14] "Anti-fanatical Religion and Free Philosophy," *Essays on Several Important Subjects in Philosophy and Religion* (London, 1676), pp. 21–22. Another important contemporary account of Latitudinarian views on the atonement, by Edward Fowler, bears out my suggestion that these churchmen are not, strictly speaking, Arminians. According to Fowler, their doctrine was "a middle one betwixt the *Calvinists* and *Remonstrants* [Arminians]" which preserved a belief in election while rejecting the notion of reprobation. In the terms of this compromise, all men are offered the possibility of that salvation of which some are assured by election. See *The Principles and Practices of Certain Moderate Divines of the Church of England* (London, 1670), pp. 228–30.

[15] See, for example, the pamphlet by A. M., "a Countrey Gentleman," entitled *Plain Dealing* (London, 1675). The author, a particularly uncompromising Anglican layman, is equally opposed to toleration for the Dissenters and to the notion that

was himself inclined to a less rigid attitude toward the heathen pointed out, not all conformists in the Church of England shared the views of their more rigorous brethren on this question. "A second sort of Conformists," Richard Baxter noted, "were those called *Latitudinarians,* who were mostly *Cambridge*-men, *Platonists* or *Cartesians,* and many of them *Arminians* with some Additions, having more charitable Thoughts than others of the Salvation of Heathens and Infidels."[16] This was written in 1665. By 1682, these "more charitable Thoughts" had spread beyond the immediate circle of Cambridge Platonists and Cartesians to a wider and somewhat later group of Latitudinarians who were still conscious that their views were not yet shared by all Anglicans. Cautiously, even deferentially, these Latitudinarians offered their notions on the salvation of the heathen as a not unreasonable hypothesis which they supported by some or all of the three arguments we saw mentioned by their earliest defender: "evidence in Scripture," "the concurrent testimony of the primitive Church for above four hundred years," and "their agreement both with the Divine Attributes and the easy suggestions of their own minds." In spite of the scarcity of other specific answers to the objection of the Deist at this early date, therefore, Dryden could still find ample precedent among his Latitudinarian contemporaries for his tactic of invalidating the Deist's argument by asserting that the necessity of revelation does not exclude the heathen from salvation.

Dryden offers two arguments in support of his position, one of which is drawn from "evidence in Scripture," the other from the divine attributes. He begins with an appeal to the divine attri-

the heathen may be saved. The fact that the charitable notions concerning the heathen expressed by Parson Adams and by Heartfree are in each case violently rejected by a clergyman of the Church of England (Barnabas in *Joseph Andrews* and the Newgate ordinary in *Jonathan Wild*) seems to indicate Fielding's belief that as late as the middle of the eighteenth century some of the lower clergy still held to Calvinist views on the subject.

[16] *Reliquiae Baxterianae* (London, 1696), p. 386. On this issue Baxter shared the sentiments of the Latitudinarians. Elsewhere in the same book he wrote: "Yet am I not so much inclined to pass a peremptory Sentence of Damnation upon all that never heard of Christ; having some more reason than I knew of before, to think that God's dealing with such is much unknown to *us!* And that the Ungodly here among us Christians are in a far worse Case than they" (*ibid.,* p. 131). This view is premised in Baxter's involved answer to Lord Herbert's version of what was to become the standard objection of the deist (*More Reasons for the Christian Religion* [London, 1672], pp. 82–116), but his answer is nevertheless very different from Dryden's.

butes of wisdom, goodness, and mercy which we noticed Glanvill emphasizing as a common Latitudinarian tactic:

> Of all Objections this indeed is chief
> To startle Reason, stagger frail Belief:
> We grant, 'tis true, that Heav'n from humane Sense
> Has hid the secret paths of *Providence*:
> But *boundless Wisedom, boundless Mercy,* may
> Find ev'n for those *be-wildred* Souls, a *way*:
> If from his *Nature Foes* may Pity claim,
> Much more may *Strangers* who ne'er heard his *Name.*
> And though *no Name* be for *Salvation* known,
> But that of his *Eternal Sons* alone;
> Who knows how far transcending Goodness can
> Extend the *Merits* of *that Son* to *Man*?
> Who knows what *Reasons* may his *Mercy* lead;
> Or *Ignorance invincible* may plead?
>
> [ll. 184–97]

In offering this hopeful interpretation which Dryden says that "Charity" bids him believe, he argues that his views agree with what we know of the divine attributes. But like the Latitudinarians described by Glanvill, he reinforces his own view by arguing that the opposite doctrine of the Calvinists denies and contradicts not only God's mercy and goodness but His justice as well. In the preface to the poem he writes:

It has always been my *thought,* that Heathens, who never did, nor without Miracle cou'd hear of the name of Christ were yet in a possibility of Salvation. Neither will it enter easily into my belief, that before the coming of our Saviour, the whole World, excepting only the Jewish Nation, shou'd lye under the inevitable necessity of everlasting Punishment, for want of that Revelation, which was confin'd to so small a spot of ground as that of *Palaestine.* Among the Sons of *Noah* we read of one onely who was accurs'd; and if a blessing in the ripeness of time was reserv'd for *Japhet,* (of whose Progeny we are,) it seems unaccountable to me, why so many Generations of the same Offspring, as preceeded our Saviour in the Flesh, shou'd be all involv'd in one common condemnation, and yet that their Posterity shou'd be Intitled to the hopes of Salvation: As if a Bill of Exclusion had passed only on the Fathers, which debar'd not the Sons from their Succession. Or that so many Ages had been *deliver'd over* to Hell, and so many *reserv'd* for Heaven, and that the Devil had the first choice, and God the next.

158

Dryden's scathing account of the Calvinist doctrine as a disparagement of divine justice, "as if a Bill of Exclusion had passed only on the Fathers, which debar'd not the Sons from their Succession," is almost certainly an attempt to identify this belief with the Dissenters. A few months earlier he had taken great pains in *The Medal* to suggest that the principal support for Shaftesbury's Bill of Exclusion came from the Dissenters, who "for God's Cause their Monarchs dare dethrone," yet whose harsh religious notions are at odds with those of their political leader; for his "God and Theirs will never long agree":

> A Tyrant theirs; the Heav'n their Priesthood paints
> A Conventicle of gloomy sullen Saints;
> A Heav'n, like *Bedlam*, slovenly and sad;
> Fore-doom'd for Souls, with false Religion, mad.
> [ll. 283–86]

Only such Christians as these, he now suggests, could comfortably square their notions of God as a tyrant with the idea that the heathen are condemned to reprobation.

In his positive argument on behalf of the heathen in the poem itself, certain features deserve particular attention, for they show that there is no basis for any charge that Dryden is succumbing to Pelagianism or deism. He begins by conceding "that Heav'n from humane Sense / Has hid the secret paths of *Providence*," and in his choice of language (as in his repeated use of the words "may" and "who knows") he is careful to offer his solution as no more than a conjecture agreeable to God's known attributes of goodness and mercy. More important, he insists that any such conjecture must be premised upon the admission that "*no Name* be for *Salvation* known, / But that of his *Eternal Sons* alone." Thus he makes short work of the deist view that revelation is unnecessary, for upon Dryden's premise one must assume some revelation, whether by miracle, missionary, or some other means. But the Pelagian notion that men can be saved by their own merits alone receives a summary dismissal as well. For by suggesting that God will find some way to "extend the *Merits* of *that Son*" to the heathen, Dryden makes perfectly clear that the infidel's salvation will come, not from nature, but from the justifying grace of the atonement.

The Latitudinarians, who have fared so badly at the hands of modern inquisitors, qualified their "charitable Thoughts" toward the heathen with similar cautions. In a famous series of sermons, "Of the Necessity of Good Works," Archbishop Tillotson declared

that there is no need so uncharitably to conclude (as some of the ancients have done, not all, nor the most ancient of them neither), that there were no good men among the heathen, and that the brightest of their virtues were counterfeit, and only in show and appearance. For there might be several good men among the gentiles, in the same condition that Cornelius was before he became a Christian. . . . And if he had died in that condition, before Christ had been revealed to him, I do not see what reasonable cause of doubt there can be concerning his salvation; and yet it is a most certain and inviolable truth, "that there is no other name under heaven given among men, whereby we must be saved, but the name of Jesus; neither is there salvation in any other." And good men in all ages and nations from the beginning of the world, both before the law, and under the law, and without the law, such as "feared God, and wrought righteousness," were accepted of him in that name and by the meritorious sacrifice of that Lamb of God, which, in respect of the virtue and efficacy of it, is said to have been "slain from the foundation of the world."[17]

In his elaborate defense of the Latitudinarians, Bishop Fowler offers a dialogue between "Theophilus," a spokesman for the moderate divines, and "Philalethes," a friend. The latter asks: "What say you to the Heathens, that never heard of Christ, or saw one letter of the Bible? Are not they under a fatal necessity of being damned? And is not God wanting to them, think you?" Theophilus replies:

To say the truth, many of them, for all their not having heard of Christ, and their being strangers to the Bible, have out-done most *Christians,* to our great shame be it spoken. . . . For my part, I will not say that they are any of them saved; but I would not for a world, neither, pronounce them all damned. I know that *there is no name under heaven whereby men can be saved, but onely the name of Jesus Christ;* but I am nowhere told, that those which never heard of him cannot be saved by him, without faith in him. . . . So that if I were bound to give my sense of the honestest of the Heathens, I would chuse to judge on the right hand: but we have nothing to do with them; nor can any Argument drawn from the consideration of their circumstances, establish the [Calvinist] doctrine against which we have so freely expressed our selvs.[18]

[17] *The Works of Dr. John Tillotson* (London: J. F. Dove, 1820), IX, 18–19.
[18] *Principles and Practices of Certain Moderate Divines,* pp. 249–53. For a similar view by an anonymous clergyman of the Church of England, see *Religio Clerici* (London, 1681), pp. 107–10.

Each of these writers—Dryden, Tillotson, and Fowler—guards the orthodoxy of his individual opinion by quoting and agreeing with the famous passage in Scripture which declares that no one can be saved except in the name of Christ (Acts 4:12); he then suggests that this need offer no insuperable difficulty to the heathen by expressing a hope that these words will bear a more favorable interpretation than they have sometimes received.[19]

Dryden's second argument is drawn from Scripture:

> Not onely *Charity* bids hope the *best,*
> But *more* the great Apostle has exprest:
> *That, if the* Gentiles, (whom no Law inspir'd,)
> *By Nature did what* was by *Law requir'd;*
> *They, who the written Rule had never known,*
> *Were to themselves both Rule and Law alone:*
> *To Natures plain indictment they shall plead;*
> *And, by their Conscience, be condemn'd or freed.*
> Most righteous Doom! because a *Rule reveal'd*
> Is *none* to *Those,* from whom it was *conceal'd.*
> Then those who follow'd *Reasons* Dictates right;
> Liv'd up, and lifted high their *Natural Light;*
> With *Socrates* may see their Maker's Face,
> While Thousand *Rubrick-Martyrs* want a place.
>
> [ll. 198–211]

The lines in italics are a paraphrase of a famous passage from St. Paul:

For when the Gentiles, which have no law, do by nature the things of the law, these, having no law, are a law unto themselves; in that they show the work of the law written in their hearts, their conscience bearing witness therewith and their thoughts one with another accusing or else excusing them. [Rom. 2: 14–15]

[19] The more liberal interpretation of this passage was confirmed a few years later. In his *Exposition of the Thirty-Nine Articles* (London, 1699) Gilbert Burnet offered the following comment on Article 18, which contains the statement that "Holy Scripture doth set out unto us only the Name of Jesus Christ, whereby men must be saved": "So in a word, all that are saved, are saved through Christ; but whether all these shall be called to the Explicit Knowledge of him, is more than we have any good ground to affirm. . . . This in general may be safely believed, That God will never be wanting to such as do their utmost endeavours in order to the saving of their Souls: But that as in the case of *Cornelius,* an Angel will be sent, and a Miracle be wrought, rather than that such a person shall be left to perish. But whether any of them do ever arrive at that state, is more than we can determine, and it is a vain attempt for us to endeavour to find it out" (p. 174). In the eighteenth century, every candidate for ordination was enjoined to study Burnet's *Exposition,* and the book played an important part in the spread of Latitudinarianism.

These verses of St. Paul had long assumed importance because they offered scriptural sanction to the Greek and Roman theories of natural law, identifying this law with the unwritten law of the Christian God. Consequently, some allusion to them, either expressed or implied, is to be found in almost every Christian discussion of the law of nature. Hooker, for example, turns to these verses for support in his great discourse on the law of nature in Book I of the *Laws*:

The Apostle St. Paul having speech concerning the heathen saith of them, "They are a law unto themselves." His meaning is, that by force of the light of Reason, wherewith God illuminateth every one which cometh into the world, men being enabled to know truth from falsehood, and good from evil, do thereby learn in many things what the will of God is; which will himself not revealing by any extraordinary means unto them, but they by natural discourse attaining the knowledge thereof, seem the makers of those Laws which indeed are his, and they but only the finders of them out.[20]

It will be noticed that Hooker contents himself with concluding from this passage that even the heathen can know the will of God; he draws no corollary as to whether this might enable them to be saved. Dryden, however, proceeds to conjecture that for such individuals the law of nature will be an acceptable substitute for the supernatural law they are denied, so that adherence to this law, while not a sufficient condition for salvation, is a necessary condition upon the fulfilment of which will depend their being permitted to share in the merits of Christ's atonement. He concedes that this is no more than a conjectural interpretation of St. Paul's words, for in the preface to the poem he writes:

I have dwelt longer on this Subject than I intended; and longer than, perhaps, I ought; for having laid down, as my Foundation, that the Scripture is a Rule; that in all things needfull to Salvation, it is clear, sufficient, and ordain'd by God Almighty for that purpose, I have left my self no right to interpret obscure places, such as concern the possibility of eternal happiness to Heathens: because whatsoever is obscure is concluded not necessary to be known.

---

[20] *Of the Laws of Ecclesiastical Polity* (London, J. M. Dent and Sons, 1954), I, 176–77 [I, viii, 3]. (All subsequent references to the *Laws* will be to book, chapter, and section, as in the reference here in brackets.) For a similar use of this passage, see *ibid.*, I, xvi, 5. Thomas Aquinas also quotes this same passage from St. Paul as his single authority in giving a positive answer to the question "Whether there is in us a natural law?" (*Summa Theologiae*, I IIae, 91, 2).

Dryden's conjecture that a diligent observance of the law of nature will be the means whereby the heathen may win divine favor and receive the gift of justifying faith is a common one among the Latitudinarians of his day. Tillotson exclaims:

God forbid that we should pass so hard a judgment [as reprobation] upon those excellent men, Socrates, and Epictetus, and Antoninus, and several others, who sincerely endeavoured to live up to the light and law of nature, and took so much pains to cultivate and raise their minds, to govern and subdue the irregularity of their sensual appetites and brutish passions, to purify and refine their manners, and to excel in all virtue and goodness.[21]

It is because of these efforts "to live up to the light and law of nature" that he goes on to suggest their salvation.

Bishop Wilkins, writing in 1675, also finds grounds for a favorable view of the salvation of the heathen in the fact that they have the law of nature to guide them. He finds some support for his view in the "concurrent testimony of the primitive Church," with the usual caution that Heaven "has hid the secret paths of *Providence*."

How far the Moral virtues of meer *Heathens,* who walk answerable to the light they have, may be approved of God, I shall not now dispute. Only thus much seems clear in the general, That the Law of Nature being implanted in the hearts of men by God himself, must therefore be esteemed to be as much his Law, as any positive Institution whatsoever: And consequently, conformity to it must in its kind, *in genere morum,* be acceptable to him. . . . Some of the *Fathers* indeed, as *Justin Martyr,* and *Clemens Alexandrinus* and *Chrysostom,* have delivered their judgments for the salvation of such *Heathens* as live according to the light of Nature: But the general stream of the rest is for the contrary opinion. I shall not now enquire into the particular grounds and reasons of this difference. It may suffice to say in general, that the *goodness* and *mercy* of God, as well as *his judgments are a great deep;* that *he will have mercy on whom he will have mercy.*[22]

For Wilkins, as for Dryden and the other Latitudinarians, it is ultimately the divine attributes of goodness and mercy which bid us hope for that which we cannot know with certainty.

It was an Anglican layman, however, writing the same year as Wilkins, who focused public attention on the problem of the

[21] *Works of Dr. John Tillotson,* IX, 17.
[22] John Wilkins, *Of the Principles and Duties of Natural Religion* (London, 1675), pp. 396–97.

salvation of the heathen and emphasized the importance of the law of nature toward its solution. Richard Burthogge's *Causa Dei* (1675) is, as the subtitle explains, "an Apology for God" in which the "Divine both Goodness and Justice [are] Defended" against the objections of a certain "W. A.," whose letter is printed at the beginning of the book. W. A. is not, apparently, a deist, but the last of his four objections against divine justice raises the same difficulty later posed by Dryden's Deist. He asks:

How much more dismal and tremendous doth it look that those People in *America, Japan, China, Lapland,* &c. that live under an unavoidable ignorance (I mean *morally* so) that yet these poor creatures for what they cannot help, shall be cast into Everlasting Darkness, and sorrows, and that there are no reserves for their acting for a happiness they have no notice of, or very little, or if they have, yet are ignorant of the proper methods to attain it? How agrees this with Infinite and Eternal Goodness?[23]

This is clearly the most forceful of W. A.'s difficulties, and Burthogge devotes some 250 pages of his book to its solution.[24] Like Dryden, Burthogge answers this objection, not by accepting W. A.'s challenge to try to show how the dismal prospect of the heathen agrees "with Infinite and Eternal Goodness," but by denying his adversary's initial assumption that they are faced with such a prospect. He makes the heathen's "unavoidable ignorance" (Dryden's *"Ignorance invincible"*) his starting point, and argues that "no man shall be condemned for what he *could not help,* nor for what he could *not do.*"[25] Burthogge then proceeds to show that all men have inherited some remnants of the primitive revelation and have, besides, the light of nature to guide them. "The Law of Nature is the Law of God written in Nature, which Reason sheweth, and this maketh Duty."[26] By observing this duty diligently, the heathen can find the necessary "reserves for their acting for a happiness they have no notice of."

If this law of nature is a means by which it is possible for all men to participate in the benefits of the atonement, it must be available, not only to the philosopher, but to those of ordinary capacities as well. Otherwise, a fortunate few would enjoy in the law of nature the same unfair advantage which was claimed,

[23] *Causa Dei* (London, 1675), sig. A4.
[24] *Ibid.,* pp. 168–422.
[25] *Ibid.,* p. 417.
[26] *Ibid.,* p. 402.

according to the deist, by those to whom the Gospel had been preached. In the "Dedication" to *Examen Poeticum* (1693), written many years later after he had become a Catholic, Dryden declared:

The Notions of Morality are known to all Men, none can pretend Ignorance of those Idea's which are In-born in Mankind; and if I see one thing, and practise the contrary, I must be Disingenuous, not to acknowledge a clear Truth, and Base to Act against the light of my own Conscience.[27]

The same assumption underlies his treatment of the law of nature in *Religio Laici* as a common largess to mankind from a benevolent Creator who wills that all men be saved. In this context, Dryden's choice of Socrates as a candidate for salvation is dictated, not by the fact that he was a philosopher, but by the tradition that he was the most virtuous of heathens, the "Saint Socrates" of Erasmus and the other humanists.

This is a very different context from that in which Socrates appears so often earlier in the poem and in corresponding passages of the preface which I discussed in the last chapter. There, it is true, he figures as a philosopher, one "whose Wisedom *Oracles* renown'd," a member of that fortunate "few, whose Lamp shone brighter" than the minds of other men. But there the context was a discussion of natural religion, of the extent to which this can provide an adequate knowledge of God, and of the practical limitation of this knowledge to a few philosophers. Here the context is a discussion of natural law, a matter of practical morality for which no such limits exist.

In the long tradition extending from Thomas Aquinas, through Hooker, to the physico-theologians as well as Dryden himself, this distinction between the infrequency of natural religion and the universality of natural law is a common one. On the one hand, natural religion, theoretically within the capacity of human reason, is in practice limited to the unaided discovery of certain philosophers, although it can be readily demonstrated to any man. On the other hand, natural law is discernible to every normal mind without the necessity of superior intelligence or the instructions of another person better qualified. I described this tradition earlier as one founded on an empirical theory of knowl-

[27] *The Poems of John Dryden,* ed. James Kinsley (Oxford: Clarendon Press, 1958), II, 791. (Hereafter referred to as *Poems.*)

edge. The maxims of natural law, if commoner, are nevertheless no more innate than is the knowledge of the existence of God, according to this tradition. It is true that the empiricists frequently describe these notions as "inscribed," "implanted," or "in-born," and even Hooker refers to them on occasion as having been written on the hearts of men by the hand of God.[28] The scriptural warrant for this metaphor is, of course, to be found in St. Paul's words about "the law written in their hearts." But it is no more than a metaphor. As Bishop Parker, a prominent empiricist of the time, explained, "these Phrases are not to be taken in exact propriety of Speech, but only in a loose and popular way of Expression; and so they were intended by those that first used them, that only alluded to the known Customs and Solemnities of enacting Laws, that were always wont to be declared and published to the Subject by Writing or Proclamation."[29]

The basic reason why the ingredients of natural law are more common than those of natural religion is because of an essential difference, not in their origin, which is empirical in every case, but in the manner of reasoning employed in their discovery. Natural religion is, as we have seen, a matter of demonstration available only to those who are capable of such an effort. Natural law, however, consists of maxims which are the effect of common experience shared by all men and which are, in fact, incapable of demonstration. "The main principles of Reason," Hooker explained, "are in themselves apparent. For to make nothing evident of itself unto man's understanding were to take away all possibility of knowing any thing. . . . In every kind of knowledge some such grounds there are, as that being proposed the mind doth presently embrace them as free from all possibility of error, clear and manifest without proof." All of the ingredients of natural law, he goes on to show, are axioms of this kind, although some are more general and others less:

Axioms less general, yet so manifest that they need no further proof, are such as these, "God to be worshipped"; "parents to be honoured"; "others to be used by us as we ourselves would be by them." Such things, as soon as they are alleged, all men acknowledge to be good; they require no proof or further discourse to be assured of their goodness.

---

[28] See, for example, *Laws*, I, xvi, 5, and III, ix, 3.
[29] Samuel Parker, *A Demonstration of the Divine Authority of the Law of Nature and of the Christian Religion* (London, 1681), p. 6.

Yet in spite of the fact that these notions of morality are common to all men, Hooker insists that they are not innate, but derived from experience. He adds: "Notwithstanding whatsoever such principle there is, it was at the first found out by discourse, and drawn from out of the very bowels of heaven and earth."[30]

Dryden makes explicit use of this distinction between the infrequency of natural religion and the universality of natural law in the preface to *Religio Laici* when he explains the difference between the maxim "God to be worshipped," properly understood, and the erroneous notions of "Deism, or the Principles of Natural Worship." He has no quarrel with the idea, common to deists and Christian exponents of natural law alike, that all men feel a natural obligation to offer praise and prayer to some superior being whom they call God. Such practices had obviously always existed among even the most remote tribes. Dryden objects to the way in which the deist has confused the universal obligation of natural law with the infrequent discoveries of natural religion in proclaiming that all mankind has been able to erect a system "of *Natural Worship,* built on *Pray'r* and *Praise,* / *To One sole* GOD," or as he expresses it in the preface, worship due to "one Supream Agent or Intellectual Being which we call God." His antidote to such confusion is to offer the account of the gradual corruption of the primitive revelation discussed in the last chapter, according to which the greatest part of mankind "lost by little and little the Primitive and Purer Rites of Divine Worship, retaining onely the notion of one Deity; to which succeeding Generations added others." He then adds the significant sentence: "Revelation being thus Eclipsed to almost all Mankind, the light of Nature as the next in Dignity was substituted; and that is it which St. *Paul* concludes to be the Rule of the Heathens; and by which they are hereafter to be judg'd." Thus, while most men eventually lost all trace of the rites of worship commanded in the primitive revelation, they retained, in the corrupted form of polytheism, something of the notion of a deity disclosed by God to Adam and taught by Noah to his sons. In this state of affairs, men could still find in the law of nature the obligation to divine worship which the primitive revelation had once required of

[30] *Laws,* I, viii, 5. In the other tradition of Christian rationalism discussed in chapter 4, that of "our Modern Philosophers" and "some of our Philosophising Divines" whom Dryden attacks, the maxims of natural law are considered to be genuinely innate.

them; but their notions of the deity to whom this worship must be offered were derived, not from the reason of every man, but from the vestiges of this revelation. Years later, after he had become a Catholic, Dryden returned to the subject briefly in his "Discourse concerning Satire" (1693) while discussing the rise of poetry. He wrote:

Mankind, even the most Barbarous, have the Seeds of Poetry implanted in them. The first Specimen of it was certainly shewn in the Praises of the Deity, and Prayers to him: And as they are of Natural Obligation, so they are likewise of Divine Institution. Which *Milton* observing, introduces *Adam* and *Eve,* every Morning adoring God in Hymns and Prayers. The first Poetry was thus begun, in the wild Notes of Nature, before the invention of Feet, and Measures. The *Grecians* and *Romans* had no other Original of their Poetry. Festivals and Holydays soon succeeded to Private Worship, and we need not doubt but they were enjoyn'd by the true God to his own People; as they were afterwards imitated by the *Heathens;* who by the light of Reason knew they were to invoke some Superiour Being in their Necessities, and to thank him for his Benefits.[31]

His notions on the subject have undergone no change. "God to be worshipped" is commanded both by divine institution and by natural obligation. But if the heathen peoples could learn by the light of reason of the necessity of praise and prayer "enjoyn'd by the true God to his own People," they offered them, nevertheless, not to the true God—the *"One sole* GOD*"* confidently envisioned by the deist—but to "some Superiour Being" among the wide choice of gods offered by the Greek and Roman religions.

Before leaving Dryden's second argument on behalf of the heathen, we ought to give some attention to the closing couplet. The hyperbole of his conclusion that those virtuous heathens "who follow'd *Reasons* Dictates right" perhaps "with *Socrates* may see their Maker's Face, / While Thousand *Rubrick-Martyrs* want a place" has given rise to some misunderstanding. The usual interpretation of *"Rubrick-Martyrs"* is represented by Kinsley's gloss: "contained in the calendar of saints."[32] If this were Dryden's meaning, his orthodoxy would indeed be suspect. For in awarding the preference to virtuous heathens over all those devout Christians who are numbered among the saints, and in fact raising doubts as to whether the latter are in heaven at all, he would certainly

---

[31] *Poems,* II, 622.
[32] *Ibid.,* IV, 1937.

be elevating the law of nature above that of the Gospel in the manner of his deist adversary. But this is not his intention.

By a *"Rubrick-Martyr"* Dryden means one who is a martyr not for the faith itself but for the sake of some rubric; that is to say, a ceremonial regulation of relatively minor importance. Such individuals are far different from those early witnesses to Christianity of whom Dryden had spoken earlier, *"Starving* their *Gain,* and *Martyrdom* their *Price,"* nor are they to be found in Foxe's *Book of Martyrs.* They may have suffered and even died in promoting trivial observances and some of them, in Dryden's view, may even be included among the "popish saints," but if they neglected good works they have missed salvation.

In teaching that faith must be accompanied by good works, the Latitudinarians were naturally led to attack the Calvinist doctrine of justification by faith alone. An exclusive emphasis upon faith, they argued, could encourage a neglect of moral duties. In his series of sermons "Of the Necessity of Good Works," Tillotson gives considerable attention to this distortion of true religion. He traces its appearance among the ancient Jews, of whom he remarks: "How soon did their religion degenerate into external observances, purifications and washings, and a multitude of sacrifices, without any great regard to the inward and substantial parts of religion, and the practice of those moral duties and virtues, which were in the first place required of them, and without which all the rest found no acceptance with God." He goes on to describe in some detail the degeneracy of the mediaeval church, in which "the primitive fervour of piety and devotion was turned into a fierce zeal and contention about matters of no moment and importance." Such matters as "the pope's absolute and universal authority . . . ecclesiastical liberties and immunities; and the exemption of the clergy" he describes contemptuously as "the great points which Thomas a Becket contended so earnestly for, calling it the cause of Christ, and in the maintenance whereof he persisted to the death, and was canonized as a saint and a martyr."[33] On these terms, Becket would be a *"Rubrick-Martyr"* such as Dryden describes, forced to give place to a Socrates who, deprived of the true faith, yet "follow'd *Reasons* Dictates right" by observing the law of nature, for which he may be permitted to share in the benefits of the atonement.

[33] *Works of Dr. John Tillotson,* IX, 4–9.

Dryden concludes his answer to the objection of the Deist by anticipating, and answering in advance, a possible rejoinder by his adversary. He has insisted all along that the Christian position on the necessity of revelation does not exclude the heathen from all hope of salvation as the Deist avows. Yet his antagonist could reply, in the manner of some modern critics, that Dryden is misrepresenting the Christian position in adopting so charitable a view and might appeal for support, not only to some of the more rigorist members of Dryden's own church and of other Protestant communions, but to certain ancient Christian writers as well. For as we have noticed Tillotson and Wilkins conceding, the Fathers themselves were divided on the question of the salvation of the heathen. Dryden proceeds to disarm his opponent by disposing of one of the best known weapons of this kind that might be used against himself: the prefatory anathemas to the Athanasian Creed.

> Nor does it baulk my *Charity*, to find
> Th' *Egyptian* Bishop of another mind:
> For, though his *Creed Eternal Truth* contains,
> 'Tis hard for *Man* to doom to *endless pains*
> All who believ'd not all, his Zeal requir'd;
> Unless he first cou'd prove he was inspir'd.
> Then let us either think he meant to say
> *This Faith,* where *publish'd,* was the onely way;
> Or else conclude that, *Arius* to confute,
> The good old Man, too eager in dispute,
> Flew high; and as his *Christian* Fury rose
> Damn'd all for *Hereticks* who durst *oppose*.
> [ll. 212–23]

He begins by conceding that the Athanasian Creed is a profession of eternal truths, but goes on to offer a deductive argument, in the form of an enthymeme, against accepting the anathemas in the preface to the creed as applicable to all those who do not accept the propositions which follow in the creed itself. His major premise is that only God, or a prophet demonstrably inspired by God for this purpose, possesses the authority to condemn to reprobation all members of mankind who fail to believe in a particular body of truths. His minor premise, understood but not stated, is that Athanasius could not prove that he was so inspired. We must conclude, then, that Athanasius possessed no authority to proclaim a universal anathema; consequently we must assume either that he meant only to condemn unbelievers in the Christian parts of the world, or else that, carried away by zeal, he really did intend a universal anathema which, because he exceeded his authority, enjoys no sanction.

This is the stanza to which Dryden refers in the preface to *Religio Laici* when he speaks of the objections of his "judicious and learned Friend" to whom he showed the poem before it was published. As David Brown has pointed out very perceptively, there is no warrant for the common idea that Dryden's friend—possibly Tillotson—objected to his charitable thoughts concerning the heathen, or even to his interpretation of the preface to the Athanasian Creed.[34] Dryden simply remarks that his friend "amongst some other faults recommended to my second view, what I have written, perhaps too boldly on St. *Athanasius*: which he advised me wholly to omit." He is clearly referring to his gratuitous suggestion that the saint was carried away by intemperate wrath, or "*Christian* Fury" as Dryden ironically describes it. This personal reflection on the great Doctor of the Church is merely the second of two alternative hypotheses Dryden offers to account for the preface to the creed, the other being his suggestion that the anathema was only intended for unbelievers in Christian lands. He might easily have adopted his friend's suggestion, but he refused to tamper with the poem. "I am sensible enough that I had done more *prudently* to have follow'd his opinion: But then I could not have satisfied my self, that I had done honestly not to have written what was my own." Instead, as Brown has shown, he makes amends in the preface to his poem by developing his alternative hypothesis at length and wholly omitting his personal reflections on the saint. He writes:

And now for what concerns the Holy Bishop *Athanasius,* the Preface of whose Creed seems inconsistent with my opinion; which is, That Heathens may possibly be sav'd; in the first place I desire it may be consider'd that it is the Preface onely, not the Creed it self, which, (till I am better inform'd) is of too hard a digestion for my Charity. 'Tis not that I am ignorant how many several Texts of Scripture seemingly support that Cause; but neither am I ignorant how all those Texts may receive a kinder, and more mollified Interpretation. Every man who is read in Church History, knows *that* Belief was drawn up after a long contestation with *Arrius,* concerning the Divinity of our Blessed Saviour, and his being one Substance with the

---

[34] See "Dryden's 'Religio Laici' and the 'Judicious and Learned Friend'," *Modern Language Review,* 56 (1961): 66–69.

Father; and that thus compild, it was sent abroad among the Christian Churches, as a kind of Test, which whosoever took, was look'd on as an Orthodox Believer. 'Tis manifest from hence, that the Heathen part of the Empire was not concerned in it: for its business was not to distinguish betwixt Pagans and Christians, but betwixt Hereticks and true Believers. This, well consider'd, takes off the heavy weight of Censure, which I wou'd willingly avoid from so venerable a Man; for if this Proportion, *whosoever will be sav'd*, be restrained onely, to those to whom it was intended, and for whom it was compos'd, I mean the Christians; then the Anathema, reaches not the Heathens, who had never heard of Christ, and were nothing interested in that dispute.

In this passage, written to satisfy his friend, Dryden has introduced a new argument besides repeating and greatly expanding the first of the two alternatives in the poem itself. He now argues that, in the first place, the anathemas in question appear only in the preface to the creed which presumably carries less weight of authority than the creed itself, and secondly, as in the poem, that *"This Faith,* where *publish'd,* was the onely way."* To neither of these arguments could his friend have demurred. Indeed, they follow so closely the two arguments in Gabriel Towerson's *Briefe Account of Some Expressions in Saint Athanasius His Creed* (1663) as to suggest that Dryden was using this pamphlet, or a similar one by some other Anglican divine, possibly lent by his friend. Towerson discusses the prefatory anathemas in the Athanasian Creed and then declares:

1. That *those passages* are *no part* of the Creed it selfe, and that it cannot be thought, *our Church* intended to burthen us with them. . . .
2. . . . I will conclude this briefe discourse with a passage of Dr. *Hammonds,* and I do it the rather because he is known to have been *one of this Churches greatest Champions.* It is in his *Treatise of Fundamentalls.* c. 10. Sect. 3. "As for the censures annext *to the Athanasian Creed* . . . I suppose they must be interpreted by their *opposition* to those *Heresies* that had invaded the *Church,* and which were acts of *carnality* in them that broached, and maintained them, against the *Apostolick Doctrine,* and contradictory to that *foundation* which had bin resolv'd on, as *necessary* to bring the world to the *obedience of Christ,* and were therefore to be *anathematiz'd* after this manner and with *detestation* branded and banished out of the *Church;* Not that it was hereby defin'd to be a *damnable sin,* to faile in the *understanding,* or *believing* the full matter of any of those *explications* before they were *propounded,* and when it might more

reasonably be deem'd not to be any fault of the *will,* to which this were imputable."[35]

As Towerson implies, sentiments which could be traced to the famous Henry Hammond, chaplain to Charles I, carried an authority which not many Anglicans were likely to question.

It is Dryden's arguments, however, rather than the use of authorities which would have been rejected in any case, which must be presumed to have silenced his deist adversary. This interlocutor is heard no more, and Dryden is ready to turn his attention to a second and more formidable antagonist, "the learned Father *Simon.*"

[35] *A Briefe Account of Some Expressions in Saint Athanasius His Creed* (Oxford, 1663), pp. 8–9.

6

DEFENDER OF THE FAITH:
ANGLICAN vs. CATHOLIC

The greatest paradox in *Religio Laici* is unquestionably the ambiguous relationship between that poem and Father Simon's *Critical History of the Old Testament* in the translation of Henry Dickinson. On the one hand, the entire second half of the poem is an answer to Simon's book in which Simon himself assumes the role of nonce adversary played by the Deist earlier in the poem and, like his predecessor in that role, goes down to defeat before the onslaught of Dryden's arguments. On the other hand, the second half of the poem opens with a digression to the translator of Simon's book which not only eulogizes Dickinson for having translated the history but praises Simon in the most respectful terms and credits his book with having "bred" the notions on revelation Dryden has offered in the earlier part of his poem. Confronted with such a staggering paradox, commentators on the poem have either ignored the praise and concentrated on the assault, or else have failed to see any signs in *Religio Laici* of an attack on Simon and have insisted that Dryden was an enthusiastic admirer of the French Oratorian, to whose influence the poem is an impressive monument.[1]

Modern interpretations of Simon's own character and motives

---

[1] Studies which regard *Religio Laici* as a poem written in agreement with Simon, or favorably influenced by him, include Louis I. Bredvold, *The Intellectual Milieu of John Dryden* (Ann Arbor: University of Michigan Press, 1934), *passim*, especially pp. 106–7; Victor M. Hamm, "Dryden's *Religio Laici* and Roman Catholic Apologetics," *PMLA*, 80 (1965): 190–98; Donald R. Benson, "Who 'Bred' *Religio Laici?*" *Journal of English and Germanic Philology*, 65 (1966): 238–51. For Bredvold, Simon and Dryden share the same fideistic outlook. Hamm overlooks the function of the nonce adversary in the poem and treats Simon's two speeches as expressions of

are equally rich in contradiction. The most influential modern study of Dryden offers a description of Simon and his *Critical History* with which every student of the poet is familiar. According to this view, Father Simon was a particularly acute and subtle apologist for the Catholic church who employed his *Critical History* as a controversial weapon carrying "the full impact of fideistic thought," by which he hoped "to make people sceptics" in order to "reduce them to the authority of Rome." His tactic, employed with unparalleled skill, was to convince Protestants of the obscurity and difficulty of the Scriptures, to raise doubts in their minds of its intelligibility and integrity, and to drive them to despair of its reliability so that they would seek refuge in the infallible authority of the Catholic church. The unfriendly reception which Simon's efforts met from Bossuet and the members of his own religious congregation has been seen as due to the fact that many Catholics "were afraid of 'higher criticism' as a controversial weapon" and recognized that fideism, however well intentioned as a polemical tool, is a heresy repeatedly condemned by the Catholic church.[2] This view has been put forward so convincingly that most recent critics, whether they feel that Dryden agreed with Simon or opposed him, have accepted the picture of the French Oratorian as an antirationalist, an antiscripturist, and an unusually formidable Catholic apologist.[3]

Readers whose knowledge of Father Simon has been gleaned exclusively from modern studies of Dryden may be surprised to learn that the interpretation I have been describing is practically unknown outside their own circle and is diametrically opposed, in almost every respect, to the judgment shared by his countrymen until quite recently. Simon has understandably received much more attention in France than in English-speaking countries. Until some twenty-five years ago, a nearly unanimous opinion of Simon and his *Critical History* prevailed among Frenchmen. For literary historians and critics such as Sainte-Beuve, Lanson, and Hazard, as well as for religious writers such as Claudel or

Dryden's own thought, a common mistake in commentaries on the poem. Benson, whose article appeared after this chapter was written, argues that Dryden was ignorant of the actual contents of Simon's book and thought he was praising it, but "unwittingly" discounted its basic assumptions.

[2] See Bredvold, *Intellectual Milieu*, pp. 73–77 and 98–107.

[3] Two exceptions are the article by Hamm, cited above, and Elias J. Chiasson, "Dryden's Apparent Scepticism in *Religio Laici*," *Harvard Theological Review*, 54 (1961): 207–21.

the author of the article on Simon in the *Dictionnaire de la bible,* the French Oratorian is the great rationalist, the ally of Spinoza and forerunner of the critical deists in his assault upon the religious faith of his countrymen. For these writers, Simon was indeed an antiscripturist, but in attacking the reliability of the Bible he was deliberately undermining the foundations of Christianity in the interest of free thought. Like his contemporaries Bayle and Spinoza, and his successors Voltaire and the Encyclopedists, Simon is intent on assaulting revealed religion in the name of reason.[4]

If we ask which of these two irreconcilable views of Simon and his *Critical History* is correct, the answer is that both are equally wide of the mark. In the past quarter of a century a remarkable rehabilitation of Simon's reputation has gradually taken place. No responsible historian today would describe Simon as an antiscripturist or attribute to him either of the devious motives we have been considering. There is general agreement at the present time that Simon was trying to restore the Scriptures, not attack them, and he has won a tardy acceptance in his own church and country as the founder of modern biblical criticism, a man so far ahead of his time that he met only distrust and misunderstanding from Catholic and Protestant churchmen from whom he deserved the highest praise.[5]

Simon was no more a narrow apologist than he was a freethinker. He was a remarkably objective scripturist who was engaged on a project, suggested to him by the Protestant ministers of Charenton, of producing an ecumenical translation of the

[4] For an example from each kind of writer, see the article on Simon by A. Ingold in the *Dictionnaire de la bible,* ed. F. Vigouroux, Vol. V (Paris: Letouzey et Ané, 1912), cols. 1743–46, and Paul Hazard, *The European Mind: The Critical Years (1680–1715),* trans. J. Lewis May (New Haven: Yale University Press, 1953), pp. 180–97 (this originally appeared in 1935 as *La Crise de la conscience européene*). A valuable history and bibliography of Simon's checkered reputation will be found in the article on Simon by A. Molien in the *Dictionnaire de théologie catholique,* ed. A. Vacant *et al.,* Vol. XIV (Paris: Letouzey et Ané, 1939–41), cols. 2094–2118.

[5] The most important contribution to the revision of Simon's reputation is the excellent study by Jean Steinmann, *Richard Simon et les origines de l'exégèse biblique* (Bruges: Desclée de Brouwer, 1960). An earlier effort in this direction was the article in the *Dictionnaire de théologie catholique,* cited above. For evidence that this re-estimate is becoming familiar in the English-speaking world, see the recent discussions of Simon, from a Protestant and a Catholic respectively, by Norman Sykes, "The Religion of Protestants," *Cambridge History of the Bible,* ed. S. L. Greenslade (Cambridge: At the University Press, 1963), pp. 194–95, and F. J. Crehan, "The Bible in the Roman Catholic Church from Trent to the Present Day," *ibid.* pp. 218–21.

Bible more accurate and less slanted in favor of one particular communion than any which had yet appeared. "He had the idea," his most recent biographer explains, "of a new translation purely scientific and interconfessional, that of a French Bible common to Catholics and Protestants. Naturally this Bible would avoid all tendentious translations and all partisan notes. It would be as exact a reflection of the text as possible."[6] The *Critical History of the Old Testament* (1678), to be followed by a companion volume on the New Testament, was intended to supply the prolegomena to this translation. Simon explained the design of the *Critical History* in the first chapter of his book:

Seeing this study is at this time neglected, and there are few that apply themselves to it with diligence, by reason of the great difficulties they meet with, I thought I might be profitable to the publick in giving them a critical History of the Texts of the Bible from *Moses* to our time, and of the chief Translations which have been made as well by Jews as Christians: to which I have added a project of a new Translation of the Bible, after having mark't the defects of most of those which have hitherto been made; last of all I have concluded this Work with a Criticisme upon the best Commentaries on the Bible, to the end one might not onely be instructed in the Text of the Holy Scriptures, but also in the way whereby we ought to explain them. I am perswaded one cannot read the Bible with profit, if one be not first of all instructed in that which regards the Criticisme of the Text, and one shall find herein several remarks touching the style of the Scripture, which is much more obscure than people usually think it.[7]

The kind of inquiry he had undertaken in his *Critical History* was an essential preliminary to an accurate translation of the Bible, Simon felt, because of the carelessness of his predecessors. Catholics and Protestants alike were translating and commenting on the Scriptures while grossly ignorant of, and happily indifferent to, the nature of the original texts, the conditions under which they had been written, and the manner in which they had been transmitted from one copyist to the next. In this state of affairs, rigorous textual criticism must precede the task of translation; the original version must be restored and the errors of the copyists eliminated before any thought could be given to rendering the

[6] Steinmann, *Richard Simon*, p. 93 (my translation). See pp. 91–96 for an account of the origin of the *Critical History* in the project of an ecumenical translation of the Bible.

[7] *A Critical History of the Old Testament*, trans. Henry Dickinson (London, 1682), Book I, pp. 2–3.

text of the Scriptures in another language. Furthermore, confusion had been compounded by the translators who had preceded Simon; in their ignorance of the Hebrew, with its difficult grammar and highly equivocal vocabulary, they had added their own errors to those of the copyists. Finally, the numerous commentators on the Bible had added their own share to the misunderstanding of the Scriptures: ignorant of the customs of the Middle East, of the literary forms of the various books of the Old Testament, and of the purpose of their authors, they had contributed misinterpretation to the fund of faulty translators and careless copyists. Hence the *Critical History* is divided into three books in which the histories of "the Hebrew Text of the Bible from *Moses* to our time," "the chief Translations of the Bible," and the principal commentaries on it are related respectively, the mistakes of each are discussed, and "the method for the well translating of the Scripture is treated of."

In the pursuit of his ideal of a pure and scientific biblical text free from all corruptions, Simon spared neither Catholic nor Protestant translators and commentators. As Henry Dickinson was to complain:

I could wish this Criticism had been made by some of our own Communion, who might have alter'd nothing of the substance of it, but have left out onely some small reflexions upon the Protestants; Father *Simon* however is less inveterate and makes fewer of his reflexions than could be expected from a Roman Catholick Doctour; which thing is yet more pardonable in him in that he spares not even them of his own Church.[8]

An example chosen at random from the *Critical History* will give something of Simon's tone, of the relentless argument, ironic wit, and scarcely concealed contempt for his predecessors which proved so irritating to many of his contemporaries. Brian Walton, the great English scripturist of the early seventeenth century, had repeated "the common receiv'd Opinion amongst Divines," derived from Genesis, that God had taught Adam and Eve their language in the Garden of Eden, that this language was Hebrew, and that He had later caused the diffusion of languages at the building of the Tower of Babel. To Simon this was absurd. Instead, he ascribes "the invention of all Languages to our reasonable Nature; God has given men onely an understanding to reason with, which

8 *Ibid.*, sig. A2v.

men have made use of for the expressing of their thoughts by inventing of Languages: and as this opinion does not wholly agree with the words of *Genesis*, [I lay] down for a principle that it is the usual style of the Scripture to ascribe most things to God, as if he was the onely Authour of them."[9] In answer to the generally accepted opinion expressed by Walton, Simon cites one of the Fathers, not because he is a more reverend authority, but for this reason: "I think we ought herein to prefer the Opinion of St. *Gregory* of *Nyssa*, before the common receiv'd one, because he reconciles as much as possibly he can, Faith with Reason, Philosophy with Divinity, and does not easily multiply miraculous and extraordinary things." Indeed, a profane philosopher, denounced from every Christian pulpit, can serve Simon's purpose of discarding a received opinion on the Scripture as well as any Father of the Church. He remarks:

As men have not sufficiently consider'd the several expressions of the Scripture, they have multipli'd the Miracles, and *Walton* has herein follow'd the most common Opinion. To conclude: Although I have quoted several things out of *Lucretius*, to show that Tongues were invented by the first men, I have not alledged them as Proofs, but only more clearly to explain St. *Gregory* of *Nyssa*'s Opinion upon this Subject, which I have preferr'd before any other, because he reconciles Reason with Religion. Besides, as the Question concerning the invention of the first Tongues, belongs as well to Philosophy as Divinity, it was in a manner necessary to joyn the Opinions of the Philosophers with those of the Divines, to reconcile them together if possible.

Finally, in a passage characteristic of many in the *Critical History*, Simon takes up Walton's opinion, proceeds to show that it arises from a misunderstanding of what the author of Genesis was trying to do, and ends by turning it to ridicule.

As for what *Walton* in the same place affirms, that man was no sooner created but he talk'd familiarly with God; that he gave Names to all Animals; and that *Eve* spoke to the Serpent; he can demonstrate nothing from thence, because the Scriptures set down only Matters of Fact, without taking notice of the Times when they hapned; and we cannot for example say, that *Cain* and *Abel* were born at the same time, because their birth is in the same place related. The History of the Scripture is only an Abridgement of what was thought fit to be given to the People; and therefore we ought not to conclude, that the things there related, hap'ned at the same time, because they are joyn'd

[9] "An Answer to Mr. Spanheim's Letter," *ibid.*, pp. 47–48.

together in the Discourse. Besides, we understand not well enough what Tongue *Adam* and *Eve* spoke to God and the Serpent in, thence to conclude that they were born with this first Tongue, which has since been communicated to their Posterity: For we may also thence conclude, that the Serpent was born with this same Tongue, which however has not been communicated to his Posterity.[10]

It is a mistake, of course, to conclude from Simon's manner that he was a scoffer at religion, an irreverent rationalist who ridiculed the notion that the Bible contains divine revelation; he revered the Scriptures as the word of God, but he was no respecter of persons, much less of time-honored opinions about the Bible, and he felt an undisguised contempt for those ignorant persons and mistaken opinions which had been responsible for disfiguring the sacred books. He had developed a "method for the well translating of the Scripture" which consisted in subjecting the original texts to the same rigorous scrutiny, critical and grammatical, which his contemporary, Richard Bentley in England, was soon to apply to classical texts. If this method produced results which ran counter to "the common receiv'd Opinion amongst Divines," such as the belief that Moses was the author of the Pentateuch, so much the worse for those errors inherited from the past. Like Gregory of Nyssa he would strive "to reconcile Reason with Religion." If he was a sceptic, he was one in Bacon's sense, not in that of either a Montaigne or a Bayle.

In reading Simon's book, however, it is easy to understand how the rumor that he was a freethinker began. It started in his own lifetime, on the eve of the publication of the *Critical History*, and it was to follow him to his grave. Many Christians were scandalized by his book. They had no quarrel with the commonly expressed ideal of reconciling reason with religion, but the method Simon adopted in pursuing it, that of applying the same critical standards to the Bible as to any other literary text and of rejecting the "common receiv'd Opinion amongst Divines" with such evident relish, struck them as profane and impious. All but a few copies of the *Critical History* were seized from the printer and burned by the police of Paris, the book itself was suppressed by the Council of State and later placed on the *Index of Forbidden Books,* and Simon was expelled from the Oratory. Bossuet began a crusade against Simon which he was to carry on

[10] *Ibid.,* Book III, pp. 154–55.

for the rest of his life. To the Catholic bishop, Simon was no better than an atheist, his book "a mass of impiety," "full of principles and conclusions pernicious to faith," and containing "wicked maxims."[11] Many Protestants took their cue from Bossuet and the Catholic authorities of Paris; they were not disposed to welcome the work of one who had fouled his own nest and was now in disgrace, not for having expounded heresy, but for undermining the foundations of Christianity. Friedrich Spanheim, the younger, a Calvinist, having read one of the few surviving copies of the *Critical History*, quickly issued a reply.[12] Less intemperate than Bossuet, and unwilling to attribute bad faith to Simon, he nevertheless agreed with the Catholic bishop in seeing pernicious consequences to Christianity itself in the *Critical History*. He accused Simon of impiety for having undertaken, without divine mission or authority, to meddle with the Scriptures, "as if," Simon remarked, "it were necessary for one to be directed by the Spirit of God to write upon a matter of Criticism and Grammar."[13]

The reactions of people like Bossuet and Spanheim, although they made more noise, were by no means universal. Not every educated person, Protestant or Catholic, who saw one of the few surviving copies of the *Critical History* in 1678, or read it in the Amsterdam edition of 1680, detected a threat to Christianity. Some, like Simon's Protestant friend Henri Justel, saw it as a daring, but immensely valuable, contribution to the Christian cause. Not many people could appreciate the enormous advance in biblical criticism which the book represented, or were interested in finding it, but Christians of every communion were anxious to find ammunition to add to the arsenal of apologetics. Simon realized this, of course, and in the preface to the *Critical History*, written to win the favor of his Catholic countrymen for the book, he discusses four "benefits" to be drawn from his work, which he is careful to distinguish from the "design" he had in writing it in the first place. Two of these benefits concern criticism: a thorough understanding of the different states of the biblical text, and the resolution of many difficult questions concerning the chronology and genealogies of the Scripture. The other

[11] See the account of Bossuet's attacks on Simon in Steinmann, *Richard Simon*, pp. 124–30.
[12] *Lettre à un amy où l'on rend compte d'un livre, qui a pour titre, Histoire Critique du Vieux Testament* (Amsterdam, 1679).
[13] "An Answer to Mr. Spanheim's Letter," *Critical History*, p. 41.

two benefits concern religious apologetics. One of these is a matter of what I have been calling "Christian apologetics." Simon points out that his book contains "many usefull principles for the resolving of the greatest difficulties of the Bible, and at the same time answering of the Objections which are usually brought against the Authority of the Holy Scriptures." He is referring to the cavils against inconsistencies in the text of the Scriptures which had been used to question the authenticity and inspiration of the Bible, but which could easily be explained, thanks to his study, as due to the conditions under which it was written or the alterations made by the transcribers. "We may by this same principle easily answer all the false and pernicious consequences drawn by *Spinosa* from these alterations or additions for the running down the Authority of the Holy Scripture."[14]

This benefit was one which all Christian apologists, Protestant as well as Catholic, might find useful in defending their religion. His last benefit, however, concerns Catholic apologetics alone. The great alterations which have been introduced into the text of the Bible in the course of time, as shown by his study, negate the Protestant principle that the Bible alone is the rule of faith, according to Simon, and make clear the necessity of joining tradition with the Scripture in the manner of the Catholics.

Instead of believing with the Protestants that the shortest and most certain way of deciding the questions of Faith is to consult the Holy Scriptures, we shall on the contrary find in this Work that if we join not Tradition with the Scripture, we can hardly affirm any thing for certain in Religion. We cannot be said to quit the word of God by joining therewith the Tradition of the Church, since he who refers us to the Holy Scriptures has also refer'd us to the Church whom he has trusted with this holy pledge.[15]

This was a "benefit" which some Protestant readers could gladly dispense with, and even deny, while agreeing that the *Critical History* was in many other respects an important and useful book. Charles Marie Du Veil, a French Protestant living in England, read one of the few copies of Simon's book which escaped confiscation in 1678 and immediately published a reply, translated into English five years later in 1683. Unlike Spanheim, Du Veil is not afraid that the *Critical History* will prove a danger to Christianity itself. He is solely concerned with the fact that Simon "pretends

[14] "The Author's Preface Translated out of French," *ibid.*, sigs. alv–a2.
[15] *Ibid.*, sig. bl.

182

to prove in that Work, that nothing for certain can be asserted in Religion, unless Tradition be joyned with the Scripture for the Decision of Questions of Faith."[16] To this common Catholic position he proceeds to offer the standard Protestant rejoinder.

These two earliest Protestant answers to Simon's *Critical History* by Spanheim and Du Veil, both written soon after its appearance, initiate two separate traditions of Protestant reaction to his book which were to become prominent in the next few years. On the one hand there are those like Spanheim who agree with Bossuet in regarding the book as a threat to the foundations of Christianity, in regretting its appearance, and in favoring its suppression or total condemnation. On the other hand there are those like Du Veil who regret or even answer its implications concerning the Protestant principle of *Scriptura sola* but see no danger to the authenticity and inspiration of the Bible in the book. Indeed, some of the latter even agree with Simon in regarding his study as a confirmation of the authority of the Scriptures and a valuable weapon of Christian apologetics against those who question that authority.

One of these latter was Henry Dickinson, the young Anglican layman who began to translate the *Critical History* in May of 1681 in order to bring it before the Protestant public in England. Except for the regretful reference we have noticed to "some small reflexions upon the Protestants," Dickinson ignores the "benefit" Simon had offered his fellow Catholics of disproving the Protestant doctrine concerning the rule of faith, although he scrupulously includes it in his translation. Instead, he selects Simon's other benefit to apologetics, that of proving the authority of the Bible against the cavils of anti-Christians, and presents it in his own preface "To the Reader" as his reason for making the *Critical History* available to a wider public. But in place of Spinoza, who had received much less attention in England than on the Continent, he anglicizes the cavilers against the authority of the Scripture and offers Simon's book as an effective answer to the deists. He writes:

Having seriously perus'd this Work in its Original, I thought I might

[16] *A Letter to the Honourable Robert Boyle, Esq.* (London, 1683), p. 1. Spanheim too had objected to Simon's position on tradition, as any Protestant would, but it is not the principal burden of his complaint. In his "Answer to Mr. Spanheim's Letter" (*Critical History*, pp. 41–91), Simon found it necessary to spend only three pages out of fifty on this objection of Spanheim's (pp. 87–89).

be serviceable to the publick by giving in English a Piece of so much Learning, and from whence we may draw convincing Arguments for the confuting of all the atheistical Opinions of our Age. There are a sort of half-learned men, who, searching out of the Bible those things onely which at the first sight seem to destroy the authority of it, and having found any seeming contradiction, or what they think is erroneous, will be sure to exercise their wit in publishing to the world what, in their judgment, makes any thing against the authority of those holy Books which have, through all Ages, been look'd upon, by the learned and judicious, as composed by Prophets or men inspir'd by God; without considering that, to the most understanding persons, they onely shew their ignorance, in that they understand not how to give solutions to the difficulties of the Scriptures, which belongs onely to the learned, or else their wilfull obstinacy, in resolving to oppose whatever shall be authoris'd either by Divine or Humane Authority. We have a fresh example of what I have been saying in the person of him, who, not many years ago, occasion'd the publishing of that excellent Piece, intituled, *A Letter to a Deist,* wherein the Authour has onely answer'd the Objections propos'd to him; but if the person that was so desirous to have his Scruples answer'd, or any one else, have any more of such like Objections, they may here either find them particularly discuss'd, or else be instructed in the way how to resolve them themselves.[17]

Thus the French Catholic priest, properly naturalized and put into English dress, can bear arms alongside Bishop Stillingfleet against the English deists, his unfortunate prejudice against the Protestant principle of *Scriptura sola* politely ignored.

Just as in the case of the original, the translation ran into difficulties on the eve of publication, and on the very same grounds: a fear that the book was an attack against the foundations of Christianity. Jacob Tonson had agreed in advance, in May, 1681, to publish Dickinson's translation, had accepted the copy when it was delivered later in the year, and had arranged to have it printed by Miles Fletcher.[18] He could not have been ignorant of the fact that the author was a Catholic, one "Father Simon, Priest of the Congregation of the Oratory," as the title page was to declare. He must have been aware, therefore, that it would contain "some small reflexions upon the Protestants" including, in

[17] "To the Reader," *Critical History,* sigs. A2–A2v.

[18] For the details of the complicated publishing arrangements of the *Critical History,* taken from Tonson's Bill of Complaint against Dickinson dated June 13, 1683, I am indebted to the informative article by Charles E. Ward, *"Religio Laici* and Father Simon's *History," Modern Language Notes,* 61 (1946): 407–12.

view of the subject, some objection to the Protestant principle of *Scriptura sola*. Dickinson assured him to his satisfaction, however, that "it was a learned discourse & contained nothing but what was agreeable to sound doctrine and good manners," an honest enough appraisal considering the translator's view that the *Critical History* was full of arguments confirming the divine authority of the Scriptures against the deists of the age. Toward the end of the year, when the printing was nearly finished, Tonson heard a rumor that the original version "had been publicly burnt in Paris and did contain several things which might bring the publisher into some danger." Clearly the rumor that alarmed Tonson was of Simon's supposed attempt to undermine Christianity; he could scarcely have imagined that the authorities of Paris would have objected to, much less destroyed, a book for attacking the Protestant doctrine of the rule of faith. In these circumstances, Tonson refused to publish the translation, "being apprehensive of danger," and turned over the sheets of the book to Dickinson, in return for the young man's promise to pay the costs of paper and printing.

At this point Dickinson persuaded Walter Davis, a bookseller associated with Tonson, to act as publisher, and the book appeared under the latter's imprint about January 14, 1682.[19] Warned by Tonson's reaction, and apprehensive that others would take alarm at what they believed to be an anti-Christian tract, he included this admonition in his preface "To the Reader": "If notwithstanding what I have already said, there shall be any who, at the first sight, shall be scandaliz'd with this Authour's free way of handling the Holy Scriptures, I give this caution to all such persons, either to let it alone and not concern themselves with it, or else to read it clear through, by which time I doubt not but they will be satisfy'd of their too nice scruples."[20]

Dickinson's fears proved to be well founded. His translation had scarcely been published two months when, on March 19, John Evelyn wrote an impassioned letter to John Fell, the Bishop of Oxford, beginning:

It cannot but be evident to your Reverend Lordship, to how great danger and fatal consequences the "Histoire Critique," not long since

---

[19] The book was advertized in the *Loyal Protestant and True Domestick Intelligence* on that date, according to Ward.

[20] "To the Reader," *Critical History*, sig. A2v.

published in French by Père Simon, and now lately translated (though but ill translated) into English, exposes not only the Protestant and the whole Reformed Churches abroad, but (what ought to be dearer to us) the Church of England at home, which with them acknowledges the Holy Scriptures alone to be the canon and rule of faith; but which this bold man not only labours to unsettle, but destroy. From the operation I find it already begins to have amongst divers whom I converse with, especially the young men, and some not so young neither, I even tremble to consider what fatal mischief this piece is like to create, whilst they do not look upon the book as coming from some daring wit, or young Lord Rochester revived, but as the work of a learned author, who has the reputation also of a sober and judicious person. And it must be acknowledged that it is a masterpiece in its kind; that the man is well studied in the oriental tongues, and has carried on his project with a spirit and address not ordinary amongst critics; though, after all is done, whether he be really a Papist, Socinian, or merely a Theist, or something of all three, is not easy to discover; but this is evident—as for the Holy Scriptures, one may make what one will of them, for him.[21]

Evelyn continues at some length, denouncing this "more pernicious plot than any that yet has alarmed us," a book full of "deadly blows which sap the roots," in words reminiscent of Bossuet's description of the *Critical History*. It is perfectly clear that Evelyn shares Bossuet's alarm and that his tremors are caused by something far more serious than yet another Catholic polemic against the Protestant doctrine of *Scriptura sola*.[22] It is true that this doctrine makes the Protestants particularly vulnerable, in Evelyn's view, to the attempts of any "bold man," whether a Spinoza or a Simon, not only "to unsettle, but destroy" the Holy Scriptures. But his allusion to Rochester, his fears that the book will create a "fatal mischief" among the young men of the time (generally considered susceptible to the wits and scoffers of the age), and his suspicion that Simon is a Socinian or theist (Evelyn's regular term for deists) all make apparent his conviction that the foreigner's "deadly blows" are aimed at the roots of Christianity itself. How many Anglicans joined in Evelyn's private complaint is a matter for conjecture, but presumably he was not alone.

The following month several Dissenters joined the hue and

[21] *The Diary and Correspondence of John Evelyn,* ed. John Forster (London: G. Bell and Sons, 1881), III, 264–65.

[22] Professor Bredvold prints the letter, but interprets it as the discovery of an ingenious Catholic plot against the Protestants (*Intellectual Milieu,* pp. 104–5).

cry over Dickinson's translation. William Lorimer published *An Examination of a Considerable Part of Père Simon's Critical History of the Old Testament*. The author's answer is in the tradition of Spanheim. He wastes no time over the Protestant rule of faith, which Du Veil had been concerned to justify, but goes to the defense of the Mosaic authorship of the Pentateuch, against the objections of not only Simon but Spinoza as well. By denying this, he feels, Simon had raised serious doubts as to the divine inspiration of the first five books of the Old Testament. To this little book the leading English Dissenter, Richard Baxter, contributed a preface, dated April 7, in which he explains that there has "been lately Published in *English,* a Book of *P. Simon's,* Intituled, *A Critical History of the Old Testament*" to which the accompanying pamphlet offered an admirable rejoinder.[23]

By late spring it was apparent that all this hostility was seriously prejudicing the sale of the translation. The printer was still unpaid, and Tonson, "sensible that he stood engaged for the paper and printing" which he had himself commissioned from Miles Fletcher, agreed to make the best of a bad bargain. He paid off the printer, took over the remaining sheets of the book, and reissued them in May under his own imprint, in spite of his former misgivings. He was later to complain of "not having heard of the offence that the said book had given," referring, apparently, to the clamor caused by the translation, since he had shown himself perfectly aware some months earlier of the trouble in Paris over the original version of the book. Somewhat disingenuously perhaps, Dickinson assured him that no exception had been made to the translation; if he was referring to an official exception, the statement was technically correct, for the book had not been presented by a grand jury. The two men showed that they were perfectly aware that something must be done to allay public hostility toward the book, however, and two steps in that direction were taken before it was reissued.

First of all, Dickinson translated Simon's reply to Spanheim, written under the pseudonym of a theologian of the Faculty of

[23] *An Examination of a Considerable Part of Père Simon's Critical History of the Old Testament, wherein all his objections, with the weightiest of Spinosa's, against Moses's being the author of the first Five Books of the Bible are answered* (London, 1682), p. 62. The pamphlet is the second part of *An Excellent Discourse Proving the Divine Original and Authority of the Five Books of Moses* by "Mr. Dubois de la Cour" (Jean Filleau de La Chaise).

Paris, and gave it to Tonson to include in his reissue of the *Critical History*. Simon had published separate answers to Spanheim and Du Veil, both of which were available to Dickinson. His decision to translate only the former is significant. There was no need for Simon's reply to Du Veil; no issue had yet been raised in England concerning Simon's attack on the Protestant doctrine of the rule of faith, and in any case it would have been tactless to have published the French priest's reply, which dealt exclusively with his defense of the Catholic position on this question. Spanheim, however, had raised the very issues that were disturbing English critics of the translation, and it was a clever tactic to introduce Simon's rejoinder, with its spirited apologia for his "free way of handling the Holy Scriptures" which was causing so much scandal. Thus, when the reissue appeared, the new title page was able to boast "a Supplement, being a Defence of *The Critical History*, in Answer to Mr. *Spanheim*'s Treatise against it."

Secondly, commendatory poems with which to introduce the new issue were solicited from prominent poets. When the translation reappeared in May it carried a new initial gathering which included, besides the new title page with Tonson's imprint, three poems: "To his Friend the Translatour of Father Simon" by Richard Duke, "To the Ingenious Translatour of the Admirable Simon" by Nathanael Lee, and "To the Authour and Translatour of the following Book" by Nahum Tate; six months later when Tonson published Dryden's *Religio Laici*, the poem included a substantial *"Digression to the Translatour of Father Simon's Critical History of the Old Testament."*

It is commonly assumed that all this poetic production is a tribute to the friendship Dickinson enjoyed with some of the leading poets of his time. Yet there is no evidence of his having been previously acquainted with any of these men except Duke. The latter had been a classmate of Dickinson's at Trinity, Cambridge, and is the only one of the poets to refer to the translator as his friend in the title of his poem. Duke, who had been winning attention for his poems since 1679 and possessed a wide circle of friends, could certainly have introduced his former classmate to the other poets. But it is difficult to believe that this obscure young man, about whom almost nothing is known, was on sufficiently intimate terms with these prominent poets and playwrights to ask and win the favor of their writing poems to him.

It has never, I believe, been noticed that a remarkable coinci-

dence occurred at just this time. Since November of the previous
year, Tonson had been publishing Dryden's *Absalom and Achitophel* in a joint arrangement with Walter Davis, and the sales
had been extremely encouraging. In the spring of 1682 the poem
had reached a third edition, and Tonson had enlarged the little
book by including three commendatory poems to introduce Dryden's work. The three poems were by Richard Duke, Nathanael
Lee, and Nahum Tate, the same trio who were now, within a few
weeks, called upon to boost another book published by Tonson
and sold by Davis.[24]

If these three poet-playwrights had been Grub Street hacks, or
in Tonson's employ, we might easily conclude that they were
required to puff Tonson's productions in the way Dryden apparently performed a similar service in prose for Henry Herringman
at the start of his career. But they were not hack writers nor young
men who still had to make their way in the world, and none of
them was in Tonson's employ. Lee was by this time one of the
foremost dramatists in London, Tate had already achieved prominence as a poet and playwright and within ten years was to become
Poet Laureate, and Duke, while younger, was a poetaster and
friend of courtiers, who could write to please himself. Furthermore, Tonson was not even the regular publisher of any of the
three men, although he was certainly acquainted with Lee and
Tate and had published a play for each of them.[25]

The link between Tonson and these three poet-playwrights is
Dryden. Tonson had been Dryden's regular publisher since 1679,
and in 1680 the two men had begun the series of business ventures in translations and miscellanies which were to link their
fortunes closely for the remainder of Dryden's life. Duke, Lee,
and Tate were not only friends of Dryden, they were all active
collaborators with him at this time. Dryden and Lee, who had
already collaborated on *Oedipus* (1679), were busily engaged on
the joint authorship of *The Duke of Guise* in the spring of 1682,
from about the beginning of April until the end of June. As soon

[24] The poems by Duke and Lee were added to the second edition (Macdonald 12 e)
at the end of 1681 or beginning of 1682. Tate's poem was added to the third edition
(Macdonald 12 f) early in 1682, the three poems appearing together in this and all
subsequent editions. See Hugh Macdonald, *John Dryden: A Bibliography of Early
Editions and of Drydeniana* (Oxford: Clarendon Press, 1939), pp. 23–24.

[25] Lee's regular publisher was Richard Bentley, but Tonson published his *Lucius
Junius Brutus* in 1681. Tate made use of a variety of publishers, Tonson publishing
his *Brutus of Alba* in 1678.

as this task was finished, Dryden stood engaged to Tonson to collaborate with Tate on *The Second Part of Absalom and Achitophel,* which was finished early in the following autumn. Duke had been one of Dryden's collaborators in the translation of *Ovid's Epistles* (1680) for Tonson two years earlier.

It was therefore appropriate that these three men should have contributed commendatory verses to the later editions of *Absalom and Achitophel.* In this case their efforts were purely honorific, for their friend's poem was selling perfectly well by itself. But in the case of the *Critical History,* I suggest that Tonson turned to Dryden in his difficulties, and that Dryden solicited the aid of his friends and collaborators as a favor to Tonson. In this event, the initiative would have come from Tonson rather than from Dickinson. The latter, now quit of his financial obligations for the book, had nothing at stake but a young man's vanity in his first work. Tonson, however, stood in danger of losing a sum equal to half of Dryden's annual salary as Poet Laureate. If my supposition is correct, Dryden's interest in the *Critical History* was not enlisted at once upon its original publication in January, as Ward and others have supposed, but was more probably awakened by Tonson in April or May of 1682.[26]

The commendatory poems which Duke, Lee, and Tate proceeded to write betray their origin as a rescue operation. In the first place, they devote far less attention to the translator of the *Critical History,* to whom the verses were ostensibly written, than to its original author. This is understandable, since it was not Dickinson who had attracted such unfavorable attention from English readers, but Simon; the poets now attempt to restore the balance by lavish encomia of the French priest. Secondly, they pick up the two points Dickinson had already stressed in his preface "To the Reader" and develop them repeatedly: Dickinson had praised Simon's book as "a Piece of so much Learning," and the poets set about emphasizing this as its principal virtue; the young translator had expounded its beneficial use for confirming the authority of the Scriptures, and the poets declare that its availability for this purpose is nothing less than providential. Finally, the poets adopt the offensive and freely attack the critics of Simon's book.

[26] For the older view, see Ward, "*Religio Laici* and Father Simon's *History*," pp. 411–12, and the same author's *Life of John Dryden* (Chapel Hill: University of North Carolina Press, 1961), p. 179.

Whereas the other two poets practically ignore the translator whom they are addressing, Duke, who was his friend, does at least begin by contrasting Dickinson to his advantage with the other translators of recent works from France. While they have wasted their efforts frivolously on novels, farces, and plays, Dickinson has been rendering "this noble Piece" into English. This allows Duke to praise Simon's book for its great learning before turning on its critics and answering them:

> Nor let ill-grounded, superstitious fear
> Fright any but the fools from reading here.
> The sacred Oracles may well endure
> Th'exactest search, of their own truth secure;
> Though at this Piece some noisy Zelots bawl,
> And to their aid a numerous Faction call
> With stretch'd out arms, as if the Ark could fall;
> Yet wiser heads will think so firm it stands,
> That, were it shook, 'twould need no mortal hands.

Lee, after a passing compliment to Dickinson for his courage, because "this Master-piece you dare produce, / Which Providence design'd for wondrous use," launches at once into a eulogy of Father Simon:

> So strong, so true, so just his Deathless Fame,
> All Pens must draw his Triumph to proclaim,
> And all conspire to bless the Father's name.

He too emphasizes the enormous learning of the *Critical History*, "All Arts, all Sciences together hurld, / As if his Library had been the World," before rounding on its critics. Just as Duke had described them as zealots, so Lee dismisses them as fanatics:

> He then that dares to reade and not admire,
> Let him fry on in his Fanatick Fire,
> Be bound to Nonsense, all his life a Slave,
> And lye forgotten in a common Grave.

Tate ignores the book's critics and concentrates on its great benefit to religion. He praises Simon, in terms more often applied at the time to Bacon, as the restorer of learning who has rescued sacred truth from the errors of the past:

> So you, from Chains of Darkness which they wore,
> The Captiv'd *Oracles* themselves Restore.
> Hail, inspir'd *Father,* who couldst force thy Way
> Through Nights vast Empire to the Realm of Day.

191

Simon is reminiscent of Bacon too in his discovery of a new method which is responsible for his remarkable achievement in reinforcing the divine authority of the Scriptures:

> One Age dissolves (such Force your Judgment bears)
> The settling Clouds of many Thousand years.
> To Vindicate the Sacred Books, a New,
> But onely Certain Method, you pursue,
> And shewing Th' are Corrupted, prove 'em True.

Let us turn now to the *"Digression to the Translatour of Father Simon's Critical History of the Old Testament"* with which Dryden introduces the second half of *Religio Laici*, after finishing his answer to the objection of the Deist.

> Thus far my Charity this path has try'd;
> (A much unskilfull, but well meaning guide:)
> Yet what they are, ev'n these crude thoughts were bred
> By reading that, which better thou hast read,
> Thy Matchless Author's work: which thou, my Friend,
> By well translating better dost commend:
> Those youthfull hours which, of thy Equals most
> In *Toys* have *squander'd,* or in *Vice* have *lost,*
> Those hours hast thou to Nobler use employ'd;
> And the severe Delights of Truth enjoy'd.
> Witness this weighty Book, in which appears
> The crabbed Toil of many thoughtfull years,
> Spent by thy Authour, in the Sifting Care
> Of *Rabbins* old Sophisticated Ware
> From Gold Divine; which he who well can sort
> May afterwards make *Algebra* a Sport.
> A Treasure, which if *Country-Curates* buy,
> They *Junius,* and *Tremellius* may defy:
> Save pains in various readings, and Translations;
> And without *Hebrew* make most learn'd quotations.
> A Work so full with various Learning fraught,
> So nicely pondred, yet so strongly wrought,
> As Natures height and Arts last hand requir'd:
> As much as Man cou'd compass, uninspir'd.
> Where we may see what *Errours* have been made
> Both in the *Copiers* and *Translaters Trade*:
> How *Jewish, Popish,* Interests have prevail'd,
> And where *Infallibility* has *fail'd.*
>
> [ll. 224–51]

One cannot fail but see that this long stanza is a digression in a far more important sense than the obvious one that Dryden has interrupted his discourse to turn to, and for the first time directly address, the "Friend" to whom his Horatian epistle is written. It is a digression also because the form and structure of this stanza deviate radically from those of the remainder of the poem. Whereas the rest of the poem is in the form of a polemical discourse possessing a logical structure in which issues are raised and arguments adduced to answer them in a modification of the Horatian epistle, this stanza is a complete and perfect example of the commendatory verse epistle, an entirely different poetic form the purpose of which is panegyric, not polemic; its structure one of amplification, not sequential argument. Among Dryden's own verses, this stanza is much closer to such poems as "To my Honour'd Friend, Dr. Charleton, on his learned and useful Works" or "To my Honored Friend, Sir Robert Howard, On his Excellent Poems" than to the rest of the poem of which it forms a part.

Furthermore, these commendatory verses to the translator of Father Simon are remarkably similar to those, of about the same length, which Dryden's three friends had written. Although they are immensely superior to these other efforts as poetry, Dryden's verses elaborate essentially the same themes. The greatest share of his eulogy is reserved for Simon and his accomplishment rather than for the translator he is addressing. Like Duke, he begins by contrasting Dickinson to his advantage with the young man's contemporaries who have wasted their "youthfull hours," but the compliment acquires its force from the importance of the book which Dickinson has spent his time in translating. This leads him to praise Simon's work for its enormous learning, as his friends had done. For Duke the book was "With various learning, knowledge, strength of thought, / Order and art, and solid judgment fraught." For Dryden too it is "a Work so full with various Learning fraught, / So nicely pondred, yet so strongly wrought" that it commands admiration. Finally he stresses, like his friends, Simon's achievement in restoring the Scripture from ancient error, "Where we may see what *Errours* have been made / Both in the *Copiers* and *Translaters Trade*," and implies that it reinforces the divine authority of the Bible. Indeed, he declares that his notions in the first half of *Religio Laici,* including his proofs that the Scriptures are the repository of divine revelation, were bred by reading Simon's book.

193

In view of these facts, *Religio Laici* may have originated in a short commendatory poem, "To the Translatour of Father Simon's *Critical History of the Old Testament*," which Dryden wrote in April or May of 1682 when he was soliciting similar poems from his friends. On this supposition, the poem, of less than thirty lines, was intended to take its place alongside those of his friends at the beginning of Tonson's new issue of the *Critical History*.[27] But Dryden apparently changed his mind, perhaps before his verses were even in final shape, as he began to see the possibility of a much more ambitious undertaking. In this case, he would have set the verses aside to await the opportunity of greater leisure which, in view of his present commitments, could not have been available much before the end of the summer.[28] Tonson, offered the prospect of a major poem by his most distinguished writer, could only have rejoiced in such an arrangement.

Neither Tonson nor anyone else, of course, could have persuaded Dryden to write even the briefest of verses in praise of Simon's *Critical History* if his reaction to the book had not squared with this proposal. Fifteen years later he stubbornly refused to acquiesce in Tonson's suggestion that he promote the sale of his own *Virgil* by writing a dedication to William III, whom he considered a usurper. A scriptural critic like Simon who challenged entrenched opinion, raised doubts concerning the judgment of ancient commentators, and boldly proposed a new method of dealing with the problems of exegesis was not likely to alienate an admirer of Bacon. Simon stood revealed as just such a sceptical critic as Dryden had long considered himself to be, and the fact that the Frenchman had attracted the hostility of obscurantists would have further insured Dryden's sympathy. As I pointed out in an earlier chapter, freedom of inquiry ought

[27] A poem of this length, which would have required both sides of a single leaf, could easily have been included in Tonson's new preliminary gathering. As it stands now, the first leaf of the gathering is a blank fly leaf, the new title page appearing on the recto of the second leaf, the commendatory verses on the third and fourth leaves. It is the function of the fly leaf in Restoration books to carry the imprimatur of the licenser on the verso, facing the title page. Dickinson's translation carries no license, however, the Licensing Act having temporarily lapsed at this time. By a different imposition of the type pages, the title page could have appeared on the first leaf of the gathering, saving another leaf for commendatory verses.

[28] Dryden contributed only about two hundred lines to *The Second Part of Absalom and Achitophel*. He must therefore have been quit of his share of this poem of over eleven hundred lines some time before Tate, who did not finish the task until the end of September or perhaps even October.

not to apply to matters of religion in the opinion of Dryden and most of his contemporaries. But this was the very point on which Simon and his defenders differed from those who had taken scandal at his book. His critics, Simon charged, were guilty of confusing criticism and grammar with religion, yet "there is a great deal of difference betwixt that which concerns the Articles of our Faith, and that which belongs simply to Criticisme."[29] The Scriptures were no more exempt from the disciplines proper to textual study than any other writings, and the biblical critic was entitled to apply these disciplines in a spirit of freedom of inquiry without being accused of impiety or considered a religious innovator. "They who search after truth it self without prejudice," Simon had proclaimed, "value not persons names nor their antiquity, especially in things not relating to Faith."[30]

The poem of some 450 lines which Dryden began in the late summer or early autumn of 1682 was no longer designed as a tribute to either Simon or Dickinson, nor as a favor to Tonson, who had long since written off the *Critical History* as a loss and bartered most of the copies with other booksellers. Dryden's lines "To the Translatour of Father Simon's *Critical History of the Old Testament*" could provide the nucleus of the poem he now began to write, but it need not have first suggested the subject of *Religio Laici*. He may previously have meditated some kind of answer to one or both of the opponents of his Church, deists and Catholics, with whom he deals in his poem. During the preceding twelve months, Dryden had emerged as a public orator, "armed with the power of verse," who spoke on political issues with persuasive authority. In short order he had written *Absalom and Achitophel* and *The Medal,* and had collaborated in the writing of *The Duke of Guise* and *The Second Part of Absalom and Achitophel,* all undertaken to defend the Crown and assault its enemies. Conceivably, Dryden, or some of his friends, may have reasoned that one who could so ably defend the state ought to bring his peculiar talents to bear in defending the church as well, and in attacking some of its enemies. From long habits of occasional composition, he had come to appreciate the advantage of some recent event—the striking of a medal, for example—in providing the opportunity for his poems. At this juncture, the unfavorable pub-

[29] *Critical History,* Book I, p. 8.
[30] "The Author's Preface," *ibid.,* sig. b2.

licity which followed the appearance of Dickinson's translation would have offered him the excuse he was seeking for a defense of the Church of England against deists and Catholics alike.

The *Critical History* provided a perfect link between these completely different adversaries, thanks to the two benefits for religious apologetics which Simon had claimed in his preface, and to Dickinson's modification of one of these to suit English needs. Here was a book which was supposed to assert the divine authority of the Scriptures, to the confusion of the deists according to Dickinson, but at the same time to proclaim the Catholic view of the rule of faith, to the dismay of all good Protestants. The first was an advantage which Dickinson and his supporters had been quick to acclaim; the second was an embarrassment which so far they had preferred to ignore. By adding or altering the opening and closing lines of the little complimentary poem to Dickinson, Dryden could make it the fulcrum of his polemical discourse; a perfectly appropriate digression to the person to whom his Horatian epistle was addressed which could serve at the same time as a remarkably smooth transition between the two halves of the poem. In a fictitious explanation of his occasion for addressing a lengthy epistle to the translator, Dryden can declare that his thoughts in the first half of the poem, where he had defended the divine authority of the Scriptures against the cavils of the deists, had been bred by reading Simon's book, which was supposed to promote this identical advantage. But at the same time he had naturally objected to Simon's equally prominent predilection for tradition and his severe reflections on the Protestant doctrine of *Scriptura sola.* Therefore he proceeds in the second half of his poem to answer Simon's criticism and to defend the Protestant position on this question.

I have called this explanation fictitious, as rhetorical strategy frequently is; there is no more literal truth in the statement that Dryden's notions in the first half of *Religio Laici* were bred by reading Simon's *Critical History* than there is in the modest pose which describes his views on the salvation of the heathen as "crude thoughts," or in the convention of the Horation epistle which represents the verses as a letter to an intimate friend. We have already seen where Dryden got his arguments against the Deist; he did not take them from Simon's book, nor could he have found them there if he had looked. It is enough that Simon and Dryden had each, in very different ways, supported the divine authority of the Scriptures for Dryden's claim to appear sufficiently plausible to serve as a transition to the second half of the poem, where the *Critical History* assumes real importance. Even as a preparation for this latter part of the poem, Dryden's assertion that he has been reading Simon's book need not refer to any prolonged activity. He certainly would have read "The Author's Preface," which describes the book's "benefits," and he may have glanced at the "Table of Chapters," which briefly summarizes the contents of each, and the opening chapter, which explains the author's "design." An acquaintance with these, and perhaps a brief look at some of the chapters of Books II and III which deal with the Protestant translators and commentators, would have been enough to furnish Dryden with the two rhetorical interjections he attributes to Simon in the poem, the first to state the Catholic position, the second to raise an objection to Dryden's arguments.

Rhetorical strategy also accounts for the bantering tone of some, but not all, of Dryden's lines in praise of the *Critical History*. To the poet, it is a "weighty Book" in every sense, ponderous as well as heavy, deep but also dull, filled with "the crabbed Toil of many thoughtfull years, / Spent by thy Authour," who had not yet celebrated his fortieth birthday when the book was suppressed; a work "which he who well can sort / May afterwards make *Algebra* a Sport." Furthermore, its probable benefit to many of the clergy is something less than the high hopes expressed by its author and its translator:

> A Treasure, which if *Country-Curates* buy,
> They *Junius,* and *Tremellius* may defy:
> Save pains in various readings, and Translations;
> And without *Hebrew* make most learn'd quotations.
>
> [ll. 240–43]

Dryden apparently relished this witticism at the expense of the country clergy. Fifteen years later he was to repeat it in slightly different form in the "Dedication to the *Aeneis*": "If I desir'd to appear more Learned than I am, it had been as easie for me to have taken their Objections and Solutions [out of Macrobius and Pontanus], as it is for a Country Parson to take the Expositions of the Fathers out of *Junius* and *Tremellius*."[31] An even greater

---

[31] *The Poems of John Dryden,* ed. James Kinsley (Oxford: Clarendon Press, 1958), III, 1038. (Hereafter referred to as *Poems.*) Simon discusses the shortcomings of Junius and Tremellius in the *Critical History,* Book II, p. 155.

show of learning can be made by the country curate who has the foresight to purchase a copy of the *Critical History*; he can effortlessly detail the errors of these two great translators of the Bible to the amazement of his rural congregation.

Dryden's apparent stupefaction on turning these pages bristling with recondite learning is not meant to detract from the importance of Simon's book; it serves his rhetorical purpose by helping to establish an appropriate subjective *ethos,* reinforcing his self-portrait as "a much unskilfull, but well meaning guide." We are reminded once again that the poet is only a layman, with a "due sense of my own weakness and want of Learning," to whom this monument of scriptural exegesis makes about as much sense as a treatise on algebra. The reminder comes at a crucial point in the poem. Up to now he has been dealing with the Deist, a coffee-house wit of no great learning, one of that breed who can repeat the slogans of Lord Herbert but who "onely shew their ignorance," as Dickinson remarked, "in that they understand not how to give solutions to the difficulties of the Scriptures." Such an opponent is an easy target for another layman who shows some understanding of the rules of logic and an acquaintance with the traditional "reasons for the Christian religion." But "the learned Father *Simon*" is another matter. Before attempting to challenge this adversary on even a single point, Dryden cheerfully admits that he cannot match his great learning. His only weapon against this Goliath, he implies, is a sturdy common sense, tempered with a sense of humor. His actual tactics, of course, are not quite so ingenuous, but they reveal all the same his canny refusal to fight on his opponent's ground, choosing instead a terrain better suited to his own resources.

These resources include, in the first place, those "helps" he spoke of in the preface to his poem, "taken from the Works of our own Reverend Divines of the Church of *England.*" Such helps were plentiful. In challenging the Protestant principle of *Scriptura sola,* Simon had not introduced some new and unheard of issue into the arena of religious polemics. He had merely alluded to one of the basic sources of disagreement between Catholics and Protestants, the subject of numerous debates between apologists for the two churches for more than a century. Simon had no wish to set this controversy on a new footing, for he believed that apologetics was out of place in a serious historical investigation such as he was conducting. Indeed, for Scripture studies "we ought not to rely upon Authors who have writ upon matters of Controversie; because in Disputes the Medium is seldom kept, which is necessary to be observ'd for the finding out of Truth. An Author ought no longer to be credited when he declares himself to be of a Party, because he suits all things to his Prejudices."[32] He was content, therefore, to suggest that the results of his own independent investigation could be used by those who favored the Catholic side of this long-standing debate, the principles of which remained unchanged. As a result, Dryden did not have to rely on a Protestant answer to Simon in particular, which was fortunate, since the only such reply devoted to the issue of the sufficiency of Scripture which had yet appeared, Du Veil's in the original French version, was a tedious compendium of quotations, as useless as Stillingfleet's *Letter to a Deist* would have been for the earlier half of *Religio Laici*.

Instead, he had at his disposal a long series of Anglican classics which had expounded the Protestant position of *Scriptura sola* in the course of forgotten debates with earlier Catholic antagonists who had shared Simon's view of the question: William Chillingworth's *Religion of Protestants a Safe Way to Salvation* (1638), the famous *Relation of the Conference betweene William Lawd and Mr. Fisher the Jesuite* (1639), Edward Stillingfleet's *Rational Account of the Grounds of Protestant Religion* (1665), and Tillotson's *Rule of Faith* (1666), to name only a few of the best known and most frequently reprinted classics of this kind. Hooker's *Of the Laws of Ecclesiastical Polity*, although the result of an engagement with Elizabethan Puritans, was another well-known treatment of the Anglican view of the place and use of the Scriptures with which Dryden was certainly familiar, for he quotes from it in the preface to *Religio Laici*. In addition to these and other classics of controversy, a steady stream of tracts and pamphlets, supplemented by sermons preached from the pulpit and later issued from the press, endlessly repeated the arguments on behalf of *Scriptura sola* in the face of Catholic criticism.

With such a wealth of material at his disposal, Dryden did not have to rely on a single book as he had done in the case of Wolseley's answer to the relatively recent challenge of deism. His reference, in the plural, to the "Works" of "Divines" implies that he consulted several books, at least, besides Hooker's *Laws*, which

[32] *Ibid.*, Book III, p. 140.

was in front of him when he wrote the preface to *Religio Laici*. But of course most of these arguments must have been familiar to him already if he was in the habit of attending church and listening to the sermons with any attention. His different manner of gathering the "helps" he used against each of his opponents is obvious in the two halves of his poem. In the first half of *Religio Laici* the arguments are tightly compact. Dryden compresses a long series of arguments into his verse, since he is closely following a single source and wishes to abridge a considerable amount of material from this book. For example, one passage of 42 lines includes five major arguments which Wolseley had required 78 pages to develop adequately. In the second half of the poem, however, which consists of almost exactly the same number of lines as the first, the arguments are far fewer and they are developed at greater length. The compact manner of the first part of the poem gives way to a more expansive approach, and in place of the bookish quality of his earlier arguments Dryden exhibits greater independence.

Enjoying more freedom, perhaps because of greater familiarity with his material, Dryden is able to exploit other resources besides books of Anglican apologetics and to display his own peculiar talents as a controversialist in the course of using the helps provided by his more learned confreres. These other resources, more congenial to his own talents, include a remarkable facility for employing other modes of persuasion besides *logos*; in particular, he gives careful attention to *ethos*. It is hardly a coincidence that all three of his overt uses of subjective *ethos* in the poem itself, carefully designed to establish a self-portrait that will win the reader's sympathy and assent, occur in the second half of *Religio Laici*. Nor is objective *ethos* absent. Whereas Dryden makes no attempt to characterize his opponent in the first half of his poem (except for the use of abusive epithets like "vain, wretched Creature" and "poor Worm") so that the Deist remains a generalized portrait, he is careful to particularize Father Simon in some detail. His opponent is learned yet pedantic, intelligent yet sly—and not even, as we shall see, completely sincere—all modifications designed to place him at something of a disadvantage. But in addition to these time-honored modes of persuasion, Dryden offers a pyrotechnic display of rhetorical strategies for winning an argument, scoring debating points against his opponent with obvious enjoyment.

His opening gambit avoids a frank assault on his learned adversary in favor of a more subtle ploy: he claims Simon and his admirable book for his own side. Dryden prepares the way for this maneuver toward the end of the *"Digression to the Translatour."* After expressing wonder at the erudite contents of the *Critical History* and wryly musing on the possible uses to which they may be put, he abandons his bantering tone and in the four lines beginning "A Work so full with various Learning fraught" offers a genuine tribute to the book in terms reminiscent of those applied to it by his friends. But when he goes on to explain the importance of the *Critical History* in the closing lines of the stanza, it begins to appear that the book offers another benefit which Dickinson and the other poets had unaccountably overlooked:

> Where we may see what *Errours* have been made
> Both in the *Copiers* and *Translaters Trade*:
> How *Jewish, Popish,* Interests have prevail'd,
> And where *Infallibility* has *fail'd.*
>
> [ll. 248–51]

These lines, which contain the hints for two separate arguments Dryden is about to develop, suggest a startling paradox. This book by a Catholic priest is actually a godsend for Protestant apologists. The Church of England has nothing to fear from "the severe Delights of Truth" contained in Simon's work, for truth is on the side of the Protestants.

Dryden begins his opening argument by suggesting that Simon was by no means unaware of this paradox himself:

> For some, who have his secret meaning ghes'd,
> Have found our Authour not too *much* a *Priest*:
> For *Fashion-sake* he seems to have recourse
> To *Pope,* and *Councils,* and *Traditions* force:
> But he that *old* Traditions cou'd subdue,
> Cou'd not but find the weakness of the *New*:
> If *Scripture,* though deriv'd from *heav'nly birth,*
> Has been but carelesly preserv'd on *Earth*;
> If *God's own People,* who of *God* before
> Knew what we know, and had been promis'd more,
> In fuller Terms, of Heaven's assisting Care,
> And who did neither *Time,* nor *Study* spare
> To keep this Book *untainted, unperplext*;
> Let in gross *Errours* to corrupt the *Text*:
> Omitted *paragraphs,* embroyl'd the *Sense*;

201

With vain *Traditions* stopt the gaping Fence,
Which every common hand pull'd up with ease:
What Safety from such *brushwood-helps* as these?
If *written words* from time are not secur'd,
How can we think have *oral Sounds* endur'd?
Which *thus* transmitted, if *one* Mouth has fail'd,
Immortal Lyes on *Ages* are intail'd:
And that some such have been, is prov'd too plain;
If we consider *Interest, Church,* and *Gain.*

[ll. 252–75]

The first two lines of this stanza have been quoted as often as any in the poem. Taken out of context, they have been cited repeatedly by Hazard and others as one more piece of testimony that Simon was a scoffer at Christianity. In the context of this stanza and the preceding one, however, it is perfectly clear that Dryden is merely suggesting, in line with his rhetorical strategy here, that Father Simon is "not too *much* a *Priest*" of the Catholic church; for *"Fashion-sake"* he mechanically repeats the appeals "to *Pope, and Councils,* and *Traditions* force" expected of one of his cloth, but he is far too intelligent to have missed the a fortiori argument Dryden urges here: "If *written words* from time are not secur'd, / How can we think have *oral Sounds* endur'd?" Surely "he that *old* Traditions cou'd subdue, / Cou'd not but find the weakness of the *New*": in his heart, Simon is a Protestant!

Whatever Dryden may have thought of the sincerity of Father Simon's profession to be a loyal Catholic, the fact is that he completely misunderstood what the French priest meant by tradition. The latter might very well have regarded as unexceptionable Dryden's argument, "If *written words* from time are not secur'd, / How can we think have *oral Sounds* endur'd," without thereby abandoning any part of Catholic belief. For he would have demurred at the notion that tradition consisted of oral sounds. In "The Author's Preface" he explains what he means by tradition:

As for the New Testament, the Gospel was established in many Churches before any thing of it was writ, and since that time S. *Irenaeus, Tertullian* and the other first Fathers have not, in their disputes against Hereticks, had recourse so much to the word of God contained in the Holy Scriptures, as to this same word which was not written but preserv'd in the chief Churches which had been founded by the Apostles.

When these Bishops were assembled in Councils they every one declar'd the belief of their own Church; so that this belief receiv'd in the first Churches serv'd afterwards as a rule for the explaining of the difficult places of the Scripture. Wherefore the Fathers of the Council of *Trent* wisely ordain'd that no one should interpret the Scripture against the common opinion of the Fathers; and this same Council made the not written Traditions to be of equal authority with the word of God contain'd in the Holy Scriptures, because it suppos'd that those Traditions which were not writ proceeded from our Saviour who communicated them to his Apostles, and from thence they at last came down to us.

We may call these Traditions an abridgment of the Christian Religion, which has been since the beginning of Christianity in the first Churches apart from the Holy Scripture. By this ancient abridgment of the Christian Religion we ought to explain the difficulties of the Scripture.[33]

In referring to the famous decree of the Council of Trent which accepted tradition as sharing equal authority with Scripture, both of which comprise the rule of faith, Simon is careful to use the words "not written" (*non scripta*) by which the council had described tradition.[34] He consistently employs this expression in alluding to tradition, never Dryden's term "oral," which is not synonymous.

"A doctrine is called 'not written'," Cardinal Bellarmine explained, "not because it has never been written, but because it was not written by a first author [i.e., one of the Evangelists]. Take, for example, the Baptism of infants. Infant Baptism is called a not written apostolic tradition, because it is not found written in any apostolic book, although it is written in the books of nearly all the ancient Fathers."[35] Similarly, an English Jesuit declares: "Neither do we distinguish Tradition from the written word, because Tradition is not written by any, or in any booke or writing; but because it is not written in the scripture or Bible."[36]

That Simon also understood the words "not written" in this sense is clear from his account of the rise of tradition. It first emerged as the Gospel preached by the Apostles "before any thing of it was writ." It continued to be preached by their successors in

---

[33] "The Author's Preface," *ibid.*, sigs. bl–blv.
[34] Fourth Session, April 8, 1546.
[35] Robert Bellarmine, *Disputationes de Controversiis Christianae Fidei* (Paris: 1608), Vol. I, col. 162. My translation.
[36] Edward Knott, *Infidelity Unmasked, or, The Confutation of a Booke Published by Mr. William Chillingworth under This Title, The Religion of Protestants a Safe Way to Salvation* (Ghent, 1652), p. 254.

the churches founded by the Apostles even after the New Testament was written, and so was transmitted orally until the time of the "first Fathers." "When these Bishops were assembled in Councils," they appealed to this still recent tradition of their churches in deciding matters of faith. These conciliar decrees and the other writings of the Fathers, embodying the beliefs "preserv'd in the chief Churches which had been founded by the Apostles," constitute the not-written, because nonscriptural, tradition which "serv'd afterwards as a rule for the explaining of the difficult places of the Scripture," and which was accepted as authoritative by the Council of Trent in ordaining "that no one should interpret the Scripture against the common opinion of the Fathers."

Many Anglican laymen besides Dryden assumed that the tradition upheld by the Catholic church was oral; they were scarcely to blame for this error since it was encouraged by certain English Catholic apologists who shared the same mistake.[37] Tillotson, who was better informed, found it necessary in fact to explain the Catholic sense of the expression "not written" to an English apologist for that church who persisted in defending oral tradition.[38] Dryden need not have been acquainted at this time, however, with the writings of any of these misinformed apologists. He probably derived his notion of oral tradition from Hooker, who was encouraged in this mistake by certain English Catholic apologists of his own day, particularly Thomas Stapleton.[39] In upholding the Protestant principle that the rule of faith consists in *Scriptura sola*, to the exclusion of tradition, Hooker regularly assumes that the tradition he is opposing is oral. He therefore uses much the same argument Dryden was to employ against Simon, pointing out that tradition, being oral, is far less certain than Scripture, which is written. He declares:

They that so earnestly plead for the authority of tradition, as if nothing were more safely conveyed than that which spreadeth itself by report, and descendeth by relation of former generations unto the ages that succeed, are not all of them (surely a miracle it were if they should be) so simple as thus to persuade themselves; howsoever, if

[37] See George H. Tavard, *Holy Writ or Holy Church: The Crisis of the Protestant Reformation* (New York: Harper Brothers, 1959), an excellent account of the controversy over the rule of faith down to the end of the sixteenth century, for a discussion, among other matters, of the misconception of "oral" tradition.
[38] See *The Rule of Faith* (London, 1666), pp. 279–92.
[39] For a discussion of Stapleton's peculiarities, see Tavard, *Holy Writ or Holy Church*, pp. 230–31.

the simple were so persuaded, they could be content perhaps very well to enjoy the benefit, as they account it, of that common error. What hazard the truth is in when it passeth through the hands of report, how maimed and deformed it becometh, they are not, they cannot possibly be ignorant.[40]

As a riposte to someone like Stapleton, the argument was obviously more pertinent than it was to Simon, who had not raised the issue of oral tradition at all. Dryden's admission that *"written words* from time are not secur'd" owes nothing to Hooker, of course, but everything to Simon's researches, so that Hooker's implied contrast between the uncorrupted Scriptures and uncertain oral tradition becomes an a fortiori comparison in which the insecurity of the written word enhances the uncertainty of oral report.

At this point Father Simon interjects the Catholic position *"Of the Infallibility of Tradition, in General"* in the words of the marginal rubric. Since Dryden has already suggested that this does not express the "secret meaning" of one who is "not too *much a Priest,"* we are meant to assume that Simon is merely repeating his church's doctrine for *"Fashion-sake":*

> Oh but says one, *Tradition* set aside,
> Where can we hope for an *unerring Guid?*
> For since th' *original* Scripture has been lost,
> *All* Copies *disagreeing, maim'd* the *most,*
> Or *Christian Faith* can have no *certain* ground,
> Or *Truth* in *Church Tradition* must be found.
>
> [ll. 276–81]

Dryden need have gone no further than "The Author's Preface" to the *Critical History* to have found Simon declaring:

The great alterations which have happened, as we have shewn in the first Book of this Work, to the Copies of the Bible since the first Originals have been lost, utterly destroy the Protestants and Socinians Principle, who consult onely these same Copies of the Bible as we at present have them. If the truth of Religion remain'd not in the Church, it would be unsafe to search for it at present in Books which have been subject to so many alterations, and have in many things depended upon the pleasure of Transcribers.[41]

---

[40] *Of the Laws of Ecclesiastical Polity* (London: J. M. Dent and Sons, 1954), I, 213 [I, xiii, 2]. (All subsequent references to the *Laws* will be to book, chapter and section, as in the reference here in brackets.)

[41] "The Author's Preface," *Critical History,* sig. a4v.

In these verses, Dryden allows his opponent to set the limits of their debate, just as the Deist had been permitted to do earlier in the poem.

The subject of this debate is the interpretation of Scripture. In suggesting that "the great alterations" he had uncovered in the texts of the Bible destroy the Protestant principle of *Scriptura sola,* Simon was simply adducing new evidence in support of the traditional Catholic position that the Scriptures by themselves are not entirely clear but must be interpreted in the light of tradition. "Let us not think," an English Catholic apologist writes, "that the Gospel lyes in the Words of Scripture, but in *their sense.*" Therefore, "this Sacred written Word faithfully *Interpreted,* And the unwritten *Deposited Word also* most *Infallibly Proposed,* is our *Form,* our *Rule and perfect Analogy of Faith.*"[42] Another English Catholic explains the relation between these components of their rule of faith:

The chief *Tradition,* the necessity and benefit of which is pretended by the Church, is not the *delivering* of any *additional* doctrines, descended from the Apostl's times *extra Scripturas,* i.e. such doctrins, as have not their foundation at least in Scripture; but is the *preserving,* and delivering of the *primitive* sense, and Church-explication of that which is written in the Scriptures, but many times not there written so clearly.[43]

In excluding tradition from the rule of faith, therefore, the Protestants simultaneously denied its necessity for interpreting the essential articles of faith contained in Scripture. Their principle of *Scriptura sola* not only insisted that "the Bible only is the religion of Protestants," in Chillingworth's famous phrase, but declared that the Scripture alone is sufficiently clear and manifest as to the necessary articles of faith so that it can be understood by itself. So Hooker declares that "Scripture therefore is not so hard, but that the only reading thereof may give life unto willing hearers," and Tillotson states: "Our Principle is, That the Scripture doth sufficiently interpret it self, that is, is plain to all capacities, in things necessary to be believed and practised."[44]

---

[42] Edward Worsley, *Protestancy without Principles, or, Sectaries Unhappy Fall from Infallibility to Fancy* (Antwerp, 1668), pp. 165, 295.

[43] Abraham Woodhead, *A Rational Account of the Doctrine of Roman-Catholicks concerning the Ecclesiastical Guide in Controversies of Religion* (2d ed.; n.p., 1673), p. 138.

[44] *Laws,* V, xxii, 14; *The Rule of Faith,* p. 106.

DEFENDER OF THE FAITH: ANGLICAN VS. CATHOLIC

The various statements by Catholic apologists I have just quoted which refer to tradition as something *"Infallibly Proposed"* or as "Church-explication of that which is written in the Scriptures" suggest the essential role taken by the church itself in the Catholic view of the rule of faith. For Catholics, the repository of tradition is the Church itself. The expression of the authentic meaning of the Scripture is found in the teachings of the living Church, Simon's *"unerring Guid,"* interpreting the word of God in the light of its tradition and preserved from error by the Holy Spirit. "If any new controversy in faith arise," writes an English Jesuit, "the Church, always living and present, can determine it by some new Decree or Declaration. These conditions are wanting in scripture, which is always the same, and wil be no more cleare, or of any larger extent for the contents thereof, tomorrow, than it is to day; nor can it speake and declare it selfe by it selfe, but only can be declared by some living Judg or Interpreter."[45] This is the *"Church Tradition"* to which Simon refers in the poem; the *"Infallibility"* which Dryden ascribes to tradition in his marginal rubric is conferred by the church which propounds it. The Protestants, rejecting the necessity of an infallible interpreter, or living "judge of controversies," counter this notion with their principle of private judgment. "Every man," Chillingworth declares, "is to judge for himselfe with the *Judgement of Discretion*. . . . But that there is any man, or any company of men appointed to be judge for all men, that we deny."[46]

Dryden answers Simon's appeal to an *"unerring Guid,"* therefore, by denying that such an infallible interpreter exists or is even necessary:

> Such an *Omniscient* Church we wish indeed;
> 'Twere worth *Both Testaments,* and cast in the *Creed*:
> But if *this Mother* be a *Guid* so sure,
> As can all *doubts resolve,* all *truth secure,*
> Then her *Infallibility,* as well
> Where Copies are *corrupt,* or *lame,* can tell;
> Restore *lost Canon* with as little pains,
> As *truly explicate* what still *remains*:
> Which yet no *Council* dare *pretend* to doe;
> Unless like *Esdras,* they cou'd *write* it new:
> Strange Confidence, still to *interpret* true,

---

[45] Edward Knott, *Infidelity Unmasked*, pp. 253–54.
[46] *The Religion of Protestants a Safe Way to Salvation* (Oxford, 1638), p. 57.

Yet not be sure that all they have explain'd,
Is in the blest *Original* contain'd.

[ll. 282–94]

The gross misunderstanding to which the first two lines of this stanza have given rise illustrate the importance of paying attention at all times to the context in which Dryden's words appear. Interpreting the lines as a moving expression of heartfelt yearning, his recent biographer comments: "Dryden's desire now for an omniscient Church competent to pronounce on doubtful points of Scripture helps to point the way to his eventual conversion to Roman Catholicism."[47] If this wish, expressed in the course of debate, augurs impending conversion, a general exodus from the Church of England might be foretold. Chillingworth asked: "Who doth not see, that supposing the Bishop of Rome, had been appointed Head of the Church, and Judge of Controversies, that it would have been infinitely beneficiall to the Church, perhaps as much as all the rest of the Bible."[48] Another Anglican apologist declared in similar terms that "to the Romish pretence of Infallible guidance, we say still, could it be made good, there would be no more to doe, but every man, upon understanding the termes and sense of her Definitions, to submit his reason and judgement without farther enquiry."[49] The question, of course, is not whether an *"unerring Guid"* in religion is desirable—a point which any Protestant would be willing to concede—but whether God has in fact provided such a benefit, and committed it to the care of the Catholic church. Dryden proceeds to deny this unequivocally.

His argument is ingenious; if it misrepresents his opponent's position, this is all but concealed by a display of logical dexterity. He constructs a hypothetical proposition: "If *this Mother* be a *Guid* so sure, as can all *doubts resolve*, all *truth secure*; then her *Infallibility,* as well where Copies are *corrupt,* or *lame,* can tell." If this proposition is accepted as true, the logic of Dryden's demonstration is impeccable. His minor, "which yet no *Council* dare *pretend* to doe," denying the consequent, has been established

[47] Ward, *Life of John Dryden,* p. 190. See also Bredvold, *Intellectual Milieu,* p. 126, for a similar comment that these lines "reveal how strong a hold the notion of authority already had on his mind, despite his vigorous rejection of the doctrine of infallibility."

[48] *Religion of Protestants,* p. 104.

[49] Henry Ferne, *Of the Division between the English and Romish Church upon the Reformation* (London, 1652), pp. 84–85.

by Simon himself: the corrupted state of the scriptural texts, carefully set forth in the *Critical History*, had obviously escaped the previous notice of the Church. The unstated conclusion, denying the antecedent, is therefore inescapable. Father Simon might well have been surprised at the notion that the Catholic church is supposed to be infallible in matters of textual criticism, however, and he certainly would have denied Dryden's major. The stratagem which allows Dryden to construct his apparently innocent proposition is so simple that it has escaped notice. It consists in equating infallibility with omniscience; "her *Infallibility*," referred to in the fifth line of the stanza, is treated as being synonymous with the notion of an *"Omniscient* Church," mentioned in the first line. The two characteristics are, of course, quite different. The infallibility actually claimed for the Catholic church, a purely negative quality, consists in nothing more than a preservation from error in matters of faith and morals which does not extend to textual criticism. Omniscience, a positive quality no Catholic apologist ever claimed for his church, consists in the possession of all knowledge, including the proper variants in the scriptural texts, and is an attribute applicable only to God.[50] Dryden's interchange of the two is so muted, however, that his proposition appears perfectly plausible. As far as I am aware, this contribution to the fund of Anglican apologetics against the infallibility of the Catholic church is original. It is an *ad hoc* response suggested by Simon's recent discovery of the uncertain state of the biblical texts, and it depends on a tactic of juggling words that would not have appealed to Dryden's more learned confreres.

Having disposed of oral tradition and the notion of an infallible Church, Dryden offers the common Protestant alternatives of *Scriptura sola* and private judgment:

> More Safe, and much more modest 'tis, to say
> *God wou'd not leave Mankind without a way*:
> And that the *Scriptures,* though not *every where*
> Free from Corruption, or intire, or clear,
> Are uncorrupt, sufficient, clear, intire,
> In *all* things which our needfull *Faith* require.
> If *others* in the *same Glass better* see

---

[50] Cf. Dryden's couplet in "Palamon and Arcite," "This Law th' Omniscient Pow'r was pleas'd to give, / That ev'ry Kind should by Succession live" (*Poems,* IV, 1527).

'Tis for *Themselves* they look, but not for *me*:
For MY Salvation must its Doom receive
Not from what OTHERS, but what *I* believe.
[ll. 295–304]

He begins by qualifying his previous admission that the biblical texts are *"corrupt,* or *lame"* by making an important distinction: the Scriptures, it is true, are "not *every where* / Free from Corruption," but "in *all* things which our needfull *Faith* require" they are completely uncorrupt. The basis of this assumption is a corollary drawn from the notion of Providence: *"God wou'd not leave Mankind without a way"* of salvation; therefore Providence must have preserved the essential passages of Scripture from corruption. This tactic of transferring from the Church to the Bible the idea of infallibility, in the sense of divine protection from error in matters pertaining to faith and morals, is common among Anglican apologists. So Chillingworth speaks of "the watchfull eye of divine providence: the goodnesse whereof will never suffer, that the Scripture should be depraved and corrupted, but that in them should be alwaies extant a conspicuous and plain way to eternall happinesse."[51] Similarly, Tillotson argues that "if they were written by men Divinely inspired, and are of use to Christians, as is acknowledged (at least in words) on all hands; nothing is more credible than, that the same Divine Providence which took care for the publishing of them, would likewise be concerned to preserve them entire."[52]

These apologists had expressed their confidence that the Scriptures are "uncorrupt" and "entire" before Simon had published the results of his investigation, but they would certainly have responded to this discovery by drawing the same distinction Dryden makes between those things in Scripture "which our needfull *Faith* require," the special care of Providence, and the rest of the Bible, which could be safely allowed to have suffered some corruption. For it had long been customary to employ this distinction in putting forward the other two attributes of Scripture Dryden mentions: "sufficient" and "clear." Hooker explained that

of things necessary to all men's salvation we have been hitherto accustomed to hold (especially sithence the publishing of the Gospel of

[51] *Religion of Protestants,* p. 61.
[52] *Rule of Faith,* p. 25.

Jesus Christ, whereby the simplest having now a key unto knowledge which the Eunuch in the Acts did want, our children may of themselves by reading understand that, which he without an interpreter could not) they are in Scripture plain and easy to be understood.[53]

This qualification, "things necessary to all men's salvation," is essential to the Anglican principle that "Scripture interprets itself." So Tillotson writes, "that the Books of Scripture are sufficiently plain, as to all things necessary to be believed, and practised," while Chillingworth declares: "And then wee suppose that all the necessary points of Religion are plaine and easie, & consequently every man in this cause to be a competent Judge for himselfe."[54]

The notion of private judgment which Chillingworth arrives at here is an inevitable corollary of the principle we have been considering. As he explains: "So that those places which containe things necessary, and wherein errour were dangerous, need no infallible interpreter because they are plaine: and those that are obscure need none because they contain not things necessary, neither is errour in them dangerous."[55] Similarly, Dryden pleads, in the last four lines of the stanza, that since the terms of salvation are clearly set forth in the Scripture for all to see, no man can surrender to another a responsibility he must answer for himself: "For MY Salvation must its Doom receive / Not from what OTHERS, but what *I* believe." As another Anglican apologist had written earlier,

private Christians have their *private judgement,* or *judgement of Discretion* for themselves onely, which is in the discerning and receiving to themselves, as the will of God, what is delivered, and propounded to them; for they must answer also for themselves, and live by their owne faith, which cannot be without allowing them due use of their reason and judgement, to see the evidence of that, to which they must assent.[56]

At this point an interruption occurs and we listen to an *"Objection in behalf of Tradition; urg'd by Father* Simon," in the words of the marginal rubric. The Catholic priest asks:

[53] *Laws,* V, xxii, 14.
[54] *Rule of Faith,* p. 10; *Religion of Protestants,* p. 59. Cf. Stillingfleet, *Origines Sacrae, or A Rational Account of the Grounds of Christian Faith* (3d ed.; London, 1666), pp. 612–13.
[55] *Religion of Protestants,* p. 59.
[56] Ferne, *Of the Division between the English and Romish Church,* p. 47.

Must *all Tradition* then be set aside?
This to affirm were Ignorance, or Pride.
Are there not many points, some needfull sure
To saving Faith, that Scripture leaves obscure?
Which every Sect will wrest a several way
(For what *one* Sect Interprets, *all* Sects *may*:)
We hold, and say we prove from Scripture plain,
That *Christ* is GOD; the bold *Socinian*
From the *same* Scripture urges he's but MAN.
Now what Appeal can end th' important Suit;
Both parts *talk* loudly, but the *Rule* is *mute?*

[ll. 305–15]

Dryden had found Simon voicing this objection before he was well into the "Author's Preface" to the *Critical History*:

Those Protestants without doubt are either ignorant or prejudic'd who affirm that the Scripture is plain of it self. As they have laid aside the Tradition of the Church, and will acknowledge no other principle of Religion but the Scripture it self, they were obliged to suppose it plain and sufficient for the establishing the truth of Faith without any Tradition.

But if we but consider the conclusions which the Protestants and Socinians draw from the same principle, we shall be convinc'd that their principle is not so plain as they imagin, since these conclusions are so different and the one absolutely denies what the other affirms.[57]

Dryden's rejoinder to "the learned Father *Simon*" is prefaced by another overt ethical appeal, reminding us once again of his modest role as "a much unskilfull, but well meaning guide":

Shall I speak plain, and in a Nation free
Assume an honest *Layman's Liberty?*
I think (according to my little Skill,
To my own Mother-Church submitting still:)
That many have been sav'd, and many may,
Who never heard this Question brought in play.
Th' *unletter'd* Christian, who believes in *gross,*
Plods on to *Heaven;* and ne'er is at a loss:
For the *Streight-gate* wou'd be made *streighter* yet,
Were *none* admitted there but men of *Wit.*
The few, by Nature form'd, with Learning fraught,
Born to instruct, as others to be taught,
Must Study well the Sacred Page; and see

Which Doctrine, this, or that, does best agree
With the whole Tenour of the Work Divine:
And plainlyest points to Heaven's reveal'd Design:
Which Exposition flows from *genuine Sense;*
And which is *forc'd* by *Wit* and *Eloquence.*

[ll. 316–33]

To Simon's question, "Are there not many points, some needfull sure / To saving Faith, that Scripture leaves obscure?" Dryden answers a qualified affirmative. There are many points which Scripture leaves obscure, but none of them is needful to saving faith. Scripture "interprets itself" only in things necessary to salvation; these the *"unletter'd* Christian" may understand for himself and "plod on to *Heaven."* The rest of the Bible does not concern his eternal happiness and can safely be left to the "few with Learning fraught" whose business it is to interpret obscure passages. This basic distinction is at the heart of the Anglican conception of private judgment, and qualifies the *"Layman's Liberty"* considerably. Hooker sets forth the distinction in unequivocal terms when he writes:

Some things are so familiar and plain, that truth from falsehood, and good from evil, is most easily discerned in them, even by men of no deep capacity. And of that nature, for the most part, are things absolutely unto all men's salvation necessary, either to be held or denied, either to be done or avoided. For which cause St. Augustine acknowledgeth, that they are not only set down, but also plainly set down in Scripture; so that he which heareth or readeth may without any great difficulty understand. Other things also there are belonging (though in a lower degree of importance) unto the offices of Christian men: which, because they are more obscure, more intricate and hard to be judged of, therefore God hath appointed some to spend their whole time principally in the study of things divine, to the end that in these more doubtful cases their understanding might be a light to direct others.[58]

The opening question of Father Simon's objection, "Must *all Tradition* then be set aside?" echoes the first line of his original interjection: "Oh but says one, *Tradition* set aside." The important change is the addition of the word *"all."* When the question is phrased this way, Dryden is willing to give a negative answer. Still speaking of the role of the "few with Learning fraught" in explaining difficult passages of the Scripture, he writes:

---

[58] *Laws,* "Preface," iii, 2.

> Not that Traditions parts are useless here:
> When general, old, disinteress'd and clear:
> That Ancient Fathers thus expound the Page,
> Gives *Truth* the reverend Majesty of *Age*:
> *Confirms* its force, by biding every *Test*;
> For best *Authority*'s next *Rules* are best.
> And still the nearer to the Spring we go
> More limpid, more unsoyl'd the Waters flow.
> Thus, *first Traditions* were a proof alone;
> Cou'd we be *certain* such they *were,* so *known*:
> But since some Flaws in long descent may be,
> They make not *Truth* but *Probability*.
> Even *Arius* and *Pelagius* durst provoke
> To what the *Centuries preceding* spoke.
> Such difference is there in an oft-told Tale:
> But Truth by its own Sinews will prevail.
> *Tradition written* therefore more commends
> *Authority,* than what from *Voice* descends:
> And this, as perfect as its kind can be,
> Rouls down to us the Sacred History:
> Which, from the *Universal Church receiv'd,*
> Is *try'd,* and *after,* for its *self* believ'd.
>
> [ll. 334–55]

Dryden's carefully qualified acceptance of tradition here is a precise exposition of Anglican doctrine. The Church of England differed from the other Protestant communions in refusing to set aside all tradition, a fact which even the Catholics recognized. Father Simon writes of "those who in *England* are call'd *Episcoparians*." These Protestants "differ not so much from the Catholicks, especially in Ecclesiastical Discipline as the others. Wherefore they consult not the Scripture as their only Rule, but they have a respect for the ancient Doctors of the Church, and for Tradition."[59]

While there is some truth to this statement it requires careful qualification. It is incorrect to say that the Anglicans "consult not the Scripture as their only Rule," if Simon is referring to the rule of faith, for in this respect "the Bible only is the religion of Protestants" of the Church of England as well as of any other Reformed Church. Nevertheless, where "the few with Learning fraught" apply themselves to the interpretation of those more obscure passages where the Bible is not "plain and easy" to the understanding of all Christians, Archbishop Laud points out

[59] *Critical History,* Book III, p. 152.

214

that "we never did, nor never will refuse any *Tradition* that is *Universall,* and *Apostolike,* for the better *Exposition* of the Scripture."[60]

What constitutes "universal and apostolic" tradition, however? Two characteristics are requisite according to the Anglicans. First of all it must be written, and therefore the Anglicans, along with all other Protestants, reject the notion of a "living church" tradition. As Dryden declares, *"Tradition written* therefore more commends / *Authority,* than what from *Voice* descends." Secondly, it must be ancient and confined to the Fathers and Councils of the first three, four, or five centuries of the Christian Era (the number varies from one apologist to another). In Dryden's words: "That Ancient Fathers thus expound the Page, / Gives *Truth* the reverend Majesty of *Age."* Thus Laud appeals to "the joynt and constant Beliefe of the *Fathers,* which lived within the *first foure or five hundred yeares after Christ,* when the Church was at the best; and [to] the *Councels* held within those times."[61] This notion that antiquity confers particular authority on tradition written "when the Church was at the best" is a common assumption; as Dryden expresses it, "still the nearer to the Spring we go / More limpid, more unsoyl'd the Waters flow." Thus Joseph Glanvill, restricting this golden age within more narrow limits, explains that the Latitudinarians

read the *Histories* of the Church, and applyed themselves to a careful perusal of the *Fathers* of the *three first* Centuries: In *them* they looked for the Doctrine and Practices that were in the *beginning*: They consider'd, that Religion was most *pure* in those *Primitive* Times of *Holiness* and *Martyrdom*; and that by knowing what was the *belief* and *use* then, they might be enabled to judge better of the more *Modern* Ways and Opinions: That though *other* Knowledge *grew,* and was much advanced by Time, yet *Divinity* was in its *perfection,* in the days of the *Apostles,* and *nearest* Ages to them; and had still been *degenerating* (more or less) in following Times.[62]

Similarly, another contemporary writer, describing the same group, writes that they derive their doctrine "from the Sacred writings of the Apostles and Evangelists, in interpreting whereof, they

---

[60] *A Relation of the Conference betweene William Lawd and Mr. Fisher the Jesuite* (London, 1639), p. 53.
[61] *Ibid.*
[62] "Anti-fanatical Religion and Free Philosophy," *Essays on Several Important Subjects in Philosophy and Religion* (London, 1676), pp. 9–10.

carefully attend to the sense of the ancient Church, by which they conceive the modern ought to be guided," explaining that they consult "all the genuine Monuments of the ancient Fathers, those especially of the first and purest ages," since those opinions "are justly to be suspected, whereof there are no footsteps to be discerned in that golden age of Christianity, that was tryed and purifyed in the fire of persecution."[63]

For all the esteem in which they held this ancient written tradition as a means of expounding the Scripture, the Anglicans did not consider it an infallible interpreter. The protection of Providence which preserved the Bible from material error and rendered it infallible in matters pertaining to salvation did not extend to the writings of the ancient Fathers. As Dryden declares: "But since some Flaws in long descent may be, / They make not *Truth* but *Probability*." The same qualification is noted by Tillotson: "As for obscure and more doubtful Texts, we acknowledge the Comments of the *Fathers* to be a good help, but no certain Rule of interpretation."[64]

Dryden proceeds to anticipate and express in his own words what the marginal rubric refers to as *"The Second Objection,"* encouraged by his concession to tradition: "The partial *Papists* wou'd infer from hence / *Their* Church, in last resort, shou'd Judge the *Sense*."

His *"Answer to the Objection"* follows immediately:

> But first they wou'd assume, with wondrous Art,
> *Themselves* to be the *whole*, who are but *part*
> Of that vast Frame, the Church; yet grant they were
> The handers down, can they from thence infer
> A right t' interpret? or wou'd they alone
> Who brought the Present, claim it for their own?
> The *Book*'s a *Common Largess* to *Mankind*;
> Not more for *them*, than *every* Man design'd:
> The *welcome News* is in the *Letter* found;
> The *Carrier*'s not Commission'd to *expound*.

---

[63] S. P. of Cambridge, *A Brief Account of the New Sect of Latitude-Men* (Cambridge, 1662), p. 9. A canon of the Convocation of Canterbury of 1571 orders preachers to teach nothing "but that which is agreeable to the doctrine of the olde Testament, or the newe, and that which the catholike fathers, and auncient Bishops have gathered out of that doctrine" (*A Booke of Certaine Canons, concernying some parte of the Discipline of the Churche of England* [London, 1571], p. 23).

[64] *Rule of Faith*, p. 106.

It *speaks* it *Self,* and what it does contain,
In all things *needfull* to be *known,* is *plain.*

[ll. 358–69]

Dryden's rejoinder to this attempt to draw an unwelcome corollary from his concession involves two points. First of all, the right of the few, "born to instruct," to expound the "Sacred Page" by referring to "Traditions parts" cannot be equated with the claim of the Church of Rome to interpret Scripture for the benefit of all Christians in the light of church tradition. For the Church of Rome is only one part of the Catholic, or universal, church and possesses no authority over the other churches of Christendom. So Laud, making the same distinction between ancient tradition and the church tradition appealed to by Catholics, writes that "though they would seeme to have us believe the *Fathers,* and the *Church of old,* yet they will not have us take their *Doctrine* from their owne *Writings,* or the *Decrees of Councels:* because (as they say) wee cannot know by reading them, what their mean-ing was, but from the *Infallible Testimony of the present Romane Church teaching by Tradition.*" This is absurd, he adds, because

they ascribe as great Authority (if not greater) to a *part* of the *Catho-like Church,* as they doe to the *whole,* which wee believe in our *Creede;* and which is the Society of all Christians. And this is full of *Absurdity* in *Nature,* in *Reason,* in *All things,* That any *Part* should bee of equall *worth, power, credit,* or *authority* with the *Whole.*[65]

Therefore the Church of Rome has no right to interpret even the more obscure passages of Scripture for the sake of Anglicans, for as Laud explains later, "the *Romane Church* and the *Church of England* are but two distinct members of that *Catholike Church* which is spread over the face of the earth. Therefore *Rome* is not the House where the *Church* dwels, but *Rome* it selfe, as well as other Particular Churches, dwels in this great *Universall House.*"[66]

Second, the fact that it is only the less essential parts of Scrip-ture that require to be explained by resort to tradition obviates the Roman Church's claim to regulate the faith of Christians. "The *Carrier*'s not Commission'd to *expound*" the *"welcome*

[65] *Relation of the Conference,* pp. 62–63.

[66] *Ibid.,* pp. 311–12. Cf. Tillotson's denial of the Church of Rome's claim to infallibility because "there is no reason why any particular church should pretend to be catholic, or universal; or, to speak plainer, why a part should pretend to be the whole" (*The Works of Dr. John Tillotson* [London: J. F. Dove, 1820], IX, 614).

News" of salvation which is already "in the *Letter* found." Therefore Dryden reiterates the Anglican position that "in all things *needfull* to be *known*" the Scripture interprets ("*speaks*") itself and is plain to the capacity of every man.

In the ensuing stanza he offers a historical account of how the Roman Church came to "infer a right t' interpret" for others a book which was meant as "a *Common Largess* to *Mankind*." He explains:

> In times o'ergrown with Rust and Ignorance,
> A gainfull Trade their Clergy did advance:
> When want of Learning kept the *Laymen* low,
> And none but *Priests* were *Authoriz'd* to *know*:
> When what small Knowledge was, in them did dwell;
> And he a *God* who cou'd but *Reade* or *Spell*;
> Then *Mother Church* did mightily prevail:
> She parcel'd out the Bible by *retail*:
> But still *expounded* what She *sold* or *gave*;
> To keep it in *her Power* to *Damn* and *Save*:
> *Scripture* was *scarce*, and as the Market went,
> Poor *Laymen* took *Salvation* on *Content*;
> As needy men take Money, good or bad:
> *God*'s Word they had not, but the *Priests* they had.
> Yet, whate'er *false Conveyances* they made,
> The *Lawyer* still was *certain* to be paid.
> In those dark times they learn'd their knack so well,
> That by long use they grew *Infallible*:
> At last, a knowing Age began t' enquire
> If *they* the *Book*, or *That* did *them* inspire:
> And, making narrower search they found, thô late,
> That what they thought the *Priest*'s, was *Their* Estate:
> Taught by the *Will produc'd*, (the written Word)
> How long they had been *cheated* on *Record*.
> Then, every man who saw the Title fair,
> Claim'd a Child's part, and put in for a Share:
> Consulted Soberly his private good;
> And sav'd himself as cheap as e'er he cou'd.
>
> [ll. 370–97]

This is, of course, the standard version of church history given by Protestant apologists in which the "golden age" of the first few centuries of Christianity was succeeded by the Dark Ages in which the Roman clergy "parcel'd out the Bible by *retail*" until, at last, "by long use they grew *Infallible*." Chillingworth, for example, writes:

> So the *Church of Rome,* to establish her tyranny over mens consciences, needed not either to abolish or corrupt the holy Scriptures, the Pillars and supporters of Christian liberty. . . . But the more expedite way, and therefore more likely to be successfull, was to gain the opinion and esteem of the *publique and authoriz'd interpreter* of them, and the Authority of adding to them what doctrine she pleas'd under the title of *Traditions* or *Definitions*. . . . this being once setled in the mindes of men, that *unwritten doctrines, if proposed by her, were to be receav'd with equall reverence to those that were written:* and that *the sense of Scripture was not that which seem'd to mens reason and understanding to be so, but that which the Church of Rome should declare to be so, seem'd it never so unreasonable, and incongruous.*[67]

The notion that the Reformation represented a recovery of the pristine religion as a result of consulting the Bible itself is of course the inevitable conclusion of such a history. The metaphorical language, borrowed from the marketplace, in which Dryden recounts the history of Christianity all derives from his basic metaphors of the *"Will,"* for the Old and New Testaments, and of the "Estate," for the Christian religion. In these terms it is possible to represent the teaching authority claimed by the Roman Church as a monstrous cheat in which the faithful were deprived of their rightful inheritance provided by Christ's Testament. Since in the legal sense a testament is a will, the basic metaphor may have suggested itself to Dryden. But if, as is not unlikely, he consulted as one of his "helps" the famous *Relation of a Conference betweene William Lawd and Mr. Fisher the Jesuite,* he would have found a long marginal comment quoting the use of this metaphor by several of the Fathers and declaring that these same Fathers, unlike the Roman clergy, "appeale to the *Written* Will, and make that the *Judge* without any Exception, when a matter of Faith comes in Question."[68]

Finally, as he had done in the case of the Athanasian Creed toward the end of the first half of *Religio Laici,* Dryden anticipates a still unspoken rejoinder to the position he has been taking.

[67] *Religion of Protestants,* pp. 51–52.
[68] Laud, *Relation of the Conference,* p. 194.

He writes:

> 'Tis true, my Friend, (and far be Flattery hence)
> This good had full as bad a Consequence:
> The Book thus put in every vulgar hand,
> Which each presum'd he best cou'd understand,
> The *Common Rule* was made the *common Prey;*
> And at the mercy of the *Rabble* lay.
> The tender Page with horney Fists was gaul'd;
> And he was gifted most that loudest baul'd:
> The *Spirit* gave the *Doctoral Degree*:
> And every member of a *Company*
> Was of *his Trade,* and of the *Bible free.*
> Plain *Truths* enough for needfull *use* they found;
> But men wou'd still be itching to *expound*:
> Each was ambitious of th' obscurest place,
> No measure ta'n from *Knowledge,* all from GRACE.
> *Study* and *Pains* were now no more their Care;
> *Texts* were explain'd by *Fasting,* and by *Prayer*:
> This was the Fruit the *private Spirit* brought;
> Occasion'd by *great Zeal,* and *little Thought.*
> While Crouds unlearn'd, with rude Devotion warm,
> About the Sacred Viands buz and swarm,
> The *Fly-blown Text* creates a *crawling Brood;*
> And turns to *Maggots* what was meant for *Food.*
> *A Thousand daily Sects rise up, and dye;*
> *A Thousand more the perish'd Race supply.*
> So all we make of Heavens discover'd Will
> Is, not to have it, or to use it ill.
> The Danger's much the same; on several Shelves
> If *others* wreck *us,* or *we* wreck our *selves.*
>
> [ll. 398–426]

By seizing the initiative and addressing his words to Dickinson rather than to Simon, Dryden implies that the Church of England is well aware of the abuses to which unrestrained private judgment can lead and is fully prepared to safeguard herself from them. The objection which he anticipates here was one frequently made by Catholic apologists, who pointed to the proliferation of Protestant sects, whose number was legion, as the logical consequence of the principle of private judgment. Critics have often commented on the sharply satirical language of this stanza. But the reason for this language is not merely the contempt for Dissenters which Dryden shared with most members of his church.

By posing this common rejoinder in his own carefully chosen words, he manages to convey something of the distance between the Anglican conception of private judgment and that of the Dissenters, and to forestall the objection before it can be raised by his opponent.

First of all, whereas he has been advocating the calm "judgment of discretion" upheld by his own church, the growth of the dissenting sects is described as "the Fruit the *private Spirit* brought; / Occasion'd by *great Zeal,* and *little Thought*." If the Anglicans have espoused private reason, they are scarcely to blame for irrational enthusiasm, the very negation of reason, "no measure ta'n from *Knowledge,* all from GRACE." "When they and their Bibles were alone together," Hooker wrote of the Puritans of his own day, "what strange fantastical opinion soever at any time entered into their heads, their use was to think the Spirit taught it them."[69]

Second, whereas Dryden has been careful to distinguish, with his church, between "plain *Truths* enough for needfull *use*," the proper subject for private judgment, and the more obscure passages of Scripture, reserved for "the few, by Nature form'd, with Learning fraught, / Born to instruct, as others to be taught," the Dissenters make no such distinction. For them "the *Spirit* gave the *Doctoral Degree*" and every ignorant tradesman, or member of a City company, "was of *his Trade,* and of the *Bible free*." The "study and pains" of the learned commentators gave place to the private inspiration of the rabble, and instead of being satisfied with "necessary truths," "each was ambitious of th' obscurest place." "Which opinion being once inserted into the minds of the vulgar sort," Hooker warned, "what it may grow unto God knoweth."

Thus much we see, it hath already made thousands so headstrong even in gross and palpable errors, that a man whose capacity will scarce serve him to utter five words in sensible manner blusheth not in any doubt concerning matter of Scripture to think his own bare *Yea* as good as the *Nay* of all the wise, grave, and learned judgments that are in the whole world: which insolency must be repressed, or it will be the very bane of Christian religion.[70]

On these grounds, the Church of England cannot accept responsibility for the behavior of the sects. The judgment of discretion,

[69] *Laws,* "Preface," viii, 7.
[70] *Ibid.,* II, vii, 6.

Dryden points out, is a bark which steers between the opposite shoals of an infallible interpreter, where *"others* wreck *us,"* and the private spirit, where *"we* wreck our *selves."*

He exploits this conception of the Anglican position as a *via media* between two extremes in the concluding stanza of his argument, where he recapitulates his principal points and adds a safeguard against excess:

> What then remains, but, waving each Extreme,
> The Tides of Ignorance, and Pride to stem?
> Neither so rich a Treasure to forgo;
> Nor proudly seek beyond our pow'r to know:
> Faith is not built on disquisitions vain;
> The things we *must* believe, are *few,* and *plain*:
> But since men *will* believe more than they *need*;
> And every man will make *himself* a Creed:
> In doubtfull questions 'tis the safest way
> To learn what unsuspected Ancients say:
> For 'tis not likely *we* shou'd higher Soar
> In search of Heav'n, than *all the Church before*:
> Nor can we be deceiv'd, unless we see
> The *Scripture,* and the *Fathers disagree.*
> If after all, they stand suspected still,
> (For no man's Faith depends upon his Will;)
> 'Tis some Relief, that points not clearly known,
> Without much hazard may be let alone:
> And, after hearing what our Church can say,
> If still our Reason runs another way,
> That private Reason 'tis more Just to curb,
> Than by Disputes the publick Peace disturb.
> For points obscure are of small use to learn:
> But *Common quiet* is *Mankind's concern.*
>
> [ll. 427–50]

On the one hand, there is no need to forego so rich a treasure as the Bible if one applies private judgment with proper discretion: easily comprehending "the things we *must* believe" and, "since men *will* believe more than they *need*," consulting the written tradition of the ancient Fathers on more obscure points. In declaring that "the things we *must* believe are *few,* and *plain*" Dryden adds the qualification *"few"* to that of *"plain"* for the first time. This development of the principle of private judgment, associated with the Latitudinarians, was designed as a further safeguard against the need for an *"unerring Guid."* As Glanvill, describing the characteristic beliefs of the Latitudinarians, explained:

They made this one of their main Doctrines; That *The principles which are necessary to Salvation are very few, and very plain, and generally acknowledg'd among Christians.* . . . They saw . . . That *Papism,* which in those times of distraction began to spread even here, would drop to the ground, if it were believed, That the *necessary principles of Religion were few,* and *plain,* and those *agreed* on: For then there would be no need of an *Infallible Interpreter,* and *Judge.*[71]

On the other hand, there is no danger that we will "proudly seek beyond our pow'r to know," acting like the fanatics who form new sects and "by Disputes the publick Peace disturb," if we adopt the safeguard of "hearing what our Church can say" and curbing private reason where it conflicts with the public teaching of the Church. This can violate no man's conscience, for "points obscure are of small use to learn" and do not concern salvation. Dryden has been accused of yielding here "an obedience to the Church of England as by law established, more strict than it theoretically could claim, and more blind than that Church, in its fear of being identified with Popery, would want to claim."[72] Yet this claim was repeatedly made by Anglican writers, and it is difficult to see how they could have maintained any semblance of church unity without such a safeguard restraining private judgment. Hooker had asked:

Is it meet that when publicly things are received, and have taken place, general obedience thereunto should cease to be exacted, in case this or that private person, led with some probable conceit, should make open protestation, "I Peter or John disallow them, and pronounce them nought"? . . . As though when public consent of the whole hath established any thing, every man's judgment being thereunto compared were not private, howsoever his calling be to some kind of public charge. So that of peace and quietness there is not any way possible, unless the probable voice of every entire society or body politic overrule all private of like nature in the same body.[73]

The abuse of private judgment for which Hooker reproved the Elizabethan Puritans did not disappear in the following century;

---

[71] "Anti-fanatical Religion and Free Philosophy," *Essays on Several Important Subjects,* pp. 25–26.

[72] Bredvold, *Intellectual Milieu,* p. 126.

[73] *Laws,* "Preface," vi, 6.

if anything, it increased, so that it was frequently necessary to caution obedience to the Church's teachings. In the mid-seventeenth century another Anglican writer declared: "Now for the using their reason and judgement against the Church, or their dissenting from the definitions and practise of it, We give no encouragement to that." He went on to explain that

> Wee teach all Inferiors, whether People or Priests, when they finde cause of doubt or question against such definitions or practise, to instruct their owne reason, and rather rely upon the publick Judgement then their owne in every doubtfull case. . . . If they cannot finde satisfaction so, as inwardly to acquiesce, yet to yeild externall obedience, and peaceable subjection, according as the condition of the matter questioned will bear. In a word, we require all that submission of judgment and outward compliance, that may be due to an Authority, not infallible, yet guiding others by an infallible Rule.[74]

The Act of Uniformity (1662) was designed to deal with abuses of private judgment by expelling from the Church large numbers of those who disturbed the public peace by disputes, in the manner described by Dryden. But it could not quell the danger of further disputes, and it was still necessary for another Anglican, writing a few years later, to declare categorically: "All Men are bound, whatever their private Sentiments may be, to submit externally to the sentence of the Church, in matters which entrench not on the Fundamentals of their Faith, because the teaching of such Doctrines must be of lesser moment then the preservation of the Churches peace."[75] This is Dryden's principle exactly.

Once we restore Dryden's arguments to their proper context, his position in the latter half of *Religio Laici* can be seen, not as the anguished compromise of one who is already struggling with doubts which must lead him eventually to the Catholic church, but as an articulate expression of the Anglican *via media*. To Walter Travers and the other Puritan members of the Church of England, the attempts of Hooker and his successors to mediate between the claims of church authority and private judgment and to appeal to ancient written tradition as well as to Scripture for settling "indifferent matters" had been taken as evidence that their church was not yet fully purified of "popery." When *Religio Laici* appeared, however, twenty years after the Act of Uniformity, the

[74] Ferne, *Of the Division between the English and Romish Church*, pp. 49–50.
[75] Daniel Whitby, *An Answer to Sure Footing* (Oxford, 1666), p. 61.

time had long passed when such charges could be taken seriously by members of the Church of England. No objections to the poem were forthcoming, and it can be assumed that most Anglican readers, like Dryden's "judicious and learned Friend," were "pleas'd to approve the body of the Discourse." It was a very different reception from that which was to be accorded his next venture into religious apologetics.

7

ENIGMATIC CONVERT

On May 29, 1687, exactly four and a half years after the appearance of *Religio Laici, The Hind and the Panther* was published. The issues raised in the second half of *Religio Laici* were aired once again in Part II of *The Hind and the Panther;* on this occasion, however, the Panther expressed in faltering accents the position which Dryden himself had confidently defended in his earlier poem, while the Hind, stoutly urging the views offered before by Father Simon, pressed forward to an easy victory over her helpless opponent.

Modern critics and biographers of Dryden, anxious to dispel charges of inconsistency leveled at the poet, have tried to find signs of an approaching change in *Religio Laici* which would make his *volte-face* in *The Hind and the Panther* less startling.[1]

---

[1] See Louis I. Bredvold, *The Intellectual Milieu of John Dryden* (Ann Arbor: University of Michigan Press, 1934), p. 126; Charles E. Ward, *The Life of John Dryden* (Chapel Hill: University of North Carolina Press, 1961), p. 190; Victor M. Hamm, "Dryden's *Religio Laici* and Roman Catholic Apologetics," *PMLA*, 80 (1965): 190–98. Professor Hamm cites various analogues between passages in *Religio Laici* and statements by Catholic apologists. Such analogues are not hard to find, but they do not prove that Dryden was influenced by, or even acquainted with, the writings of Catholic apologists as early as 1682. The first half of *Religio Laici*, which belongs in the tradition of Christian apologetics, contains arguments which were common to both Protestant and Catholic defenders of Christianity. Since Dryden was writing as an Anglican, it seems more reasonable to suppose that he is drawing these common arguments from Protestant rather than Catholic sources. The two speeches by Father Simon in the second half of the poem are assumed by Professor Hamm to be expressions of Dryden's own views and to be evidence of his acquaintance with a number of Catholic apologists who naturally shared many of Simon's religious views. Since both these speeches are, as I have shown, close paraphrases of Simon's remarks in "The Author's Preface" to the *Critical History*, there is no need to assume any other source for them.

The evidence produced in the last chapter shows, however, that
Dryden's position in the second half of *Religio Laici* accords completely with that of other Anglican apologists, none of whom later
left the Church of England; if Dryden had died at the end of
1682, no one, I venture to suggest, would ever have suspected
from this poem that he was moving toward the Catholic church.
The fact is that the Anglican and Catholic positions on the issues
debated in the second parts of *Religio Laici* and *The Hind and
the Panther* are totally inconsistent, and anyone who chooses to
discuss them twice, first as an Anglican and then as a Catholic,
will necessarily contradict his earlier views on the second occasion. Conversion itself involves inconsistency, but where the conversion is sincere, inconsistency need not draw reproof.

The charge that Dryden's conversion was motivated by hopes
of personal profit, which he found it necessary to answer in a passage of *The Hind and the Panther,* has now been conclusively dis-
proved.[2] No one is likely to question the sincerity of his motives
today, or to deny that his change of religion was a matter of intellectual conviction. The attempt to portray this conviction as a
long-standing distrust of human reason which led Dryden to seek
refuge in an infallible church can no longer be taken seriously,
however, in view of the evidence in the preceding chapters. A different approach has been taken by a recent critic who seeks to
trace the convictions behind Dryden's conversion to the political
concerns he expressed in numerous works written between the
time of the Exclusion Crisis and the revolution. According to this
view, Dryden joined the Catholic church when he became convinced that "the Church of England was moving in a political
direction opposite from his own," toward that of the Whigs, and
that only the Catholic church could arrest the religious ferment
of the nation and "guarantee the integrity of the Christian Church
in England and of English society at large."[3] Yet the views Dryden
expressed, even after he became a Catholic, do not support this
theory. Only the firm belief that Catholicism would once again
become the religion of most Englishmen could have justified the
sanguine hopes attributed to him of seeing the religious ferment of the nation arrested and the integrity of English society

[2] See Louis I. Bredvold, "Notes on John Dryden's Pension," *Modern Philology,* 30
(1933): 267–74.
[3] Donald R. Benson, "Theology and Politics in Dryden's Conversion," *Studies in
English Literature,* 4 (1964): 393–412.

227

restored by his newly adopted church. But the fable of the martin and the swallows in Part III of *The Hind and the Panther*, as well as Dryden's letter to Etherege, make perfectly clear that he expected the English Catholics to remain a small and precarious minority.[4] To suggest that Dryden's motives in becoming a Catholic were political and pragmatic rather than religious and intellectual is to revive in a new form the discredited notion that they were not disinterested.

It would be fruitless to deny, of course, that politics and religion were more closely intertwined in the seventeenth century than in most other periods of English history. But the movement of influence was usually from religion to politics, and seldom in the opposite direction. Many Englishmen took their politics from their religion, as Dryden was fond of pointing out. In the latter half of the preface to *Religio Laici,* he argues at some length that faction and rebellion are the inevitable accompaniment of Catholicism and Dissent, and that the Popish Plot and the Exclusion Crisis are merely the practical corollaries of these two religions respectively. Again, in both *Absalom and Achitophel* and *The Medal* Dryden is at pains to suggest that the Dissenters are behaving with perfect consistency to their religious beliefs in supporting the political activities of Shaftesbury. But neither Dryden nor his contemporaries were in the habit of suggesting that many Englishmen took their religion from their politics. At all events, they would not have made the mistake of supposing that such behavior was above reproach.

The fact that politics and religion were closely connected in the Restoration period does not mean that Englishmen could not separate the two when they became topics for discussion. To see *Religio Laici* as a political poem and its publication as a political act is to fail to appreciate this distinction.[5] The poem, as we have seen, is a contribution to religious apologetics, and the first half of the preface, besides supplying the remedial introduction I discussed in chapter 2, is devoted to clarifying some of the religious arguments offered in the first part of the poem. But it was published the same year as *The Medal* and *The Duke of Guise,* and the poet's thoughts still turned to the issues raised by the

---

[4] See the lucid discussion of Dryden's views on this subject in Bredvold, *Intellectual Milieu,* pp. 164–84.

[5] See E. N. Hooker, "Dryden and the Atoms of Epicurus," *ELH*, 24 (1957): 177–90; Benson, "Theology and Politics in Dryden's Conversion," p. 395.

Popish Plot and the Exclusion Crisis. He therefore proceeds, in the remainder of his preface, to suggest the political corollaries which proceed from some, though not all, of the religious errors he has dealt with in the poem. Such suggestions do not alter in any way, however, the essentially religious purpose and subject of the poem they accompany.

In *The Hind and the Panther,* on the other hand, Dryden chooses to deal with both politics and religion in the poem itself, as he points out in the preface. But at any given moment in the poem he is dealing with "Matters either Religious or Civil," to use his own words, never with both topics simultaneously. In Part II his subject is "Church Authority," considered not as a matter of ecclesiastical polity for the English nation, but as a question of the divine economy of salvation which Christ provided for his church. As such, Part II raises many of the same issues discussed in the latter half of *Religio Laici* and is as exclusively religious as was the earlier poem. Part III, on the other hand, raises the question of political toleration for the Catholics and its subject is therefore "Civil" rather than religious. In Part I both topics are introduced, but they are kept completely separate. In the case of three of the beasts described there, the Fox, the Wolf, and the Panther, the first appearance of each becomes the occasion for a long discussion, in the poet's own voice, of a subject connected with the group whom the animal represents. The mention of the Wolf introduces a long political discussion, first, of the Presbyterians' "innate antipathy to kings" and of the political consequences of their activity and, second, of the advantages of civil toleration. The introduction of "False *Reynard*" and of the Panther, on the other hand, leads in each case to the discussion of a purely religious topic: that of Transubstantiation in the first instance; and of the hedonistic motives of the reformers, the Anglican attitude toward the Real Presence, and the Church of England's lack of religious authority in the other.

The temptation to seek clues to Dryden's religion in his politics is understandable. In the first place, while his religious beliefs changed, his political convictions did not. His Toryism is a principle of continuity in the changing world of Dryden's convictions which proves attractive to those who seek a consistent and predictable development of his ideas. Secondly, politics was a subject on which Dryden continued to write during the interval between *Religio Laici* and his conversion to the Catholic faith. *The Vin-*

229

dication of the Duke of Guise (1683), the "Postscript" to *The History of the League* (1684), *Albion and Albanius* (1685), and *Threnodia Augustalis* (1685) express his political views in steady succession during a period when he maintained a tantalizing silence on the subject of religion. The biographer, ready to grasp at any straw in frustration, may turn to these works in the hope of finding some clue to the imminent change in Dryden's religion. He will find plentiful references to the political consequences of Catholicism and Dissent of the kind already offered in *Absalom and Achitophel, The Medal,* and the latter part of the preface to *Religio Laici.* But he will find no hint of the change of faith that was taking place in the poet's mind and heart. On that matter of crucial importance he remained deliberately silent.

Only after an uncertain interval of time had elapsed following his conversion was Dryden to come forward once more and express his views on religious questions in two works issued a few months apart. The first was *A Defence of the Papers* (1686), part of a debate with Stillingfleet over the *Copies of Two Papers* which had been published earlier the same year.[6] The second was *The Hind and the Panther.* The one was a polemical pamphlet in prose; the other, as I have tried to show in chapter 2, a work of religious apologetics in verse. Neither is an attempt to explain his reasons for becoming a Catholic. Against Stillingfleet, Dryden carried on a personal debate in which he could rely on his own resources as a skilled controversialist. In order to deal with the far wider issues raised in *The Hind and the Panther,* on the other hand, he turned for help to the works of other religious apologists, as he had done in the case of *Religio Laici,* drawing this time on Catholic writers. This outside aid is employed to buttress his own arguments, of course, and as long as we recognize their polemical orientation we can accept them as expressing Dryden's views as a Catholic. What they will not tell us, however, is the motive for a conversion which had already taken place. *The Hind and the Panther* is not Dryden's *Apologia pro Vita Sua.*

The chief accusation against his former church which Dryden returns to repeatedly in *The Hind and the Panther* is her lack of

---

[6] Professor Ward has recently argued that *A Defence of the Papers* is entirely from Dryden's hand, not just the last part dealing with the third paper (*Life of John Dryden,* pp. 219, 359). For an answer to Ward's attribution, see Earl Miner, "Dryden as Prose Controversialist: His Role in *A Defence of the Royal Papers,*" *Philological Quarterly,* 43 (1964): 412–19.

innate religious authority. In Part I of the poem he introduces her as "the *Panther* sure the noblest, next the *Hind*, / And fairest creature of the spotted kind" (I, 327–28). He alludes to her doctrines with far less asperity than he applies to the other Protestant churches, concluding that she is "least deform'd, because reform'd the least" (I, 409). But when he turns to the matter of ecclesiastical jurisdiction he becomes more caustic, raising an issue which is to be explored at greater length in Part II of the poem:

> Fierce to her foes, yet fears her force to try,
> Because she wants innate auctority;
> For how can she constrain them to obey
> Who has herself cast off the lawfull sway?
> Rebellion equals all, and those who toil
> In common theft, will share the common spoil.
> Let her produce the title and the right
> Against her old superiours first to fight;
> If she reform by Text, ev'n that's as plain
> For her own Rebels to reform again.
> As long as words a diff'rent sense will bear,
> And each may be his own Interpreter,
> Our ai'ry faith will no foundation find:
> The word's a weathercock for ev'ry wind:
> The *Bear*, the *Fox*, the *Wolfe*, by turns prevail,
> The most in pow'r supplies the present gale.
> The wretched *Panther* crys aloud for aid
> To church and councils, whom she first betray'd;
> No help from Fathers or traditions train,
> Those ancient guides she taught us to disdain.
> And by that scripture which she once abus'd
> To Reformation, stands herself accus'd.
> What bills for breach of laws can she prefer,
> Expounding which she owns herself may err?
> And, after all her winding ways are try'd,
> If doubts arise she slips herself aside,
> And leaves the private conscience for the guide.
> If then that conscience set th' offender free,
> It barrs her claim to church auctority.
>
> [I, 452–80]

The suggestion that the weakness Dryden exploits here was a compelling motive in his own conversion cannot be dismissed lightly. It was often alluded to by English converts to Catholicism as an important consideration in their decision to leave the Church of

231

England. Edward Knott, for example, a Jesuit who engaged in a famous series of debates with Chillingworth, offered the following as the last and most important of a list of motives for abandoning the Established Church: "Because by denying all humane authority, either of Pope or Councels, or Church, to determine controversies of Fayth, they have abolished all possible meanes of suppressing Heresy, or restoring Unity to the Church."[7] That Dryden thought this a powerful argument is certain from the fact that he expounds it in the passage I have just quoted and elsewhere in *The Hind and the Panther*. That he found it a forceful motive in his own conversion a few months earlier is quite possible, but the hypothesis acquires no certainty from the fact that he chooses to concentrate on the problem of church authority in *The Hind and the Panther*. For this was one of the principal issues of debate between Anglicans and Catholics at the time and it is the subject of many works of apologetics written by both sides.

It is true, as his biographer has pointed out,[8] that Dryden expressed frequent concern with the excesses of private judgment, as practiced by the sects, long before he wrote *The Hind and the Panther*. Whether he is justified in assuming that this is an important clue to Dryden's conversion is not so certain. The fact is that none of these attacks on the Dissenters' abuse of private judgment, expressed in his political writings, moves beyond his admission in *Religio Laici* that these excesses existed, and the sharp reproof he offered the sects in that poem. In *The Medal,* for example, written a few months before *Religio Laici,* he had complained of the Dissenters:

> They rack ev'n Scripture to confess their Cause;
> And plead a Call to preach, in spight of Laws.
> But that's no news to the poor injur'd Page;
> It has been us'd as ill in every Age:
> And is constrain'd, with patience, all to take;
> For what defence can Greek and Hebrew make?
> Happy who can this talking Trumpet seize;
> They make it speak whatever Sense they please!
> 'Twas fram'd, at first, our Oracle t' enquire;

---

[7] *Motives Maintained, or, A Reply unto M. Chillingworthes Answere to His Owne Motives of His Conversion to Catholike Religion* (n.p., 1638), p. 23.
[8] See Ward, *Life of John Dryden*, pp. 212–13.

> But, since our Sects in prophecy grow higher,
> The Text inspires not them; but they the Text inspire.
>
> [ll. 156–66]

Two years later, in the "Postscript" to *The History of the League,* he returned to this favorite subject of how the Dissenters took their seditious politics from their fondness for private judgment in religion:

> But the beginning of leagues, unions, and associations, by those who called themselves God's people, for reformation of religious worship, and for the redress of pretended grievances in the state, is of a higher rise, and is justly to be dated from Luther's time; and the private spirit, or the gift of interpreting scriptures by private persons without learning, was certainly the original cause of such cabals in the reformed churches; so dangerous an instrument of rebellion is the holy scripture in the hands of ignorant and bigotted men.

He goes on to declare that "the Anabaptists of Germany led up the dance" in Luther's time, recounting the first stirrings of the sect, until at last

> they had the impudence to pretend to inspiration in the exposition of scriptures; a trick which since that time has been familiarly used by every sect in its turn, to advance their interests. Not content with this, they assumed to themselves a more particular intimacy with God's holy spirit; as if it guided them, even beyond the power of the scriptures, to know more of him than was therein taught. For now the Bible began to be a dead letter of itself; and no virtue was attributed to the reading of it, but all to the inward man, the call of the Holy Ghost, and the engrafting of the word, opening their understanding to hidden mysteries by faith. And here the mountebank way of canting words came first in use; as if there were something more in religion than could be expressed in intelligible terms, or nonsense were the way to heaven. This of necessity must breed divisions amongst them; for every man's inspiration being particular to himself, must clash with another's, who set up for the same qualification; the Holy Ghost being infallible in all alike, though he spoke contradictions in several mouths.[9]

Lastly, he relates how these religious notions were transplanted into Scotland and England.

These passages make clear that before his conversion Dryden

[9] *The Works of John Dryden,* ed. Sir Walter Scott and George Saintsbury (Edinburgh: William Paterson, 1882–93), XVII, 157–59.

consistently condemned the sectaries' method of interpreting the Scripture in terms from which the Church of England was wholly exempt. He regularly describes this method, both here and in *Religio Laici,* as the "private spirit," or a pretense "to inspiration in the exposition of scriptures"; there is no hint here or in *Religio Laici* that this has anything to do with the Anglican appeal to private judgment, his term for which is "private reason." From the time of Hooker, numerous Anglican apologists, in the course of upholding this ideal of private judgment, had condemned and ridiculed the Puritan appeal to the private spirit, often in terms much harsher than any Dryden uses. The Anglican notion of their own private judgment as a *via media* equally distant from Puritan and Catholic theories of scriptural interpretation is expressed by Dryden as well in the preface to *Religio Laici* when he writes:

But, by asserting the Scripture to be the Canon of our Faith, I have unavoidably created to my self two sorts of Enemies: The Papists indeed, more directly, because they have kept the Scripture from us, what they cou'd; and have reserv'd to themselves a right of Interpreting what they have deliver'd under the pretence of Infalibility: and the Fanaticks more collaterally, because they have assum'd what amounts to an Infalibility, in the private Spirit.

That the sectaries' pretense to inspiration in expounding the Scriptures was a misuse and corruption of the original Protestant principle of "private conscience" was undeniable to Dryden and his contemporaries. The abuse was almost as old as the principle itself, and "is justly to be dated from Luther's time," as Dryden remarked. But the fact that "this good had full as bad a Consequence," which he conceded in *Religio Laici,* had resulted, not from the encouragement of the Church of England, but in spite of her warnings.

After he had become a Catholic and had assumed the role of apologist for his new church, it is understandable that Dryden should have attributed the fragmentation of English Protestantism to the principle of private conscience, blaming the Established Church for upholding a principle which encouraged the growth of the sects. But we must remember that when he repeatedly levels this accusation against the Church of England in *The Hind and the Panther,* Dryden is alluding to a historical phenomenon which had already taken place, just as he attributes the creation of the

Established Church itself to the lust of Henry VIII. All of the major sects in England had arisen by the middle of the seventeenth century; "the *Bear,* the *Fox,* the *Wolfe,*" fully grown and ranging the forest alongside the Panther, are a standing reproach to the elder beast who has long been unable to "constrain them to obey."

If Dryden, as an Anglican, experienced growing concern over the ill effects of private conscience, it is unlikely that he expected educated Englishmen to succumb to the private spirit, which he had defined as "the gift of interpreting scriptures by private persons without learning." It is much more probable that his confidence in the Church of England's own alternative of private reason, expressed with such assurance in *Religio Laici,* began to wane shortly afterwards. As a matter of fact, a serious crisis of authority, which has escaped the attention of historians, was taking place at this very time within the Church of England. Its battleground was not the private spirit, long condemned by that church, but the very principle of private reason which she upheld.

In 1674, Martin Clifford, master of the Charterhouse, published a prose pamphlet, entitled *A Treatise of Humane Reason,* which ignited a furious controversy in the Church of England, lasting for ten years and involving at least as many contributors before it had run its course.[10] The pamphlet responsible for all these polemics is an assault on the authority of the Church of England to regulate the beliefs and practices of its own members. What is unusual about this attack is the fact that it proceeds from the pen, not of one of the usual enemies of the Established Church— atheists, deists, Dissenters, or Catholics—but of one of its own members addressing his fellow Anglicans. Clifford has no quarrel with the Scripture; he grants the necessity of revelation as willingly as any other Christian. "True it is," he writes, "that the best and truest *Humane Reason* could not have found out of it self, that *wisdom of God in a mystery, even that hidden wisdom which God ordained before the world,* which is the mystery of *Christ Jesus;* but it was necessary it should first be revealed by that Spirit,

---

[10] The late E. N. Hooker suspected the existence of this controversy, although he was aware of only three of the contributions to it, including Clifford's pamphlet. Probably because of his limited knowledge of its dimensions, he does not appear to have suspected its real implications; he concluded, erroneously, that *Religio Laici* was itself a contribution to this controversy, and that its character was purely political. See "Dryden and the Atoms of Epicurus," pp. 180–82.

which can only search and discover the deep things of God."[11]

His concern, therefore, is with the interpretation of the Scriptures he accepts as a Christian and with the right of his church to exact obedience from its members. Clifford appeals to the Protestant principle of private conscience as upholding the right of every individual to interpret the Scriptures for himself; by private conscience he means private reason, for he explicitly rejects the private spirit, along with General Councils and ecclesiastical tradition, as completely useless for explaining the Bible. But setting aside the traditional Anglican limitation of private reason to the discovery of plain truths necessary to salvation, he insists that the principle of private conscience, proclaimed by the reformers, extends to the more obscure passages of Scripture as well, eliminating the Anglican caution "that private Reason 'tis more Just to curb, / Than by Disputes the publick Peace disturb." "From whence then shall we say it proceeds," he asks, "that since the Reformation open'd a way to this Freedom of Conscience, so much Blood and Confusion, and almost Desolation, has followed in all those Countries which admitted it. *Germany, France,* the *Low-Countries,* and *Scotland* are sufficient witnesses of this; and I could wish that miserable *England* had not been added to the number of these sad Examples." The cause of all these wars of religion "I can find to be no other, than the strange and uncharitable Pride of those men, who having with just cause vindicated their own Reason from the tyranny of unnecessary bonds, endeavour nevertheless to lay them upon others; so that not the use of such Liberty, but the appropriating of it to our selves only, is the true, and, I think, the sole fountain of these Disorders."[12] If the benefits of the Reformation are ever to be realized, then, the exercise of church authority ought to be abandoned in favor of unrestricted private reason, for "it is impossible that ever any man should have been, is, or can hereafter be guided by any thing else but his own *Reason,* as in other things, so also in matters of Religion."[13]

That Clifford's motives in publishing his pamphlet were political, as E. N. Hooker suggested, seems certain. The political consequences of his theory, if accepted, would have been com-

[11] *A Treatise of Humane Reason* (London, 1674), pp. 57–58.
[12] *Ibid.,* pp. 10–11.
[13] *Ibid.,* p. 81.

plete civil toleration for all Protestants, and his patron, the Duke of Buckingham, was about to introduce such a bill in Parliament, on November 16, 1675, in a bid for the support of the Dissenters. What Hooker failed to perceive, however, is that the outcry which the pamphlet aroused was not primarily political, but religious, for Clifford had attacked the right of the Church of England to teach or enforce religious discipline. The history of the controversy is a curious one in which Clifford's supporters are politically motivated like himself, coming to the aid of his principles in order to promote the Country Party's strategy of toleration, whereas every one of his opponents concentrates on the religious issues he has raised, either ignoring or briefly dismissing the political corollary of his position. All of the participants save one, on both sides of the controversy, are members of the Church of England engaged in a purely domestic quarrel.

The first to answer Clifford was a layman. A. M., "a Countrey Gentleman," was incensed at the suggestion that toleration be extended to the Dissenters, but he was even more scandalized at Clifford's plea for unlimited private judgment, and it is to combating this that he devotes most of his pamphlet. His answer is to resort to the standard Anglican position on the interpretation of the Scripture expounded in *Religio Laici* and elsewhere. Where the common people are concerned, he writes, "it is the safest way for them, to relie upon the Church, especially in all matters of indifferency and of unnecessary disputes: and upon some of those Guides which the Church hath lawfully called and authorized in all cases of conscience."[14] This advice clearly depends on the distinction noticed in the last chapter between things necessary to salvation, which are left to private reason, and other matters of religion, which must be left to the authority of the church. "Read the Scriptures in English," he advises his fellow laymen, "and practise those things that are plain and easie in them: and as for difficult disputes either let them quite alone, or else consult in all difficulties the directions of your own Church, the Church of *England,* by those guides which she hath set over you."[15]

[14] *Plain Dealing: or, A Full and Particular Examination of a Late Treatise, Entituled, Humane Reason* (London, 1675), p. 108. This pamphlet is often erroneously attributed to Andrew Marvell. The author's point of view contradicts Marvell's in almost every respect.
[15] *Ibid.,* p. 112.

The same year, 1675, an Anglican clergyman, Edward Stephens, answered Clifford in milder accents than A. M. had used, but the burden of his complaint was the same; Clifford was for setting aside the directions and helps offered by the Church of England in favor of unrestrained private reason. "I shall here leave it to our Authors consideration, whether those Directions, and Helps may not more reasonably be said to be the guide of our Reason in its search, than Reason which is to make the search, and therefore to be guided, be said to be the guide it self."[16]

John Warly, fellow of Clare Hall, Cambridge, attacked Clifford in two sizable books, published in 1676 and 1677 respectively. The first, which challenges Clifford's view of the motives of credibility, need not concern us here.[17] The second, however, written "to assert the Authority of the Church," quarrels with Clifford over the same issues as A. M. and Stephens had raised. "I assert Ecclesiastical Authority with its due right," he declares, "above private Judgment of single persons, who so far become the Proselytes of humane Reason in that sense, which a late Author [Clifford] asserted it, as they appeal to nothing but the evidence of their own Reason conducted by its own natural Method, only having the information by reading the Scriptures; and fortifying their Opinions with mere natural Arguments (without any respect to the consent or authority of the Church)."[18] By this point the dust of battle has obscured the traditional distinction between private interpretation of things necessary to salvation and the acceptance of indifferent matters from the voice of the church. The issue has become a simple choice between private judgment and ecclesiastical authority, with Clifford's opponents defending the latter. A sign that the controversy was beginning to create more heat and less light is indicated by the fact that the next person to attack Clifford, a certain W. H. writing in 1679, mistook his opponent for a deist and charged "thus manifestly doth this

[16] *Observations upon a Treatise Intituled, Of Humane Reason* (London, 1675), p. 11.

[17] See *The Natural Fanatick, or, Reason Consider'd in Its Extravagancy in Religion, and (in Some Late Treatises) Usurping the Authority of the Church and Councils* (London, 1676). The other treatise referred to in Warly's title is Robert Boyle's *The Reconcileableness of Reason and Religion*. Warly accuses Clifford of Pelagianism for considering the motives of credibility purely rational and omitting any mention of divine grace.

[18] *The Reasoning Apostate: or Modern Latitude-Man Consider'd, as He Opposeth the Authority of the King and Church, Occasion'd by Several Late Treatises* (London, 1677), pp. 39–40. Only Consideration III of this book (pp. 38–64) deals with Clifford.

Opinion evacuate the necessity of Revelation, and derogate ex-treamly from the Mercy and Goodness of God in Blessing the World with knowledge of his Gospel."[19]

Some measure of equilibrium was restored the following year by Albertus Warren, who came to Clifford's defense. The book is dedicated to Shaftesbury and the author's political motives are clear, for he is chiefly interested in supporting Clifford's plea for toleration. But in order to answer A. M., he must deal with the religious issues involved, and he offers a useful reminder at this point that the question involves reason *vs.* authority, not reason *vs.* revelation: "For the Question is not amongst Christians, whether the Scripture be true or no; but this, what the meaning is of par-ticular Texts therein: or if any man can shew me any other way to understand it but Reason, I shall be very thankful; if then there be no other way but the Mediation of Reason, Reason, and bare Reason, is to be followed."[20] In challenging the Church of England's right to impose her authority upon believers, Warren pointed to what he considered a fatal weakness in her position: a church which has abrogated all claim to infallibility has likewise abdicated her right to impose her beliefs upon the faithful. "I am satisfied," he writes, "we have Religion well stated here [in England], but for all that, we do not pretend to infallibility; wherefore, for us to impose, being our selves fallible, is a little severe: as to the *Romanists,* they have something more colour, they pretending to Infallibility."[21]

Sir George Blundell, an Anglican layman who undertook to answer Warren as well as Clifford three years later, found it nec-essary to deal with this disturbing objection. He replied:

---

[19] *The Spirit of Prophecy. . . . Together with the Divine Authority of Christian Religion and the Holy Scriptures, the Insufficiency of Humane Reason, and the Reasonableness of the Christian Faith, Hope, and Practice, Deduced therefrom, and Asserted against Mr. Hobbs, and the Treatise of Humane Reason* (London, 1679), p. 216. Only chap. vi, sect. 3 (pp. 214–22) is concerned with Clifford. The book was written at the command of Peter Gunning, Bishop of Ely, known as "the hammer of the schismatics" because of his severity toward nonconformity, who read and approved it before publication. The common attribution of the book to William Hughes, the Dissenter, is therefore probably erroneous. Hughes did not conform to the Church of England until after 1680, according to Anthony Wood, who does not include this book in his list of Hughes's works (*Athenae Oxonienses* [3d ed.; London: F. C. and J. Rivington, 1820], IV, 541–45).

[20] *An Apology for the Discourse of Humane Reason, Written by Mr. Clifford, Esq.; Being a Reply to Plain Dealing* (London, 1680), p. 13.

[21] *Ibid.,* p. 24.

Thus much then we acknowledge, that we do not think our selves obliged to believe the Pastors of Holy Church (upon the bare account of Humanity) to be absolutely infallible, neither do we attribute to them so high Illuminations and Gifts as the first planting of the Gospel did require, and Christ's Conversation afforded his Apostles, who likewise were not altogether exempt from mistakes: but yet we rely upon the Spirit of Truth (which our Saviour promised to send to the Apostles and their Successors after his Ascension) to preserve them from teaching such Errors as are inconsistent with the Divine Oeconomy in Affairs of Religion, and the harmony of the Scriptures.[22]

This response involves a decidedly different view of the church's role from the one which appears in rejoinders to Catholic apologists. Henry Ferne, for example, contrasting the Church of England with the Church of Rome, declares: "Therefore we say also, the Guides and Pastors of the Church doe guide and teach not Infallibly, but Morally, by way of doctrine and perswasion."[23] Blundell, however, hard pressed by an opponent to whom moral authority is no authority at all, draws a distinction between "absolute infallibility," which he acknowledges that the pastors of the Church of England lack, and a limited infallibility, restricted to the divine economy of salvation, which these same pastors enjoy under the guidance of the Holy Spirit and which confers a sanction on their teachings.

This claim, put forward by a layman in the heat of debate, is negligible in itself, but it illustrates how embarrassing Warren's challenge proved to be and what little comfort the doctrine of moral authority could offer in this new crisis. Early in the controversy with Clifford, a Catholic apologist, one T. P., had exploited this embarrassment to the advantage of his own church. The only practicable alternatives, he argues, are an unlimited private judgment pushed to the extremes that Clifford wishes, or else a church whose infallibility permits her to decide controversies authoritatively. "And in Truth," he writes, "if each Man's Reason (Promiscuously) must be Umpire in this Rational Strife, men may Play at this Sport to Perpetuity and never win nor lose: But certainly our Blessed Saviour has not left the Condition of Mankind in this endless Confusion, but has miraculously Founded, and

[22] *Remarks upon a Tract, Intituled, A Treatise of Humane Reason. And upon Mr. Warren's Late Defence of It* (London, 1683), p. 30.
[23] *Of the Division between the English and Romish Church upon the Reformation* (London, 1652), pp. 47–48.

Signaliz'd a Church to end all Controversyes, if Men (that talk so much of Reason,) would but rightly use it."[24]

We can isolate two principal arguments, then, which were being raised by some of her own members to challenge the teaching authority of the Church of England. One of these is Warren's argument that only a church which claims to be infallible has the right to demand submission to her interpretation of Scripture. The other is the argument used by Clifford, that the logical outcome of the Reformation is the rejection of all church authority and the pursuit of private reason to wherever it may lead the individual Christian. This latter argument is also used by the Duke of Buckingham, whose own pamphlet in support of Clifford's plea for political toleration, although it was not published until 1705, many years after his death in 1687, was almost certainly circulated in manuscript at this time. Buckingham writes:

But when the Reformers had cast off the unsufferable Bondage of *Rome,* and rescu'd the Gospel from the Impositions and Impostures of that Church, one wou'd have imagined they should have cast away that odious Maxim of confining and imposing on the Consciences of those, they had set free; and never have dreamt of Persecuting them for making use of that Liberty, they had pretended to establish, by requiring an implicit Faith in them, and their Doctrines, when they wou'd not allow it to those of the Church, they had forsaken for her Errors, and Tyranny. For to me it is very unaccountable, that they should pretend to tell us, that we should now freely consult the Word of God, and at the same time deny us to understand it for our selves; since that is but to Fool us with the name of Liberty, without letting us possess the thing, and we might as well have continu'd under our old Masters, as be Slaves to new Lords.[25]

Against these two arguments no satisfactory answer was attempted by those who upheld the authority of the church. Except for Blundell's not very convincing attempt to appeal to a limited

---

[24] *Reason Regulated or, Brief Reflections, upon a Late Treatise of Human-Reason* (n.p., 1675), p. 45.

[25] "Letter to Mr. Clifford. On His Humane Reason," *The Works of George Villiers, Duke of Buckingham* (3d ed.; London, 1715), II, 186–87. Henry Hallywell is probably referring to Clifford and Warren when he speaks of the *"Capricio's* of such pert persons as think themselves obliged to believe and profess nothing more then they can maintain by their own solitary Reason applying it self to the Scriptures." He offers the usual answer of upholding "the Authority of . . . our own Church so excellently well temper'd and reformed according to the Primitive Pattern" ("The Preface to the Reader," in George Rust, *A Discourse of the Use of Reason in Matters of Religion* [London, 1683], sigs. a1v–a2v).

infallibility his church was not in the habit of claiming for herself, the apologists were content to answer their opponents with assertion instead of argument. Warly's remark that it "seems only necessary that I assert Ecclesiastical Authority with its due right, above private Judgment of single persons" describes fairly well the procedure of all the apologists in this controversy.

It was while this debate was at its highest pitch that Dryden wrote *Religio Laici*. The poem is not a contribution to the dispute, for it is an answer to other opponents, deist and Catholic, both of them outside the Church of England. In the latter part of the poem, where Dryden is expounding a *via media* between the Catholics and the Dissenters in answer to Father Simon, he finds the traditional Anglican position of private reason limited by church authority a perfectly satisfactory solution. This is scarcely surprising, since that position had been developed by earlier apologists for his church as a means of answering the very objections with which Dryden finds it necessary to deal. Whether he afterwards found this position as satisfactory an answer to the objections raised by members of his own church is less certain. He obviously felt no sympathy for the goals pursued by Clifford, Warren, and Buckingham, which would have eliminated all church authority, but he may have been impressed with the dilemma they had created for the Church of England, caught in an untenable position between two alternatives, neither of which she could adopt. If Clifford and his friends preferred the one alternative of unlimited private reason, Dryden was soon to choose the other of an infallible church authority.

In *The Hind and the Panther* Dryden's assault upon the Protestant principle of private conscience is not limited to the aberration of this principle which the sects had created with their appeal to the private spirit. He now criticizes, as we might expect, the Anglican version of this principle as well. Early in Part I, speaking in his own voice, he asks: "What weight of antient witness can prevail / If private reason hold the publick scale?" (I, 62–63). It is a question he returns to repeatedly in Part II, in the course of considering the importance of church authority. In challenging the Panther's right to claim such an authority, the Hind makes good use of each of the two arguments which Clifford and his friends had brought against that claim. The first, we may recall, was the argument employed by Clifford and Buckingham that the logical outcome of the Reformation is the rejection of all church authority. The Hind quotes the Panther's own rebellious sons against her in words which closely recall the passages I included earlier from these two men's protests:

> Well may they argue, (nor can you deny)
> If we must fix on church auctority,
> Best on the best, the fountain, not the flood,
> That must be better still, if this be good.
> Shall she command, who has herself rebell'd?
> Is *Antichrist* by *Antichrist* expell'd?
> Did we a lawfull tyranny displace,
> To set aloft a bastard of the race?
> Why all these wars to win the Book, if we
> Must not interpret for our selves, but she?
> Either be wholly slaves or wholly free.
>
> [II, 275–85]

The other argument, pursued by Warren, that only a church which claims to be infallible has the right to demand submission, is also used with telling effect by the Hind against the Panther. Already in Part I Dryden had dismissed the Anglican position that she teaches "not Infallibly, but Morally, by way of doctrine and perswasion," when he asked "How answ'ring to its end a church is made, / Whose pow'r is but to counsell and persuade?" (I, 491–92). In Part II, the Hind tells the Panther:

> It then remains that church can onely be
> The guide, which owns unfailing certainty;
> Or else you slip your hold, and change your side,
> Relapsing from a necessary guide.
> But this annex'd condition of the crown,
> Immunity from errours, you disown,
> Here then you shrink, and lay your weak pretensions down.
>
> [II, 483–89]

The Hind, then, is certainly familiar with both arguments used by Clifford and his friends against their own church, and she demonstrates that they can be employed as effectively on behalf of an infallible church authority as in support of the opposite position of unlimited private reason. But we cannot therefore conclude that the Hind's creator had discovered these arguments, while still an Anglican, in the pamphlets of his Whig coreligionists or that this provides an unmistakable clue to his conversion. Both arguments, as we shall see in the next chapter, were rejoinders to the Anglican position which had been used by Catholic apologists on many occasions and could conceivably have been discovered for the first time by Dryden after his conversion when he was engaged in providing himself with weapons for his most ambitious polemical poem.

We must conclude that *The Hind and the Panther* is no more reliable a guide to the religious conversion which it followed than are *Religio Laici* and the political writings which preceded that event. It is a plausible hypothesis that the crisis over church authority created in the Church of England by the Clifford controversy may have played a part in Dryden's conversion, but there is no confirmation of this hypothesis in his writings.

At all events, if Dryden left no account of his reasons for joining the Catholic church, he made an unequivocal statement of his motives for remaining in it which focuses attention on the problem of church authority as the most compelling consideration in his choice of a church. Six months before his death, he declared in a letter to his Protestant cousin, Elizabeth Steward:

I can neither take the Oaths, nor forsake my Religion, because I know not what Church to go to, if I leave the Catholique; they are all so divided amongst them selves in matters of faith, necessary to Salvation: & yet all assumeing the name of Protestants. May God be pleasd to open your Eyes, as he has opend mine: Truth is but one; & they who have once heard of it, can plead no Excuse, if they do not embrace it.[26]

The abrupt shift Dryden makes here from an account of his beliefs to an attempt at persuasion should remind us of the proper perspective for reading *The Hind and the Panther*. When approached from the viewpoint of biography, it is a baffling document; considered as persuasive poetry, it is Dryden's most sustained performance. In the next chapter I shall consider those parts of the poem in which he exhibits his skill as a religious apologist for the last time.

[26] *The Letters of John Dryden, ed.* Charles E. Ward (Durham, N.C.: Duke University Press, 1942), p. 123. The letter is dated November 7, 1699.

8

SPOKESMAN FOR A MINORITY

When Dryden began writing *The Hind and the Panther* toward the end of 1686, his acquaintance with the writings of other Catholic apologists was presumably quite recent. He had learned something of the way in which Catholics assailed Protestant positions in 1682 when he had read the preface to Father Simon's *Critical History;* but Simon was not a religious apologist, as I pointed out in chapter 6, and he makes no attempt to enlarge on the commonplaces he repeats. Again, allusions to various Catholic authors in the preface to *Religio Laici* where Dryden is discussing the political consequences of Catholicism indicate that he had read the works of some of their authors on the vexed question of obedience to a heretical prince; but he gives no sign there or elsewhere of having read the religious apologetics on behalf of that church as early as 1682.

It seems likely that Dryden turned to the writings of Catholic religious apologists for the first time during the months preceding his conversion, when he quite naturally would have had a strong personal interest, not only in the arguments justifying the religion toward which he was now inclining, but also in the case against the church he was about to leave. After his conversion, when he decided to champion his new religion in another argumentative poem, he would have gone as a matter of course to the polemical writings of his coreligionists for "helps" as he had done, under very different circumstances, when he wrote *Religio Laici.* There was no scarcity of such writings at any time in the seventeenth century, least of all in the reign of James II.

None of the contexts of Dryden's thought has been more completely misunderstood than the tradition of Catholic apologetics in England and its relation to his religious arguments in *The Hind and the Panther*. Two assumptions have governed discussions of this tradition in relation to Dryden, both of them false. The first is that English Catholic apologetics was a monolithic body of opinion expressed by a closely organized group of writers, all of whom were in a position to speak authoritatively on behalf of their church, and any of whom can be cited to support and clarify Dryden's own position as a Catholic. The second is that it was characteristic of this group to employ fideistic arguments as "weapons against Protestantism," although "not as a part of the structure of Roman Catholic theology," since fideism is considered a heresy by that church. The premises of these writers are therefore assumed to be Pyrrhonistic, their strategy one of forcing their opponents to despair of reason as a reliable faculty in order to reduce them to utter dependence on an infallible church.[1]

The precarious situation of English Catholics in the seventeenth century was not conducive to organized activity nor even to uniform opinion, and the serious divisions in the ranks of their clergy created positive disharmony. The quarrel between the regular clergy and the secular chapter grew so intense, in fact, that it forced the retirement of the Vicar Apostolic, Richard Smith, in 1628. Gregorio Panzani, dispatched to England in 1634 with instructions to restore harmony among the Catholics there, was unable to carry out his commission, and the continued dissension among the clergy made the appointment of a successor to Smith impracticable. From 1628 to 1685, therefore, English Catholics were without episcopal jurisdiction; all the tendencies to disruption to which any underground organization is subject were allowed to materialize without interference. Instead of forming a solid phalanx against their enemies, the clergy were engaged in internecine quarrels; regulars fought with seculars, the various factions of the secular chapter fought each other, and one or the other party to a dispute would carry the matter to Rome, or even, on occasion, to the Protestant authorities at Westminster.

[1] See Louis I. Bredvold, *The Intellectual Milieu of John Dryden* (Ann Arbor: University of Michigan Press, 1934), pp. 73–129. More recent studies which have taken the fideism of Catholic apologetics for granted include Helene M. Hooker, "Charles Montagu's Reply to *The Hind and the Panther*," ELH, 8 (1941): 51–73; Thomas H. Fujimura, "Dryden's *Religio Laici*: An Anglican Poem," PMLA, 76 (1961): 205–17; Donald R. Benson, "Theology and Politics in Dryden's Conversion," *Studies in English Literature*, 4 (1964): 393–412.

In this state of affairs, Catholic apologetics was not a concerted effort but a sporadic activity carried on in the intervals between domestic engagements by men who were often no better disposed toward some of their confreres than they were toward their Protestant enemies. Living in comparative isolation and surreptitiously publishing books which had to be printed abroad or on forbidden presses nearer home, these men were free to develop eccentricities of opinion encouraged by their independence of normal supervision. Some of these eccentricities had already begun to appear in the previous century. A recent historian, referring to the earlier period, has pointed out that

the English Recusants were themselves not of one mind on Scripture and Tradition. Some of them had theological idiosyncrasies of their own. Anglicans often mistook these for "the Romish doctrine." Thus a frequent generalization ascribed to the Church of Rome a theology which had by no means been endorsed by any Catholic authority. Among Recusants as among Anglicans, extremists captured the headlines. More often than not both Recusants and Anglicans assailed positions that were defended by the least moderate of their adversaries, and did not correspond to the theology of the most intelligent minds of either side.[2]

Given free rein in the following century because of the conditions I have described, these idiosyncrasies were able to develop, in some cases, into independent theological systems. This was especially true of certain secular priests, subject only to a chapter torn by internal dissension, since the regular clergy, responsible to the English provincials of their various orders, were under greater restraint. As a result, a competitive spirit developed among the apologists which was scarcely conducive to uniformity. Something of the lengths to which this spirit could lead is indicated by the following passage:

SEVENTH DEMAND. Whether it argue not that the passion and Interest of these men is above their love of maintaining Catholick Religion to blast not only the name of an Author who has written so advantagiously and solidly for Faith, but even those very Books which so incomparably defend Faith and its Rule? Let *Rushworths Dialogues*, *Apology for Tradition* and *Controversie-Logick* be examined (to omit

---

[2] George H. Tavard, *Holy Writ or Holy Church: The Crisis of the Protestant Reformation* (New York: Harper Brothers, 1959), p. 210. For a discussion of these idiosyncrasies down to the end of the sixteenth century, see pp. 210–43.

others) and see whether ever the Heterodox party were either so solidly confuted, or Faith so radically stated; yet are these Books condemn'd too with the rest, what more disgrace to our Cause could even a *Presbyterians* heart wish? . . . *Knots* voluminous Encounter with *Chillingworth,* and *Fishers* with B. *Laud,* remain sad Instances of the Catholick cause, left dangerously exposed, not through want of grounds, but by a voluntary desertion of Catholick Principles, to follow those of Interest and Flattery.[3]

The author is an anonymous secular, writing in defense of another secular whose books of apologetics had been placed on the *Index of Forbidden Books* the previous year for theological idiosyncrasies too glaring to be passed over in silence. The two famous works of controversy with Chillingworth and Laud, on the other hand, the authors of which are here condemned for deserting Catholic principles, were both written by Jesuits. Such intemperate charges should make us wary of accepting at face value the testimony of interested parties to these disputes.

Yet the legend that most Catholic apologists employed fideistic arguments designed to encourage philosophical scepticism in the interest of their church is based entirely on the testimony of contemporary witnesses who are particularly suspect. All but one of these witnesses are Protestants engaged in controversy with Catholic adversaries whom they accuse of encouraging scepticism of the reliability of human reason.[4] Such name-calling is common to both sides in seventeenth-century religious polemics and does not deserve serious consideration. More specifically, in the controversy over the interpretation of Scripture between Anglicans and Catholics, each side accused the other of an exaggeration of its actual position. In what often became, in the heat of debate, a simplified choice between private reason and church authority, the Anglicans accused the Catholics of undervaluing reason to the point of scepticism, whereas the Catholics charged the Anglicans with exaggerating its importance to the point of Socinianism. Both accusations were useful at the time for scoring debating points; neither is trustworthy for reconstructing the actual positions of the apologists on either side.

The other witness to the sceptical tendencies of Roman Catholic apologetics in England is a contemporary Catholic priest

---

[3] *Check: or, Inquiry into the Late Act of the Roman-Inquisition: Busily, and Pressingly Disperst over all England by the Jesuits* (London, 1662), pp. 11–12.

[4] See Bredvold, *Intellectual Milieu,* pp. 85–98.

248

whose testimony at first sight appears more reliable. Thomas White—so runs the explanation—"was no critic of the reason; he was for certainty both in philosophy and in religion." Worried by the sceptical tendencies of such works of Catholic apologetics as the famous *Rushworth's Dialogues* and Hugh Cressy's *Exomologesis*, we are told, White reproved "'some of our Divines; who (raising more dust then they were able to keep out of their own eyes) seem to have unawares contributed to the hatching of this dangerous Cockatrice, *Incertitude.*'"[5] This seemingly disinterested testimony acquires a different perspective, however, when we realize that this same Thomas White, alias Blacklo, is the secular who is being so violently defended in the "Seventh Demand" quoted above, the author of *Rushworth's Dialogues* and numerous other "Books condemn'd" at Rome to the infinite consolation of Presbyterians. White's remarks clearly cannot have been directed at such books as *Rushworth's Dialogues* and Cressy's *Exomologesis*, unless he was engaging in self-criticism. He was, as his supporter declared, the author of the first and his quoted criticism is taken from his preface to that book; Cressy, at the time he wrote *Exomologesis*, was an admirer and supporter of White's theological system. The charge of scepticism is obviously directed against some other group of Catholics; it is not a disinterested observation but a highly partisan accusation from one who, a century and a half later when the controversy still smouldered, was described by another English Catholic as "precisely the boldest enemy of authority, the most daring innovator, the most violent party-man, that has ever yet distracted our small church."[6]

Many of White's activities as a "violent party-man" were connected with his leadership of a group of capitular priests, known as "Blacklo's Cabal," who were engaged in a struggle for control of the secular chapter which need not concern us here. Much more important for our purpose is White's role in developing an independent theological system and leading another, no less vio-

[5] See *ibid.*, pp. 80–84. After establishing his hypothesis by means of White's testimony and that of the Protestant controversialists, Professor Bredvold proceeds to find support for it by interpreting various passages from Catholic apologists as fideistic. As Elias J. Chiasson has shown, however, Bredvold's interpretation is based on a misunderstanding of Catholic (and Anglican) theology, and parallels for these supposedly fideistic statements can readily be found in Thomas Aquinas and in Hooker. See his illuminating article on "Dryden's Apparent Scepticism in *Religio Laici*," *Harvard Theological Review*, 54 (1961): 207–21.

[6] Charles Plowden, *Remarks on a Book Entitled Memoirs of Gregorio Panzani* (Liege, 1794), p. 256.

lent, party of apologists who employed his system in controversy with the Anglicans over the rule of faith. This system of White and his partisans offered an alternative view to that of other Eng-lish Catholics on most of the religious issues raised in *The Hind and the Panther*. The tradition of English Catholic apologetics available to Dryden, to which he could turn for arguments with which to supply the Hind, consisted, therefore, not of a uniform body of opinion, but of two mutually antagonistic systems of thought. It is impossible to understand Dryden's own position and its relation to Catholic apologetics without some knowledge of the difference between these two systems, the relative strength of their adherents, and Dryden's unquivocal preference for one system rather than the other.

The minority party in this dispute was certainly White's; it attracted so much attention, however, by the novelty of its doc-trines, that it assumed far greater importance in the controversy between Anglicans and Catholics than the number of its adher-ents would suggest. Tillotson, whose famous *Rule of Faith* (1666) was written in answer to one of the members of this party, John Sergeant, provided a complete roll of its members. Referring to Sergeant, he writes of "the chief of *his Brethren of the Tradition, viz.* Mr. *Rushworth*, Dr. *Holden*, Mr. *Cressy*, and Mr. *White*, who besides Mr. *S*[ergeant] and one *I. B.* [John Belson] are (so far as I can learn) all the publick Patrons that ever this Hypothe-sis of Oral Tradition hath had in the World; and if Mr. *White* (as I have reason to believe) was the Authour of those *Dialogues* which pass under *Rushworth*'s name, the number of them is yet less."[7]

Tillotson, an admittedly hostile witness, is nevertheless relating certain facts about a division among Catholic apologists which was well known to both Anglicans and Catholics at the time. The party he mentions consisted of a group of seculars who took their theological idiosyncrasies from their leader, Thomas White. As Tillotson suspected, William Rushworth was not a member of the group. At his death in 1637, he left some dialogues in manu-script which White altered and expanded to suit his own peculiar ideas before publishing them in 1640.[8] In many other books, pub-

---

[7] *The Rule of Faith* (London, 1666), p. 119.

[8] Since Rushworth's manuscript no longer exists, it is impossible to assess White's share of the first edition of the book (1640), consisting of three dialogues. The second edition (1654), "Corrected and Enlarg'd by Thomas White," contains a fourth dia-

lished under his own name, White developed his system more fully. Before returning to England to join the secular chapter there, White had taught at Douay, where many members of the English mission received their training. One of his students at Douay was Henry Holden, who came under the influence of his teachings. Later Holden became a professor at the Sorbonne, where Hugh Cressy became his own student and absorbed White's teachings at second hand. It was while Cressy was still fresh from Holden's tutelage that he published *Exomologesis* (1647), in which he expressed White's views; later he joined the Benedictine order and recanted his earlier teachings.[9] John Sergeant, alias Holland, thirty years White's junior, was his close friend and private secretary before becoming secretary of the secular chapter.[10] In *Sure Footing* (1665) (answered by Tillotson in *The Rule of Faith*) and numerous other books, Sergeant expounded the notions he had acquired from his friend and patron and added his own refinements. John Belson was apparently also, like Holden, a student of White's. When Belson published his defence of *Rushworth's Dialogues,* entitled *Tradidi Vobis* (1662), Sergeant contributed the preface, in which he declared that Belson had written the book out of "a grateful respect to that incomparable and much envied Master of his, the great *Explainer* of *Tradition* [White]; to the defence of whose Doctrine he owes the imploy-

logue which White acknowledged as his own "besides a very considerable polishment of the whole." It seems to have been generally assumed that White modified Rushworth's text until it became practically his own, as Tillotson implies. Robert Pugh declared that White "printed some Controversiall Dialogues, composed by Mr. *Rushworth,* whose name they bore: a treatise good in its self, yet he [White] left the print of his foot in it by foisted errors" (*Blacklo's Cabal Discovered in Severall of Their Letters* [2d ed.; n.p., 1680], no pagination or signatures). Pugh was a bitter enemy of White's and his testimony cannot be taken at face value; however, White's friends also seem to have considered him the author of the book. The author of *Check,* previously quoted, attributes it to White, as does John Belson, who refers to *Rushworth's Dialogues* and the later *Apology* for them as "those two Pieces of Mr. Whites."

[9] At least according to Peter Talbot, *Blakloanae Haeresis Olim in Pelagio et Manichaeis Damnatae, Nunc Denuo Renascentis, Historia et Confutatio* (Ghent, 1675), p. 121. As is evident from the title, Talbot was not an impartial witness.
[10] See George Leyburn, "A List of the More Noteworthy Priests Who are to Be Found at Present among the English Secular Clergy," *The Douay College Diaries, Third, Fourth and Fifth, 1598–1654,* ed. Edwin H. Burton and Thomas L. Williams (London: Catholic Record Society, 1911), II, 549–50. Leyburn's judgments of White, Sergeant, and the other members of their cabal are extremely tendentious, but his facts are generally sound.

ment of that strength the same Doctrine had given him."[11] The
two most prominent members of the little group were obviously
White, who was responsible for the innovations his followers
adopted, and Sergeant, known to his enemies among the English
Catholics as "Blacklo's Philip," because he played Melancthon
to White's Luther.[12]

Sergeant and his friends acquired many such enemies among
their confreres for the views they expressed on the rule of faith.
We have already noticed that all White's works, "both printed
and in manuscript," had been placed on the *Index of Forbidden
Books* in 1661. Completely undeterred by this setback, he continued to defend his views. George Leyburn, president of Douay,
was White's most violent antagonist and published a series of
books warning the English clergy to beware of the "profane
novelties" and "divers naughty, erroneous, and scandalous doctrines" contained in White's works.[13] When Sergeant began to
publish his own series of books expounding White's system, the
furor in the Catholic camp grew more intense than ever. In 1675,
Peter Talbot, the Catholic archbishop of Dublin, published a
large volume, entitled *Blakloanae Haeresis*, in which he discussed
a formidable list of heresies of which Sergeant was guilty, but
which had originated with White.

The Blackloists found it necessary, therefore, to carry on

[11] "The Publisher to the Reader," in Belson, *Tradidi Vobis: or The Traditionary
Conveyance of Faith Cleer'd, in the Rational Way, against the Exceptions of a
Learned Opponent* (London, 1662), sig. A2v.

[12] See Charles Plowden, *Remarks on a Book Entitled Memoirs of Gregorio Panzani*,
p. 285. Part III of this book (pp. 255–97) is devoted entirely to White, Holden, and
Sergeant. Plowden was Provincial of the English Jesuits at the end of the eighteenth
century, and his bias against the secular clergy is apparent. Nevertheless, his account
of English Catholic affairs in the seventeenth century is a valuable corrective to
Charles Dodd's *Church History of England* (1737–42), on which Professor Bredvold
seems to have relied implicitly. Plowden is very severe on Dodd, whom he calls "a
partial and passionate writer, who has not equal charity for all his neighbours, and
is therefore equally unworthy of credit, in what he prints and in what he conceals"
(p. 186); there is some justice to his charge that Dodd acts as apologist for White and
his party throughout the *Church History* (p. 263). The truth probably lies somewhere between Plowden and Dodd.

[13] See *An Epistle Declaratorie, or Manifest Written by G. L. to His Brethren
Residing in England* (n.p., 1657). See also *The Summe of Doctor Leyburnes Answere
to a Letter Printed against Him by Mr. Blacloe* (n.p., 1657), which discusses seven of
White's "profane novelties," and *Dr. Leyburns Encyclicall Answer to an Encyclicall
Epistle Sent to Our Brethren of England* (Douay, 1661), which includes another list
of White's heresies on pp. 69–75. For a catalogue of Catholic writers who attacked
White's doctrines as heretical, see Plowden, *Remarks*, pp. 257–58.

their warfare on two fronts. While they engaged with some of the most formidable apologists in the Anglican camp, their own coreligionists were assailing them from the rear. Their Anglican adversaries were only too ready to capitalize on this disadvantage and to quote Catholic authorities against them. One of Tillotson's most telling maneuvers against Sergeant in *The Rule of Faith* is to quote the Council of Trent, the Roman Catechism, Cardinals Bellarmine and Perron, and Edward Knott in direct opposition to what he calls "Mr. *Rushworth*'s new Rule of Faith."[14] In the same manner, Stillingfleet points out that Sergeant "apparently opposes himself to the whole current of their own authors," and taunts him and his party with the fact that "their Books are censured at *Rome,* their opinions disputed against, and their persons condemned."[15]

It is important that we become aware of the host of enemies, Catholic as well as Protestant, created by those who expounded "Mr. *Rushworth*'s new Rule of Faith," in order to realize the serious division of opinion among English Catholics on this question and the confusion which results from citing various Catholic apologists indiscriminately in an attempt to construct a unanimous point of view. But the hostility which Simon's *Critical History* evoked from Bossuet and many of his coreligionists should remind us of the hazards of trying to elicit a writer's opinions from the accusations of his enemies, even when they belong to his own church. These charges become even more suspect when we remember that White and Sergeant were the leaders not only of a theological party but of a clerical cabal engaged in a struggle with other seculars for control of the chapter. Charges of heresy were a powerful weapon in the hands of the cabal's enemies when they appealed to Rome for a decision on the dispute. We must turn, therefore, to the polemical writings of the Blackloists themselves in order to understand something of their theological system.

It is perhaps misleading to use the term "theological system" in connection with the arguments of these active controversialists. They were interested first of all in winning debates rather than

14 See *The Rule of Faith,* pp. 279–92.

15 *A Reply to Mr. J. S. His 3rd Appendix, Containing Some Animadversions on the Book Entituled, A Rational Account of the Grounds of Protestant Religion* (London, 1666), pp. 52–53. A copy of Talbot's *Blakloanae Haeresis* now in the British Museum bears the following inscription on the flyleaf: "The Gift of D. Stillingfleet, Dean of S. Pauls, to Tho. Tenison."

in engaging in theological speculations. But their tactics were novel and their arguments were immediately challenged not only by their Protestant opponents but by their Catholic confreres. In this situation the traditional role of the religious apologist—that of devising arguments in support of the position already espoused by his own church—proved inadequate. With growing frequency they were forced to turn their attention to the theological premises behind their arguments.

Like many Catholic apologists, the Blackloists began by challenging the Protestant position on the rule of faith. Against the exclusive emphasis on *Scriptura sola* as the rule of faith, Catholics had customarily responded by urging that tradition be given an equal share with Scripture, and by arguing that the latter alone was inadequate. It was perhaps inevitable that in the heat of controversy some faction among the Catholics, impatient with attempts to qualify their opponents' rule of faith, should have rejected it altogether and presented the debate as a simple choice between Scripture and tradition. At all events, this was to be the procedure of the Blackloists, whose "new Rule of Faith" consists entirely of tradition, to the exclusion of Scripture. Christ "instituted *Tradition* alone to be the means and rule of the receit of his doctrine," White declares, "and [gave] *Scripture* only for superabundant instruction and consolation."[16] In fact, "the principal end perhaps for which the *Scripture* was deliver'd and recommended to us" was purely homiletic, "[the Evangelists'] intention being, not so much literally to teach the Articles of Christian doctrin, as to perswade and make what is already believ'd sink into the Auditory, with a kind of willingness & easiness, that their faith be quickned into a principle of action to govern their lives."[17]

White's "new Rule of Faith" is the subject of Belson's *Tradidi Vobis*, which is divided into two parts, the first entitled "Scripture not the Rule of Faith" and the second "Tradition the Rule of Faith." Sergeant adopts the same format in *Sure Footing*. After establishing the properties of a rule of faith in the first discourse of the book, he devotes the next three discourses to showing "that Scripture's Letter Wants All the Forementioned Properties Be-

---

[16] *Rushworth's Dialogues, or, The Judgment of Common Sence in the Choyce of Religion* (2d ed.; Paris, 1654), p. 40. See also pp. 46 and 166.

[17] *An Apology for Rushworth's Dialogues* (Paris, 1654), pp. 34–35. See also pp. 40–42 and 46–47.

longing to the Rule of Faith."[18] He then proceeds to argue in the fifth discourse that these properties are to be found exclusively in tradition, which, as he was to insist in other books as well, is "the only Conveyor of Christs Doctrine hitherto."[19] Their fellow Catholics protested in vain against the Blackloists' exclusive attention to tradition. "You are raving [*insanis*], Sergeant," Archbishop Talbot declared, "when you exclude Holy Scripture from the rule of faith."[20] To the Blackloists such criticism from their own camp was a betrayal which only made them more obdurate.

Not content to oppose tradition to Scripture by simple assertion, the Blackloists attempted to show that the properties of a rule of faith were such as could be possessed only by tradition. In order to do this, they found it necessary to challenge the usual conception of the nature of faith. We noticed in chapter 4 that it was commonly held that moral arguments were the best that reason could bring in support of the Christian religion, whose revelation had taken place in the distant past and had been recorded in books almost as ancient as the events they related. The historical evidence for the genuineness of this revelation as found in Scripture, such as Dryden offered in the first half of *Religio Laici*, might be extremely probable, yet it could not prove the matter beyond all doubt. As Archbishop Laud declared: "For though this Truth, *That Scripture is the Word of God*, is not so Demonstratively evident, *a priori*, as to enforce Assent: yet it is strengthen'd so abundantly with probable Arguments, both from the Light of *Nature* it selfe, and *Humane Testimony*, that he must be very

---

[18] *Sure Footing in Christianity, or Rational Discourses on the Rule of Faith* (London, 1665), p. 39.

[19] *Reason against Raillery* (n.p., 1672), p. 189. On this important question Cressy did not follow the other members of the party. His allegiance to the group was only temporary, as I have pointed out, and it was never complete. Even in *Exomologesis* (Paris, 1647) he maintains that "the entire Rule of Faith . . . [consists] not onely in Scripture, but likewise in unwritten Traditions" (p. 123). As Tillotson was quick to point out, the view which "Mr. *Cressy* likewise (not very consistently to himself) layes down, is as contrary as can be to Mr. *Rushworth's* new Rule of Faith" (*Rule of Faith*, p. 284). It is worth noticing that *Exomologesis* has a much wider scope than the books by the other Blackloists and lacks the polemical tone of their writings. Most of the peculiarly Blackloist tenets in the book, which the author later recanted, are found in Section III (pp. 246–487). The first two sections contain many things that would have been unexceptionable to any Catholic reader, and include various analogues to passages in *The Hind and the Panther*, although these analogues are certainly not unique.

[20] *Blakloanae Haeresis*, p. 277. My translation. See pp. 273–90 for Talbot's discussion of the differences between the Blackloist notion of the rule of faith and the one held by most Catholics.

wilfull, and selfe-conceited, that shall dare to suspect it."[21] This admission, of course, is at the very heart of the classical distinction between science and faith, or knowledge and belief, common to both churches. Faith is a theological virtue precisely because rational arguments, although they are the foundation of belief, are not sufficient to maintain it without the intervention of the will strengthened by divine grace to produce conviction; "to which firmnesse of *Assent*," as Laud explained, "by the Operation of *Gods Spirit*, the *Will* conferres as much, or more *strength*, then the *Understanding, Clearenesse*, the whole *Assent* being an *Act* of *Faith*, and not of *Knowledge*."[22]

The Blackloists willingly conceded that historical evidence for the divine authorship of the Scriptures could yield only probable arguments, but on these very grounds they concluded that Holy Scripture does not possess the properties of a rule of faith. For they stoutly denied the classical distinction between science and belief, insisting that faith, where genuine, is a matter of clear and certain knowledge derived from evidence not essentially different from any other kind. White declares "that the means of comming to the assent of Faith, are really so firm and certain, that a man may, and all such as goe exactly to work, doe arrive at so rationall a fixednesse in it, that no opposition of reason, duly managed, can draw them from it."[23] This means of coming to the assent of faith is, as Sergeant explains, "*orall* or *Practical Tradition*. By which we mean a Delivery down from hand to hand (by words, and a constant course of frequent and visible Actions conformable to those Words) of the Sence and Faith of Forefathers."[24] As interpreted by the Blackloists, tradition becomes a process whereby the faithful themselves preserve their beliefs and practices from generation to generation by passing them on from father to son within each family, the generality of Christians, as Sergeant writes,

practising the same external Actions which determin to a certain degree the sence of the Words they have been inur'd to; and (since the practice of those Actions was instill'd from their Infancy, and serious) *holding* consequently the Principles of those Actions; that is, the same Points of Faith with the former Age. And this goes on not

[21] *A Relation of the Conference betweene William Lawd and Mr. Fisher the Jesuite* (London, 1639), p. 77.
[22] *Ibid.*, p. 115.
[23] "Preface," *Rushworth's Dialogues*, sigs. ✱✱✱7v–✱✱✱8.
[24] *Sure Footing*, p. 41. Cf. White, *Apology for Rushworth's Dialogues*, p. 126.

by leaps from an hundred years to an hundred, or from twenty to twenty, but by half-years to half-years, nay moneths to moneths, and even less.[25]

This oral or practical tradition, according to the Blackloists, is a trust accepted by the community of the faithful which it is impossible to believe that they would violate by permitting errors and innovations to alter the beliefs and practices they have inherited from their parents. "When a whole age agrees universally to acknowledge a Tradition under that notion," Cressy declares, "neither freinds nor enemyes contradicting, it is impossible that such a report should be false."[26] For as Belson explains, "it being the nature of man to speak truth, and the number of men being, in this case beyond all temptations, whether of hopes, fears, or whatever else may be imagined should prevail with them to contradict their nature, I cannot see but a little reflexion must needs make you acknowledge 'tis beyond the power of imagination it self to put any deceit in their testimony."[27] If this is the case, then faith depends on evidence as indubitable as any other; what is commonly styled belief is really "knowledge from report or Tradition," which, in Cressy's words, is "as truely certaine as that from sence or demonstration."[28]

As the Blackloists perceived, their conception of the nature of faith was the basic premise of their entire system of controversy; if this were once accepted, they reasoned, their Protestant opponents would be forced to adopt the "new Rule of Faith" which was its logical corollary. They therefore hammered unceasingly at the classical distinction between knowledge and faith, ridiculing the notions of probable or moral arguments on behalf of revealed religion, of the intervention of the will in the act of faith, and even of the necessity of divine grace for Christian belief.[29] In attacking this time-honored distinction, however, they found themselves in conflict with the members of their own church as

---

[25] *Sure Footing*, p. 45. The subject is discussed at length on pp. 41–47. Cf. White, *Apology for Rushworth's Dialogues*, pp. 70–77, and his *Tabulae Suffragiales* (London, 1655), p. 96.

[26] *Exomologesis*, p. 297. See also p. 313.

[27] *Tradidi Vobis*, p. 295.

[28] *Exomologesis*, p. 296. See also pp. 317–18.

[29] See White, "Preface," *Rushworth's Dialogues*, sigs. *7v–*8v; Cressy, *Exomologesis*, pp. 433–35; and the following works by Sergeant: *Sure Footing*, pp. 25–27; *Reason against Raillery*, sig. d1v and p. 167; *Faith Vindicated from Possibility of Falshood, or, The Immovable Firmness and Certainty of the Motives to Christian Faith* (Louvain, 1667), pp. 157–58.

well. If most Anglicans, with the exception of the "Philosophising Divines" attacked by Dryden in the preface to *Religio Laici,* had preserved the distinction between knowledge and faith, they were maintaining a tradition which Hooker had inherited from Thomas Aquinas and which was shared by most Catholics of Dryden's time.[30] When White characterized his Anglican opponents as "these delicate Believers [who] content their easie and civil natures with a dow-bak't probability, as if they were little concern'd, whither the Religion they profest were true or fals," he quickly added: "Yet I'le not do them the wrong to say, they had not some ground or rather occasion out of some of our Divines; who (raising more dust then they were able to keep out of their own eyes) seem to have unawares contributed to the hatching this dangerous Cockatrice, *Incertitude,* which these bold Reformers have at last shewed to the world."[31] He is referring here, as Tillotson pointed out, to "the generality of their *School-Divines;* whom he calls *Scepticks,* because they do not own his *Demonstrative* way."[32] But it was not only the Schoolmen of the Middle Ages and the Anglicans of his own day whom White described as *"Scepticks."* He also applied this term of abuse freely to contemporary Catholics who maintained the Thomistic conception of faith in the face of his *"Demonstrative* way."[33] Seen in this light, White's accusation of scepticism, which has beclouded modern discussions of Roman Catholic apologetics in England, acquires an altogether different perspective.

Before we leave the Blackloists, we should notice one other corollary of their theological system. If faith can be preserved from all possibility of error by purely human tradition, there is no need for the supernatural protection of the Holy Spirit. The concept of an infallible authority unerringly interpreting the sense of Scripture becomes irrelevant once this Scripture has been degraded in importance and the Christian religion comes to depend on the natural truthfulness of the whole body of the

---

[30] For an extended discussion of the Blackloist conception of the nature of faith in the light of the majority opinion among Catholics, see Talbot, *Blakloanae Haeresis,* pp. 51–110.

[31] "Preface," *Rushworth's Dialogues,* sig. ✳7.

[32] *Rule of Faith,* p. 287.

[33] See especially White's practice in his *Exetasis scientiae requisitae in theologo ad censuras sententiis theologicis inferendas. Oblata . . . Cardinalibus Congregationis S*tae *Inquisitionis, ad purgationem librorum suorum a criminibus quae Sceptici moderni eisdem objiciunt* (n.p., 1662).

faithful offering a consensus of belief and practice which even determines "the sence of the Words they have been inur'd to." Deprived, in this view, of the protection of the Holy Spirit, the teaching authority of the church may even succumb to error. " 'Tis evident whatever the Church speaks and delivers *for Tradition,*" White declares, "is agreed on by all Catholicks to be certain and unrefusable."[34] Nevertheless, he writes, "it is not impossible that a Pope or Council would attempt to [depart from tradition], and by this attempt would fall into error, and would even proclaim it."[35] Belson too points out that "the Rule, even of Councils themselves, is *Tradition,* and were it possible they should contradict it, we are taught to adhere to *Tradition* against both them, and Angels too."[36] In *Exomologesis,* Cressy gives an account of his conversion—"that *famous passage* (which hath given so much offence to several of his own Church)," as Tillotson calls it[37]—in which he relates how for a long time he was unable to become a Catholic because he could not accept infallibility in the sense of immunity from error on the part of a pope or council; it was only when he came to understand—from Henry Holden, presumably—that infallibility could be redefined as simply the authority of these leaders to enforce dogmas that he was able to overcome his scruples and join the Catholic church.[38] The Blackloists' denial that Catholics need believe in an inerrant hierarchical authority was challenged even by their Protestant opponents, besides giving scandal to the members of their own church.[39]

The divisions among Roman Catholic apologists in Restoration England over theological issues were therefore real, important, and widely recognized among Anglicans and Catholics alike. If the Blackloists commanded a good deal of attention because of

[34] *Rushworth's Dialogues,* p. 197.

[35] *Tabulae Suffragiales,* p. 277 (my translation). On the possibility of error by a pope or council, see also White's *Sonus Buccinae* (Paris, 1654), pp. 366–72.

[36] *Tradidi Vobis,* pp. 299–300. For Sergeant's similar views, see *Sure Footing,* p. 212.

[37] *Rule of Faith,* p. 125.

[38] See *Exomologesis,* pp. 284–87 and 367–79. Cressy declares that he consulted Holden while writing his book (see pp. 112–13). It was printed with Holden's "*approbatio.*"

[39] See Stillingfleet's remarks in *A Reply to Mr. J. S. His 3rd Appendix,* pp. 6–8. For a full discussion of the Blackloist denial of infallibility in the light of Catholic teaching, see Talbot, *Blakloanae Haeresis,* pp. 110–48.

the novelty of their ideas, the traditional position of the majority of Catholics who opposed such novelties continued to receive articulate expression from other apologists. These latter included some of the secular clergy, such as George Leyburn, as well as the regular clergy, the most prominent of whom were the Jesuits. Those two classics by Jesuits of an earlier generation, Knott's "voluminous Encounter with *Chillingworth*" and Fisher's with Archbishop Laud, remained popular with most English Catholics for all that the Blackloists considered them "sad Instances of the Catholick cause." To these were shortly added the numerous contributions of later Jesuits such as James Mumford and Edward Worsley, whose books, until the accession of James II, had been printed abroad and smuggled into England. Finally, several Catholic laymen had preceded Dryden in taking up the cause of their church against the Anglicans; the most prominent of these were Abraham Woodhead and Obadiah Walker, who ranged themselves with the majority of their coreligionists against the novelties of the Blackloists.[40] At a time when Catholic apologists fought under the standard of one or the other of these two conflicting groups, it would have been practically impossible for Dryden to have remained neutral. When we examine the religious arguments of *The Hind and the Panther* against this background, Dryden's complete allegiance to the moderate majority among his coreligionists appears unmistakable.

He begins his poem with a description of the beasts among which the Hind lives, all of them symbolizing various English Protestant communions except for the *"Buffoon Ape,"* briefly mentioned as a symbol for the atheists, and the Fox, described as follows:

> With greater guile
> False *Reynard* fed on consecrated spoil:
> The graceless beast by *Athanasius* first
> Was chas'd from *Nice*; then by *Socinus* nurs'd
> His impious race their blasphemy renew'd,
> And natures King through natures opticks view'd.
> Revers'd they view'd him lessen'd to their eye,
> Nor in an Infant could a God descry:

---

[40] See, for example, Woodhead's attack on White, Holden, and Sergeant for their teachings concerning the nature of faith in *A Rational Account of the Doctrine of Roman-Catholicks concerning the Ecclesiastical Guide in Controversies of Religion* (2d ed.; n.p., 1673), pp. 352–55.

New swarming Sects to this obliquely tend,
Hence they began, and here they all will end.

[I, 52–61]

The Fox's "impious race" includes both the ancient Arians, condemned at the Council of Nicaea and denounced by Athanasius, and their modern counterparts the Socinians, who like the Arians denied the divinity of Christ.

Dryden's purpose in introducing here the Arians and Socinians, despised as heartily by Protestants as by Catholics, is to suggest that these heretics shared two characteristics with the Protestants, who are of course the real target of his attack. The first of these is a fondness for private judgment, which is to be the subject of extended discussion in Part II and is therefore appropriately denounced here at the very outset of the poem:

What weight of antient witness can prevail
If private reason hold the publick scale?
But, gratious God, how well dost thou provide
For erring judgments an unerring Guide?
Thy throne is darkness in th' abyss of light,
A blaze of glory that forbids the sight;
O teach me to believe Thee thus conceal'd,
And search no farther than thy self reveal'd;
But her alone for my Directour take
Whom thou hast promis'd never to forsake!
My thoughtless youth was wing'd with vain desires,
My manhood, long misled by wandring fires,
Follow'd false lights; and when their glimps was gone,
My pride struck out new sparkles of her own.
Such was I, such by nature still I am,
Be thine the glory, and be mine the same.

[I, 62–77]

Dryden's tactic of comparing the Protestants to the Arians and Socinians on the grounds that all these groups depend on private judgment was a popular one among Catholic apologists. Abraham Woodhead's *The Protestants Plea for a Socinian* (1686) is a dialogue between a Protestant and a Socinian in which the latter quotes Chillingworth and other Anglican divines on behalf of private judgment and then proceeds to use this privilege to interpret Scripture as denying Christ's divinity. James Mumford's *The Question of Questions* (1658) presents an "Arian Cobler"

261

who employs the Protestant principle of private judgment for the same purpose.[41]

Dryden opposes to private judgment an "unerring Guide," the infallible church symbolized in the poem by the Hind and described here as a "Directour" whom God has "promis'd never to forsake." This conception of a church protected from error by the Holy Spirit will be developed more fully later in the poem, but it is already clear from the outset that Dryden's notions on this score contradict those of the Blackloists, who denied infallibility in this sense.

I have already discussed the latter portion of the above passage in chapter 2 as an ethical appeal in which Dryden anticipates and defends himself from the charges of inconsistency and insincerity which were certain to be leveled against the author of *Religio Laici*. Its more immediate purpose, which justifies its inclusion at this point in his argument, is to exemplify in his own life the contrast he is drawing between Catholic submission to an "unerring Guide" and the dependence of all other groups, Protestant as well as Socinian, on the principle of private judgment first invoked by the Arians of the fourth century: "New swarming Sects to this obliquely tend, / Hence they began, and here they all will end." The humility of his present attitude, asking only that he be allowed to follow an "unerring Guide," is deliberately contrasted with his "thoughtless youth" and early manhood in which the principle of private judgment, abetted by his own pride, encouraged him to follow "wandring fires" and "false lights."

Dryden now turns to a second characteristic of the Arians and Socinians which their Protestant enemies share. In describing the Fox's progeny, Dryden had alluded to their denial of Christ's divinity, which rendered them abhorrent to every Christian sect. The source of this heresy, in his view, is that the mystery of the Incarnation has proved an insuperable barrier to those who will believe no farther than their senses can perceive. To such individuals, who "natures King through natures opticks view'd," the

---

[41] See *The Question of Questions, Which Rightly Resolv'd Resolves All Our Questions in Religion: This Question is, Who Ought to be Our Judge in all these Differences* (2d ed.; London, 1687), pp. 23–25. *The Protestants Plea for a Socinian* (London, 1686) is a separate reprint of the "Fourth Discourse" of Woodhead's *Rational Account of the Doctrine of Roman-Catholicks.* See also Edward Worsley, *Protestancy without Principles, or, Sectaries Unhappy Fall from Infallibility to Fancy* (Antwerp, 1668), pp. 136–39, for a similar debate between Matthew Poole and an Arian who employs his opponent's own principle of private judgment against him.

human nature assumed by Christ at his birth effectively concealed his divine nature: "Revers'd they view'd him lessen'd to their eye, / Nor in an Infant could a God descry." He proceeds now to imply that the situation of the Arians and Socinians is analogous to that of the Protestants who, because their senses can perceive only the accidental appearances of bread and wine in the Eucharist, are unwilling to accept through faith Christ's corporal presence there and consequently deny the Catholic doctrine of Transubstantiation. Returning to the present again after his description of his Protestant past, Dryden writes:

> Good life be now my task: my doubts are done,
> (What more could fright my faith, than Three in One?)
> Can I believe eternal God could lye
> Disguis'd in mortal mold and infancy?
> That the great maker of the world could dye?
> And after that, trust my imperfect sense
> Which calls in question his omnipotence?
> Can I my reason to my faith compell,
> And shall my sight, and touch, and taste rebell?
> Superiour faculties are set aside,
> Shall their subservient organs be my guide?
> Then let the moon usurp the rule of day,
> And winking tapers shew the sun his way;
> For what my senses can themselves perceive
> I need no revelation to believe.
>
> [I, 78–92]

Dryden is offering here the a fortiori argument that since the Christian readily accepts through faith matters beyond the reach of reason, he should more easily assent to doctrines, such as that of Transubstantiation, which exceed the perception of the senses: "Superiour faculties are set aside, / Shall their subservient organs be my guide?" A series of rhetorical questions, cast in the first person immediately following Dryden's account of his youth and early manhood as a Protestant, reminds his antagonists of some of the doctrines above the reach of his understanding that he had been taught to believe as a Protestant: the mysteries of the Trinity, the Incarnation, and the Redemption. After such flights as these, he now declares, the distance was but a short one which carried him beyond his "imperfect sense" to an acceptance of the doctrine of Transubstantiation.

It is not my purpose to consider in detail Dryden's arguments

on behalf of Transubstantiation, which occupy some seventy lines
at this point (I, 78–151) and to which he returns on two further
occasions in the poem (I, 410–29, and II, 29–49). I need only
remark that Dryden is pursuing a line of argument throughout
this passage which was often used by Catholic apologists. Abraham
Woodhead and Edward Worsley, for example, both use Dryden's
tactic of defending the doctrine of Transubstantiation by citing
analogous articles of belief accepted by Protestants, drawn both
from mysteries above reason, such as the Trinity, and from biblical events which contradict the testimony of the senses, such as
the example Dryden uses (I, 93–105) of the occasions on which
Christ, following his Resurrection, appeared in the midst of his
disciples, "the doors being shut."[42]

Our concern, however, is not with the thesis Dryden is trying to
prove, but with the common ground he shares with his antagonists.
In arguing that the senses do not deserve greater respect than is
paid to reason in matters of faith, he can begin with the assumption that most Anglicans and Catholics agree on the proper relation between reason and faith. We are forcefully made aware of
this by the fact that some of Dryden's lines here echo, perhaps
deliberately, phrases in the opening stanza of *Religio Laici*, where
he had been employing commonplaces of Christian apologetics
familiar to both churches. Thus he now declares that if the senses
are to be the criteria for accepting or rejecting the truths of revelation, "then let the moon usurp the rule of day, / And winking
tapers shew the sun his way"; the lines recall his use of the same
metaphor in his earlier poem to express a similar caution concerning reason: "DIM, as the borrow'd beams of Moon and Stars / To
lonely, weary, wandring Travellers, / Is *Reason* to the *Soul*."
Again, when he urges a little later that the doctrine of Transubstantiation is beyond the reach of the understanding, he declares:
"Let reason then at Her own quarry fly, / But how can finite
grasp infinity?" (I, 104–5); the words remind us of the lines in
the earlier poem in which he had emphasized the inevitable limitations of reason in all matters pertaining to religion: "How
can the *less* the *Greater* comprehend? / Or *finite Reason* reach
Infinity?"

[42] See Woodhead, *A Discourse of the Necessity of Church-Guides, for Directing
Christians in Necessary Faith* (n.p., 1675), pp. 38–42 and 142–44; Worsley, *Protestancy
without Principles*, p. 159; Worsley, *The Infallibility of the Roman Catholick Church
and Her Miracles Defended against Dr. Stillingfleets Cavils* (Antwerp, 1674), pp.
193–209.

The conception of faith which Dryden takes for granted here is of a voluntary act in which reason assents to the articles of belief not because they are self-evident or demonstrable but under the impetus of the will. When he asks, "Can I my reason to my faith compell, / And shall my sight, and touch, and taste rebell?" he assumes that the first line will win an affirmative answer from any Anglican who agrees with Archbishop Laud that *"Faith* is a mixed Act of the *Will* and the *Understanding,* and the *Will* inclines the *Understanding* to yeeld full *approbation* to that whereof it sees not full *proofe."*[43] It is because "full *proofe"* is lacking where reason has been able to offer only probable or moral arguments that the intervention of the will is necessary. Years later, in his "Life of Lucian" (1696), Dryden declared:

We have indeed the highest probabilities for our revealed religion; arguments which will preponderate with a reasonable man, upon a long and careful disquisition; but I have always been of opinion, that we can demonstrate nothing, because the subject-matter is not capable of a demonstration. It is the particular grace of God, that any man believes the mysteries of our faith; which I think a conclusive argument against the doctrine of persecution in any church.[44]

The notions which Dryden sets forth of probable arguments on behalf of revealed religion, of the intervention of the will in the act of faith, and of the necessity of divine grace before the Christian can believe were all rejected by the Blackloists, as we have noticed. In the writings of the moderate majority among English

[43] *Relation of the Conference,* p. 106. In his recent book, *Dryden's Poetry* (Bloomington: Indiana University Press, 1967), which appeared after this study was completed, Earl Miner declares that Dryden agrees with Cressy in accepting a "rational faith" in which the will plays no part, and that, in fact, *"Exomologesis* is the clearest model for Dryden's poem" (see pp. 184–86). This view apparently follows from the fact that Professor Miner, while rightly locating Dryden in the tradition of Thomas Aquinas and Hooker, mistakenly identifies the notion that faith involves the participation of the will with "voluntarism," a doctrine opposed by both these divines. However, the conception of faith as an assent of the intellect determined by the will is accepted by both Thomas Aquinas and Hooker (see *Summa Theologiae,* II IIae, 2, 1, and *Laws,* V, lxiii, 1–2); it has nothing to do with voluntarism in either the philosophical sense (the theory that knowledge is subordinate to the will) or the theological sense (the theory that God's essence is will rather than intellect).

[44] *The Works of John Dryden,* ed. Sir Walter Scott and George Saintsbury (Edinburgh: William Paterson, 1882–93), XVIII, 66. Watson omits this section of the "Life" from his edition of the *Essays* on the grounds that it consists for the most part of "material explicitly translated or adapted from continental treatises and commentaries" (*Of Dramatick Poesy and Other Critical Essays,* ed. George Watson [London: J. M. Dent and Sons, 1962], I, 17). This particular passage, however, unquestionably expresses Dryden's own views.

Catholic apologists, however, they were a commonplace; every one of Dryden's ideas on the subject is repeated so often by Knott, Mumford, Leyburn, Worsley, and Woodhead that quotation would be tedious.[45]

Later in the passage we are considering, Dryden, still stressing the analogy between reason and the senses where faith is concerned, offers an argument which makes especially clear the identity between his present views on the relation of reason to revelation and those which he had held as an Anglican, discussed in chapter 4. He anticipates an objection to the doctrine of Transubstantiation:

> 'Tis urg'd again that faith did first commence
> By miracles, which are appeals to sense,
> And thence concluded that our sense must be
> The motive still of credibility.
> For latter ages must on former wait,
> And what began belief, must propagate.
>
> [I, 106–11]

The objection was a common one among Anglican apologists.[46] Dryden proceeds to offer an answer:

> But winnow well this thought, and you shall find,
> 'Tis light as chaff that flies before the wind.
> Were all those wonders wrought by pow'r divine
> As means or ends of some more deep design?
> Most sure as means, whose end was this alone,
> To prove the god-head of th' eternal Son.
> God thus asserted: man is to believe
> Beyond what sense and reason can conceive.
> And for mysterious things of faith rely
> On the Proponent, heav'ns authority.
> If then our faith we for our guide admit,
> Vain is the farther search of humane wit,
> As when the building gains a surer stay,

[45] See Leyburn, *Holy Characters, Containing a Miscellany of Theologicall Discourses* (Douay, 1662), I, 68–77; Knott, *Mercy and Truth,* in Chillingworth, *The Religion of Protestants a Safe Way to Salvation* (Oxford, 1638), p. 313; Woodhead, *Rational Account of the Doctrine of Roman-Catholicks,* pp. 350–56; Woodhead, *Dr. Stillingfleets Principles, Giving an Account of the Faith of Protestants* (Paris, 1671), p. 94; Worsley, *The Infallibility of the Roman Catholick Church,* pp. 141–48; Mumford, *The Question of Questions,* pp. 357–58, 488.

[46] See, for example, Stillingfleet, *A Rational Account of the Grounds of Protestant Religion* (London, 1665), Part I, chap. v.

We take th' unusefull scaffolding away:
Reason by sense no more can understand,
The game is play'd into another hand.

[I, 112–27]

This passage alone would be enough to forestall any suspicion that Dryden had become a fideist on joining the Catholic church or that he was any less inclined now than formerly to acknowledge that reason fulfils an essential, if subordinate, function as one of the grounds of religion. It is the function of reason—to which he now adds the senses for the sake of his argument—to make morally certain the divine authorship of revelation. This done, its function ceases, for the "mysterious things of faith" are assented to on the authority of the divine "Proponent" who is omniscient and cannot deceive. This was, of course, Dryden's very point in the preface to *Religio Laici* when he declared: "Let us be content at last, to know God, by his own Methods; at least so much of him, as he is pleas'd to reveal to us, in the sacred Scriptures; to apprehend them to be the word of God, is all our Reason has to do; for all beyond it is the work of Faith, which is the Seal of Heaven impress'd upon our humane understanding." As we noticed in chapter 4, Dryden, as a moderate Anglican, had thus taken up a position midway between the fideists who denied reason any function in religion and the "Philosophising Divines" of his church "who wou'd prove Religion by Reason" through an attempt to demonstrate the mysteries of their faith. As a Catholic, he now follows a similar course equally removed from fideism and from the policy of the "Philosophising Divines" of his new church, the Blackloists, who would "prove Religion by Reason" through their "*Demonstrative* way." Among the moderate Catholics he could, of course, find ample support for this traditional position of both churches, as I have already indicated.

In the remainder of Part I, Dryden divides his attention between the Presbyterian Wolf and the Anglican Panther. The political discussion to which the introduction of the Wolf leads is, like the dialogue on toleration between the Hind and the Panther in Part III, outside the scope of the present study. The introduction of the Panther allows Dryden to mention the hedonistic motives of the reformers and to allude again to the Anglican attitude toward the Real Presence before launching an attack on the Church of England's lack of innate religious authority in a pas-

267

sage, discussed in the last chapter, which is simply a prelude to the fuller discussion of this topic in Part II.

The dialogue between the Hind and the Panther "concerning Church Authority" in Part II of the poem is Dryden's contribution to the tradition of apologetics made famous by the Jesuits and Catholic laymen I have already mentioned. The question raised in Part II concerns the necessity of a hierarchical "judge of controversies" or infallible guide in matters of religion. The altercation between the two beasts begins and ends with this question and all other issues are subordinate to it. It is a question which was irrelevant to the Blackloists, who denied the infallibility of the teaching church, but it was the central concern of such apologists as Woodhead, Mumford, and Worsley, who issued book after book with such titles as *The Guide in Controversies, The Infallibility of the Roman Catholick Church,* and *A Discourse of the Necessity of Church-Guides.*

In considering this question Dryden found it necessary to refer once again to many of the issues presented in the second half of *Religio Laici,* such as the respective claims of Scripture, tradition, private judgment, and an infallible church. But the enormous difference in the way these same issues are handled in the two poems does not result from Dryden's offering opposite answers to the same question. In each poem he raises an entirely different question which he considers to be the crucial one because of his religious orientation at the time. The important question to Dryden as an Anglican, which he brings up in the latter half of *Religio Laici,* concerns the interpretation of Scripture. He is chiefly interested in the means by which the individual Christian is to discover the revealed truths which are necessary for his salvation.

> If *others* in the *same Glass better* see
> 'Tis for *Themselves* they look, but not for *me*:
> For MY Salvation must its Doom receive
> Not from what OTHERS, but what *I* believe.

> [ll. 301–4]

The problem he considers, therefore, is whether these truths are contained in Scripture "uncorrupt, sufficient, clear, intire, / In *all* things which our needfull *Faith* require," so that every Christian may discern them by the judgment of discretion, or whether the written word must be explained by an infallible church in the light of its unwritten tradition.

The essential question to Dryden as a Catholic, on the other hand, which he raises in Part II of *The Hind and the Panther*, concerns the judge of controversies among Christians. He is primarily interested in the means by which the community of believers is to preserve the same faith, and in the regulating authority which is to settle their differences in doctrine. The problem he considers, therefore, is whether the Scripture itself, interpreted by every individual, is sufficiently clear and unambiguous to insure uniformity of belief among Christians, or whether disputes concerning the written word are bound to arise which can only be settled by a living judge, protected from error by the Holy Spirit and deciding differences by consulting tradition.

It is a question about infallibility by the Panther which initiates the long argument between the two beasts. After several preliminary exchanges concerning the recent behavior of the two churches, she declares that

> shunning long disputes, I fain wou'd see
> That wond'rous wight infallibility.
> Is he from heav'n this mighty champion come,
> Or lodg'd below in subterranean *Rome*?
> First, seat him somewhere, and derive his race,
> Or else conclude that nothing has no place.
>
> [II, 64–69]

The Hind points out in reply that if, which she denies, there is important disagreement as to where infallibility is "lodged," nevertheless "the doubtfull residence no proof can bring / Against the plain existence of the thing." She continues:

> I then affirm that this unfailing guide
> In Pope and gen'ral councils must reside;
> Both lawfull, both combin'd, what one decrees
> By numerous votes, the other ratifies:
> On this undoubted sense the church relies.
> 'Tis true, some Doctours in a scantier space,
> I mean in each apart, contract the place.
> Some, who to greater length extend the line,
> The churches after acceptation join.
> This last circumference appears too wide,
> The church diffus'd is by the council ty'd;

As members by their representatives
Oblig'd to laws which Prince and Senate gives:
Thus some contract, and some enlarge the space;
In Pope and council who denies the place,
Assisted from above with God's unfailing grace?

[II, 80–95]

The Panther's taunt was a frequent one from Anglican apologists. Chillingworth's was particularly famous, and is worth quoting because of the use Dryden seems to be making of it:

Some of you say, the Pope alone without a Councell may determine all Controversies: But others deny it. Some, that a Generall Councell without a Pope may doe so: Others deny this. Some, Both in conjunction are infallible determiners: Others againe deny this. Lastly, some among you, hold the Acceptation of the decrees of Councells by the Universall Church to be the only way to decide Controversies: which others deny, by denying the Church to be Infallible.[47]

The number, order, and wording of the theories listed by Chillingworth are sufficiently close to Dryden's verses to suggest that he may have had this famous passage in mind. As Dryden presents the argument, however, these conflicting opinions are placed in the mouth, not of the Panther, but of the Hind, who is thus able to seize the initiative and, with the words "'tis true," proceed to detail the extent of the disagreement among her "Doctours" with an air of open honesty. It is the same tactic Dryden had used so effectively in *Religio Laici* when, with the words "'tis true, my Friend," he forestalled a familiar Catholic objection to private judgment by proceeding to condemn on his own initiative the abuse of this principle by the Protestant sects.

Those who "in each apart, contract the place," attributing infallibility exclusively to either the pope or general councils, are the papalists and conciliarists respectively, who had debated their claims since the later Middle Ages. The opinion of those who join "the churches after acceptation" to the notion of infallibility, insisting that the decrees of a pope and council must be accepted by the various national churches before they can be considered infallible, is the Gallican theory popular in France in the late seventeenth century and lately embodied in the fourth of the

---

[47] *The Religion of Protestants,* p. 130. For another example, see Henry Ferne, *Of the Division between the English and Romish Church upon the Reformation* (London, 1652), pp. 163–65.

famous Gallican Articles of 1682.[48] The remaining theory, that infallibility inheres in the decrees of general councils which have been ratified by the pope, is proclaimed by the Hind as the correct one. It is presented as a sensible *via media* between the views of the extremists, among whom "some contract, and some enlarge the space." The Hind's view was the one usually offered by moderate Catholic apologists in Dryden's time. James Mumford, for example, answering Henry Ferne's use of the Panther's taunt, declares: "All and every one of us (without the least disagreement) do and will unanimously say, That all those Definitions declare an infallible Truth, which are set forth by the Pope defining together with a general Council."[49]

The Hind defends this moderate view of infallibility against the Gallican theory by comparing the form under which the Catholic church is governed to the political structure familiar to the English people: "The church diffus'd is by the council ty'd; / As members by their representatives / Oblig'd to laws which Prince and Senate gives." Dryden is probably indebted for this peculiarly English argument to Mumford, who had used it to defend the same position:

Now this is easily understood by that manner of Government which we had here in *England,* from the Conquest to our days; according to which, all the Decrees and Ordinances by which we were govern'd or directed, were to be made by a lawful King jointly with a lawful Parliament. This Representative, and their Decrees are call'd the Decrees of the Kingdom. Just so, the particular manner by which the Church diffused or universal is directed and govern'd, is by a lawful Pope, as supreme Pastor, jointly with a lawful Council: And this Assembly is call'd the Church Representative, and their Decrees are call'd the Decrees of the Church.[50]

Mumford's use of the past tense to describe a government "by a lawful King jointly with a lawful Parliament" is explained by the fact that he was writing in 1658 under the Protectorate.

[48] Cressy refers to Chillingworth's list of these theories in *Exomologesis,* where he declares in favor of the last, or Gallican, opinion (see pp. 442–43). However, he is not speaking of infallibility in the usual sense, but in his own special sense of the Church's authority to enforce her discipline (see p. 422). According to Leyburn, the Blackloists as a whole were Gallican in their sympathies. See *Douay College Diaries,* II, 546–47.

[49] *The Question of Questions,* p. 378. See also pp. 10–11 and 373–74.

[50] *Ibid.,* p. 382. Earl Miner has recently suggested that Dryden was a Gallican (see *Dryden's Poetry,* p. 184). The poet's explicit attack at this point on one of the most important of the Gallican Articles would seem to contradict this view.

Having proclaimed that the infallible authority of the church is exercised by the pope and general councils acting together, "both lawfull, both combin'd, what one decrees / By numerous votes, the other ratifies," the Hind proceeds to declare that it is by means of such decrees or canons that the judge of controversies settles all disputes:

> Those Canons all the needfull points contain;
> Their sense so obvious, and their words so plain,
> That no disputes about the doubtfull Text
> Have, hitherto, the lab'ring world perplex'd:
> If any shou'd in after times appear,
> New Councils must be call'd, to make the meaning clear.
> Because in them the pow'r supreme resides;
> And all the promises are to the guides.
>
> [II, 96–103]

Dryden's point is that a judge of controversies, in order to be effective, must be living and vocal as well as infallible, so that it can settle new disputes when they arise. As Knott had explained to Chillingworth,

you are in a great errour, if you conceive that we hold any one Writing or Decree, to be sufficient for deciding all Controversyes; But we say, that the Church upon severall exigents can declare her mynd, either by explicating former Decrees, or by promulgating new ones, as necessity shall require. . . . If we did yield to any one writing the sufficiency of ending all emergent Controversyes, God forbid we should deny it to holy scripture![51]

The Hind now turns to an attack on the Protestant notion that Holy Scripture, interpreted by themselves, is an adequate authority for settling controversies in religion:

> This may be taught with sound and safe defence:
> But mark how sandy is your own pretence,
> Who setting Councils, Pope, and Church aside,
> Are ev'ry man his own presuming guide.
> The sacred books, you say, are full and plain,
> And ev'ry needfull point of truth contain:
> All who can read, Interpreters may be:
> Thus though your sev'ral churches disagree,

---

[51] *Infidelity Unmasked, or, The Confutation of a Booke Published by Mr. William Chillingworth under This Title, The Religion of Protestants a Safe Way to Salvation* (Ghent, 1652), p. 254.

Yet ev'ry Saint has to himself alone
The secret of this Philosophick stone.
These principles your jarring sects unite,
When diff'ring Doctours and disciples fight.

[II, 104–15]

She continues at some length, maintaining that the resort to Holy Scripture as a final authority, far from settling controversies, has merely encouraged them.

This long opening speech by the Hind has established the question at stake between her and the Panther and has set forth their respective positions. It is a method we noticed Dryden following in each half of *Religio Laici,* where the respective positions of the poet and his nonce adversary, the Deist or Father Simon, were carefully explained as a preliminary to debate. In the earlier poem, however, Dryden had extended his nonce adversaries the minimal courtesy of permitting them to express their views in their own words. Here it is not the Panther who presents her position, but the Hind, in words highly colored by her own antipathy to this view. It is a mode of procedure Dryden is to follow throughout Part II of his poem. We noticed in chapter 2 the enormous disparity in length between the Hind's speeches and those of the Panther. The latter's remarks, all but two of which consist of less than ten lines apiece, are obviously too brief to allow her to develop any arguments in detail. Only rarely, moreover, does she attempt to offer even the most abbreviated argument; as a result, there is seldom any genuine debate between the two beasts. For the most part, the Panther's remarks consist of brief defensive qualifications of her own position, unsupported accusations against the Hind which provide the latter with an opportunity to answer them, and questions designed to elicit information from her opponent. In short, this one-sided dialogue is actually a platform for the Hind in which the role of the Panther, for all her hostility, is simply that of the interlocutor who provides the speaker with his cues by asking the right questions.

Once we perceive that Part II of *The Hind and the Panther* is essentially a long speech by the Hind, infrequently interrupted, on the authority of the Catholic church to decide controversies, we can follow its organization without difficulty. The Hind has two basic tasks. She must first of all establish the necessity of a living judge of controversies, at the same time showing that Holy

273

Scripture, interpreted by private judgment, is inadequate for settling disputes. Secondly, she must prove that this living judge of
controversies is to be found in the Catholic church, at the same
time showing that it is not present in any other church. The logical pattern Dryden adopts here is an obvious choice for his purpose and had already been used by other Catholic apologists
arguing the same question. Thus Mumford's *The Question of
Questions,* which gives independent status to the two subtopics I
have mentioned, consists of the following four parts: (1) That
there must be an infallible judge of controversies; (2) That the
Scripture is not this infallible judge; (3) That the Church is this
judge; (4) That this church is the Roman church.

The Panther's single demur to the Hind's characterization of
the Anglican position is a reminder that only matters necessary
for salvation are supposed to be plain to every reader's capacity in
the Scripture (a point Dryden had developed at length in *Religio
Laici*): "Yet, *Lady,* still remember I maintain, / The Word in
needfull points is onely plain." The Hind replies:

> Needless or needfull I not now contend,
> For still you have a loop-hole for a friend,
> (Rejoyn'd the Matron) but the rule you lay
> Has led whole flocks, and leads them still astray
> In weighty points, and full damnation's way.
> For did not *Arius* first, *Socinus* now,
> The Son's eternal god-head disavow,
> And did not these by Gospel Texts alone
> Condemn our doctrine, and maintain their own?
> Have not all hereticks the same pretence
> To plead the Scriptures in their own defence?
>
> [II, 145–55]

We noticed Dryden comparing the Protestants to the Arians and
Socinians in Part I of the poem because of the fondness they shared
for private judgment. Here it is the dependence of all these groups
on the principle of *Scriptura sola* which the Hind reproves.

Dryden had encountered this standard Catholic argument in
the preface to Father Simon's *Critical History* years earlier. We
saw in chapter 6 that Simon remarked that "if we but consider
the conclusions which the Protestants and Socinians draw from
the same principle, we shall be convinc'd that their principle is
not so plain as they imagin, since these conclusions are so differ-

ent and the one absolutely denies what the other affirms." Dryden had versified this in *Religio Laici* as the *"Objection in behalf of Tradition; urg'd by Father* Simon":

> Are there not many points, some needfull sure
> To saving Faith, that Scripture leaves obscure?
> Which every Sect will wrest a several way
> (For what *one* Sect Interprets, *all* Sects *may*:)
> We hold, and say we prove from Scripture plain,
> That *Christ* is GOD; the bold *Socinian*
> From the *same* Scripture urges he's but MAN.
>
> [ll. 307–13]

The argument was a favorite one among Catholic apologists. Worsley, for example, in the course of answering Stillingfleet, declared:

The Learned *Socinians,* the learned *Arians* with others, read and ponder the same Scripture you read Mr. Dr. They want no more the Faculty of discerning between Truth and falshood then you. They pretend to have as much of Gods grace as you can pretend to, and are as loth to damn themselves by maintaining a wilful errour against Scripture, as you. Yet this matter of fact is evident, That they plainly contradict you in the belief of Necessaries, and so doe other most learned Christians also.[52]

Continuing her allusion to the Arian controversy, the Hind asks:

> How did the *Nicene* council then decide
> That strong debate, was it by Scripture try'd?
> No, sure to those the Rebel would not yield,
> Squadrons of Texts he marshal'd in the field;
> That was but civil war, an equal set,
> Where Piles with piles, and eagles Eagles met.
> With Texts point-blank and plain he fac'd the Foe:
> And did not *Sathan* tempt our Saviour so?
> The good old Bishops took a simpler way,
> Each ask'd but what he heard his Father say,
> Or how he was instructed in his youth,
> And by traditions force upheld the truth.
>
> [II, 156–67]

Again the argument is one Dryden was familiar with from reading

---

[52] *The Infallibility of the Roman Catholick Church,* p. 46. See also the same author's *Protestancy without Principles,* pp. 165–66.

275

the preface to the *Critical History,* where, as we noticed in chapter 6, Simon remarked that "when these Bishops were assembled in Councils they every one declar'd the belief of their own Church; so that this belief receiv'd in the first Churches serv'd afterwards as a rule for the explaining of the difficult places of the Scripture." In the interval, Dryden had almost certainly encountered other uses of the same argument by English Catholic apologists. Mumford, for example, had explained how the earliest councils proceeded in settling controversies which had arisen: "The Votes therefore of the Fathers assembled in Council are demanded, not only of what they think to be conformable to Gods Word written in Scripture, but also how conformable such a Point is, or is not, to that Tradition which they have all receiv'd from the Fathers of their Church, as deliver'd to them from their Fathers for Gods Word, by Tradition committed to their Forefathers as such, from the Apostles themselves."[53]

The Panther responds by accepting, as Dryden had done in *Religio Laici,* such written tradition as is drawn from the Fathers and Councils of the earliest centuries. When, she asks, "were those first Councils disallow'd by me? / Or where did I at sure tradition strike, / Provided still it were Apostolick?" She goes on to explain that she decides which traditions are "sure" and "Apostolick" by applying to them the standard of Holy Scripture.

The Hind replies that the Panther uses the same criterion to determine which traditions are acceptable as she uses to decide controversies: the Scripture, which is as inadequate a judge of the one question as it is of the other.

> Suppose we on things traditive divide,
> And both appeal to Scripture to decide;
> By various texts we both uphold our claim,
> Nay, often ground our titles on the same:
> After long labour lost, and times expence,
> Both grant the words, and quarrel for the sense.
> Thus all disputes for ever must depend;
> For no dumb rule can controversies end.
>
> [II, 196–203]

Dryden's point here that no rule of faith which is "dumb" or mute can settle disputes was the basic objection to Scripture as

---

[53] *The Question of Questions,* pp 395–96. See also pp. 13–14, 111.

the judge of controversies by Catholic apologists. As Knott explained to Chillingworth:

The name, notion, nature, and properties of a Judge cannot in common reason agree to any meere writing, which, be it otherwise in its kind, never so highly qualified with sanctity and infallibility; yet it must ever be, as all writings are, deaf, dumb, and inanimate. By a Judge, all wise men understand a Person endued with life, and reason, able to hear, to examine, to declare his mind to the disagreeing parties . . . There is a great and plain distinction betwixt a *Judge* and a *Rule*. For as in a Kingdome, the Judge hath his rule to follow which are the received Lawes and Customes; so are not they fit or able to declare, or be Judges to themselves, but that office must belong to a living Judge. The holy Scripture may be, and is a Rule, but cannot be a Judge.[54]

The Panther's only reply to the Hind's argument is a question: "If not by Scriptures how can we be sure / (Reply'd the *Panther*) what tradition's pure?" The Hind answers that the same church which decides controversies must be the judge of which traditions are acceptable. She then proceeds to argue that the Church of England, by attempting to maintain a precarious balance between private judgment and church authority, and between the total acceptance of tradition by the Catholic church and its complete rejection by the other Protestant churches, is caught in a hopeless dilemma.

> Your friend the *Wolfe* did with more craft provide
> To set those toys traditions quite aside:
> And *Fathers* too, unless when reason spent
> He cites 'em but sometimes for ornament.
> But, Madam *Panther,* you, though more sincere,
> Are not so wise as your Adulterer:
> The private spirit is a better blind
> Than all the dodging tricks your authours find.
> For they, who left the Scripture to the crowd,
> Each for his own peculiar judge allow'd;
> The way to please 'em was to make 'em proud.
> Thus, with full sails, they ran upon the shelf;
> Who cou'd suspect a couzenage from himself?
>
> [II, 246–58]

The Presbyterians, for all that their premises are mistaken, at least pursue them to a logical conclusion; they therefore display a con-

[54] *Mercy and Truth,* p. 42.

sistency and a worldly wisdom which the Church of England lacks.

Dryden is of course presenting here the same Anglican *via media* he had praised in the concluding stanza of *Religio Laici*. By his choice of language, he skilfully alters his earlier image of a church adeptly steering a perilous but successful middle way between the extremes of Catholicism on the one hand and of the sects on the other. He had expressed this idea earlier in a nautical metaphor: "The Danger's much the same; on several Shelves / If *others* wreck *us*, or *we* wreck our *selves*" (ll. 425–26). He repeats this metaphor here as a means of describing the sects, who wreck themselves: "Thus, with full sails, they ran upon the shelf." But he now introduces a new figure of speech for the Church of England:

> But you who *Fathers* and traditions take,
> And garble some, and some you quite forsake,
> Pretending church auctority to fix,
> And yet some grains of private spirit mix,
> Are like a *Mule* made up of diff'ring seed,
> And that's the reason why you never breed;
> At least not propagate your kind abroad,
> For home-dissenters are by statutes aw'd.
> And yet they grow upon you ev'ry day,
> While you (to speak the best) are at a stay,
> For sects that are extremes, abhor a middle way.
>
> [II, 261–71]

The Church of England is now like a mule, sterile hybrid from a Catholic mare and a Presbyterian ass, while the Catholic church itself has been eliminated from Dryden's earlier metaphor; the opposite shoals now represent the sects on either side of the Anglican compromise: "for sects that are extremes, abhor a middle way." The metaphorical language is Dryden's own; but the notion that no church can successfully temporize between private judgment and ecclesiastical authority was a common argument used by Catholic apologists, as when Knott declared that "there is really no middle way betwixt a *publique externall*, and a *private internall* voyce; and whosoever refuseth the one, must of necessity adhere to the other."[55]

The Hind continues to argue at some length that the Panther's sons, having seen their own mother rebel against church authority,

---

[55] *Ibid.*, p. 48.

will scorn any compromise which seeks to prevent their following unlimited private judgment. Her antagonist ignores this argument,

> nor cou'd the *Panther* well enlarge
> With weak defence against so strong a charge;
> But said, for what did *Christ* his Word provide,
> If still his church must want a living guide?
> And if all saving doctrines are not there,
> Or sacred Pen-men cou'd not make 'em clear,
> From after ages we should hope in vain
> For truths, which men inspir'd, cou'd not explain.
>
> [II, 297–304]

For the first and last time in Part II of the poem, the Panther has roused herself sufficiently to challenge the Hind on logical grounds. She argues, a fortiori, that if the Evangelists, eyewitnesses to Christ's ministry who wrote under the special inspiration of the Holy Spirit, were unable to explain in Scripture "all saving doctrines" in a manner sufficiently clear for settling controversies, it is even less likely that later pastors of the church, expounding a subsequent tradition, should be able to perform the task.

The Hind begins her long reply to this argument by explaining that the Panther is mistaken in assuming that Holy Scripture is more ancient than unwritten tradition; in reality, the chronology is just the reverse:

> Before the Word was written, said the *Hind*:
> Our Saviour preach'd his Faith to humane kind;
> From his Apostles the first age receiv'd
> Eternal truth, and what they taught, believ'd.
> Thus by tradition faith was planted first,
> Succeeding flocks succeeding Pastours nurs'd.
> This was the way our wise Redeemer chose,
> (Who sure could all things for the best dispose,)
> To fence his fold from their encroaching foes.
> He cou'd have writ himself, but well foresaw
> Th' event would be like that of *Moyses* law;
> Some difference wou'd arise, some doubts remain,
> Like those, which yet the jarring *Jews* maintain.
> No written laws can be so plain, so pure,
> But wit may gloss, and malice may obscure,
> Not those indited by his first command,
> A Prophet grav'd the text, an Angel held his hand.

Thus faith was e'er the written word appear'd,
And men believ'd, not what they read, but heard.

[II, 305–23]

The unwritten tradition which the Church uses in settling controversies, therefore, is more ancient than the Scripture and is based on the preaching of Christ himself and of the same "men inspir'd" who later became the "sacred Pen-men" of the Scriptures.

The Hind proceeds to explain why the Apostles eventually committed their catechesis to writing:

But since th' Apostles cou'd not be confin'd,
To these, or those, but severally design'd
Their large commission round the world to blow;
To spread their faith they spread their labours too.
Yet still their absent flock their pains did share,
They hearken'd still, for love produces care.
And as mistakes arose, or discords fell,
Or bold seducers taught 'em to rebell,
As charity grew cold, or faction hot,
Or long neglect, their lessons had forgot,
For all their wants they wisely did provide,
And preaching by Epistles was supply'd:
So great Physicians cannot all attend,
But some they visit, and to some they send.

[II, 324–37]

Dryden's whole account here of the origin of tradition in the preaching of the Apostles and of the reasons which led them afterward to write the New Testament was probably familiar to him from many sources. In chapter 6 we noticed Simon asserting in the preface to his *Critical History* that "the Gospel was established in many Churches before any thing of it was writ." Many English Catholic apologists as well argued, in the words of Edward Worsley, "that there was Divine Doctrin Taught by the very Founders of Christianity before the Writing of Scripture. There was a Plat-form of Christian Religion made by the very Apostles before they Separated Themselves, and began their Preaching to several Nations."[56] According to this account, as the multitude

---

[56] *Protestancy without Principles*, p. 293. Cf. Knott, *Mercy and Truth*, p. 49; Mumford, *The Question of Questions*, pp. 242–43, 351. On the basis of Dryden's lines declaring that the oral catechesis preceded the written, Professor Miner has recently argued that he adopted a "radical" position on the rule of faith, magnifying tradition at the expense of Scripture to a degree farther than Cressy had been willing to go

of Christians increased and spread throughout the Roman world, the Gospels were written in order to provide the "absent flock" with eyewitness accounts of Christ's life and teachings as preached by his Apostles. The Epistles, in turn, were written to the churches by these first pastors in order to settle controversies "as mistakes arose, or discords fell, / Or bold seducers taught 'em to rebell."

Some parts of the New Testament, then, were undoubtedly written in order to solve disputes; but this fact, the Hind goes on to explain, does not make the Scripture an adequate judge of controversies for succeeding ages:

> Yet all those letters were not writ to all;
> Nor first intended, but occasional,
> Their absent sermons; nor if they contain
> All needfull doctrines, are those doctrines plain.
> Clearness by frequent preaching must be wrought,
> They writ but seldome, but they daily taught.
> And what one Saint has said of holy *Paul*,
> *He darkly writ*, is true apply'd to all.
>
> [II, 338–45]

The Epistles, being occasional letters addressed to individual churches in order to settle particular disputes, cannot, therefore, suffice for judging later controversies which the Apostles could not foresee.

In urging, through the mouth of the Hind, that tradition was both an earlier and a fuller expression of the Gospel than were the Scriptures, Dryden is not trying to suggest that tradition contains necessary truths which are not present at least implicitly in the Scriptures. Instead of arguing with the Panther whether "all saving doctrines are not there," the Hind readily concedes that the Scriptures "contain all needfull doctrines"; for as George Leyburn had explained, "catholicks doe not deny, but that traditions, which are the unwritten word be contained implicitly in the writ-

(see *Dryden's Poetry*, pp. 186–91). As a matter of fact, Cressy also declared that the Gospel was preached before any of it was written (see *Exomologesis*, pp. 174–77). It was, of course, the unanimous opinion of Catholics, whatever their differences on the rule of faith, that the Apostles' oral catechesis, which began on the first Pentecost according to the second chapter of Acts, preceded the writing of any of the Gospels. Dryden's purpose in bringing forward this argument for the *temporal* precedence of the earliest tradition over Scripture is not to show that Scripture is inferior to tradition as part of the rule of faith, but to answer the Panther's view of tradition as a creation of "after ages," a body of medieval beliefs inherently less reliable than the Scriptures which antedated it by many centuries.

281

ten word of God: that is to say, as in a generall principle from whence they are deducible: and the whole word of God is contained in Scriptures."[57] Dryden's point is that tradition is fuller in the sense that these doctrines are explained more completely there than in Scripture, where they are not always plain. If the "sacred Pen-men cou'd not make 'em clear," this was not because of any failure in their inspiration but because of shortcomings inherent in the written word: "Clearness by frequent preaching must be wrought." Therefore, the Hind continues, God must have made some other provision for settling the disputes over the meaning of this written word which were bound to arise:

> For this obscurity could heav'n provide
> More prudently than by a living guide,
> As doubts arose, the difference to decide?
> A guide was therefore needfull, therefore made,
> And, if appointed, sure to be obey'd.
>
> [II, 346–50]

The Hind now gathers the various strands of her argument and pronounces her conclusions on the question:

> Thus, with due rev'rence, to th' Apostles writ,
> By which my sons are taught, to which, submit;
> I think, those truths their sacred works contain,
> The church alone can certainly explain,
> That following ages, leaning on the past,
> May rest upon the Primitive at last.
> Nor wou'd I thence the word no rule infer,
> But none without the church interpreter.
> Because, as I have urg'd before, 'tis mute,
> And is it self the subject of dispute.
> But what th' Apostles their successours taught,
> They to the next, from them to us is brought,
> Th' undoubted sense which is in scripture sought.
> From hence the church is arm'd, when errours rise,
> To stop their entrance, and prevent surprise;
> And safe entrench'd within, her foes without defies.
> By these all festring sores her councils heal,
> Which time or has disclos'd, or shall reveal,
> For discord cannot end without a last appeal.
>
> [II, 351–69]

[57] *Holy Characters,* II, 349–50.

Carefully distinguishing between a rule and a judge, the Hind declares that the rule of faith consists of both Scripture—"th' Apostles writ, / By which my sons are taught, to which, submit"— and tradition—"what th' Apostles their successours taught, / Th' undoubted sense which is in scripture sought." By means of this joint rule of faith, she declares, the church, the divinely appointed judge of controversies, "is arm'd, when errours rise, / To stop their entrance, and prevent surprise." The Hind's position, although it contradicts that of the Blackloists, for whom Scripture was no part of the rule of faith, is the usual one among the English Catholic apologists upon whom Dryden drew for his arguments. All of the elements of her position can be found, for example, in Knott's answer to Chillingworth, that "sad Instance of the Catholick cause," according to the Blackloists:

Of our estimation, respect, and reverence to holy Scripture even Protestants themselves doe in fact give testimony, while they possesse it from us, and take it upon the integrity of our custody. No cause imaginable could avert our will from giving the function of supreme and sole Judge to holy writ, if both the thing were not impossible in it selfe, and if both reason and experience did not convince our understanding, that by this assertion Contentions are increased, and not ended. We acknowledge holy Scripture to be a most perfect rule, for as much as a writing can be a Rule: We only deny that it excludes either divine Tradition, though it be unwritten, or an externall Judge to keep, to propose, to interpret in a true, Orthodoxe, and Catholique sense.[58]

The Hind concludes her case for the necessity of a living guide by offering a final argument from analogy to prove that Scripture, though a rule, is not a judge:

> for suppose debate
> Betwixt pretenders to a fair estate,
> Bequeath'd by some Legator's last intent;
> (Such is our dying Saviour's Testament:)
> The will is prov'd, is open'd, and is read;
> The doubtfull heirs their diff'ring titles plead:
> All vouch the words their int'rest to maintain,
> And each pretends by those his cause is plain.
> Shall then the testament award the right?
> No, that's the *Hungary* for which they fight;

[58] *Mercy and Truth*, p. 42. Cf. Leyburn, *Holy Characters*, II, 336; Mumford, *The Question of Questions*, pp. 7–10, 157, 257.

The field of battel, subject of debate;
The thing contended for, the fair estate.
The sense is intricate, 'tis onely clear
What vowels and what consonants are there.
Therefore 'tis plain, its meaning must be try'd
Before some judge appointed to decide.
[II, 373–88]

Once again Dryden takes over figurative language he had already used in *Religio Laici* and applies it to a very different purpose. In the earlier poem he had introduced the same metaphors of the "will" for the New Testament and of the "estate" for the Christian religion which the Hind now uses. But on the previous occasion he had employed this language to describe and justify the rejection of the authority of the Catholic church in favor of private judgment at the time of the Protestant Reformation, when the laity discovered "that what they thought the *Priest*'s, was *Their* Estate: / Taught by the *Will produc'd,* (the written Word) / How long they had been *cheated* on *Record*" (ll. 391–93). By altering the situation to one in which the estate, instead of being unjustly sequestered, is the subject of litigation, and in which the will, instead of being hidden, is contested before a court, Dryden provides the Hind with an argument against private interpretation in favor of a "judge appointed to decide." He was not the first apologist for his church to discover that the fact that the word "testament" can mean a will as well as a covenant could be exploited as readily for Catholic as for Protestant purposes. Mumford had earlier declared

that we add nothing to Gods Testament: but with all reason we still stand to have it Interpreted, not by any mans private Authority. For what Commonwealth permits the Testaments and Last wills of Man to be so Interpreted? Let us have Gods Testament both new and old, Interpreted by that publick Authority impower'd by Gods commission to this end, and we require no more. . . . No Wills worse made than those which concern many intricate Matters belonging to very several Persons, and yet prohibiting any Court in the World to interpret them, but do let the Sense be judg'd by every one concern'd in it.[59]

At this point the Hind has completed her first task of proving the necessity of a living judge of controversies and can turn to her second, that of showing that this judge is to be found only in the

[59] *The Question of Questions,* pp. 240–41.

Catholic church. The Panther, making what is to be her last interjection, provides an appropriate transition by conceding the Hind's first point and demanding that she proceed to the second:

> Suppose, (the fair Apostate said,) I grant,
> The faithfull flock some living guide should want,
> Your arguments an endless chase persue:
> Produce this vaunted Leader to our view,
> This mighty *Moyses* of the chosen crew.
>
> [II, 389–93]

Her attitude of defiance is short-lived, for the Hind immediately accepts the challenge with unexpected courage:

> The Dame, who saw her fainting foe retir'd,
> With force renew'd, to victory aspir'd;
> (And looking upward to her kindred sky,
> As once our Saviour own'd his Deity,
> Pronounc'd his words—*she whom ye seek am I.*)
> Nor less amaz'd this voice the *Panther* heard,
> Than were those *Jews* to hear a god declar'd.
>
> [II, 394–400]

In this state of apparent stupefaction, the Panther listens without further interruption to the great speech of 250 lines in which the Hind supports her claim to be the "living guide" demanded by her adversary.

In the first hundred lines of this speech, the Hind shows that no rival church can meet the two requirements of a living guide: unity of doctrine and discipline, and a claim to infallibility. She begins by reviewing the doctrinal and disciplinary dissensions which rend the Reformed churches and concludes that

> neither you, nor any sect beside
> For this high office can be qualify'd,
> With necessary gifts requir'd in such a guide.
> For that which must direct the whole, must be
> Bound in one bond of faith and unity:
> But all your sev'ral churches disagree.
>
> . . . .
>
> In short, in doctrine, or in discipline
> Not one reform'd, can with another join:
> But all from each, as from damnation fly;
> No union, they pretend, but in *Non-Popery.*
>
> [II, 448–62]

Secondly, the Reformed churches "all confess themselves are fallible" and therefore lack the other requirement of a living guide:

> Now since you grant some necessary guide,
> All who can err are justly laid aside:
> Because a trust so sacred to confer
> Shows want of such a sure interpreter:
> And how can he be needfull who can err?
> Then, granting that unerring guide we want,
> That such there is you stand oblig'd to grant:
> Our Saviour else were wanting to supply
> Our needs, and obviate that necessity.
> It then remains that church can onely be
> The guide, which owns unfailing certainty.
>
> [II, 474–84]

On this conclusive issue the question must be decided, the Hind declares, following the same reasoning as Mumford, who had written: "We put all the force of our Argument in this, That the Church, truly appointed by God for infallible Judge of Controversies, cannot possibly be any of those Churches which teach themselves not to be this infallible Judge, because they teach themselves to be fallible. . . . The Church which is truly appointed by God to be infallible Judge, must needs have this condition, That she do's own her Infallibility."[60]

In the remainder of her speech, the Hind proceeds to show that she meets this condition, by applying to herself the promises of infallibility, "all which the mother church asserts her own, / And with unrivall'd claim ascends the throne" (II, 497–98). She then continues by considering the conditions which are annexed to infallibility and which she alone possesses:

> Now, to remove the least remaining doubt,
> That ev'n the blear-ey'd sects may find her out,
> Behold what heav'nly rays adorn her brows,
> What from his Wardrobe her belov'd allows
> To deck the wedding-day of his unspotted spouse.
> Behold what marks of majesty she brings;
> Richer than ancient heirs of Eastern kings:
> Her right hand holds the sceptre and the keys,
> To shew whom she commands, and who obeys:

[60] *Ibid.*, p. 376.

With these to bind, or set the sinner free,
With that t' assert spiritual Royalty.

[II, 515–25]

These annexed conditions which she now discusses are the four *"Marks of the Catholick Church from the* Nicene *Creed,"* in the words of the marginal rubric. The first three—unity, sanctity, and catholicity—are considered briefly, with particular attention to the first in order to show that the unity of doctrine and discipline which the Hind had previously required of a living guide is to be found in the Catholic church, "one in herself not rent by schism, but sound" (II, 526). Her sanctity, she asserts, is as prominent as her unity: "As undivided, so from errours free, / As one in faith, so one in sanctity" (II, 531–32). Her catholicity, the Hind continues, is undeniable as well:

Thus one, thus pure, behold her largely spread
Like the fair ocean from her mother bed;
From East to West triumphantly she rides,
All shoars are water'd by her wealthy Tides.
    The Gospel-sound diffus'd from Pole to Pole,
Where winds can carry, and where waves can roll.
The self same doctrine of the Sacred page
Convey'd to ev'ry clime in ev'ry age.

[II, 548–55]

In two succeeding stanzas, the Hind contrasts these Catholic missionary activities with those of the Protestants, who carry on their explorations, not in order to spread Christianity, but for far less worthy ends. The English transport their convicts to the New World:

And through our distant colonies diffuse
The draughts of Dungeons, and the stench of stews.
Whom, when their home-bred honesty is lost,
We disembogue on some far *Indian* coast:
Thieves, Pandars, Palliards, sins of ev'ry sort,
Those are the manufactures we export;
And these the Missionaires our zeal has made.

[II, 559–65]

Even worse are the Dutch, who are interested only in trade, for the sake of which they "sell all of Christian to the very name" (II, 574).

Finally, the Hind turns to the fourth mark of the true church which she alone possesses:

> Thus, of three marks which in the Creed we view,
> Not one of all can be apply'd to you:
> Much less the fourth; in vain alas you seek
> Th' ambitious title of Apostolick.
>
> [II, 576–79]

She proceeds to assert at length that Catholic doctrine and discipline are "a limpid stream drawn from the native source; / Succession lawfull in a lineal course" (II, 614–15) from the Apostles.

The Hind concludes her speech by inviting the Panther to return to her discipline:

> See how his church adorn'd with ev'ry grace
> With open arms, a kind forgiving face,
> Stands ready to prevent [anticipate] her long lost sons embrace.
>
> [II, 639–41]

The Panther is unwilling to accept this offer of reconciliation, yet she is effectively prevented from renewing the hostilities by a timely intervention from heaven:

> Thus, while with heav'nly charity she spoke,
> A streaming blaze the silent shadows broke:
> Shot from the skyes a chearfull azure light;
> The birds obscene to forests wing'd their flight,
> And gaping graves receiv'd the wandring guilty spright.
>
> [II, 649–53]

On this note of supernatural approval the Hind's long discourse ends.

The evidence provided by this examination of Dryden's religious arguments in *The Hind and the Panther* conclusively disproves, I believe, the notion that there was anything idiosyncratic about his views as a Catholic. Having decided to employ his poetic and argumentative powers in the service of the small and despised minority he had joined, Dryden allied himself with the Jesuits and laymen who were in the mainstream of English Catholic apologetics. Whatever his opinion of Jesuit politics, as represented by the maneuvers of Father Petre at Court, he evidently regarded their polemical writings as unexceptionable and a valuable source for many of his own arguments. The Blackloists he ignored; it was no part of his purpose to publicize the dissensions which embarrassed his small church. He may even have been unacquainted with their writings, though he could scarcely have remained ignorant of their opinions, discussed and condemned by Anglicans as well as Catholics. At all events, these eccentric views exerted no influence on *The Hind and the Panther,* the last and longest achievement of Dryden's five-year period as a public orator on behalf of religion.

Throughout this study I have argued against the view that Dryden expressed consistent attitudes in *Religio Laici* and *The Hind and the Panther* on questions dividing the Anglican and Catholic churches. At the same time I have tried to show that there are other attitudes, perfectly compatible with membership in either church, which he persistently expresses or takes for granted, not only in his poems on religion, but in many other writings to which I have referred.

One of these is Dryden's attitude toward knowledge and belief as two distinct categories of truth which are the province of reason and revelation respectively. As I showed in chapter 1, he expressed an unswerving confidence in the efficacy of reason for apprehending truth under proper conditions and with respect to appropriate inquiries belonging to the natural order. He also believed, in spite of the fideists, that reason performs a necessary function in religion; but he denied, contrary to the "Philosophising Divines" of the two churches to which he successively belonged, that this office was to "prove Religion by Reason" in the sense of demonstrating or comprehending its mysteries. In his view, the preambles to faith must be supplied by reason, but faith itself depends on revelation for its discovery and on the authority of the proponent for its certainty. In two of the most ratiocinative poems on religion in the English language, Dryden never forgets this distinction. He is careful always to "lay no unhallow'd hand upon the Ark, but wait on it," to argue, not about the articles of faith themselves, but about the means by which they are to be discovered, interpreted, and agreed upon by the community of believers.[61]

---

[61] This is true even of the apparent exception, Dryden's defense of Transubstantiation in Part I of *The Hind and the Panther*. His concern there is not with proving this doctrine on the evidence of Scripture and tradition, but only with showing that it is not essentially different from any other articles of faith which transcend our faculties and must be believed on the authority of the divine proponent.

Another attitude no less consistently maintained is Dryden's habit of moderation: the attitude of "waiving each Extreme" in order to follow a deliberate middle course on any question he happens to be considering. At times this takes the form of a self-conscious appeal to the moderation of his own view by presenting it as a *via media* between unwelcome extremes. It is thus, both in the preface to *Religio Laici* and in the final stanza of the poem, that he presents the Anglican position as a midstream between the "several Shelves" representing the unlimited private judgment of the sects on the one hand, and the unlawful public authority of the Catholic church on the other. In the same fashion he permits the Hind, in Part II of *The Hind and the Panther,* to present Dryden's own view of infallibility as a middle ground between the views of extremists, among whom "some contract, and some enlarge the space." Such explicit appeals serve an obviously rhetorical function, of course, for they enhance the moderation which is an important part of the speaker's *ethos*. This does not mean that Dryden's moderate attitudes are simply assumed for the occasion, however. They appear so often without fanfare on other occasions that we must assume they were habitual with Dryden.

His moderation is particularly noticeable in those many confrontations with an opponent where Dryden adopts a position more temperate than that of extremists who shared his religious persuasion. We noticed in chapter 4 how he opposed the Deist's system of natural worship, not by adopting the fideist solution of condemning reason in religion, but by carefully delineating its proper limits. Again we saw in chapter 5 how Dryden met the objection of the Deist, not by appealing to the rigid view of justification upheld by the Calvinists, but by espousing a Latitudinarian view of the question sufficiently close to his opponent's to invite the unjustifiable charge that he has fallen into the Deist's snare. In chapter 6 we noticed how, in answering the Catholic view of the interpretation of Scripture in *Religio Laici,* he expressed the moderate attitude of his church toward tradition and church authority for which Hooker and Laud had been accused of "popery" by the Puritan members of their church, and for which Dryden has been made the victim of a similar charge by modern critics. Lastly, we have seen in the present chapter that he confronted the Anglicans in *The Hind and the Panther,* not by adopting the Blackloist solution of rejecting Scripture in favor of an exclusive alternative, but by qualifying the proper role of

Scripture, in keeping with the position of his more moderate coreligionists.

Dryden's habit of moderation in these poems suggests that he is less interested in condemning his opponent than in reconciling their differences. Without compromising his own position he stresses the common ground they already share and the short distance that separates them. His attitude had no appeal for the fanatics of either church, "for sects that are extremes, abhor a middle way"; but it was entirely appropriate to one who believed that "a Man is to be cheated into Passion, but to be reason'd into Truth."

APPENDIX

DRYDEN'S USE OF WOLSELEY'S
Reasonableness of Scripture-Belief

Dryden's arguments in the first half of *Religio Laici,* as I explained in chapter 4, are as follows:

    I. Necessity of Revelation (ll. 1–125)
        A. Inadequacy of natural religion (ll. 1–92)
        B. Our dependence on revelation for the means of atonement (ll. 93–125)
    II. Proofs That This Revelation Is Contained in the Bible (ll. 126–67)
        A. Superiority of its teachings to those of other religions in answering the ends of human life (ll. 126–33)
        B. Antiquity of its laws (ll. 134–37)
        C. Character and circumstances of its authors (ll. 138–45)
        D. Confirmation of its doctrines by miracles (ll. 146–51)
        E. Its remarkable reception in spite of so many hindrances, internal and external (ll. 152–67)
    III. Answer to the Objection of the Deist (ll. 168–223)

I have chosen seven popular treatises of Christian apologetics, all published during the decade preceding the composition of *Religio Laici,* which contain, I believe, the greatest number of the above arguments, excluding, of course, the third argument in answer to the objection of the Deist. They are a representative lot, as it happens, for they include the work of both clergy and laity, of Anglicans, nonconformists, and even a Continental Protestant. The list begins with the two treatises on natural religion mentioned in chapter 4 which contain chapters on divine revelation as well: Bishop Wilkins' *Of the Principles and Duties of Natural Religion* (1675), and *Natural Theology, or the Knowl-*

edge of God from the Works of the Creation (1674) by Matthew Barker, a nonconformist. It includes as well three of the two-part works of apologetics discussed in chapter 4: *A Demonstration of the Divine Authority of the Law of Nature and of the Christian Religion* (1681) by Samuel Parker, later Bishop of Oxford;[1] *The Interest of Reason in Religion* (1675) by Robert Ferguson, an Independent;[2] and *The Truth of Christian Religion* (1680), the English translation of a popular work by Hugo Grotius, the well-known Continental Protestant. Finally, it includes the separately published second parts of their authors' complete systems of Christian apologetics mentioned in chapter 4: *The Divinity of the Christian Religion Proved by the Evidence of Reason and Divine Revelation* (1677) by William Bates, a Presbyterian, and *The Reasonableness of Scripture-Belief* (1672) by Sir Charles Wolseley. In the following table I have listed by number all of Dryden's arguments which appear in each of these books, in the order in which the authors present them.

Barker	Wilkins	Parker	Ferguson	Grotius	Bates	Wolseley
I B			I B			I A
I A						I B
	II:	II:	II:	II:	II:	II:
	B	C	A	D	A	A
	C	E	B	C	D	B
	D	D	C	A	C	C
	E		D	E	E	D
	A					E

The most noticeable difference between Wolseley and the other authors is that he alone offers both of Dryden's two major arguments (Ferguson includes parts of both arguments, but neither is complete). The other remarkable difference is that Wolseley introduces all of the parts of Dryden's second argument and in exactly the same order (Wilkins includes all of them but in a somewhat different order, and he omits the first argument entirely).

The way in which Dryden used Wolseley's book in composing the first half of *Religio Laici* should become clear from an outline of Wolseley's much more elaborate discourse, in which the arguments borrowed by Dryden are indicated in italics.

---

[1] As the title indicates, this work is unusual in that the first part deals with natural law rather than with the usual ingredients of natural religion (the existence of God and the immortality of the soul).

[2] Both parts will be found in the first chapter, a complete and substantial treatise of 274 pages.

APPENDIX

I. *Necessity of Revelation* (pp. 86–178)
   A. *Inadequacy of natural religion* (pp. 86–123)
   B. Pretence of all religions to some form of revelation (pp. 123–28)
   C. Our dependence on revelation for the manner of divine worship (pp. 128–40)
   D. *Our dependence on revelation for the means of atonement* (pp. 140–62)
II. *Proofs That This Revelation Is Contained in the Bible* (pp. 178–362)
   A. General qualifications possessed by the Bible (pp. 178–98)
      1. Its majestic style, which betrays its divine origin (pp. 179–81)
      2. *Superiority of its teachings to those of other religions in answering the ends of human life* (pp. 181–84)
      3. Conformity of the Bible to natural law (pp. 184–90)
      4. Its suitable conveyance to mankind (pp. 190–94)
      5. Absence of any visible defect in the Bible (pp. 194–97)
   B. Particular proofs of the Bible's divine authority (pp. 198–362)
      1. *Antiquity of its laws* (pp. 200–227)
      2. The way and manner of its conveyance to us (pp. 227–63)
         a. *Character and circumstances of its authors* (pp. 228–40)
         b. *Confirmation of its doctrines by miracles* (pp. 240–63)
      3. Success and effects of the Bible since its first conveyance (pp. 263–97)
         a. It has been preserved entire for us through so many ages (pp. 263–88)
         b. *Its remarkable reception in spite of so many hindrances, internal and external* (pp. 289–97)
      4. The subject matter of the Bible (pp. 297–353)
         a. Internal evidence that the book was written by divine command (pp. 303–25)
         b. External testimony in confirmation of its facts by pagan historians (pp. 325–53)
III. Objections Proposed and Answered (pp. 362–447)

In the course of over 350 pages, Wolseley develops an intricate argument which far exceeded Dryden's needs. The pattern of the discourse is perfectly clear, however, for Wolseley regularly outlines his arguments at the beginning of each section of his book and conveniently recapitulates them at the close of the section. It would have been a relatively easy matter, then, for Dryden to choose the arguments he wished to use and to omit the rest.

Dryden's procedure, I believe, was to read *The Reasonableness of Scripture-Belief* from beginning to end, marking certain passages as he did so. He then went through the book a second time while writing his own verses, using the marked passages as an outline for his own arguments. That he had the book in front of him as he wrote (or notes containing verbatim passages from the book) is suggested by the many verbal parallels, some of which I have indicated in chapter 4. The closest parallels are often to be found in those paragraphs in which Wolseley conveniently summarizes a detailed argument which has occupied many pages. It is just such passages that Dryden would be likely to mark as he read the book.

On two occasions Dryden amplifies one of Wolseley's arguments by drawing on another of his arguments from another part of the book. In both cases the second argument has no independent status in the poem but is subordinated to the fuller development of the first. In the first instance Dryden is closely following Wolseley's topic II B 2 in the outline above, "the way and manner of the Bible's conveyance to us." Wolseley had drawn two arguments from this topic, one relating to the authors of the Bible, the other to the book itself. Dryden does the same thing, first announcing the topic, as Wolseley had done, in lines 138–39, and then taking up each of the two arguments in turn. In expounding the second argument, however, which concerns the way in which the doctrine contained in the Bible was confirmed by miracles, Dryden evidently recalled the logical parallel of Wolseley's final argument (II B 4 b), which concerns the way in which the facts related in the Bible were confirmed by pagan historians. He therefore includes a reference to this argument before proceeding to discuss miracles. In the other instance Dryden spends four lines (152–55) discussing the Bible's style at the outset of his final argument on the remarkable reception of Christianity. The relevance of the Bible's style, discussed separately by Wolseley under II A 1 above, to the reception of Christianity is not, perhaps, sufficiently clear in Dryden's poem. Actually, Wolseley had himself repeated this discussion of the Bible's style more briefly when considering the reception of Christianity under II B 3 b. It is perfectly relevant there, for Wolseley explains that in the absence of external helps, such as the force of arms, Christianity had to make its own way purely by means of the majestic style of Scripture which, as Dryden expresses it, "speaks no less than God in every Line," and was immediately accepted as divine by great multitudes of converts. In this case I think we can conclude that Dryden has attempted to compress too much material into a few lines. As a result, what was a perfectly coherent argument in Wolseley's book, and presumably in Dryden's mind when he read it there, appears somewhat disjointed in the poetic version.

No outline can make clear the extent to which Dryden is indebted to Wolseley for his development of these commonplace topics of argument. For example, every one of the apologists listed above, except Barker, mentions the common argument that the doctrines contained in the Bible were confirmed by miracles at the time they were proclaimed. But of all these apologists, only Wolseley goes on to stipulate, as Dryden does, that miracles confirm a doctrine solely "when what is *Taught* agrees with *Natures Laws.*"

There is not, I believe, another instance in his original poetry of Dryden's depending so heavily on a single book for his ideas. The explanation seems to be the comparative novelty of deism and the scarcity of books specifically answering this new threat to the established religion.

INDEX